VISION FOR A CANADA STRONG AND FREE

VISION

for a Canada Strong and Free

Mike Harris & Preston Manning

2007

Series editor: Fred McMahon
Director of Publication Production: Kristin McCahon
Coordination of French publication: Francis Dumouchel

Design and typesetting: Lindsey Thomas Martin
Cover design by Brian Creswick @ GoggleBox
Editorial assistance provided by White Dog Creative Inc.

Date of issue: November 2007
Printed and bound in Canada

To order printed publications of The Fraser Institute, please contact the publications coordinator: e-mail: sales@fraserinstitute.ca; telephone: 604.688.0221 ext. 580 or, toll free, 1.800.665.3558 ext. 580; fax: 604.688.8539; mail: The Fraser Institute, Fourth Floor, 1770 Burrard Street, Vancouver, British Columbia, V6J 3G7 Canada.

For media enquiries, please contact our Communications Department: e-mail: communications@ fraserinstitute.ca; telephone: 604.714.4582.

Library and Archives Canada Cataloguing in Publication Data

Harris, Mike, 1945-
Vision for a Canada strong and free / Mike Harris & Preston Manning.

Co-published by Institut économique de Montréal.
Includes bibliographical references.
ISBN 978–0–88975–223–8

1. Canada--Politics and government--21st century.   2. Canada--Economic policy--21st century. 3. Canada--Social policy.   4. Democracy--Canada.   I. Manning, Preston, 1942-   II. Fraser Institute (Vancouver, B.C.)   III. Institut économique de Montréal   IV. Title.

JL65.H374 2007   320.60971'09051   C2007-906116-8

CONTENTS

MIKE HARRIS

Michael D. Harris, ICD.D, was born in Toronto in 1945, and was raised in Callander and North Bay, Ontario. Prior to his election to the Ontario Legislature in 1981, Mike Harris was a schoolteacher, a School Board Trustee and Chair, and an entrepreneur in the Nipissing area. On June 8, 1995, Mike Harris became the twenty-second Premier of Ontario following a landslide election victory. In 1999, he was re-elected, making him the first Ontario Premier in over 30 years to form a second consecutive majority government.

After leaving office in April 2002, Mr. Harris joined the law firm of Goodmans LLP as a Senior Business Advisor, and acts as a consultant to various Canadian companies. Mr. Harris serves as a Director on several corporate Boards including Magna International Inc., Canaccord Capital Inc., and First-Service Corporation. He is Chair of the Board of Trustees for the Chartwell Seniors Housing REIT and of the Board for EnGlobe Corp. He is also a Director on the Boards of the Tim Horton Children's Foundation and the Mount Royal College Foundation.

Mr. Harris also serves on a number of corporate Advisory Boards for various companies, and is President of his own consulting firm, Steane Consulting Ltd. As well, he is a Senior Fellow with the Fraser Institute, a leading Canadian economic, social research, and education organization.

PRESTON MANNING

Preston Manning served as a Member of the Canadian Parliament from 1993 to 2001. He founded two new political parties—the Reform Party of Canada and the Canadian Reform Conservative Alliance—both of which became the Official Opposition in the Canadian Parliament. Mr. Manning served as Leader of the Opposition from 1997 to 2000 and was also his party's critic for Science and Technology.

Since retirement from Parliament in 2002, Mr. Manning has released a book entitled *Think Big* (McClelland & Stewart) describing his use of the tools and institutions of democracy to change Canada's national agenda. He has also served as a Senior Fellow of the Canada West Foundation and as a Distinguished Visitor at the University of Calgary and the University of Toronto. He is currently a Senior Fellow of The Fraser Institute and President of the Manning Centre for Building Democracy.

Mr. Manning continues to write, speak, and teach on such subjects as the revitalization of democracy in the Western world, relations between Canada and the United States, strengthening relations between the scientific and political communities, the development of North American transportation infrastructure, the revitalization of Canadian federalism, the regulation of the genetic revolution, and the management of the interface between faith and politics.

ACKNOWLEDGMENTS

The Canada Strong and Free series is the work of many minds and hands, and we therefore have a number of people to thank. Former Fraser Institute Executive Director, Michael Walker, and the current Executive Director, Mark Mullins, were instrumental in initiating this project and guiding it. Fred McMahon, Director for the Centre for Globalization Studies at The Fraser Institute once again did a superb job as series editor. Francis Dumouchel of the Montreal Economic Institute generously lent us his considerable expertise and directed the translation in French. We would also like to thank the President of the Montreal Economic Institute, Paul Daniel Muller, and Martin Masse, who directed the translation of earlier volumes.

This volume summarizes the work of the previous volumes in the series and also contains much new material. For help with the new material, we thank the following Fraser Institute staff: Gerry Angevine, Senior Economist, Energy Studies; Jason Clemens, Director of Research Quality and Resident Scholar in Fiscal Studies; Senior Fellow Gordon Gibson; Heather Holden, Director of the Risk, Regulation, and Environmental Centre; Amela Karabegović, Associate Director of the Centre for Globalization Studies; Senior Fellow Rainer Knopff; Sylvia LeRoy, Senior Policy Analyst; Milagros Palacios, Senior Research Economist; and Niels Veldhuis, Director of Fiscal Studies.

Both Jean Marie Clemenger, Preston Manning's secretary and researcher, and Elaine Pritchard, Mike Harris's assistant, did exemplary work in keeping us on track. Jean Marie was especially helpful in editing innumerable rough drafts. Kristin McCahon, Director of Publication Production, skillfully steered the book through production. Dean Pelkey and Leah Costello, both of The Fraser Institute, and Phil von Finckenstein have contributed much to our work by managing communications and arranging CSF-related events. White Dog Creative Inc. provided valuable editorial assistance.

For policy work on our earlier volumes, we would also like to thank the following Fraser Institute staff: Nadeem Esmail, Director, Health System Performance Studies; Claudia R. Hepburn, Director, Education Policy; Senior Fellow Rainer Knopff; Senior Fellow Robert Knox; former intern Kate Mullock; and Brett Skinner, Director, Health and Pharmaceutical Policy Research and Director, Insurance Policy Research. University of Calgary Professor Barry Cooper provided important material on rebalancing Canada's democracy. André Turcotte's polling provided valuable information for our first volume.

We also thank Nicholas Gafuik of the Manning Centre for Building Democracy for his work on democratic reform, Mary Manning for her work on the reform of foreign aid, and Michael Hart, Simon Reisman Professor of Trade Policy at the Norman Paterson School of International Affairs, Carleton University.

Of course, we take full responsibility for the ideas and interpretations presented here. While we have relied on the insights of many, we set the analysis and the policy choices this document reflects.

FOREWORD

WHAT CANADA COULD BE

In April of 2005, in response to the lament that no truly inspirational vision existed in Canada to guide public policy decision makers and legislators, The Fraser Institute launched its Canada Strong and Free project.

The vision we offered to Canadians was that of a nation whose people enjoy the highest quality of life in the world; have access to good jobs, high incomes, and quality goods and services provided by the best performing economy in the world; and exercise their freedom in the security of the best-governed democratic federation in the world. We further envisioned a Canada that attains new levels of influence and leadership on the international stage.

No dimension of this vision is beyond our reach—if we resolve to achieve it and are prepared to implement the policies that will make it a reality.

FIRST PRINCIPLES

"Whereas Canada is founded upon principles ..." With these words our *Charter of Rights and Freedoms* begins. Principles are essential to realizing our vision of a Canada as truly "strong and free," as our national anthem boasts. We have therefore based our public policy recommendations on the following principles.

♣ Freedom is the supreme value; but while fundamental freedoms of conscience, speech, and assembly are well protected in Canada, no less vital freedoms have been unjustifiably curtailed in our federation, in particular freedom of choice, freedom of enterprise, and freedom to trade both domestically and internationally.

♣ Acceptance of responsibility is an essential corollary to the possession and exercise of freedom.

♣ The inherent equality of citizens before the law, and their right to choose, direct, and dismiss their governments, are the basic principles of democracy.

♣ Poverty is sooner and more permanently alleviated by broader distribution of the "Tools of Wealth Creation"—property rights, markets and improved access to capital, financial instruments, information, technology, education, and health services—than by redistributing wealth itself.

♣ There is an optimal division of activity and resources between the public and private sectors and among the three levels of government, and public policy should seek to achieve this division.

♣ Respect for the constitutional division of powers between our federal and provincial governments requires "rebalancing" the exercise of those powers where that division has not been respected.

♣ *Subsidiarity*, the principle that government services, especially social services, are most effectively delivered by the level of government closest to those being served, needs to be respected in our federation.

♣ Transparency and accountability on the part of governments and private sector organizations are prerequisites to securing and retaining public trust.

THESE PRINCIPLES APPLIED

In the five previous volumes of our Canada Strong and Free series, we applied these principles (as described and elaborated in Volume 1) systematically to the development of forward-looking public policies for Canada:

♣ To improve Canadians' quality of life through reforming the provision of health, education, child care, and social assistance services (Volume II).

♣ To improve democratic governance by restoring accountability and transparency, and enhancing citizen input through any of a variety of measures enumerated in a "menu" of democratic reforms (Volume III).

♣ To improve the effective exercise of federalism by rebalancing the powers and responsibilities of our federal and provincial governments (Volume III).

✤ To improve the performance of the Canadian economy through optimizing the size of government, reducing the burden of excessive taxation and regulation, and eliminating inter-provincial barriers to trade (Volume IV).

✤ To strengthen Canada's role as an international leader through championing trade liberalization, increasing our influence with the United States, and reforming our approach to providing foreign aid (Volume V).

Now, in this sixth and final volume of the Canada Strong and Free series, we endeavor to do two things: to provide a holistic snapshot of market-oriented public policy thinking in Canada at the beginning of the 21st century; and, no less importantly, to present an agenda for inquiry, development, innovation, and action to implement market-oriented policies for the future.

MARKET-BASED APPROACHES TO PUBLIC POLICY
In the following pages you will therefore find an anthology of our previous analysis and recommendations with respect to four critical areas of challenge.

✤ *Quality of life*: education, welfare, health care, childcare;
✤ *Economic vitality*: economic freedom, size of government, regulation, free domestic trade;
✤ *Responsive democracy*: accountable government, federal-provincial balance, policy development, citizen input;
✤ *International standing*: Canada-US relations, international trade liberalization, foreign aid.

Secondly, you will find seven Monographs highlighting additional challenges to public policy in which there is a clear benefit to be gained from a more assertive application of market-oriented thinking. These include both fields in which market-based approaches are well accepted, but could be more rigorously practiced, and others where the application of market-based approaches will represent a break with conventional thinking.

GOVERNMENT INERTIA PERSISTS
These and other ideas contained in the following pages offer promising new alternatives to a range of failed or costly (often both) existing policy approaches. We regret to observe however that Canadian governments have often been terribly slow to adopt plainly necessary changes of course—even when those enjoyed broad public support.

For example, as early as 1984 there was significant polling evidence that Canadians were ready to support action to restrain out-of-control public spending and eliminate the federal budget deficit. Yet it was not until 1998—14 years later—that the federal budget was finally balanced. What other enterprise in the country could take so long to implement such a self-evidently necessary measure and still survive? Sadly, this inertia persists in other policy areas.

CANADA NEEDS YOU

The ideas offered in the following pages emerged from exchanges between researchers associated with Canada's largest market-oriented think tank, The Fraser Institute, and ourselves, two political practitioners with an interest in reform framed on conservative principles. If you are a student, supporter, developer, or advocate of market-oriented public policy thinking, we hope this volume will provide you with a useful overview of workable, pragmatic, and powerful new approaches to help Canada become the best country in the world to live in.

Without you and similarly engaged Canadians however, these liberating and empowering ideas are likely to remain no more than words on a page. We therefore encourage you to exercise your own democratic rights to press for the changes that must be made if our richly blessed land is to become an example to the world of excellence, prosperity, compassion, and liberty—a Canada indeed "strong and free."

Mike Harris
Toronto, Ontario

Preston Manning
Calgary, Alberta

SUMMARY OF RECOMMENDATIONS

Throughout the Canada Strong and Free series, we have promoted a vision of Canada that brings the best quality of life, the highest levels of prosperity, and the fullest experiences of democracy to the citizens of this great nation, and a presence on the world stage befitting our potential. We have argued that policies based on freedom and responsibility are not only intrinsically valuable in their own right but have the greatest potential to achieve these goals for Canadians. Here we outline the recommendations that arise from this vision.

CARING FOR CANADIANS: QUALITY OF LIFE
"The highest quality of life in the world"—the steps forward

To equip our children to lead the world in educational preparedness for success in later life:

1.1 Give families the resources to take advantage of the growing number of education alternatives by making available vouchers worth 50% of the total cost per student of public education for parents opting for independent education.

1.2 Facilitate the choice of alternative education for children with special needs by making available vouchers worth 75% of the total cost per student of public education.

1.3 Hold all K-12 schools accountable for results, while giving them freedom to innovate. Parents allowed to choose their children's schools will choose those that produce the best results. Money will follow students. Schools that succeed will prosper and grow.

To give Canadians in need a meaningful path out of dependence and poverty:

2.1   Eliminate the federal Health and Social Transfer and have the federal government vacate equivalent tax room for the provinces to raise their own funds for the purpose of sustaining welfare programs.

2.2   Take advantage on the provincial level of these additional resources, and have the provinces fulfill their constitutional responsibility by redesigning their welfare schemes to emphasize the "helping hand" over the "warehouse" of long-term dependency.

2.3   Open both the administration of welfare and program delivery at the provincial level to competitive bidding from for-profit companies as well as the non-profit sector.

2.4   Focus assistance on restoring independence through employment. To this end, welfare payments should be structured to present a clear incentive toward employment, while earned income should be subject to the lowest possible marginal tax rates.

2.5   Make return to work not only an explicit goal of welfare programs but a mandated condition of assistance, with clear time limits for receiving benefits.

2.6   Include "pre-benefit" components in social assistance programs to help applicants avoid welfare altogether by pursuing every viable alternative.

2.7   Provide those Canadians with disabilities so severe that they can never be fully independent with sufficient support for them to live in dignity and eliminate "clawbacks" that limit their ability to supplement this support with earned income.

To ensure that Canadians receive the best health care in the world, without either delay or regard to income:

Federal-provincial responsibilities

3.1   Have the federal government return health-care resources and responsibility to the provinces.

3.2   Spend federal dollars where it makes the most sense, on health-care science and research; the collection and provision to consumers of information about best medical practices; the portability of benefits between provinces; and the coordination of a national response to health threats that do not respect provincial borders, such as those posed by SARS, BSE, and predicted pandemics.

3.3 Right-size provincial health ministries, to fund and regulate—but not manage—health-care delivery.

3.4 Increase accountability. Many provinces already report to their citizens how long they will need to wait for certain kinds of care and how many people are ahead of them in the queue. The idea behind these initiatives should be extended to help patients make sound decisions about which hospital or health provider will best meet their needs.

Individual responsibilities

3.5 Give Canadians the freedom to care for themselves. Canadians in every province should be free to contract for private health-care services and to buy insurance that would pay for those services.

3.6 Encourage patients to make more informed decisions. Co-insurance, deductibles, and co-payments can increase efficiency in health delivery and reduce costs though public support should ensure that no Canadian, no matter how poor, is denied health care.

3.7 Consider implementing a solution common in Europe—"social insurance"—essentially, a system of either private or public insurers (or both) at arm's length from government that provide coverage for health-care costs.

3.8 Help Canadians save for future medical needs. A creative approach to this is individualized "medical savings accounts" for long-term care.

Management responsibilities and structure

3.9 Work with the private sector. International experience indicates that public-private partnerships (P3s) could result in more creatively designed health-care facilities, while lowering lifecycle costs by between 20% and 30%.

3.10 Pay hospitals for the care they deliver. Give hospitals a financial incentive to provide better access and a more comfortable environment to attract more patients.

3.11 Free Canada's medical schools to train the doctors Canadians need.

To help Canadian parents provide strong emotional, social, intellectual and spiritual foundations for their children:

4.1   Stop penalizing child-care choices with biased tax breaks. Government policy should not privilege formal, paid daycare over care by a parent or another family member.

4.2   Restore federal-provincial balance by eliminating conditional grants. Canada is a large and diverse country, a diversity reflected in the different choices that parents in different provinces make for the care of their children. A Canada that believes in strong and free families must respect these differences.

4.3   Support self-employed parents as well as the employed. Legislation should be enacted to allow self-employed parents to fund their own parental leave by accessing their RRSP savings, in the same way that individuals can borrow these funds for home purchases or life-long education.

Recommended in Monographs

Social Entrepreneurship
+ Examine ways to open up provision of social services to competitive bidding from the for-profit and not-for-profit sectors.

Aging
+ Increase the retirement age and undertake the required investigation to determine the appropriate age.

A MORE DYNAMIC ECONOMY: UNLEASHING PROSPERITY
"The most productive, prosperous economy in the world"—the steps forward

To achieve world-leading levels of economic performance:

5.1   Maximize, at all levels of government, the economic freedom of Canadians.

To achieve the optimal size of government relative to the rest of the economy:

6.1   Adopt spending and taxation policies at all levels of government that would move the total government share of GDP to 33% or less within five years.

To reduce the tax load on Canadian business and allow Canadians to achieve our full economic potential:

7.1 Accelerate the complete elimination of all corporate capital taxes. This is largely a provincial issue, as the federal government has already committed itself to eliminating capital taxes rappidly.

7.1 Reduce corporate income tax rates. Specifically, the federal government should reduce its rate to 12.0% from 21.0% over the next five years. The provinces are encouraged to reduce their corporate income-tax rates by a minimum of 30%, with a target rate of 8%.

7.3 Increase aggressively the amount of income eligible for the "preferential" federal and provincial small-business tax rate. Over time, this "preference" should be eliminated entirely, not by raising the small-business tax rate but rather by reducing the general corporate income-tax rate.

7.4 End the practice of applying sales tax to business inputs in the five provinces that have maintained it, namely British Columbia, Saskatchewan, Manitoba, Ontario, and Prince Edward Island. These provinces are further encouraged to harmonize their provincial sales taxes with the federal goods and services tax (GST), which already exempts business inputs.

To reduce personal income taxes and harness the productive energies of workers, business owners, and entrepreneurs across country:

7.5 Move toward a single-rate personal income tax on both the federal and provincial levels. Removing the disincentives for work, saving, investment, and entrepreneurship inherent in increasing tax rates as incomes rise, will encourage productive activity and make the Canadian economy more efficient.

7.6 Raise the thresholds at which higher rates apply for jurisdictions that retain multiple tax rates. One of the problems in the current Canadian personal income-tax system is that "middle" and "upper" income-tax rates are applied at relatively low levels of real income.

To encourage savings and investment:

7.7 Eliminate capital gains taxes. As a small, open economy struggling to compete for business capital, it is critical that Canada create and maintain a strongly attractive investment climate. Eliminating levies on capital gains would not only remove one of the most economically costly of tax types but also send a strong pro-development and investment signal to potential investors.

7.8 Retain taxes on investment income at competitive rates. The ideal would be to move toward a single-rate, integrated, tax system. Failing that more fundamental reform, however, it is critical that Canada and its provinces ensure that our treatment of savings, dividend, and interest income remains strongly competitive internationally, especially with the United States.

7.9 Eliminate contribution limits for RRSPs and RPPs. The majority of Canadians save exclusively in tax-deferred accounts such as RRSPs. Greater flexibility in their use would have beneficial economic effects.

7.10 Introduce tax-pre-paid savings accounts. These are essentially the reverse of RRSPs, in that the tax is pre-paid but earnings are tax-exempt, as are any withdrawals.

To improve the effectiveness and efficiency of regulation:

8.1 Follow up on the Smart Regulation Initiative. We are encouraged that the 2007 federal budget contains a pledge to finalize and extend the "smart regulation approach" under the new label of "Creating a Performance-Based Regulatory System."

8.2 Require government officials and interest groups proposing new regulations to submit detailed benefit/cost estimates, including estimates of compliance as well as administrative costs.

8.3 Require Parliament and legislatures, or their appropriate committees, to hold regular "de-legislation/deregulation" sessions where the only item of business is to strike obsolete, unnecessary, and overly restrictive laws and regulations from the books.

8.4 Enact compulsory "sunset" provisions with every new regulation. All new or renewed regulations should automatically expire in five years unless specifically extended for a similar term.

To remove costly and unproductive barriers to internal trade:

9.1 Secure acceptance by all provincial and territorial governments and the federal government of the principle of an open domestic market. The purpose of such acceptance would be to establish that all Canadian governments understand that measures they undertake must not operate as barriers to trade, investment, and worker mobility.

9.2 Seek and achieve agreement by all governments to:

* establish rules to define what would be considered a barrier; these might be similar to those in the current Agreement on Internal Trade (AIT);
* define under what circumstances a measure presenting a barrier to trade might be permitted; this could be based on the "legitimate objective" provision in the AIT;
* remove or change any measures, policies, or practices that create an unjustifiable barrier;
* support the creation of a quasi-judicial Canada Internal Trade Tribunal to enforce the foregoing trade rules;
* take the necessary legislative steps to ensure that these rules can be enforced in relation to measures in their jurisdiction.

9.3 Establish a Canada Internal Trade Tribunal. The purpose of the Tribunal would be to enforce the trade rules established under the principle of an open domestic market. It would be a standing tribunal that would hear complaints from individuals, businesses, or governments against measures that may be barriers to trade, investment, and worker mobility.

9.4 Establish a Canada Internal Trade Council. The purpose of the Internal Trade Council would be to provide an advisory and political forum for issues not covered by the general agreement referred to in Recommendation 9.2 above. As such, it should be made up of ministerial representatives from all governments.

9.5 Investigate federal constitutional powers to free internal trade. In particular, initiate a federal reference to the Supreme Court asking it to clarify, first, the extent of the present federal commerce power (i.e., the power of the federal government under the present Constitution to strike down inter-provincial barriers to trade) and, second, what kind of amendment would be required, if necessary, to give the federal government that power.

9.6 Negotiate the geographic extension of the Trade, Investment, and Labour Mobility Agreement (TILMA) between Alberta and British Columbia across Canada. While TILMA is not a perfect agreement, it is a step in the right direction.

Recommended in the monographs

Productivity

+ Eliminate all capital taxes to encourage increased capital expenditure.

+ Reduce substantially overall business taxes to allow increased capital accumulation. In particular: reduce corporate income taxes and eliminate all corporate capital taxes.

+ Harmonize provincial sales taxes with the federal goods and services tax (GST) to ensure that business inputs are exempt from sales taxes.

+ Reduce substantially middle and upper personal income-tax rates to harness the productive energies of workers, business owners, and entrepreneurs across the country.

+ Move towards a single-rate personal income tax.

+ Increase school choice in Canada to improve the foundations for human capital improvement.

Energy

+ Deregulate the price-setting dynamic at both the wholesale and retail level where electricity demand and supply are large enough to ensure that electricity prices could be determined by competitive market forces.

+ Embed the costs of environmental protection in the energy pricing process where possible, so that price-sensitive consumers are have an incentive to use cleaner types of energy.

+ Streamline regulatory processes, including those pertaining to environmental issues, to ensure that energy project applications are dealt with as efficiently and quickly as possible.

+ Locate energy projects and facilities (subject to public-interest considerations imposed by regulation) on the basis of sound economic principles rather than political pressure.

Environment: Water

+ Implement policies to require universal water metering and progressive volume pricing, based on the full cost (capital plus operation and maintenance) of delivery from source and research-based estimates of the cost of ensuring an adequate supply of water into the future.

✦ Phase out all subsidies for water delivered for agricultural or industrial purposes under existing arrangements and shift water charges , over time, to a "full-cost" basis.

✦ Give local governments the authority to create "secondary" water markets, where the density of industrial presence justifies it, together with appropriate funding to provide the infrastructure connections that such a market would require.

REBALANCED AND REVITALIZED: RESPONSIVE DEMOCRACY
"The best governed democracy in the world"—steps forward

To ensure that elected representatives and public officials answer to the citizen:

10.1 Bring all of government into the light by broadening the scope of Canada's Access to Information Act 1985 to include any entity that meets a broad list of criteria that might include: Is it funded by taxpayers' money? Does the government own, or partially own, it or its parent entity? Does it perform a service essential to the public interest in a federal jurisdiction?

10.2 Ensure that Canadians know, clearly and with confidence, who did what, by requiring public officials to document their actions and decisions and preserve the public's right to access these records.

10.3 Put the health and safety of Canadians before the secrecy of government, by requiring (subject to limited exceptions) that public bodies disclose any information about a risk of significant harm to the environment, to the health and safety of the public or a group of people, or where the disclosure is clearly in the public interest.

10.4 End mandatory exclusion of Cabinet confidences from the right of request under the Access to Information Act; instead these confidences should receive a *presumption* of exclusion, subject to independent review by the Information Commissioner.

10.5 Enact legislation (taking Sarbanes-Oxley and New Zealand's Fiscal Responsibility Act as models) empowering Canadian citizens to hold government to legally enforceable standards of disclosure, transparency, and accountability at least as high as those required of public corporations, and holds those in charge to account.

10.6 Require deputy-ministers to sign contracts of employment making them personally responsible for the department's performance.

10.7 Increase protection of whistle-blowers but without putting further constraints, beyond those already contained in the Privacy and Access to Information Acts, on public access to information or the right of whistle-blowers (and those accused) of seeing and correcting the appropriate files.

10.8 Fund the Auditor General's budget independently of the government of the day, through a special Parliamentary appropriation for that purpose.

10.9 Increase the capacity of the Auditor General to compel compliance with his or her recommendations by giving the office the power to freeze funding to programs temporarily, pending their demonstration of compliance or further investigation, and to impose penalties for non-compliance or ineffective compliance.

10.10 Convene a national conference to outline the measures necessary to create a credible and objective report card on government performance in Canada, modeled on the report cards on individual aspects of government performance pioneered by The Fraser Institute.

To give citizens an effective voice and confidence in the democratic process:

11.1 Encourage citizens, interest groups, and political parties interested in democratic reform to review, debate, and decide on those reforms most deserving of their support from a menu of democratic reforms which includes: civic education, citizens' assemblies, fixed election dates, reform of the electoral system, referendums, citizens' initiatives and recall, "third party" advocacy and electoral financing, the court challenges program, freer voting in Parliament and legislatures, responsible government for aboriginals, reform of party financing and processes, development of political infrastructure.

11.2 Strengthen in particular non-partisan, non-ideological civic education in Canada.

11.3 Call together Citizens' Assemblies to consider other democratic reform options, investing in referendums supported by educational campaigns to let informed voters decide whether or not a particular reform should be adopted.

11.4 Implement freer voting in legislatures and in Parliament, particularly on measures directed at advancing democratic processes and institutions.

To revive the intent of Confederation by respecting the Constitutional balance of jurisdictions and strengthening the provincial role:

12.1 Remove the federal government from the fields of social assistance, child care, and health care and all other areas of provincial responsibility.

* Coordinate with this withdrawal a reduction in federal revenues by the current value of federal fiscal transfers to the provinces in support of these services, vacating the equivalent tax room to the provinces.

* Have the provinces assume in full their constitutional responsibility for providing essential social services (education, health care, child care, and social assistance) and for developing whatever national standards are desirable in these areas by means of inter-provincial agreements facilitated by the Council of the Federation.

* Amend the current equalization formula to provide additional revenues to lower-income provinces for which a "tax point" is worth less than for higher-income provinces, to the effect that no province be "worse off" after the transfer of tax points than under the current system.

12.2 Strengthen the federal government in key areas by having it focus on:

* foreign policy;
* defence and military capability;
* external trade arrangements and the elimination of trade barriers within Canada;
* a sound currency and monetary policy;
* intellectual property law;
* criminal law and the provision for public safety;
* the discharge of federal responsibilities toward aboriginal peoples.

12.3 Increase the use of Memorandums of Understanding (MOUs) by all provinces and territories to pursue common objectives and interests, facilitated and supported by the Council of the Federation.

12.4 Negotiate an increasing number of Trade Investment and Labour Mobility Agreements (TILMAs) among provinces.

12.5 Provide a stronger check on the executive by strengthening the bicameral nature of Parliament, in particular by democratizing (electing) the Senate; to this end Bills C-43 and S-4 should be passed.

12.6 Strengthen the powers of parliamentary and legislative committees by giving them an earlier role in the legislative process, giving their members (especially their elected chairs) more security of tenure, and giving them the resources (budgets, staffs, research capacity) required to discharge their responsibilities effectively.

12.7 Establish a pre-appointment hearing or confirmation process for appointments to the Supreme Court by an appropriate parliamentary committee to improve the transparency and balance of those appointments.

12.8 Pursue a constitutional amendment to shift the power of appointing justices to provincial courts of appeal from the federal government to the provincial governments.

12.9 Recognize the "notwithstanding" clause as a legitimate and necessary part of our Constitution and encourage its proper use through refining and democratizing its application.

Recommended in Monographs

Aboriginal empowerment

* Separate administration of program funds from their political structure in aboriginal bands.

* Give parents and students a choice in education, provided through school vouchers and a legal framework supportive to the establishment of charter schools.

* Encourage private property ownership on reserves; in particular, home ownership should be ceded to individuals and families.

* Send to individuals and families the $5 billion now sent by government to chiefs and councils, with a concurrent provision to allow bands to tax back some of this money to fund their activities.

Regional disparity

* Factor into the calculation of inter-provincial equalization payments regional differences in the cost of providing comparable public services.

* End regionally extended entitlements to Employment Insurance (EI).

* Reduce taxes to spur citizen's productive potential in have-not provinces.

* Adopt in the provinces of Atlantic Canada an agreement structured on the Trade, Investment, and Labour Mobility Agreement (TILMA) struck between Alberta and British Columbia.

A MODEL TO THE WORLD: INTERNATIONAL LEADERSHIP
"A model of international leadership"—steps forward

To enhance Canada's international trade:

13.1 Eliminate the last vestiges of the protectionist National-Policy mindset, from supply management and business subsidies to ownership restrictions in transportation, telecommunications, and financial services to allow Canadian firms to become more productive and competitive in international markets.

13.2 Pursue a customs union and common external tariff with the United States, using the process to lower remaining tariffs and reduce cross-border transaction costs.

13.3 Institute full cost recovery from clients of government export promotion programs, including clients of the Export Development Corporation. The long-term goal should be to hand over such activities to private sector institutions.

13.4 Let markets decide with whom Canadians trade, either as exporters or as consumers. Ideologically driven efforts to diversify trade patterns substitute political and bureaucratic preference for market judgment and impoverish rather than enrich Canadians.

13.5 Continue to support Canadian exporters by working to expand market access, resolve specific trade problems where possible, and fully exercise Canada's trade agreement rights. At the same time, Canada should live up to its own commitments and ensure that our domestic market is fully open to foreign competition.

13.6 Pursue free-trade agreements with minor partners only to the extent that they do not interfere with key Canadian trade goals.

**To advance Canada's interests within a secure,
integrated North American economy:**

14.1   Devote priority resources at the federal level to the management of our relationship with the United States.

14.2   Work with the United States to update the architecture of our relationship and
develop a joint approach to the governance of our common economic and
security space, working together to create both a more open and more secure
common border for the movement of people and goods.

14.3   Revisit the decisions not to participate in the Ballistic Missile Defence program
and not to broaden the mandate of NORAD, in order to place the Canada-US
security relationship on the most mutually advantageous basis.

14.4   Negotiate with the United States to create a customs union involving a common external tariff, a joint approach to the treatment of third-country goods,
a fully integrated energy market, a common approach to trade remedies, and
an integrated government procurement regime, in order to facilitate further
economic integration.

14.5   Work with the United States to promote regulatory convergence to obtain maximum advantage from economic integration.

14.6   Negotiate with the United States a comprehensive agreement embracing all
of the foregoing, and institutionalize measures to realize the greatest possible benefits from deeper economic and security integration for both our
nations.

**To ensure that Canada's assistance to less fortunate
nations is effective and reflects our national values:**

15.1   Adopt the Tools of Wealth Creation as the centerpiece of development aid, to
equip poor people with the resources to pull themselves out of poverty. These
include a broader distribution of:

- property rights;
- access to capital;
- human capital development;
- access to technology; and
- access to trade markets.

15.2 Use Public-Private Partnerships, where appropriate, to undertake projects that would otherwise be unfeasible in developing countries and create multiple winners among local governments, donors, the private sector, and local citizens. P3s are particularly suited to developing infrastructure and vaccines.

15.3 Strengthen internationally active NGOs in Canada by encouraging consolidation, economies of scale, and specialization in the sector.

15.4 Transform CIDA by:

- requiring greater accountability to the government and Canadian public;
- improving operational efficiency;
- replacing a "made-in-Ottawa" approach to aid with an "on-the-ground" approach;
- adopting a "90-10" rule—90% of development aid to low-income countries and 10% to middle-income countries;
- buying in research rather than duplicating existing expertise;
- creating a market place for aid projects; and
- demanding execution, leadership, and sound management at CIDA.

15.5 Reform food aid by:

- completely untying food aid;
- refocusing efforts on rural development; and
- supporting market-based approaches to managing environmental risks, such as drought insurance.

15.6 Improve post-conflict aid by:

- recognizing the new paradigm of conflict- and post-conflict aid;
- increasing the amount of aid allocated to both conflict-prone nations and post-conflict situations;
- demanding accountability for post-conflict aid disbursements and giving the military responsibility for aid delivery if necessary;
- realigning Canada's aid and peacekeeping priorities to focus on Africa;
- using aid money and Canadian expertise to facilitate bottom-up institution building and governance initiatives in post-conflict nations; and
- improving the timing of post-conflict aid.

15.7 Adopt a reasoned, evidence-based, foreign-aid budget target rather than the current random, analytically arbitrary monetary target of 0.7% of GDP by 2015.

VISION FOR A CANADA STRONG AND FREE

KEEPING CANADA'S PROMISE

A FOUNDING VISION

When Canada was conceived, its founders had a vision. They foresaw a strong, prosperous, and independent nation on the northern half of North America and took action to make that vision a reality. They adopted the constitution of a democratic federal state, protecting personal liberties; created an economic union and national market; built a transcontinental railway, opening up vast new territories; extended the rule of law; and developed independent trade and foreign policies to advance Canada's interests.

Generations that followed built on that foundation. In the twentieth century, Canadians participated in two World Wars in defence of freedom and democracy abroad. We welcomed immigrants from all corners of the globe to strengthen our economy while expanding our cultural diversity. We survived the Great Depression and laid the foundations of a comprehensive social safety net for our citizens. We helped create the United Nations and invent international peacekeeping. We entered into the largest bilateral trade agreement the world has ever seen with our closest neighbour, the United States. Canada was one of the most respected and influential voices in the world, and we backed our words with real commitments of money, personnel, and national resolve.

Without a doubt, we accomplished great things together—in the past. But where are we now? And what of the future? Where is that strong, clear vision for the future that will unite and guide Canada for the twenty-first century? What choices and public policies will make that future a reality?

ADRIFT

Over the past two decades, Canada has lost its momentum along with its direction. Our standard of living, relative to our economic peers and other developed countries, has slipped. We have conspicuously fallen behind the United

States. In fact, Canada has barely kept pace with major European nations, which themselves have experienced poor economic performance in recent years. (See Figure 0.1 for a comparison of key nations.) Too many Canadians pay higher and higher taxes, for fewer and poorer government benefits. For example, in health care: in theory, we have universal access to good quality health-care services, but too many of our citizens find themselves waiting months and even years for services that are far from number one in the world (Esmail and Walker, 2006). With respect to the productivity of our economy, on which our jobs and international competitiveness depend, we have allowed a widening gap to open with our largest trading partner. Indeed, Canada's productivity performance over the last 20 years has been one of the worst in the developed world. (See Figure 0.2 for a comparison of key nations.)

Our foreign policy increasingly failed to serve Canadian interests and values. Canada became known more for its preachiness in world affairs than for its willingness to back its sermons with anything more than token support. Although the new government has been moving to correct past problems, the Canadian military, once a source of national pride, was for many years starved of funding, equipment, and personnel. While we maintain the form and processes of democracy in Canada, its spirit and practice are on the wane. Increasing numbers of Canadians, particularly the young, hold Parliament, political leaders, and candidates for public office in contempt. Only 64.7% of eligible voters cast a ballot in the last federal election.

Figure 0.1: GDP in selected countries, constant local currency

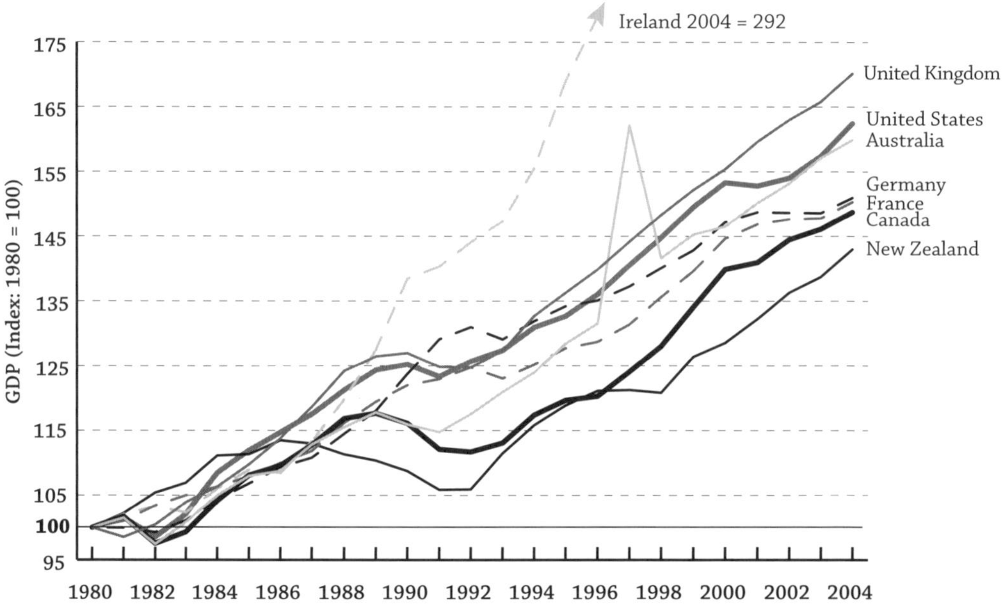

Source: World Bank, 2006.

Figure 0.2: Manufacturing output per hour

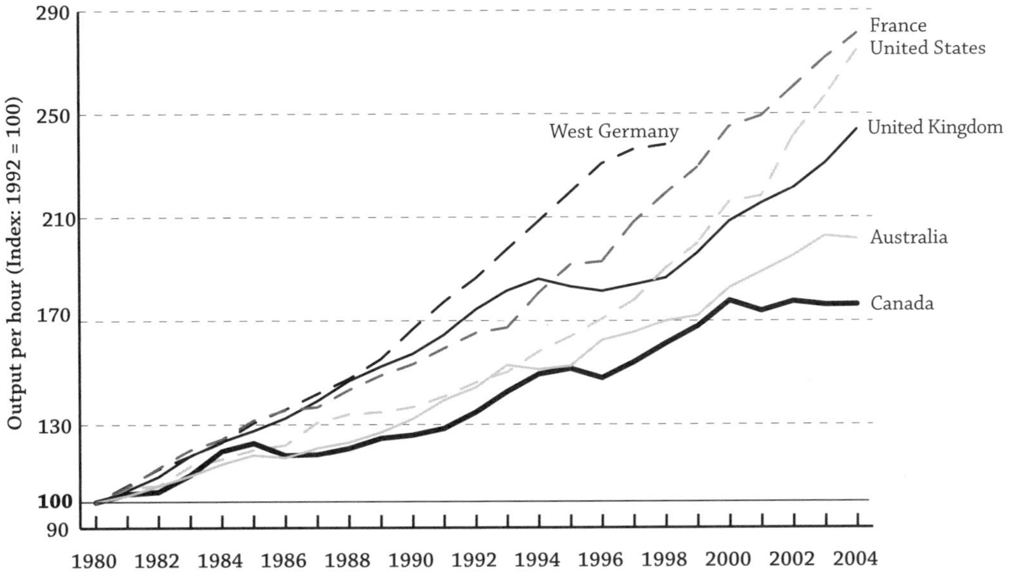

Source: US Bureau of Labor Statistics, 2007.

This is not what Canada's founders envisaged. It is not what today's generation of Canadians should settle for. A nation endowed with more resources and opportunities per capita than any other people on earth is capable of achieving so much more—socially, economically, democratically, and internationally.

This is no abstract goal. In very practical terms, it is possible for you and your children to enjoy better health care, education, social security, and environmental quality than you do today. It is possible for you to earn a higher income from a better job than the Canadian economy presently provides, and to keep more of it than the tax system currently allows. It is possible for your voice and vote to make a real difference in public affairs, and for the vast majority of our citizens in every region to feel truly accepted and at home in their own country. And it is possible to regain the world's respect for Canada, even to surpass the level of regard this country enjoyed following the Second World War. It is possible, in short, to restore the justifiable pride that all Canadians long to feel for our country.

TO THE SUMMIT

Canada's first peoples used to visit the high and sacred places of their territories to dream dreams and see visions of the future. Just so, we invite you to climb in your mind's eye to the high and inspirational places of our country, and to look out toward the horizon of what the future could hold for Canada, for you and for your family. We also invite you to examine the barriers that impede us from reaching that future, and the policy paths that could break through those obstacles. We hope that the pages ahead will offer a useful guide for that journey.

Our vision for Canada embodies four goals—high, but obtainable:

+ achieving for Canadians the highest quality of life in the world;

+ improving Canada's economic performance to achieve and sustain the highest living standards in the world;

+ making Canada the best-governed democratic federation in the world;

+ establishing Canada as a model of international leadership and citizenship.

QUALITY OF LIFE

Quality of life means different things to different people. But we suggest it may be defined and measured in terms of:

+ services like health care, education, childcare, public safety, transportation, communications, and retirement security;

+ physical environment—the quality of the air we breathe, the water we drink, the food we eat, and our relationships to the lands, forests, and animals with which we share this planet;

+ relationships with others—spiritual, cultural, family, and community relationships, including our relationships with those less fortunate than ourselves;

+ economic opportunities and rewards—more and better jobs and investment opportunities, higher incomes and more dollars in our pockets, better quality and choice of goods and services, and better value for our personal and collective (tax) expenditures;

+ an effective voice in our government and influence over the policies that affect us, regardless of our province of residence.

It is precisely because quality of life means different things to different people that expanding Canadians' freedom of choice, securing the means to exercise that freedom, and accepting the responsibilities that accompany its exercise, are prerequisites to achieving the highest quality of life in the world.

The subject of health care provides a particular instance in which market-oriented solutions to an important quality of life challenge have been willfully neglected. In both Volumes I and II of A Canada Strong and Free, we outlined the way to provide Canadians with the best health care in the world. We recommended a combination of universal coverage regardless of ability to pay (the best feature of our current system) with a mix of public and private providers of health-care insurance, financing, and delivery—the distinguishing feature of all those European health-care systems whose medical outcomes surpass our own. Nevertheless, despite increasing delays for care, and costs that consume an ever-larger and plainly unsustainable share of provincial budgets, reform of Canadian

THE IRISH INSPIRATION

For motivation, let's quickly take a look at the nation with the most radical experience of accelerated growth in the western world: Ireland (figure o.1). Less than 20 years ago, Ireland was a high-tax nation, burdened even more heavily than Canada. Ireland's unemployment rate was at Newfoundland levels, reaching close to 20% of the workforce. The best and the brightest in Ireland were fleeing to other shores. Ireland was a desperately poor nation. On a per-person basis, Canada was two and one-half times richer than Ireland. Now here's a shocker. Today the average Irish person produces about 20% more wealth than the average Canadian.

Manus O'Riordan, head of research for Ireland's largest union association, the Services Industrial Professional Union once said: "There are whole areas of this city [Dublin] where there is no culture of employment. Taxes are a disincentive to work. We need incentives to work" (McMahon, 2000a: 82). Tax reductions in Ireland provided those incentives and today the country is more troubled by labour shortages than job shortages (Chambers of Commerce of Ireland, 2003). Just as Canadians might have been saddened by Ireland's huge numbers of unemployed 20 years ago, the Irish would be appalled by the unnecessarily high unemployment rates Canadians tolerate today.

Our Vision for Canada aspires to the same dramatic increase in economic well-being in this country. It was achieved in Ireland by the most radical shift of economic policy that any advanced economy has made in peacetime. Government spending and taxes were reduced by far more than they were by Margaret Thatcher or Ronald Reagan. And what was the net result? Astonishing economic growth and a dramatic increase in the Irish standard of living.

Measures to establish government spending and taxation, and thus the size of government, at levels that optimize the quality of public services and economic growth, are not "left wing" or "right wing." They are simply good economic policy. Canadians should ignore ideological labels and resolve to adopt and support sensible economic policies—ones that create jobs and wealth for average Canadians. There is an abundance of evidence throughout the industrialized world that the path to growth, employment, and poverty reduction is found by expanding economic freedom and reducing the weight of government where it has become excessive and counterproductive. We'll give our analysis of this data, and our recommendations, in chapters 5 and 6 of this book.

health policy inches forward at a glacial pace. Such protracted inaction is unjusti-fiable. We again call on Ottawa and the provinces to act on an urgent basis.

In a new monograph in this volume, we also examine the demographic time bomb Canada faces and its potential impact on future quality of life. As our population ages, the demands placed upon our health-care and pension sys-tems will become financially unsupportable. Hundreds of thousands of senior citizens face fear, uncertainty, and a declining quality of life. This prospect is unavoidable without a fundamentally different approach to providing Cana-dians with adequate income and health care during their sunset years. The principles of personal responsibility, federal rebalancing, and subsidiarity, as well as the dynamism of social entrepreneurship, also examined in this mono-graph, offer a more effective and cost-efficient alternative than the existing pay-as-you-go, taxpayer-funded system.

PRODUCTIVE ECONOMY

Improving our economic performance is not an end but a means. It is essential to provide Canadians with the financial resources to accomplish their individual goals in life on their own terms. It is the single most important thing we can do to secure the goods and services that will provide Canadians with the world's highest standard of living. Indeed, without a better economic performance, Can-ada's existing social safety net cannot even be maintained, let alone expanded.

In Volume IV of this series, *Building Prosperity in a Canada Strong and Free*, we asked what percentage of Canada's Gross National Income should be left in the hands of consumers to spend and businesses to invest, in order to maxi-mize our ability to generate jobs and incomes for Canadians. After examining the research, we came to the following conclusions.

❧ An optimal balance between the public and private sectors of the economy would see the former (total spending by all governments) consume no more than 33% of GDP.

❧ Since governments currently consume about 39% of GDP, spending restraint and tax reductions should be instituted that would transfer about $390 billion from state control to citizens' hands over a five-year period.

❧ In order to realize the improved economic performance that would result from this rebalancing of resources, Canadian governments need not cut spending in absolute terms but only constrain the increase in their spending to .9% per year for 60 months.

But not one major government in Canada has come remotely close to limiting its spending increases to less than .9% per year. The average increase last fiscal year among the provinces was 5.1% while it was 5.2% at the federal level. Each has its excuse. A booming province like Alberta insists, "We must spend more, not less, to cope with growth." Less affluent provinces offer the justification that, "We must spend more, not less, to create growth." In major cities, it is argued, "We have to spend more, not less, to serve larger populations." In rural municipalities, that, "We have to spend more, not less, in order to stem a decline in population." And, in the case of the federal government, the argument is made that, "We have to spend more, not less, to correct fiscal imbalances with the provinces and meet increasing international obligations."

But in every case the consequence is the same: a dramatic increase in public spending and the total tax burden borne by Canadians, rather than their necessary attrition, leaving less wealth in Canadians' hands to finance our personal, family, and corporate aspirations. Here we once again urge governments to restrain their spending to the level required to raise Canadian productivity, strengthen Canadian firms, and provide this and future generations of Canadians with the highest standard of living in the world.

Of course, "improving economic performance" must mean more than simply increasing Canada's per-capita production of goods and services. If the quality of our natural environment is a fundamental dimension of quality of life—as we believe it is—then economic performance must be pursued in ways that are compatible with environmental conservation, not at the expense of either nature or future generations. That does not reduce the importance of improving our national economic productivity, but it does make it all the more vital that we choose the right policies to accomplish the task.

In this volume, we examine the path to environmental improvement in a new monograph. Environmental policy has all too often focused on increased government regulation of industrial activity. Without denying the utility of enlightened regulation, an even more powerful instrument is available: the market itself. Of course, it is frequently the market that generates environmental stress as a byproduct of its production of goods and services. At its most fundamental, however, the market is simply a forum in which price signals provide financial incentive to supply what consumers desire.

In principle, this dynamic can be just as effective in meeting public demand for clean air, pure water, healthy forests, and wildlife protection as it has been in providing food, shelter, energy, and a host of other goods and services. The implication seems clear: there can be no durable solution to environmental degradation that neglects market principles. The law of supply and demand, the principle of property rights, full-cost accounting in price-setting, trade instruments, financial incentives (and disincentives), and private invest-ment—all of these must be harnessed to environmental conservation.

Economic freedom and personal responsibility, exercised through market-oriented policy regimes offer flexible, efficient alternatives or complements to conventional "command and control" strategies for addressing these press-ing challenges, yet solid research to that end is extremely limited and under-funded in Canada. We therefore call on market participants, policy developers, and citizen activists, to give this approach the priority it deserves.

RESPONSIVE DEMOCRATIC FEDERALISM

We aspire to make Canada the best-governed nation in the world, deepening our commitment to democracy in its federal form. Yet, in the political sphere, Canadians grow apathetic, indifferent, or even hostile to democratic processes and institutions when:

* voters have little confidence in the fairness or effectiveness of the voting system;

* elected representatives are constrained by their parties or the executive arm of government from adequately representing their constituents' views;

* weak-kneed legislators surrender their responsibility to deal with contentious issues to judges not directly accountable to the public, who actively seek to make laws as well as interpret them;

* regional and provincial interests are inadequately represented and balanced in a federal system;

* voters are unable to make direct input to government decisions affecting them or to discipline representatives who lose their confidence between elections;

* responsibility for important services is so divided among different departments and levels of government that it becomes impossible for the public to hold anyone to account for the quality and cost of services received;

* governments or public servants cannot be held accountable for their decisions and actions.

A new strategy is required for Canada to improve fundamentally the quality and functioning of our democracy. This goal demands that we ignite a new passion for democracy among our citizens, to raise the level and quality of civic participation. It will require us to reform our democratic processes and institutions, as well as the ethical standards of those in government, to restore the accountability of political participants to the voters they serve. It will also mean adjusting the balance between crucial complementary forces in our democratic system whose proper equilibrium is vital to achieving our full potential as individuals and as a country. These include the respective roles of the public and private sectors, the various levels of government, and the conflicting demands of globalization and localization.

Yet, we cannot be satisfied with our democracy unless all our citizens are included. Sadly, too many of our aboriginal citizens are excluded from the quality of life all Canadians should share. In a new monograph in this volume, we discuss how aboriginal governance can be improved. But we go beyond this, for our fellow citizens must also have increased economic opportunity to become fully part of our democratic structure.

In Volume V of A Canada Strong and Free, we called for a complete overhaul of Canada's traditional, and demonstrably ineffectual, approach to helping poorer nations around the world, ideas that have relevance here in Canada. We urged an alternative based on wider adoption of the Tools of Wealth Creation so that those in poverty might receive not just temporary relief but the means to secure a durable prosperity and self-reliance. Like most Canadians however, we are acutely aware of—and deeply embarrassed by—this country's ongoing failure to improve the fortunes of our own First Nations. Entire provinces have also failed to partake fully in the nation's overall economic advance. The same Tools of Wealth Creation, together with the principle of democratic accountability, point the way to breakthroughs in reducing these economic disparities and the stalled progress of aboriginal governance.

EXAMPLE TO THE WORLD

Canada has much to offer the world. To realize our potential on the international stage, however, we must refocus our foreign policy so that it effectively advances Canada's interests. This is not an exclusively self-interested prescription. Our national interests include strengthening democratic and humanitarian values throughout the world and defending those values where they are threatened or abused. Two of the most effective steps we can take to that end are restoring our squandered influence with the United States and rebuilding our once proud military. There are currently promising developments in both areas.

Likewise, removing the barriers we have erected to international trade as quickly as possible will not only open new global markets for our own goods and services; it will expand opportunities for people from other nations to trade with Canada. As one of the most potent of the Tools of Wealth Creation, such expanded trade opportunities would do far more to fight poverty and improve people's lives than any amount of foreign aid that too often only reinforces the tyranny of corrupt regimes (Gwartney, Skipton, and Lawson, 2001; Devarajan et al., 2001; Easterly, 2003).

IDEAS AND VALUES THAT WORK

We believe the keys to achieving all of these goals lie in liberating Canadians' sense of personal freedom and responsibility; achieving a more productive relationship between the public and private sectors of society; and restoring a balance of resources and responsibilities among the various levels of government. By addressing the root causes of our nation's recent drift, these strategic initiatives will not only revive opportunity and living standards, personal security, and responsive government at home; they will also regain for Canada an influential place at the table of nations as we lead by shining example. The key prerequisites to the realization of our Vision for Canada are:

* a dramatic expansion of freedom of choice in every dimension of Canadian life—economic, scientific, social, cultural, religious, political—and in the world at large;

* a greater acceptance by Canadians, and better enforcement, of the responsibilities and obligations that attend any assumption or exercise of freedom;

* a strengthening of democratic freedoms and responsibilities, particularly through devolving power to the levels of government that are closest to the people (the principle of "subsidiarity"), reducing the unmanageable size of government, and restoring Parliament's role as an effective forum for the people of Canada.

FREEDOM AND RESPONSIBILITY

Freedom is of supreme importance. Each of us has the intrinsic right to determine our own future course, make choices for our lives as we see fit, read and watch what we wish, associate (or not associate) with whom we please, and participate freely in the direction of our own government. No less do we bear the responsibility for these choices.

Freedom is one face of a two-sided coin. The other is responsibility. If we wish to enjoy the fruits of freedom we must also bear responsibility, not only for the consequences of our own actions but also for helping to maintain the freedoms we all enjoy. In Canada, while our *Charter of Rights and Freedoms* gave constitutional protection to the freedom side of the coin, the responsibility side has been sadly neglected. Fear that individuals or corporations will abuse freedom has frequently prompted demands for government to intervene, extending the heavy hand of the state deeper into society. But this invariably takes away more freedom than it protects. Canadians are relieved of their democratic responsibility as citizens whenever:

* governments do for people what they can and ought to do for themselves;

* the only exercise of self-government citizens participate in is an election every four or five years;

* public policies are developed and services managed by officials who are remote and distant from those the policies affect.

The alternative is for those who seek to exercise greater freedom also to accept greater responsibility. Expanding the freedom of enterprise, trade, and scientific inquiry implies a corresponding acceptance of greater responsibility for the social and environmental consequences of exercising those freedoms. More diverse lifestyle choices entail accepting greater responsibility for the personal and social result of those choices. Assuming greater religious freedom for ourselves brings a responsibility to respect the consciences and values of others. Increased political freedom carries expanded responsibilities of citizenship.

Last, it is important to recognize that freedom and responsibility are not just intrinsically valuable. Free societies, democratically governed and marked by personal responsibility, have produced the greatest prosperity, best health, longest life expectancy, and highest levels of education this planet has ever known. This experience proves beyond doubt that individuals and families, given freedom and responsibility, look after themselves far better than government can. So consistently do individuals acting in free markets produce greater prosperity and less poverty than government intervention achieves, that it is difficult to understand why the contrary argument continues to be made.

THE RIGHT BALANCE

What public policies, especially at the national level, are required before Canadians' freedom of choice and attendant responsibilities can expand dramatically? What policies will improve our quality of life, economic performance, democratic governance, and leadership in the world? The answers to those questions, we believe, are found in the following pages. They have in common measures to give a far greater number of individual Canadians the freedom to secure their own interests as well as accept responsibility for their choices; to drive the making of public policy and delivery of services down to the level of government closest to those they affect; to restore a more productive balance of government and private sector; and to disseminate the Tools of Wealth Creation more widely both abroad and at home.

In the first section, "Caring for Canadians: Quality of Life," we discuss the application of these principles and market-oriented policy responses to the provision of services that many Canadians rightly regard as important to their quality of life: health care, social assistance (welfare), education, and child care. In the second section, "A More Dynamic Economy: Unleashing Prosperity," we look at the steps necessary to ensure that Canada's economy is sufficiently productive to ensure that Canadians—as individuals and a society—can afford the goods and services that embody the highest possible quality of life. In the third section, "Rebalanced and Revitalized: Responsive Democracy," we examine what changes in process, institutions, and practice are needed to bring the vision of Canada's founders into the twenty-first century, engaging Canadians more fully in the responsibilities of democracy and making our government the most responsive in the world. In the the fourth section, "A Model to the World: International Leadership," we identify the priorities Canada must pursue abroad in order to advance our own national interests, be of effective assistance to the world's less fortunate, and restore our international reputation through action and example.

Throughout, a series of Monographs identifies other challenging areas of public policy in which the keys of maximizing individual freedom, "subsidiarity" of government authority, and rebalanced federalism hold unrealized promise. In the first section, these look at how private-sector groups might play a greater role in delivering social programs, as well as ways to meet the future financial and health-care needs of Canada's rapidly aging population. In the second section, we suggest ways to bring a new spark to Canada's persistently sluggish productivity growth, unlock new sources of energy, and arrest (perhaps begin to reverse) environmental degradation, with a focus on the ultimate strategic liquid, water. In the third section, we discuss ways in which "rebalanced federalism" would benefit Canada's perennial "have-not" provinces and we propose that an approach using the Tools of Wealth Creation to aid underdeveloped countries be applied more vigorously to the stubborn problems of economic marginalization in our aboriginal communities.

IN SUMMARY

Canada was conceived in a vision of greatness. We too envision a nation whose citizens achieve standards of living, economic performance, and democratic governance that make Canada a model to the world. We believe this future is attainable through the expansion of freedom of choice, the acceptance of greater personal responsibility, a more vigorous democratic culture, and the implementation of public policies based on these principles. We invite you to share your own vision, insights, concerns, and reactions by visiting <http://www.fraserinstitute.ca>.

CARING FOR CANADIANS
QUALITY OF LIFE

Our vision for Canada is of a nation whose citizens enjoy the highest quality of life in the world.

"Quality of life" means different things to different people. To some, it may imply sufficient wealth to surround themselves with the latest or most luxurious material goods. To others, it may mean enough free time to enjoy relationships with family and friends. To others still, the phrase may evoke nothing more complicated than a day without pain, fear, or hunger. "Quality of life," in short, is essentially a private concept. It ought not to be government's role to define it for any citizen. On the other hand, where government can give effective assistance to help individuals improve the quality of their lives, we believe it should.

Some Canadians have allowed the same belief to lead them to the conclusion that more government must inevitably mean a better quality of life. This is a mistake. An excess of government may instead lead to a smothering, expensive, and intrusive "nanny state" that leaves little room for free citizens to define, let alone pursue, their own idea of what it means to enjoy a high quality of life.

Our convictions lead us in another direction. Just as we believe each person has the right to his or her own vision of what the best "quality" of life might be for them, we believe that individual Canadians will always make better choices than government agencies about what is best for themselves and their families. When government lends a hand, it should be in a way that maximizes individual freedom and responsibility—and minimizes state intrusion into private lives. Likewise, and in keeping with our principle of "subsidiarity," Canada's leaders should ensure that such assistance should come from the level of government closest to those being helped.

In this section, therefore, we set out both a case and an argument that the principles we identified in our introductory pages can guide Canadians toward the best quality of life on the planet—however individuals may choose to define that goal for themselves—by promoting freedom of choice for all Canadians.

We focus on four areas of life that are important to almost every Canadian: ensuring that our next generation is equipped to excel in a challenging era of global competition; the availability of a helping hand in times of adversity; health care; and nurturing, supportive care for our children. As we will see, empirical evidence strongly supports our contention that when provinces are free to act with energy on their constitutional authority, and when families and individuals enjoy the greatest freedom of choice together with personal responsibility for outcomes, the results shine. The evidence also shows that the more those conditions are impaired, the less satisfactory the results become. The weight of evidence, we argue, should persuade every Canadian that the path to the best quality of life on the planet lies in maximizing Canadians' individual freedom; and that this can best be realized by rebalancing government activity back into line with the intent of our Constitutional framers, both to limit government's intrusion into private decision-making and to ensure that when government does act, it does so at the level of authority closest to those whose lives are affected.

To that end, the chapters just ahead examine in detail the experience in Canada and elsewhere in public education, social assistance ("welfare"), health insurance and public assistance with child-care. As well, our first Monographs look at two other quality-of-life areas where the same principles hold a largely unacknowledged, even unexpected, degree of promise: the provision of social services by private agencies, and the looming crisis in financial support for Canada's expanding ranks of seniors. In all of these fields, market-oriented approaches deliver real advantages over state-monopoly strategies. In education: a wider choice of public and affordable private schools, strongly motivated to meet your family's priorities while equipping your children to achieve a better life. In social assistance: escape from the "welfare trap" of dependent poverty into a new life of self-confidence, choice, and economic independence. In health care: meaningful incentives to make your own decisions regarding your health and well-being, more timely and satisfactory care, and lower overall costs. In child-care: public support for an array of choices beyond one-size-fits-all institutional daycare, with resources to help you—or a family member or friend of your own choosing—deliver the direct, personal care you want for your child.

That is far from summing up all the potential benefits to Canadians from restoring individual freedom, personal responsibility, and provincial constitutional authority in areas of social policy. As the Monographs on our aging population and privately delivered social services also illustrate, the same principles may be brought to bear beneficially on a wide range of other "quality of life" challenges as well. But wherever Canadians choose to apply these principles, we believe the evidence shows convincingly that they offer the most direct means available to achieve for ourselves the world's highest quality of life.

CHAPTER 1

EDUCATING FUTURE GENERATIONS

EDUCATION POLICY IN CANADA

We envision a day in the near future when every Canadian child enjoys the best educational opportunities on earth, one when Canada's youth lead the world in international comparisons of knowledge, skills, and achievement. The reality, we are glad to report, is much brighter here than in any other social policy realm we have examined. Canada can be proud of its educational achievement. Canadian 15 year-olds, for instance, are reported to be above the OECD mean in mathematics and problem solving (OECD, 2005b).

This is, in our view, hardly surprising: education is the only one of the four policy areas we address here in which the principle of balanced federalism is completely respected. In this field alone among those assigned them by our constitution do the provinces continue to maintain effective control of their own choices. Likewise, we find it profoundly telling that the good results are most striking in those provinces that have emphasized our other guiding principles of personal choice and responsibility. The provinces that have followed this route—Alberta, British Columbia, Manitoba, and Quebec—lead the rest in educational achievement. Alberta, which has gone furthest to encourage educational choice and responsibility, is a world leader.

THE NEED: PREPARING OUR CHILDREN TO LEAD THE WORLD

It is a truism of the 21st-century economy that knowledge is the key to personal success. Canada's children deserve the world's best education. Canadian families deserve the help they need to provide it.

All children deserve a learning environment that nurtures their knowledge, skills, and personal growth, one that equips them to seize every opportunity their lives will present. No child should be trapped in a poorly performing school. Each child is also unique and deserves a school that meets their particular needs, one that provides for the development of their individual gifts. Families should have help in accessing the educational environment that best meets the needs of their children.

Four provinces, Alberta, Quebec, British Columbia, and Manitoba, offer parents a portion of what it costs to educate their children in a public school so that they may, if they wish, choose another environment more suited to their children's particular needs. Those provinces have achieved world-class excellence in education, confirmed by international comparisons of educational achievement.

Six provinces deny school choice—except to families prosperous enough to afford it on their own. We are being unfair to those provinces' other families: the lack of choice clearly disadvantages poorer children. This is wrong. Canada should be a land of opportunity for rich and poor alike. We believe that Canadian children from one coast to the other deserve the same opportunities that children enjoy in Quebec or Alberta. Canadians in every province, from Newfoundland to British Columbia, should have access to the best educational choices available in the world.

WHAT IS BEING DONE? CREATIVE STUDIES

Canadians value education highly and appreciate the need for their children to gain a firm foundation of skills in their formative years. As a country, we reflect that in our education spending. Canada ranks well over the average in primary and secondary education spending per student, ranking seventh among the 21 OECD countries (OECD, 2001). Yet spending does not determine the quality of the education system. One Canadian province, Alberta, is an undisputed world leader in educational achievement, not because its spending is unusually high, but because it allows freedom and choice. Others are not far behind: British Columbia, Manitoba, and Quebec have attained excellence with transparent and accountable testing programs and curriculum-based school exit exams (Bishop, 1999). Children in these four provinces have won honours for their performance in national and international tests. If we care for our children's future, we adults will learn lessons from their successes.

RESPECTING PROVINCIAL AUTONOMY

Under our Constitution, Canada's provinces have exclusive jurisdiction over education policy and funding. Almost uniquely, the federal government has not sought to interfere with this authority, as it has in so many other areas of provincial jurisdiction. Provinces are entirely free to design programs that suit the needs of their citizens.

Few other countries offer their component jurisdictions so much autonomy over education—or see a fraction of the diversity in the result. Our federal government provides no funding, imposes no curriculum, and attempts no regulation of primary or secondary (K-12) education.[1] National initiatives in areas like testing and program coordination are developed solely by provincial authorities through the Council of Ministers of Education, Canada (CMEC).

This unusual level of freedom, coupled with the provinces' very different histories, founding populations, and cultures, has produced dramatically different education systems across Canada. Indeed, even the term "public education" does not mean the same thing in one province as it does in any other.

The results confirm the wisdom of this approach. In a study comparing 31 nations, Canadian students ranked second in reading, fifth in science, and sixth in mathematics (Bussière et al., 2004). Significantly, provinces that follow our other guiding principles of freedom of choice and personal responsibility also do significantly better than provinces that disregard them.

THE ALBERTA EXAMPLE

Alberta, the country's top academic scorer, provides an example of how common-sense policies can produce an education system ranked among the best in the world. This is not due to huge spending on education. Indeed, according to the most recent study of spending per student, Alberta spends less per student on education than the national average. Only three provinces spend less per student than Alberta (Figure 1.1).[2] Instead, Alberta excels in Canadian and international comparisons because it enables families to choose the best educational alternatives for their children.

Not coincidentally, the province that leads the nation in scholastic achievement also ranked first in the Canadian Education Freedom Index (Hepburn and Van Belle, 2003). In the words of the United Nations Declaration of Human Rights, Alberta gives its parents more power "to determine the kind of education that shall be given to their children."

---

1 The portion of tuition at independent religious schools that is applicable to religious instruction is eligible for the standard federal income-tax credit for charitable donations.
2 While data only applies to public schools, as noted in the text the great majority of students are in the public school system and drive the PISA (Programme for International Student Assessment, a project of the OECD) results, with educational choice improving the quality of public schools.

Figure 1.1: Total expenditure per student in public and elementary schools, 2003/04

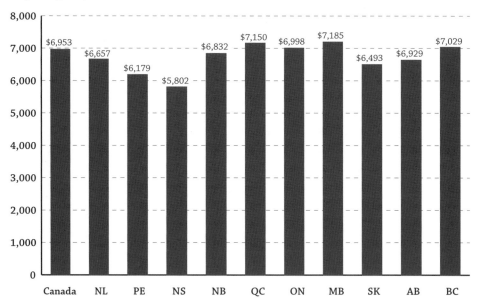

Source: Statistics Canada, Public Institutions Division, 2005.

Alberta has identified and implemented policies that international research and its own experience have proven to raise both standards and citizen satisfaction levels. These do not rely purely on either public or private delivery models but use the best in each to challenge and energize the system as a whole. First, Alberta ensures equity and choice by funding education in independent schools and at home, as well as in the public system. Accredited private schools receive subsidies worth approximately 60% of the basic per-student grant available to public schools, or approximately 35% of the total cost of educating a student in the public system (about $2,500). Children with special education needs who attend private schools receive the same funding as they would if they were attending public schools. Accredited independent schools also receive public funding for supervising the education of home-schooled students, while the parents of those children may receive public funding equal to approximately 16% of what is spent to educate a child in the public system.

Thanks to sound public-policy decisions that encourage excellence and diversity—and defying some critics' apprehensions—Alberta's parents do not always decide that the best choice for their children lies outside the public system. To the contrary. In 1994, when public funding for independent schools was increased, the government also made changes to encourage the public system to become more "goal-oriented, service-oriented, and responsive to market forces" (Bosetti, O'Reilly, and Gereluk, 1998: 2). School boards acquired more control over how they produced academic results, while becoming more accountable for those results. Other reforms included standardized testing, high-school diploma exams, and "charter schools." These last, the only ones in Canada, empower communities to start schools that respond to a local educational need. Although run independently of local school boards, charter schools are public institutions that may neither charge tuition nor exclude any student.

In fact, charter schools have not gained a large foothold in Alberta. In part, that is because Edmonton's far-sighted school superintendent, Emery Dosdall, responded to demands from parents and educators for new programs by encouraging them to open as new schools under his own board. Today, Edmonton is home to more than 30 different educational programs at more than 140 locations. The board has rid itself of "catchment areas" and instead offers elementary students bus service to their family's choice of facility. Researchers found that in 2001 only 51% of Edmonton public school students attended their neighbourhood school—49% attended another Edmonton public school (Hepburn and Van Belle, unpublished).

Calgary was initially slower to provide choices and, in the face of opposition from the local school board, became home to six charter schools.[3] But as choices multiplied in Edmonton, attracting international attention, the Calgary board began to change its stance. Between 2001 and 2004, that board opened 26 new programs or program locations. Though these choices are still meagre in comparison to Edmonton's, they are generous in comparison to much of the rest of Canada.

Educational freedom in other provinces

Alberta is not the only province that encourages equity and excellence through choice and accountability. British Columbia, Manitoba, and Quebec also provide some public funding for children attending independent schools. Like Alberta, these provinces allow the funding to be applied to operating costs and insist that the schools teach the provincial curriculum. Manitoba and Quebec allow funding for schools that operate for profit, which further increases parental choice.

Ontario flirted briefly with a refundable tax credit for parents of children at independent schools but currently provides no assistance for this choice. Saskatchewan and the Atlantic provinces offer no financial support for families that choose independent schools. Independent schools are also heavily

---

3   Charter applicants in Alberta must first apply for status to their local school board. If the school board denies them a charter, they may appeal to the minister of education, as happened in all six cases in Calgary.

regulated in these provinces, making it doubly difficult for them to provide parents with any real alternative to the public system. Tellingly, the same provinces tend to perform below the Canadian average on national and international tests (CMEC, 2005).

THE REPORT CARD ON CHOICE

Alberta gives parents the widest school choice in Canada. It also tops the provinces—and most of the world—in educational achievement. In the rankings on reading literacy, Alberta not only ranks ahead of all the other Canadian provinces, but also ranks higher than any of the other 40 nations in the study save Finland (Figure 1.2).[4] In science, Alberta again ranks ahead of all the other provinces and is outscored only by Finland and Japan, while students in Hong Kong put in a performance equalling Alberta's (Figure 1.3). In mathematics, Alberta again leads Canadian provinces, followed by British Columbia and Quebec. Only Hong Kong outranks Alberta (Figure 1.4).

Along with Alberta, the provinces that encourage some parental choice or that have parents making choices despite a lack of support from the provincial government, rank above the others. In mathematics and science, students in Alberta, British Columbia, and Quebec outperformed the Canadian average and all other provinces. For reading, students in Alberta, British Columbia, and Ontario outperformed their counterparts in other provinces and the Canadian average for all students.

Though most people agree that a choice of schools benefits children, some worry that government funding of independent schools may have negative consequences for the public system. We sometimes hear that such funding will result in "cream skimming," as the best teachers and brightest students abandon public schools, leaving them a sort of educational ghetto populated only by those who can't afford or access better private schools. International and Canadian evidence puts those fears to rest. When policies are well constructed, children in both systems wind up winners. The largest study ever done of educational efficiency, by Germany's Kiel Institute, reveals a powerful link between the health of private education and achievement in the public system. "International differences in student performance are not caused by differences in schooling resources but are mainly due to differences in educational institutions," the study concludes (Wößmann, 2000: Abstract). Competition from private schools inspires excellence among public schools.

---

4   The most recent PISA report had not been published when this publication went to press.

Figure 1.2: PISA scores for reading, 2003

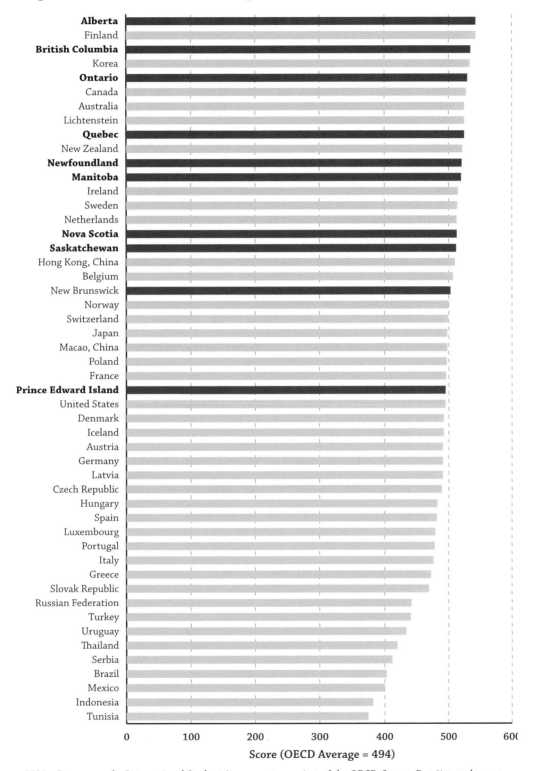

Score (OECD Average = 494)

PISA = Programme for International Student Assessment, a project of the OECD. Source: Bussière et al., 2004.

Figure 1.3: PISA scores for science, 2003

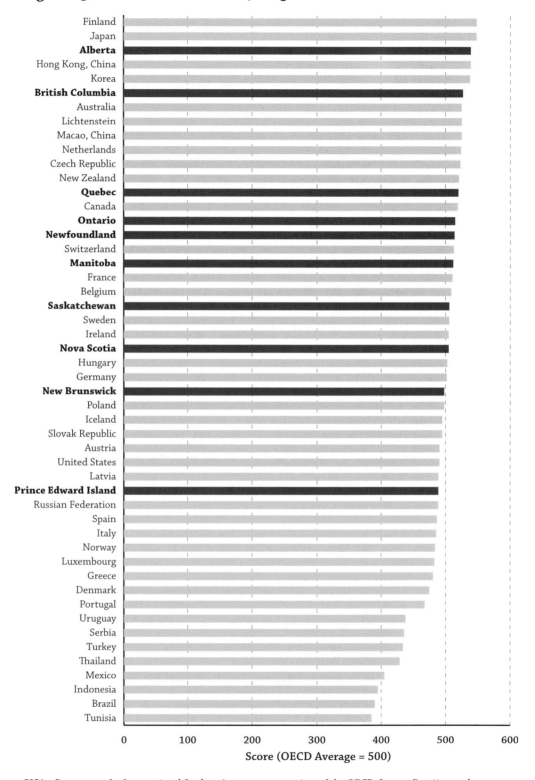

Score (OECD Average = 500)

PISA = Programme for International Student Assessment, a project of the OECD. Source: Bussière et al., 2004.

Figure 1.4: PISA scores for combined mathematics, 2003

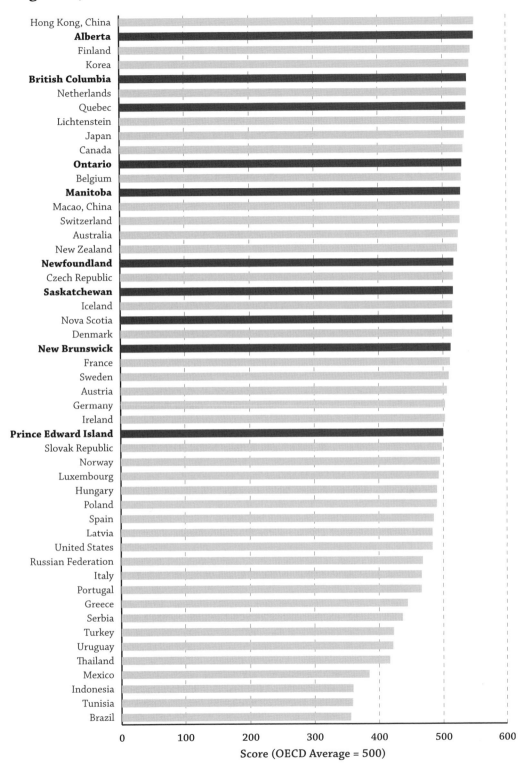

Score (OECD Average = 500)

PISA = Programme for International Student Assessment, a project of the OECD. Source: Bussière et al., 2004.

Further evidence that private-school competition improves public-school performance comes from the United States. Noted Harvard economist Caroline M. Hoxby summarized the effect in this conclusion to one of her many studies of school choice:

> It appears that public schools are induced to raise achievement when they are faced with competition and that this effect swamps any effect associated with cream skimming, reverse cream skimming or the like. The choice reforms that are currently in place do not appear to generate winners and losers, but only winners. Public school students, who are often predicted to be losers, are winners because their schools respond positively to competitive threats. This is not only good news for students; it should be welcome news to those who think that public schools have much good potential. (Hoxby, 2001: 22)

It is equally clear in Canada that public funding of private and home schools has resulted in neither a mass exodus from the public system nor a reduction in the quality of public education. Though independent-school enrolment has increased in Alberta (as in most other provinces), it remains well below the national average (Statistics Canada, 2001b). Rather than encourage a rush to private schools, Alberta seems to have given families good cause to choose public education.

CONCLUSIONS: RAISING OUR MARKS

Education is the one policy field discussed in these pages where the balance of Confederation is respected: provinces not only have the responsibility for education, they are free from federal interference. It should surprise no one that it is also the one area of social policy in which Canada clearly excels. Respecting the constitutional authority of provinces demonstrably produces superior results.

And we can do better still. The other fundamental principles we embrace—choice and personal responsibility—also provide guidance on how to increase our educational achievement. Education is, at heart, a family matter. It may be subsidized by the state, guided by provincial curricula, and monitored by public inspectors but the responsibility for choosing the best education for each child lies with parents. Families across Canada deserve the excellence of educational opportunities found where parental choice is allowed. No child should be forced to attend a school that does not meet his or her needs. These choices should reside with families, providing them the means, freedom, and responsibility to choose the best education possible for their children. In their individual choices, they will also illuminate the path to national excellence in education.

Quality, accountability, and equity are three further commonsense objectives for Canadian education policy. Ministries of education must define their objectives, teach towards them, measure their success, and inform parents and the public of their results. They must also reach out not only to the average or most able students but to those with special needs or at risk of dropping out of school.

RECOMMENDATIONS

1.1 Make available vouchers worth 50% of the total per-student cost of public education for parents opting for independent education. According to the fifteenth OISE/UT (Ontario Institute for Studies in Education at the University of Toronto) Survey, Public Attitudes Towards Education in Ontario, 2004, in 2004 only 35% of Canadian adults were confident in their province's public schools. The same survey found that only 28% of people thought the quality of high-school education was improving. A voucher system for children up to age 18 would allow these parents to find more satisfactory solutions. Families would have the resources to take advantage of the growing number of education alternatives: full-day, part-time, or after-school community programs, or e-schooling via the internet. Needless to say, both parents and government have the responsibility to ensure that these alternatives are indeed educating children and are not engaged in any inappropriate or illegal activity.

1.2 For children with special needs, make available vouchers worth 75% of the total per-student cost of public education for whose parents choose alternative education for these children. Children with special needs require special support. Although education systems across the country spend large sums on special-needs programs, parents are often dissatisfied with their results[5] and resort to home or independent schooling if they can afford them. Children with special needs cannot wait for the system to be fixed. It is only fair that their parents receive some additional help with the challenge of meeting their children's needs. Some provinces, including British Columbia, Alberta, and Manitoba, deserve credit for providing special funding for these students to attend independent schools.

---

5 See in particular the 2001 *Annual Report* of Ontario's Provincial Auditor on the failure of Ontario's public school system to serve special-needs children adequately (Government of Ontario, Office of the Provincial Auditor, 2001).

1.3 Hold all K-12 schools accountable for results, while giving them freedom to innovate. Provinces should encourage site-based management of public schools, giving principals control over budgets and staffing and holding them to account for their results. Market mechanisms can further increase public school accountability. Parents allowed to choose their children's schools will choose those that produce the best results. Money will follow students. Schools that succeed will prosper and grow.

CHAPTER 2

LENDING A HELPING HAND

WELFARE POLICY

We envision a more productive and prosperous Canada where all Canadians can build better lives for themselves and their families. We wish no less to see a caring Canada, always ready to comfort and assist individuals and families when misfortune strikes, and to offer them the opportunity to rebuild self-sufficient lives.

But what is the reality for too many Canadians? Over 1.7 million Canadians—5.4% of our fellow citizens—live on welfare (Figure 2.1). They find themselves trapped in poverty by social "assistance" programs that increase, rather than decrease, their state of dependence. In our land of opportunity and wealth, this is an unacceptable sign that we are failing too many of our fellow Canadians. We believe Canada can do better.

THE NEED: PATHWAYS OUT OF WANT

We believe Canadians on welfare, or in danger of falling onto social assistance, need and deserve a strong helping hand. Compassion should be a guiding principle in welfare reform. But compassion must go beyond a monthly cheque. Programs that leave individuals and families trapped in dependence are not compassionate. They are particularly damaging for children, who may come to believe that the doors of opportunity are closed to them. Programs must be based on the best empirical evidence and carefully designed to help individuals and families begin to build hope and prosperity for the future, to get on with productive, independent lives.

As with all government services financed by taxpayers, economy must also guide welfare reform. This is not simply out of a desire to save money. High and increasing welfare spending is not an indicator of caring programs. It is a sign that we are failing; that those already on welfare remain trapped in

Figure 2.1: Welfare dependency in Canada, 1973–2005

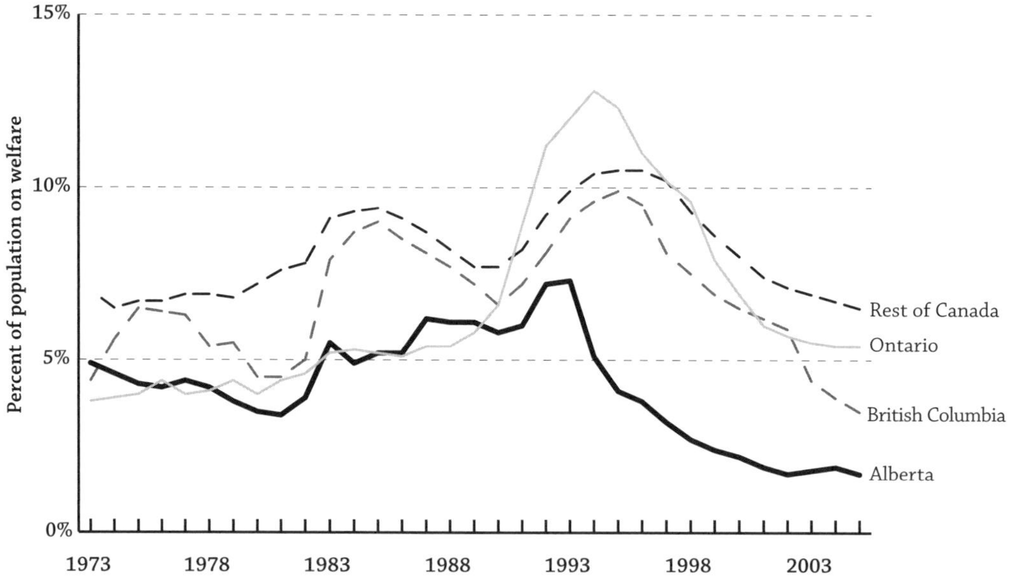

Source: Schafer, Emes, and Clemens, 2001; National Council of Welfare, 2005; Statistics Canada, 2005d.

dependency and that others are joining them. By contrast, programs that provide to Canadians in need the freedom and opportunity to take responsibility for their own lives, will by their very nature save money over time.

That said, a reduction in spending due merely to lower benefits is not, by itself, a sign of success. The sad reality is that too many Canadians are, in effect, warehoused in the welfare system—"out of sight, out of mind." They lack the help, advice, skills, motivation, and incentives they need to begin building new, more prosperous, lives for themselves and their families.

Beyond compassion and economy, the central principles guiding welfare reform must be freedom and responsibility, and the right division of responsibility between levels of government. We believe that individuals and families given the freedom to determine their own fate will look after themselves far better than any government program. In the same spirit, we believe that the government closest to the people it serves but still large enough to be able to raise sufficient funds will, given responsibility, resources, and freedom to innovate within a rebalanced federalism, best serve its citizens.

By far the best welfare outcome for most recipients is a job—paying work. We will propose in this section policies that have helped hundreds of thousands of Canadians find jobs and begin building hope and prosperity for themselves and their families. It may seem obvious to say that those who escape the welfare-dependency trap by finding work should benefit from their efforts. Sadly, this is too often not the case. "Claw-backs" often leave them little better off or even worse off. Recipients who enter the workforce need to reap the rewards and see their standard of living increase. We propose to ensure that.

True success for Canadians on, or at risk of joining, welfare rolls lies in reducing their dependency, combined with real gains in earned income. That is our goal for welfare reform. It is already being achieved in some Canadian provinces.

WHAT IS BEING DONE? LEARNING HOW TO HELP

The good news is that hundreds of thousands of Canadians have escaped the welfare trap in the last decade. As recently as 1994, over 3 million Canadians—more than 10% of our population—were on welfare. That number has been cut by nearly one-half in the last decade. How has this been achieved? In part because Canada's government did eventually follow the public's wishes and eliminate its budget deficit, spurring the economic growth that is always the best friend of the poor. Even so, previous periods of strong economic growth have not reduced welfare roles as sharply, nor did all provinces with growing economies see the same reduction this time. So other explanations must be at work.

Innovative programs in a number of provinces are giving welfare recipients what they need to begin rebuilding their lives. Teamed with experienced workers who understand their plight, Canadians on welfare are now receiving the assistance and expertise they need to re-enter the workforce. Such programs also lend every effort to ensure that Canadians in need, but not yet dependent on welfare, find better alternatives.

Driving much of this change in policy over the last decade was concern over rising welfare dependency and budgetary deficits. From 1980 to 1994, the percentage of Canadians supported by social assistance nearly doubled, from 5.4% to 10.7%. Typically, welfare rolls expanded during bad times but then failed to shrink during good times. More and more Canadians became trapped in dependency. This growing dependency was reflected in the nation's fiscal burden. In 1980, spending on all social programs amounted to 14.3% of gross domestic product (GDP); by 1992, this figure had risen to 21.1% (Battle, 1998). Far from reflecting a caring society, these increased costs were a sign of failure to help recipients renew lives and livelihoods. In effect, they were the price of a heartless willingness to warehouse needy Canadians in dependency.

In part because of this financial pressure, the provinces responded to varying degrees by reducing welfare benefits. In addition, many provinces tightened eligibility requirements, especially where government support was considered less important, as for single employables. A number of provinces adopted anti-fraud measures. These are often criticized but can be essential to the success of overall reform: people who learn how to game the welfare system are motivated to remain on its support rather than seek independence from it.

Reducing the pressure on public spending also leads to other benefits. It frees resources to focus on those in greatest need and those moving from dependency to self-sufficiency. But welfare reform must go beyond saving money, or it will fail the very people it is intended to help. Fortunately, well-designed reforms have been shown to provide great benefits for those on assistance.

Most importantly, application of the principle of "rebalanced federalism" has enabled transformation in this important area of social service, with impressive results. A willingness on the part of the federal government to respect provincial responsibilities for welfare—and to supply no-strings-attached funding for this purpose—has allowed at least some of the provinces to adopt programs that provide recipients with greater freedom of choice and the opportunity to accept more responsibility for their own well being.

FEDERAL REFORM: RESTORING RESPECT FOR PROVINCIAL RESPONSIBILITY

In 1996, the federal government replaced the Canada Assistance Plan (CAP) and the Established Programs Finance (EPF) with the new Canada Health and Social Transfer (CHST).[1] Unlike those earlier dollar-for-dollar cost-sharing initiatives, the CHST provided a block grant to the provinces for spending on welfare, health, and post-secondary education. This block grant reduced total federal funding for those services, transferring more financial responsibility to the provinces. But, critically, it also gave provinces greater authority over how welfare services were to be delivered. The only condition for receiving federal funds for welfare under the CHST (since renamed the Canada Social Transfer—CST) was that provinces must allow residents and non-residents alike to be eligible for social assistance. That is, the federal government prohibited any residency requirement but permitted any other reforms the provinces saw fit. For their part, provinces could use this new flexibility to restructure their social assistance programs.

---

1   The Canada Health and Social Transfer (CHST) was a combined transfer that provided federal support for provincial health care, post-secondary education, and social assistance and social services programs. On April 1, 2004, the CHST was replaced by the Canada Health Transfer (CHT), which provides federal support for provincial health-care programs, and the Canada Social Transfer (CST), which provides support for all other programs previously included with health care in the CHST including social assistance and social services.

PROVINCIAL REFORMS: FREEDOM—AND CHOICE

This rebalancing of responsibilities gave Canadian provinces the freedom to experiment. They were able to design programs that best suited the needs of their own people. Not all chose to pursue reform. Many were satisfied with the basic structure of their welfare programs and did little with the opportunity granted under the new federal legislation. But some provinces set out on a path to reduce dependency and restore hope to their citizens in need. They were able to learn from reforms experienced in other jurisdictions and adjust their policies accordingly. Interestingly however, no two provinces embraced exactly the same set of new policies.

Alberta

Alberta began reforming its welfare system even before the CHST, at the risk of losing federal funding. Indeed, the province's success in reducing welfare dependency actually encouraged Ottawa to establish the CHST in 1996. By the same token, the CHST legitimized Alberta's initiatives and freed the province to pursue them more rigorously.

Most importantly, the Alberta reforms strove to help people avoid welfare in the first place. This approach was based on the recognition that the propensity to receive social assistance increases dramatically after the first receipt of support. Thus, in 1993, Alberta revamped its welfare program with the primary goal of reducing the number of first-time applicants entering the system, particularly young employables. Case-workers assess the immediate needs of welfare applicants and encourage them to use every other avenue of support, including job-search and labour-market programs, before granting assistance. The goal is to offer more choices and pry open the door of opportunity before dependence sets in with its attendant sense of hopelessness. Alberta also allowed faith-based non-profit organizations to provide more social services, such as addictions counselling, daycare, homeless shelters, and seniors' lodging.

Ontario

Ontario also began reform prior to the enactment of the CHST. In 1995, the Ontario government undertook comprehensive measures to reverse a decade-long trend of rising welfare dependency. Principal among Ontario's reforms was the creation in 1996 of Ontario Works, the first work-for-welfare program in Canada. Its primary goals were to promote self-reliance through employment and provide temporary assistance to those most in need (MCFCS, 2001).

Ontario Works prepares recipients for self-sufficiency by engaging them in some level of employment, depending on their skills, education, and personal or marital status. Though agreements vary, participants typically begin a job search immediately in order to assess their level of employability (MCFCS, 2001). The province instituted private-sector work placements to expand available job opportunities (MCSS, 1999) while assigning some of those unable to find work through job searches to paid employment in the public sector.

Those who criticized Ontario's reduction in welfare benefits—to a level still 10% above the national average—ignored a significant component of this reform. Ontario allowed welfare recipients to keep the same level of total benefits available prior to the benefit reductions by reducing the government share of benefits by 22% and increasing the earnings provisions without "claw-back" by an equal amount. This move further encouraged recipients to start paid work and begin the process of re-entering the workforce and learning not only job skills but also life skills associated with having a job (time management, grooming, and so on). To develop work skills among the hardest to employ, typically welfare recipients with little or no work experience, Ontario Works assigned unpaid community service of up to 70 hours per month.

The goal of reform is to open doors of opportunity but sometimes it may also involve a push through that door. In Ontario, recipients who fail to honour their participation agreements are subject to financial penalties. Those who do not adhere to their work requirements, refuse a job without cause, or quit an assigned work placement, have their benefits reduced or cancelled for three months for the first offence, and six months for subsequent offences (Ontario Regulation 134/98). Some have called this hard-hearted but we do a disservice to those who can make better lives for themselves and their families if we allow dependence to grow.

British Columbia

In 1999, British Columbia for the first time engaged a private-sector agency, JobWave, to assist and support individuals as they rejoined the workforce and regained their independence. In addition to providing a free placement service for employers, JobWave staff provided face-to-face counselling, e-coaching, on-line seminars, and search capabilities for local employment. As of April 2007, this innovative re-employment program, one of several operated by WCG International Consultants Ltd., a company based in Victoria, had helped over 57,000 British Columbians find jobs with an average wage of $11.25 per hour—44% higher than minimum wage.

In 2002, British Columbia became the first province in Canada to experiment with time limits on welfare benefits. Under the new policy, employable recipients were limited to a cumulative two years of social assistance out of every five-year period. Upon the expiration of the time limit, employable recipients become ineligible for welfare while recipients with dependents have their benefits reduced. Effectively, time limits returned welfare to its original purpose: a short-term insurance program to provide assistance in times of emergency. While these time limits were ultimately abandoned, it is interesting to note that their introduction had a signalling effect since their abandonment has not had a large impact on welfare dependency in the province to date.

In addition to the time limits, the province required that all employable welfare recipients, including single parents with children over three years of age, seek employment or participate in job-related activities to remain eligible for assistance. Recipients failing to adhere to their work requirements are sanctioned, resulting in the reduction or cancellation of benefits for a prescribed period. Single parents with children under the age of three were exempt from work requirements. If, after two years, these single parents are not employed, their social assistance benefits were reduced by 33%; only those single parents caring for a disabled child or who are temporarily excused from seeking employment would escape this reduction.

Reforms in other provinces

Not all provinces used their new freedom under the CHST to make comprehensive changes to their welfare systems. Some, such as Saskatchewan and Quebec, implemented far less ambitious reforms. Others maintained essentially the same programs in place before 1996, with only small improvements.

Saskatchewan

Saskatchewan focused on improving incentives to make employment attractive for welfare recipients. In 1997, for example, the Youth Futures program eliminated assistance to individuals younger than 22 years of age unless their families were unable to provide for them financially—while also requiring anyone in this age group who did receive welfare to participate in school, training, or work-experience programs.

Quebec

Quebec's changes were even more limited. In 1996, the Quebec government increased the penalty for welfare recipients who failed to look for work or quit a job without legitimate reason. Changes to the treatment of liquid assets sought to ensure that applicants first exhausted all other resources. Adults pursuing vocational high-school education were transferred off welfare to the provincial student assistance plan.

Diverse responses

The introduction in 1996 of block grants with minimal constraints freed provinces to experiment with a range of policy alternatives. Some grasped the opportunity to undertake fundamental welfare reforms, adopting focused programs to help people avoid their first stretch on welfare (Alberta) or promptly re-join the workforce (Ontario). Others were content to fine-tune their programs or do very little at all, leaving the basic structure of their welfare systems intact.

THE EVIDENCE: REFORMS PAY HUMAN DIVIDENDS

Dependency rates

Between the 1970s and the early 1990s, Canada experienced a considerable increase in welfare dependency in every jurisdiction (Figure 2.1). As we have already noted, by 1994 a record 3.1 million people were receiving social assistance—more than one Canadian in 10. In the wake of reforms, this number has been cut roughly in half. In 2005, the most recent year for which data is available, just 5.4% of Canadians were receiving assistance.

The fruits of reform have differed by province (Figure 2.2). Alberta experienced a dramatic reduction in the number of people receiving social assistance. In 1993, 196,000 Albertans were on welfare—7.3% of the province's population. That percentage has fallen steadily, to 56,400 people in 2005 (about 1.7% of the population)—a dramatic 71% reduction from the 1993 peak. A similar impact occurred in British Columbia after the 1999 and 2002 reforms. Welfare dependency in that province dropped from 7.5% in 1998 to 3.5% in 2005. Today, British Columbia and Alberta are enjoying the lowest levels of welfare dependency in more than 30 years.

Welfare dependency has also fallen sharply in Ontario. In 1994, 12.8% of Ontarians were receiving welfare cheques. By 2005, that proportion was reduced to 5.4% (or about 676,500 beneficiaries)—the lowest rate of dependency since 1988. Other provinces have had less success in reducing their welfare rolls. Since 1995 when welfare dependency peaked, Saskatchewan has lowered the number of its dependent citizens from 82,200 (about 8.1% of the population) to 48,700 (4.9%). In Quebec, the rate has fallen from a high of 11.2% in 1996 to 6.8% today; still, aside from Newfoundland (at 9.4%), Quebec has the highest rate of welfare dependency in all of Canada. In the rest of Canada, where provinces were content mainly to make marginal changes to welfare policies, welfare dependency has declined from an average of 10.0% in 1994 to 6.4% in 2004. This is largely the result of a very strong economy through the late 1990s.

Self-sufficiency

Of course, dependency rates do not provide the whole picture. While leaving social assistance is a positive first step, it is also important that former recipients become self-sufficient. To that end, researchers have examined the well-being of welfare leavers in Canada in terms of employment and earnings.

Figure 2.2: Welfare dependency in Canada, 1995 & 2005

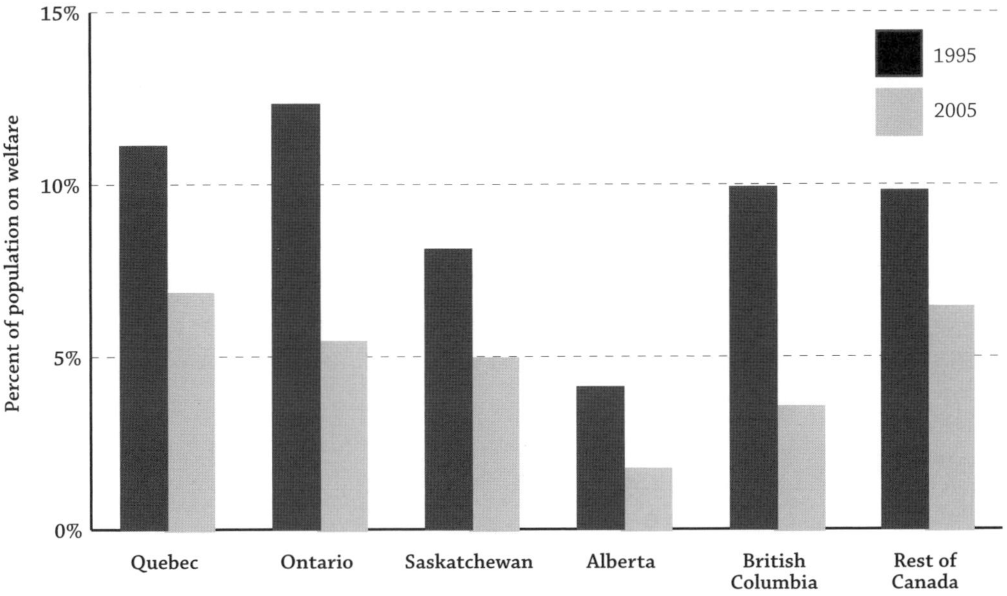

Source: Schafer, Emes, and Clemens, 2001; National Council of Welfare, 2006;
Provincial Economic Accounts, 2006.

For example, a 2003 survey suggests that British Columbia's reforms have been successful in moving recipients out of dependency and into employment. According to that research, 64% of those leaving welfare found employment, while another 7% returned to school. At the time of the survey, 60% of respondents indicated that their main activity was employment (BC Ministry of Human Resources, 2003).

Data released by Statistics Canada in March 2003 also show that most people leaving welfare have become better off (Frenette and Picot, 2003). The study, *Life after Welfare: The Economic Well-Being of Welfare Leavers in Canada during the 1990s*, found that about six out of ten former Canadian welfare recipients saw their after-tax family income improve substantially from what they had received on social assistance. In Ontario, for instance, a third of former recipients earned, on average, $13,000 more than they had received two years earlier on welfare; another third had incomes $2,500 higher than before.

THE POSSIBILITIES: FREEING THE DEPENDENT

It is critical to recognize the central role that our guiding principles of rebalanced federalism, freedom of choice, and acceptance of responsibility have played in the impressive reduction of welfare dependency over the last decade. By the standards of compassion and economy, the results have been heartening and commendable—when those principles have been most vigorously applied. Provinces that seized the opportunity to make fundamental reforms—especially those emphasizing the choices and responsibilities presented to their citizens in need—have seen their welfare rolls shrink. Most former welfare recipients in those jurisdictions have found employment and become better off. By contrast, provinces that pursued more modest changes have seen relatively smaller reductions in welfare dependency. However, these principles have yet to be fully or universally applied in social assistance policies. When one level of government provides funding and another designs and delivers programs, accountability and responsibility remained blurred; governments should be fully accountable for the money they raise and spend. Not every jurisdiction has made available to its own needy citizens the same freedom of choice, opportunity, and responsibility for their own lives that are embodied in the 1996 rebalancing of federal roles. We emphasize these points, because these principles guide our recommendations as to "where we go from here."

POLICY PROPOSALS

Getting the fundamentals right

While the reforms introduced in 1996 have allowed provinces the freedom to improve their welfare programs dramatically, the current structure of federal transfers is still imperfect. On the one hand, the existing arrangement allows provinces wide latitude to decide policies that lie clearly within their jurisdiction, does not bias their decisions other than to prohibit residency requirements, and allows them to retain surpluses in transferred funds arising from their choices. On the other hand, the transfer still creates a disconnect between the government that raises money for welfare and the government that spends it. Provinces are effectively spending money that they have not collected and thus are likely to be less prudent in the use of those funds. The same disconnect makes governments less accountable to their citizens for how much revenue is really being raised through the taxes they pay.

The federal government would do far better to reduce its revenues by the value of the transfer, vacating the tax room for the provinces to raise their own funds for the purpose of sustaining welfare programs. This gives the provinces a more direct responsibility to their citizens with greater accountability as a result. Provinces should also take this opportunity to design welfare policies suited to their unique circumstances, policies that best reflect the needs and desires of their citizens. Those provinces that have yet to do so should take advantage of this additional freedom to redesign their welfare schemes to emphasize the "helping hand" over the "warehouse" of long-term dependency.

At the same time, appropriate programs for individuals who do require long-term assistance must reflect the special financial and other needs of these individuals. All too often, disabled Canadians do not receive adequate levels of support to allow them to live in dignity. Even worse, "claw-back" measures deprive them of the chance to improve their standard of living by accepting limited employment that is within their abilities.

We have outlined several reforms below that provinces can implement in order to provide a more efficiently administered and delivered welfare program that provides short-term relief to help those in need back to their feet.

Improving the welfare "back office"

Monopolies are nearly always inimical to top performance. An effective welfare program will incorporate competition in both administration and delivery, thereby both reducing costs and improving the quality of services.

1 *Competition in the administration of welfare*

For-profit companies have certain competitive advantages over the public sector, as do those in the non-profit sector. In order to achieve the most effective administration of welfare services, the system should be open to competitive bidding among both types of organizations. (See the Monograph, "Social Entrepreneurs: The Alternative to Government Services," page 63.)

The United States has permitted the contracting of welfare intake and eligibility determination since 1996. Competition to supply these services has resulted in substantial gains. A leader in this area is Wisconsin, the first state to privatize entire areas of its welfare-delivery system through its Wisconsin Works (W-2) program. As a result of opening up eligibility determination, case management, and related services to competitive bidding, the state's taxpayers saved at least $10.25 million during the first two years of privatization (Dodenhoff, 1998). This saving came not through reduced benefits but increased efficiency.

2 *Competition in program delivery*

As with administrative functions, governments can contract out client-service responsibilities to private for-profit and not-for-profit providers through competitive bidding. As one example, private providers can assist welfare recipients to find and maintain employment through training, trial work periods, and post-employment assistance. Such contracts often incorporate a pay-for-performance standard so that providers are compensated based on their success at moving welfare recipients into employment.

One notable example of successful private delivery of welfare is the New York-based America Works. Studies of America Works have found that, of those welfare recipients placed in jobs in the prior three years, 88% were still off the welfare rolls (New York State Department of Labor, 1997). The Social Market Foundation confirmed in its study of America Works that the program had been "successful in helping the long-term unemployed to find jobs and at saving money" (Harding, 1998). Furthermore, the National Center for Policy Analysis found that America Works is capable of training workers for $5,490 per recipient, substantially less than the estimated $24,000 price tag for a comparable program run by New York City (NCPA, 2000).

Restoring independence

An effective welfare program both relieves short-term financial distress and assists in the return to economic self-sufficiency. Its objective is one of transition, not maintenance; and its measure of success, you might say, is how quickly it "loses" each client.

1   Moving forward to employment

Opportunity, self-esteem, and future prosperity are all best served by keeping the focus of welfare assistance on the ultimate objective, employment. Programs that concentrate on moving recipients quickly back to work are more effective in generating earnings and self-sufficiency than those that instead emphasize training outside the workplace. Exposure to the working world helps individuals maintain or acquire basic job skills such as punctuality, reliability, and cooperation. It provides an opportunity to network for future job openings and, perhaps most importantly, earn valuable work experience, the most common barrier to employment for welfare recipients (Reidl and Rector, 2002).

By contrast, empirical evidence largely discredits back-to-work programs that emphasize education and training first. A study by The Fraser Institute of government-sponsored training programs in the United States found that these were largely unsuccessful in reducing unemployment, increasing earnings, or diminishing welfare dependency among poor single parents, disadvantaged adults, and out-of school youth (Mihlar and Smith, 1997). Similarly, Manpower Demonstration Research Corporation found that recipients placed in employment-focused programs earn 122% more than their counterparts in education-based programs. The same study determined that the employment-first model "moved welfare recipients into jobs more quickly ... [and] had larger effects on employment, earnings, and welfare receipt ... than [did] education-focused ones" (Hamilton et al., 2001: ES-2).

2 Making work pay

We all need motivation. Incentives are an important policy tool: welfare recipients are more likely to seek and find work when earnings are subject to low effective marginal tax rates. When someone can keep most of the income they earn, they are more inclined to work.

All American states offer such incentives in the form of "earned income disregards"—referred to in Canada as "earnings exemptions"— that exclude some income when calculating welfare benefits. Most states also disregard a portion of earnings when determining eligibility (USHHS, 2003). Such exemptions are particularly effective at encouraging part-time employment—valuable in maintaining basic job skills and access to information on future employment opportunities.

Conversely, welfare benefits that exceed what can be earned in the workplace create incentives to remain (or, worse, go) on welfare rather than take employment and be self-sufficient. Thus, benefit levels must be set with regard to prevailing wage rates to ensure that working pays more than welfare.

3 Making work more than just a goal

An explicit requirement that recipients work, with sanctions for those who do not comply, serves both to hasten the transition to self-sufficiency and to make welfare less attractive to first-time applicants. It reinforces the intended temporary nature of social assistance and discourages unnecessary reliance on it.

The United States adopted work requirements with other welfare reforms in 1996. State versions cover a broad range of job related activities: unsubsidized employment, subsidized private or public-sector employment, on-the-job training, community service, vocational training, and job search. Still, the nature of the required work activity is an important consideration: there are inherent differences between private-sector and public-sector jobs. The latter have often been characterized as temporary "make-work." According to the US General Accounting Office, widespread public-service employment programs of the 1970s failed to prepare participants for unsubsidized work in the private sector (US GAO, 1978, 1979, 1980). Professor Thomas DiLorenzo of George Mason University asserts that the private sector, in contrast, has a greater capacity to develop marketable job skills and foster long-term independence, in part because people are trained in occupations that are valued by employers (DiLorenzo, 1984).

In order to enforce work requirements, every US state has adopted some form of sanctions: welfare benefits are reduced or terminated if recipients fail to participate in their assigned activity. Evidence from the Wisconsin Works (W-2) program has demonstrated that requiring most new applicants to find employment in the private sector or perform community service shortly after enrolling, reduces the number of entrants by half (Rector, 1997). Similarly the Cato Institute's Michael J. New found that "the strength of state sanctioning policies had the largest impact on caseload declines between 1996 and 2000" (New, 2002: 9).

4   *Setting time limits*

Limiting the length of time that certain recipients can receive benefits shifts welfare from being a program of entitlement to one of insurance against temporary periods of adversity. It encourages a prompt return to employment and the seeking out of other alternatives to welfare whenever possible. Jurisdictions that have established such time limits have also succeeded in reducing long-term welfare dependency. Time limits have become the norm in the United States since 1996. Under the federal Personal Responsibility and Work Opportunity Reconciliation Act (PRWORA), American states must impose a five-year lifetime limit on Temporary Assistance for Needy Families benefits. Many have legislated time limits shorter than five years.

The fact that the United States implemented numerous reforms in the late 1990s to reduce welfare dependency makes it difficult to isolate the effect of time limits alone. Nonetheless, certain studies have demonstrated their effectiveness. For instance, a recent study entitled "Welfare Dynamics under Time Limits" examined the effects of Florida's Family Transition Program five-year time limit on the receipt of welfare benefits. The study found that time limits, "in the absence of other features of the program that worked to increase welfare use, would have reduced welfare receipt by as much as 16%" (Grogger and Michalopoulos, 2003).

5   *Creating better options*

A further strategy helps applicants avoid welfare altogether by pursuing every viable alternative. This is important because one's first spell on social assistance is seldom the last. In other words, receiving social assistance for the first time tends to generate welfare dependency in the future (Blank and Ruggles, 1994; Cao, 1996; Meyer and Cancian, 1996). In Canada, Alberta has embraced this strategy with the most vigour. In a 1997 study of the province's welfare program, it was determined that "[t]he significant reduction [in the number of recipients] came from a sharp decrease in individuals who were applying for welfare for the first time" (Boessenkool, 1997: 11–12).

Where compassion counts most: increasing help for the disabled

Welfare works best as a temporary program to help people in need get back on their feet. Regrettably, many disabled Canadians can never be fully self-supporting; they may also face special financial pressures because of their disability. These citizens nonetheless deserve the opportunity to improve their quality of life. The provinces should establish separate programs for these Canadians, providing sufficient support for them to live in dignity. "Clawbacks" and other road-blocks that restrict their ability to supplement these programs with earned income should be eliminated.

CONCLUSION: RESTORING INDEPENDENCE

Our goal can be simply stated: to provide a helping hand to those in need, to help Canadians who encounter hardship regain the dignity of work and the advantages it brings, to restore their hope for a better future. The programs we have discussed are not revolutionary or even new. They have a proven track record in meeting these goals.

Only hesitancy and lack of foresight hold us back. Those are not reasons to abandon hundreds of thousands of our fellow citizens to needless dependency. We owe it to them to move ahead. In addition, let us never lose sight of the fact that the most important policies to help welfare recipients are not actually welfare policies. Instead, they are policies designed to increase prosperity, jobs, and opportunities. We will have more to say about how to achieve those objectives in the second section, A More Dynamic Economy.

RECOMMENDATIONS

2.1 Eliminate the federal Health and Social Transfer and have the federal government vacate equivalent tax room for the provinces to raise their own funds for the purpose of sustaining welfare programs.

2.2 Take advantage on the provincial level of these additional resources, and have the provinces fulfill their constitutional responsibility by redesigning their welfare schemes to emphasize the "helping hand" over the "warehouse" of long-term dependency.

2.3 Open both the administration of welfare and program delivery at the provincial level to competitive bidding from for-profit companies as well as the non-profit sector.

2.4 Focus assistance on restoring independence through employment. To this end, welfare payments should be structured to present a clear incentive toward employment, while earned income should be subject to the lowest possible marginal tax rates.

2.5 Make return to work not only an explicit goal of welfare programs but also a mandated condition of assistance, with clear time limits for receiving benefits.

2.6 Include "pre-benefit" components in social assistance programs to help applicants avoid welfare altogether by pursuing every viable alternative.

2.7 Provide those Canadians with disabilities so severe that they can never be fully independent with sufficient support for them to live in dignity and eliminate "claw-backs" that limit their ability to supplement this support with earned income.

SOCIAL ENTREPRENEURS: THE ALTERNATIVE TO GOVERNMENT SERVICES

Societies have always depended on non-profit and voluntary organizations to provide many vital public goods independently of both government and the private, for-profit sector. More than simply providing temporary aid and insurance against unforeseen economic hardship, these institutions of civil society—including family, church, charity, mutual aid societies, and other informal community associations—have helped to build social capital, encourage trust and cooperation among individuals, and develop the values and character of citizenship.

In 2003, the most recent year for which data is available, there were 161,000 organizations operating in Canada's non-profit sector.[1] Twelve percent (19,000 organizations) were devoted to social services, the vast majority of which (91%) were locally provided in a single neighbourhood, town, city, or region. Their accountability to the communities that support them with gifts of time and money make these non-profit organizations uniquely qualified to provide social services in an efficient, responsive, and compassionate manner.

TACKLING THE ROOT CAUSES OF HOMELESSNESS[2]

When a group of concerned citizens recognized Calgary's growing homelessness problem in 1983, they didn't wait for government to come to the rescue. Rather, they sought community support to tackle the root causes of homelessness by opening the doors of Simon House Residence Society, a home for homeless and indigent men actively addressing their addictions and pursuing recovery. In a sector where government funding is the norm, Simon House has steadfastly resisted all direct government funding.[3] In addition to con-

---

1 Approximately half of these organizations are registered charities. The difference between charities and non-profits is that charities are registered with, and subject to, the Canada Revenue Agency's regulations and are able to issue tax receipts and accept grants and donations from foundations.

2 This profile is drawn from LeRoy and Gudelot, 2004.

3 The non-profit social service sector in Alberta gets approximately 42% of its aggregate revenues from government. Because most direct government funding for Canadian non-profits comes from provincial and municipal levels (80% from the provinces and 12% from municipalities), the independence of the sector varies significantly by province (Statistics Canada, 2004a). Simon House has, from time to time, accepted small (less than 1% of their total revenues) provincial government employment grants that subsidized the cost of providing paid work experience to one of their social assistance clients.

cerns that such funding would contribute to mission drift, interfere with their strategic planning, and add to their paperwork and administrative burden, Simon House's volunteer board of directors felt that the organization should be community-supported. This decision has paid off. In a notoriously competitive and unstable world of non-profit fundraising, Simon House has insulated itself from unexpected changes in income by maintaining a large and diversified funding base: collecting revenue from 52 different sources, Simon House's largest donor accounts for just over one third of its total income.

In addition to supporting the organization financially, the community also provides a willing source of volunteers, who donate over 15,000 hours of their time to Simon House each year. Grateful ex-clients are among the organization's most committed volunteers, providing current residents with living proof that by making positive life choices, they too can graduate to a life of opportunity as productive members of society. This use of volunteers and careful stewardship of donated income allows them to provide their services for just $15 per day, where costs for similar programs can typically exceed $1,000 per day.

This reliance on community support as a source of volunteers and private financing has established a direct line of accountability from Simon House to the community they serve. This has produced some remarkable results. In a field where success rates can fall into the discouragingly low 5%-to-20% range, Simon House boasts a success rate of 50%.[4] In addition to earning Simon House the gratitude and respect of their clients, volunteers, and supporters, this success has made their organization a model for replication across North America.

SHOWING TEEN PARENTS LIFE AFTER WELFARE

Non-profit organizations can also bring their innovation and efficiency to bear on the delivery of government social-assistance programs. While funding three quarters of their $8-million-per-year operation with donations from private foundations and individuals within their community, the YMCA of Sarnia-Lambton is also contracted by the Ontario government to provide a Learning, Earning, and Parenting (LEAP) program. Established in 2000 as part of the province's welfare-to-work strategy, known as Ontario Works,[5] LEAP was designed to improve the lives of young parents between the ages of 16 and 21, helping them to complete high school, find and maintain employment, and enhance their parenting skills.

With over 90 years of experience serving youth in their community, the YMCA is able to draw on a 400-person volunteer workforce to deliver an enhanced array of programs and services to their clients. This added people-power is clearly evident in the LEAP program, where a single full-time equivalent (FTE) staffer is assisted by the equivalent of 16 full-time volunteers. This enables the YMCA to keep costs low while responding to local needs by offering value-added incentives to the LEAP participants, from diapers and babysitting services to mentoring and career counselling.

---

4   Simon House defines success as "a return to family, employment, community, and maintaining continuous sobriety for a period in excess of one year or longer."

5   Ontario Works was the centrepiece of reforms that coupled tough work requirements with sanctions for non-compliance to help move more than half a million people (577,300) off Ontario's welfare rolls between 1994 and 2000 (LeRoy, 2005).

The use of volunteers and the strong attention to client needs and outcomes are just two features that have made the YMCA of Sarnia-Lambton's LEAP program so successful. To date, 127 students have graduated from the YMCA's LEAP program, more than 90% of whom are no longer on the Ontario Works caseload. Even more important than the savings to taxpayers that has resulted from this partnership are the young families that have been saved from a lifetime of dependency and hardship.

CONCLUSION

Simon House and the YMCA of Sarnia-Lambton show how the innovation and entrepreneurship of the non-profit sector can be used to improve the quality of public services, and quality of life, in our communities. The fact that taxpayers fund a particular service no more means that government must provide the service than that government must form a public-sector construction company every time a government building is erected. Whether acting independently or in partnership with government, non-profit organizations are driven by the discipline of the market to make best use of scarce human and financial resources. Just as importantly, these non-profit organizations are motivated by a genuine compassion for the individual clients whose lives they come to share through many hours of heartfelt service.

RECOMMENDATION

❀ Canadian governments should examine ways to open up provision of social services to competitive bidding from the for-profit and not-for-profit sectors.

CHAPTER 3

THE WORLD'S BEST HEALTH CARE

PROVIDING CHOICE AND CARE TO ALL

We envision a health-care system in Canada that is second to none in the world. We believe Canadians should get the best medical care available regardless of ability to pay, without delay.

But what is the reality? Canadians pay top dollar for their health-care system yet receive mediocre service and outcomes. Even worse, millions of Canadians endure unnecessary anxiety and deteriorating health as they wait in lengthy queues for diagnosis or treatment to become available.

THE NEED: HELPING CANADIANS ENJOY
THE BEST POSSIBLE HEALTH

Canadians deserve the best health-care system in the world. We are certainly paying for a world-class system by international comparisons. But Canadians in need of medical services are not getting the results they deserve. Canadians requiring tests or treatment should receive them promptly. Canada's public health-care program should deliver the care Canadians desire in a time frame that gives comfort and peace of mind and—most importantly—supplies treatment when it is most effective. Every Canadian should receive the highest quality of service, without delay and without regard to income. No Canadian should be forced into an agonizing wait for inferior or insufficient care.

Where government programs fail Canadians' health-care needs, they should have the freedom to take responsibility for themselves and arrange for their own diagnostic tests and treatment. Canadians also deserve choice. They should be able to determine the health-care provider they prefer, whether it be a private for-profit, not-for-profit, or government-administered clinic or hospital. Likewise, Canadians should be able to purchase the health insurance programs that best meet their needs.

WHAT IS BEING DONE? SYMPTOMS OF DISTRESS

The good news is that Canadians are living longer and healthier lives than they were 30 years ago. The bad news is that, while Canada ranks second in expenditure on health care as a share of GDP (age-adjusted) among all the OECD countries with universal-access health systems (Figure 3.1), we place nowhere near the top in health-care outcomes from the services we actually receive (Table 3.1).

According to a recent study of age-adjusted access to health care (OECD, 2006), Canada ranked twenty-fourth among 28 countries for which data were available in the number of doctors per capita (2.3 doctors for every 1000 Canadians) (Figure 3.2). With respect to advanced medical technology, we ranked thirteenth of 24 in access to MRIs, seventeenth of 23 in access to CT scanners, seventh of 17 in access to mammographs, and were tied for second last of 20

Figure 3.1: Age-adjusted health spending (% GDP) in OECD countries with universal access, 2003

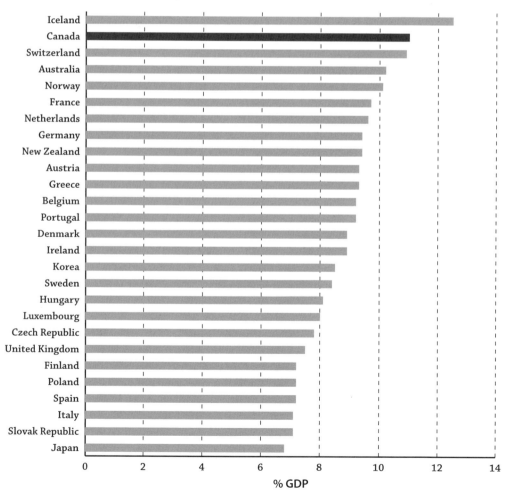

Source: Esmail and Walker, 2006: 2.

nations in our access to lithotripters (Table 3.2). In 2006, Canadians could expect to wait 17.8 weeks—more than four months—after their general practitioner or family doctor said a specialized treatment was necessary before they were actually cared for. That wait was fully 91% longer than it would have been only 13 years ago, back in 1993.

Our health is paying the price. Despite spending more on health care than any other industrialized country in the OECD except Iceland, Canadians rank sixteenth in the percentage of our life expectancy that we can expect to live in full health. We rank twenty-first in infant mortality, fourteenth in perinatal mortality, tenth in deaths due to breast cancer, ninth in the number of years of life lost to disease and fourth in avoidable deaths. We also rank second in the incidence of colorectal cancer mortality.

Figure 3.2: Doctors per 1,000 population (age-adjusted) in OECD countries, 2003

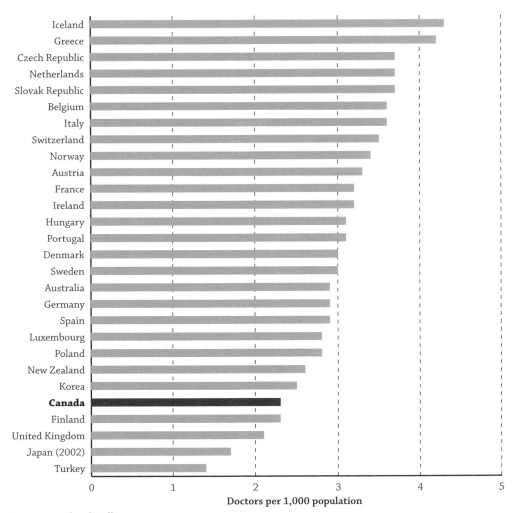

Source: Esmail and Walker, 2006: 3.

Table 3.1: Performance of health systems in OECD countries

| | Healthy Life Expectancy/Life Expectancy Rank 2002 | Mortality based on population statistics | |
		Infant Mortality Rank 2003	Perinatal Mortality Rank 2003
Australia	11	17	3
Sweden	1	3	9
Japan	2	2	2
Canada	**16**	**21**	**14**
Iceland	16	1	1
France	11	8	19
Italy	7	11	6
Switzerland	8	13	24
Norway	5	5	9
Finland	9	3	7
Luxembourg	4	19	11
Korea	27	21	5
Austria	11	16	15
Germany	2	11	13
New Zealand	21	24	17
Greece	20	8	16
Spain	5	6	11
Netherlands	10	17	21
United Kingdom	19	21	20
Belgium	16	13	16 [2]
Denmark	15	15	18
Ireland	22	20	25
Portugal	24	10	8
Poland	26	25	22
Turkey	28	28	27
Czech Republic	11	7	4
Slovak Republic	22	27	23
Hungary	25	26	26

[1] Combined mortality is the average of male and female mortality percentages.

[2] Not all information was available for all nations. Where data was unavailable, the rank of average values has been inserted.

Sources: Esmail and Walker, 2006: 7.

Mortality closely related to the effectiveness of health care

Mortality Amenable to Health Care Rank 2001	Potential Years of Life Lost Rank 2002	Breast Cancer Mortality Rank 2002	Colon/Rectum Cancer Combined Mortality Rank 2002 [1]	Cumulative Rank
3	6	5	2	1
5	2	1	9	2
2	3	11	4	3
4	**9**	**10**	**2**	**4**
16 [2]	1	4	7	5
1	12	6	11	6
6	8	11	5	6
16 [2]	4	9	1	6
8	5	8	14	9
13	7	2	14	10
16 [2]	10	6	6	11
16	21	3	7	12
10	11	16	17	13
14	14	14	12	13
15	17	13	10	15
11	13	17	19	16
7	15	21	18	17
9	16	23	16	18
17	20	15	13	19
16 [2]	*17* [2]	18	20	20
12	19	21	25	21
18	18	24	21	22
19	22	19	23	23
21	24	20	22	24
16 [2]	*17* [2]	28	28	25
20	23	25	24	26
22	25	27	26	27
23	26	26	27	28

Table 3.2: Age-adjusted availability of medical technology in the OECD, 2003

	MRI/ Million	Rank out of 24	CT Scanners/ Million
Australia	4.1	16	—
Austria	13.2	5	26.4
Belgium	6.2	11	27.0
Canada	**5.1**	**13**	**11.7**
Czech Republic	2.6	19	13.2
Denmark	9.1	9	14.4
Finland	12.6	6	13.6
France	2.6	19	7.9
Germany	5.3	12	12.6
Greece	2.0	23	15.2
Hungary	2.5	21	6.3
Iceland	20.5	2	24.6
Ireland	—	—	—
Italy	10.1	8	21.0
Japan	29.9	1	78.4
Korea	13.9	3	49.4
Luxembourg	11.5	7	27.7
Netherlands	—	—	—
New Zealand	4.3	14	13.5
Norway	—	—	—
Poland	1.1	24	7.0
Portugal	3.7	17	12.0
Slovak Republic	2.4	22	10.5
Spain	6.7	10	11.9
Sweden	—	—	—
Switzerland	13.4	4	17.0
Turkey	3.0	18	7.3
United Kingdom	4.2	15	6.4
OECD Average	7.9	—	18.9

Note: Data for the year 2000 was not available for all countries. Earlier years have been substituted where noted below.

MRI 2002 Data: Greece, Japan: CT Scanner 2002 Data: Greece, Japan; Mammograph 2002 Data: France, Greece; Mammograph 2001 Data: Canada; Lithotripter 2002 Data: Japan; Lithotripter 2001 Data: Turkey.

Source: Esmail and Walker, 2006: 63.

Rank out of 23	Mammographs / Million	Rank out of 17	Lithotripters/ Million	Rank out of 20
—	—	—	1.4	13
5	—	—	1.7	11
4	18.6	9	4.0	6
17	**21.4**	**7**	**0.6**	**18**
13	14.9	12	3.6	7
10	—	—	—	—
11	38.3	3	0.4	20
19	39.6	1	0.7	17
14	—	—	2.8	9
9	24.7	5	—	—
23	11.5	13	1.1	15
6	20.5	8	4.2	5
—	—	—	—	—
7	—	—	—	—
1	—	—	5.4	2
2	38.4	2	10.5	1
3	23.0	6	2.3	10
—	—	—	—	—
12	26.2	4	0.6	18
—	—	—	—	—
21	15.8	10	3.2	8
15	10.9	14	1.3	14
18	15.6	11	5.2	3
16	8.8	15	1.6	12
—	—	—	—	—
8	—	—	4.3	4
20	6.4	17	0.9	16
22	7.5	16	—	—
—	20.1	—	2.8	—

Canadians believe strongly that health care is vital to their quality of life, and that no Canadian should be denied medically necessary services because of an inability to pay. They may disagree about which policies are most likely to sustain and improve our health care but there is little dispute over the objective itself. Sadly, differences of opinion over which policies work best, combined with a fixation on the US health-care experience, have locked us into policies that do not serve us well. Canadians are left wanting, deserving, and paying, for more but getting less and less as time goes on.

DIAGNOSIS: BALANCE DISORDER

Canadian health care suffers from a debilitating disorder: a systemic imbalance of responsibilities and restricted freedom of choice. No other country in the developed world—even those with highly socialistic governments—goes to the lengths that Canada does to insist on a government-planned health-care monopoly, regardless of cost. The keystone of Canada's public health-care system, the Canada Health Act (CHA), explicitly denies provinces and individual citizens alike the freedom to seek out policies and services that best suit their own needs. As the federal government has thus far interpreted it, the CHA imposes on every province a public-sector monopoly on health-care insurance; it dictates that government alone finance and administer all core health-care services; and it denies Canadians the right to acquire such services from private providers. The CHA further forbids user charges, extra billing for publicly insured services, or any other market mechanisms and pricing signals that could help allocate health-care resources more efficiently. Provinces that depart from the Canada Health Act face sanction. They risk losing sizeable federal transfers for health care and social services—estimated at more than $29.8 billion in 2006/2007.

Do these monopolistic provisions result in better health care? Based on international comparisons, the answer is emphatically "No!" Among OECD countries whose citizens enjoy universal access to health care and also lose fewer years of life to disease and preventable deaths than Canadians, all also permit private alternatives to the public system and employ some form of public health-care user fee. Furthermore, only one of these countries spends more on health care than Canada, after adjusting for the age of their population (necessary, since the cost of health care varies greatly with age). All of the countries whose populations live more of their life in full health than Canadians, also have a private care sector competing to meet patient needs; over three quarters of these also have some form of cost sharing for access to the system.

When we look at mortality from breast cancer, a specific catastrophic but treatable disease, Canada ranks tenth among OECD nations. Every country with universal-access health care that does better by that measure also has private health-care alternatives and some form of user fees. All but one spend less of their GDP on health care than Canada does.

Finally, few developed countries subject their citizens to such long delays for medical treatment. Seven OECD nations have virtually no waits for care at all; every one has embraced competition, freedom, and personal responsibility throughout its health-care programs.

Canada is a rich nation. Our people, including our doctors and other health-care professionals, are talented and hard working. When Canadians receive sub-standard care, it is not for lack of wealth or talent. It is a symptom of bad policy. We believe Canada can do better.

LOOKING UP: ENCOURAGING PROSPECTS FOR CHANGE

Previous chapters have recorded how the principles of freedom of choice, personal responsibility, and appropriately balanced federalism have maintained Canada's education system in robust health and begun to restore effectiveness to provincial welfare policies. The poor condition of Canada's public health system is symptomatic of what happens when these same principles are disregarded. In short, we have been heading down the wrong road: far too great a reliance on a public-sector monopoly over the delivery of health care, far too little freedom of choice and acceptance of personal responsibility, and far too much federal interference in an area of provincial jurisdiction. But there are, at long last, encouraging signs that we are being obliged to stop going down that road and seek a new direction.

The Supreme Court's decision in the Chaoulli case in 2005 sent a powerful warning signal that the delays incurred by our current approach to health care violate Canadians' Charter rights to life and security of the person. It has always been unconscionable for a sick person in Canada to suffer or even die while waiting for public health care. The Court is now telling us—and our governments—that it is also unconstitutional, at least in Quebec. Significantly, it is Quebec that may well lead the way toward a health-care system that continues to assure universal access but allows for a choice of providers. It is moving from a system dominated by government monopoly to a "mixed system." British Columbia also appears to be open to moving towards such a "mixed" option and away from government monopoly. The medical profession, represented by the Canadian Medical Association, has also indicated a willingness to stop, look around, and consider alternatives to the status quo.

TREATMENT: WHAT MORE CAN BE DONE

Principles

Compassion, not money, should be our key concern in reforming Canada's health-care system. Our neighbours and fellow citizens in ill health or awaiting test or treatment must be our first priority. But we also believe that the formula for providing them with the prompt, effective, and compassionate care they deserve lies in the principles that underpin all of our policy prescriptions, specifically a greater respect for individual choice and responsibility, and a more appropriate balance of jurisdictional authority and resources.

The Supreme Court's 2005 decision to strike down Quebec's ban on private health insurance reflected several of these principles. We Canadians should assume greater personal responsibility for our own health and that of our families. But to do so, we must also have greater freedom to choose the health-care services we desire. Federal fiat should not limit our choice to a government monopoly. Government agencies need not run hospitals any more than doctors need be civil servants.

Nor should our provincial governments be coerced into denying Canadians alternatives that clearly lie within their constitutional authority. The provinces must be freed from federal shackles to deliver the choices Canadians deserve and demand. Here once again, the importance of balance between the federal government and the provinces can hardly be overstated. Free of federal constraint, Canada's primary and secondary schools manifest the excellence and diversity that provincial governments, closer and more responsive to their citizens' values and priorities, can mobilize. Likewise, hundreds of thousands of Canadians in need or on social assistance began to gain new hope and opportunity once the federal government recognized that the same could hold true for welfare programs.

The same principle can also lead to new hope and help for Canadians in need of prompt, effective, and appropriate medical attention. At the provincial level, we urge governments to embody the same spirit, by empowering individual Canadians and their families and communities to make their own choices. At the end of the day, health is the most personal of all concerns. Needs and preferences are specific to individuals: they differ materially from family to family, community to community. Governments, even at the provincial level, find it extremely difficult, if not impossible, to aggregate the choices and requirements of millions of individuals and still manage them well. Informed individuals, families, and local communities will always make decisions that reflect their own priorities better than government. Likewise, the health-care providers closest to those informed individuals, families, and communities will respond most effectively to their needs and wishes. They must be allowed to do so.

Information and incentive are keys to unlocking this virtuous dynamic. At present, our health-care system does little to reward Canadians who exercise responsibility by pursuing healthy lifestyles. Nor does it provide either pricing signals or metrics of quality to guide individuals, families, and communities to sound health-care choices. Nothing illustrates this perverse aspect of our health-care system better than its tortured lines of "accountability." Health-care providers get most of their revenue directly from governments rather than from the consumers they ostensibly serve. Invariably they are obliged to be more responsive to bureaucratic direction from above than to patient demand from below. The results? Either inferior, more expensive services and unacceptable waits for necessary services or acceptable levels of service provided by dedicated health-care professionals but provided in spite of the constraints and disincentives of the health-care system in which they must function.

When health-care professionals are more directly accountable to their patients, and provided with greater freedom to meet their needs, they will perform better. When individuals and families have more choices in health care—as they do in virtually every other developed nation—they are able to hold health-care providers more accountable. They can demand better, and get it. Canadians deserve no less.

Making the system work: What needs to be done

1 Federal-Provincial responsibilities

The federal government should return health-care resources and responsibility to the provinces. This priority is straightforward and compelling: Ottawa should step back from collecting taxes for health care and allow the provinces to raise their own revenues by an amount equivalent to current federal spending for health-care delivery. This proposal may alarm Canadians in some lower-income provinces. It need not. A properly structured equalization formula, implemented alongside reductions in tax rates, can protect these provinces against any negative consequences. In particular, a reformed equalization formula should provide additional revenues to those lower-income provinces for which a tax "point" is worth less than for higher-income provinces.

Federal support for health care should be directed where it does the most good: on health-care science and research; the collection and provision to consumers of information about best medical practices; the portability of benefits between provinces; and the coordination of a national response to health threats that do not respect provincial borders, such as those posed by SARS, BSE, and predicted pandemics.

Once responsibility for health care is returned to the provinces, they should aim to create better systems for their citizens rather than simply be satisfied with a continuation of the current system. Many of the problems plaguing Canadians' health care—waiting lists, lack of the latest medical equipment, shortages of doctors—arise because our system of providing care is organized mainly as a government monopoly. There are much better ways to do things, ways that are entirely consistent with the goal of providing Canadians with prompt and universal access to high-quality medical services, regardless of their ability to pay.

The provinces should not respond to the federal government's withdrawal from the health policy sphere by bulking up their own bureaucracies. Rather, provincial ministries should reorganize to fund and regulate—but not manage—health-care delivery. Governments that both manage and regulate any service face a deep conflict of interest. They should instead conclude and monitor contracts with hospitals, clinics, physicians, and other providers to deliver health services. Those contracts should establish desired outcomes—such as mortality, infection and complication rates, and patient satisfaction—that provincial authorities should monitor, making the results public to equip citizens to make the best possible choices about where to seek care. Providers who do not live up to the established benchmarks should have their contracts terminated.

On the other hand, contracted hospitals and other service providers should be legally and functionally independent of government. This will free them to conclude their own labour agreements and exercise their own judgment about such questions as how many staff to employ or what sort of equipment to acquire. Facilities that provide publicly funded care should also be accredited by a responsible and independent third party, rather than the provincial government.

Many provinces already report to their citizens how long they will need to wait for certain kinds of care and how many people are ahead of them in the queue. The idea behind these initiatives should be extended to help patients make sound decisions about which hospital or health provider will best meet their needs. However, while provinces should make more information available to citizens, they should cease to be the sole provider of that information. Governmental reviews of government's own performance are inherently suspect. Giving researchers and consumer organizations easier access to all the data on the health system's activities and performance (while of course protecting individual patients' privacy) would provide a more reliable and richer basis for consumers to determine their best health-care choices. The free, transparent marketplace for information would encourage providers to compete on the basis of quality.

2 Individual responsibilities

Canadians in every province should be free to contract for private health-care services and to buy insurance that would pay for those services. The present lack of choice in the health-care system has resulted in a common, uncontested, and mediocre standard of service, which Canadians are unable to protest by opting for a different provider. Since Canadians cannot "vote with their dollars" by patronizing providers that offer greater convenience, more timely service, better accommodations, or higher-quality care, the public health system is not motivated to offer them any of the above. Allowing a parallel private-health sector to flourish will right many of these wrongs. Allowing physicians and hospitals to work under both the privately and publicly funded regimes will serve to import innovations and efficiencies more rapidly from the private sector into the public system. This would also make better use of a valuable resource that often sits idle because of restrictions on activity or incentives created by the budgetary system.

At present, the provision or purchase of private insurance for "medically necessary" health services is generally disallowed in Canada. This policy ignores the evidence on the pitfalls of having a public monopoly in health insurance. While private health insurance will clearly not solve every health-care woe by itself, it will undoubtedly improve the provision of care to all Canadians.

Families, individuals, unions, businesses, volunteer groups, and charities should all be free to buy whatever insurance they wish for themselves or their members. Indeed, they should be encouraged to do so through a program modeled on those in Australia and Germany, where purchasers of private health insurance are partly reimbursed, or exempted from paying, the premiums that apply to the public health insurance scheme.

Actively encouraging the development of a private market in health insurance and care delivery could have many benefits, principal among them better service for patients. Patients who buy private health coverage or care with their own money also free up resources in the public system for patients who are waiting to receive them.

As well, the provinces need to reform the way the publicly funded health-care system itself interacts with patients. When individuals pay no direct charge for health care at the point of service, they have no financial incentive to restrain their use of health care and limited incentive to make an informed decision about when and where it is most appropriate to seek out care. The situation can produce excessive demand for care and waste resources.

Paying for health care through our taxes, as most Canadians do now, begets a number of other unfortunate results. With no clear connection between the money being paid into the system and the benefits being paid out, it is possible for governments to increase taxes, claiming the increases are needed to pay for health services, without dedicating the additional revenues that result to that end. As well, when citizens do not share the cost of the health services they receive at the point of access, they may resist tax increases that truly are required—failing to make (or doubting) the connection with the health care they demand as though it were free. This can lead to chronic shortfalls in health-care funding.

Co-insurance, deductibles, and co-payments can increase efficiency in health delivery and reduce costs. Of course, such mechanisms should be constrained by appropriate limits to ensure that the chronically ill and those suffering catastrophic health events are protected from financial strain. And since cost sharing can have an adverse effect on the health of the poor, these and certain other groups should be exempt from sharing the cost of care altogether.

A good solution, common in Europe, is what is known as "social insurance"— essentially, a system of either private or public insurers (or both) at arm's length from government that provide coverage for health-care costs. To ensure universal access to care, enrolment is mandatory: every citizen would have to choose, and pay premiums to, one of a number of competing social insurance providers. Some tax financing may still be required to provide coverage for the poor, the unemployed, and possibly the elderly. Still, this system is less vulnerable to politically motivated intervention than a fully tax-financed system, as independent bodies collect the insurance payments and dispense the funds for health services. In Belgium, the Czech Republic, the Netherlands, the Slovak Republic, Germany, and Switzerland, social insurers compete for customers, sometimes offering a variety of cost-sharing schemes that allow those willing to pay more out of pocket to enjoy lower premiums. At the same time, the presence of multiple purchasers of health services encourages competitive efficiencies among providers.

There may be other benefits: countries that have opted for a social-insurance system of health funding have fewer problems providing prompt care than those that have a tax-financed system (Altenstetter and Björkman, 1997). A comparison of Britain's publicly funded National Health Service with California's private, non-profit Kaiser Permanente, meanwhile, found that the per-capita costs of the two systems were similar to within 10%. Yet Kaiser members experienced more comprehensive and convenient primary care as well as quicker access to specialists and hospital admissions (Feachem, Sekhri, and White, 2002)

Another concern for the health-care system is that the proportion of Canadians older than age 65 is increasing. While this may or may not foreshadow a future crisis in health-care funding, there is no question that seniors consume more health-care dollars than non-seniors. It makes sense to prepare for that eventuality by setting aside resources now to guarantee that services are available for tomorrow's elderly without placing undue stress on the coming generation to fund their care. Quebec's Clair Commission on health care has proposed that that province institute and manage a mandatory collective savings plan to fund future, long-term care for its seniors.

But rather than yet another massive government program, why not individualized "medical savings accounts" for long-term care? As individuals reach an age when they require extra assistance they or their families—not government—could elect whether home support or institutional care best suits their needs. Measures already exist to protect someone's health and financial interests when they lose their autonomy and are unable to manage their assets. These could apply to any savings account. An even simpler approach would be to abandon contribution limits on RRSP and RPP savings plans and allow withdrawals from these existing savings instruments for health purposes. In addition, the interest earned on RRSP and RPP savings, which compounds over time, would substantially increase the resources available to individuals well beyond the actual value of their contributions. (For a more thorough discussion of the implications for Canada's social services system, including health care, resulting from the ageing of Canada's population, see Monograph 2, "An Aging Population: The Impact on Social Programs," page 87.)

3 *Management responsibilities and structure*
The provinces should re-organize the way the health-care system is managed. International experience indicates that public-private partnerships (P3s) could result in more creatively designed health-care facilities, while lowering life-cycle costs by between 20% and 30%. Other reviews are more cautious about P3s; they point to such problems as governments failing to properly enforce contractual arrangements or concluding deals with the private sector without considering competitively priced public ventures. These potential failings on the part of governments should not however obscure the ability of P3s to provide new infrastructure at lower cost and in a more timely fashion than would have been possible without competitive bidding. They deserve consideration.

More effective use of the private sector will require a change in the way hospitals are paid. In general, hospitals in Canada today receive an annual operation budget from their provincial health plan. While this system allows provinces to control expenditures, it also disconnects funding from the provision of hospital services. Hospitals have no financial incentive to provide better access or a more comfortable environment to attract more patients. Put simply, hospital administrators see empty operating rooms as savings and suffer no loss if patients decide they will be better cared for at another facility. The result: fewer services and a lower standard of patient care.

Replacing this scheme with payments based on the number and types of conditions actually treated would create powerful incentives to deliver more and better health services without dramatic cost increases. Health economists refer to this method of paying for hospital and surgical care as the "diagnostic related group" (DRG) system, although it is best considered a prospective fee-for-service regime. The idea is fairly simple: the service provider is paid a fee for each individual treated based on the expected costs of treating the patient's diagnosis at the time of admission. Such payments create incentives for hospitals to treat more patients (an idle operating room is no longer saving money but rather wasting it) and to provide the types of services that patients desire. It also sharpens competition among hospitals because the cost of performing procedures is clearly identified.

Much of the current shortage of physicians in Canada is the direct result of provincial intervention. To reduce the number of health-care providers who could "bill the system," governments chose to down-size medical schools, limit post-graduate enrolments, and resist accrediting international medical graduates. Another part of the problem is the unintended consequence of other decisions, to cap physician billings, close hospitals, and place quotas on some surgeries.

Merely relaxing the existing restrictions on medical school admissions, as is now taking place, will not resolve the problem in the long term. Instead such restrictions should be abandoned entirely, freeing medical schools themselves to determine their level of admissions. At the same time, permitting medical schools to price their training at its actual cost will allow students themselves to decide whether a career in medicine is profitable, given open supply to the marketplace. This reform would allow patients' needs—not an arbitrary funding decision—to determine the national supply of doctors. Shortages of doctors would be mitigated automatically, as students reasonably anticipate greater returns to their medical education from rising demand (more patients available to attend their practice, patients with unmet health needs, and so on), while an excess supply of physicians would have the opposite effect.

We recognize that changing the system of medical education involves not only health policy but also post-secondary education, income-tax policy, and the medical associations. It is a change not to be taken lightly; as with the other recommendations offered here, it must be thoroughly studied and properly implemented.

CONCLUSIONS: CHOOSING BETTER HEALTH CARE

Our choices are not simply between Canada's government monopoly on the funding and management of health care and the patchwork of private and public insurance and services that leaves too many of our American neighbours without affordable medical treatment. Many health-care systems around the world—in Sweden, Japan, Australia, France, Switzerland, and other nations—allow more freedom of choice and individual responsibility than Canadians enjoy, while at the same time guaranteeing to everyone, regardless of income, access to high levels of care.

We advocate following their lead and the guiding principles that have already performed so well for us in the areas of education and welfare policy. We propose freeing the provinces and the private sector from stagnant, monolithic, monopoly thinking to innovate solutions to the current health-care crisis and meet our future health-care needs. National health-care standards can be preserved by inter-provincial agreement through the Council of the Federation, while federal equalization payments continue to assist have-not provinces to meet those standards.

Our goal is to provide Canadians with the best health-care system in the world, one that will be a true example for others. Our nation possesses the resources, the talents, and the blueprints to accomplish those ambitions. We believe Canadians deserve no less.

RECOMMENDATIONS

Federal-provincial responsibilities

3.1   Have the federal government return health-care resources and responsibility to the provinces.

3.2   Spend federal dollars where it makes the most sense, on health-care science and research; the collection and provision to consumers of information about best medical practices; the portability of benefits between provinces; and the coordination of a national response to health threats that do not respect provincial borders, such as those posed by SARS, BSE, and predicted pandemics.

3.3   Right-size provincial health ministries, to fund and regulate—but not manage—health-care delivery.

3.4   Increase accountability. Many provinces already report to their citizens how long they will need to wait for certain kinds of care and how many people are ahead of them in the queue. The idea behind these initiatives should be extended to help patients make sound decisions about which hospital or health provider will best meet their needs.

Individual responsibilities

3.5   Give Canadians the freedom to care for themselves. Many of the problems plaguing Canadians' health care—waiting lists, lack of the latest medical equipment, shortages of doctors—arise because our system of providing care is organized mainly as a government monopoly. Canadians in every province should be free to contract for private health-care services and to buy insurance that would pay for those services.

3.6 Encourage patients to make more informed decisions. When individuals pay no direct charge for health care, they have no financial incentive to restrain their use of health care and limited incentive to make an informed decision about when and where it is most appropriate to seek out care. Co-insurance, deductibles, and co-payments can increase efficiency in health delivery and reduce costs though public support should ensure that no Canadian, no matter how poor, is denied health care.

3.7 Consider implementing a solution common in Europe—"social insurance"—essentially, a system of either private or public insurers (or both) at arm's length from government that provide coverage for health-care costs. To ensure universal access to care, enrolment is mandatory: every citizen would have to choose, and pay premiums to, one of a number of competing social insurance providers. Some tax financing may still be required to provide coverage for the poor, the unemployed, and possibly the elderly.

3.8 Help Canadians save for future medical needs. The proportion of Canadians older than age 65 is increasing. While this may or may not foreshadow a future crisis in health-care funding, there is no question that seniors consume more health-care dollars than non-seniors. It makes sense to prepare for that eventuality by setting aside resources now to guarantee that services are available for tomorrow's elderly without placing undue stress on the coming generation to fund their care. A creative approach to this is individualized "medical savings accounts" for long-term care. (For a more thorough discussion of the implications for Canada's social services system, including health care, resulting from the ageing of Canada's population, see Monograph 2, "An Aging Population: The Impact on Social Programs," page 87.)

Management responsibilities and structure

3.9 Work with the private sector. International experience indicates that public-private partnerships (P3s) could result in more creatively designed health-care facilities, while lowering lifecycle costs by between 20% and 30%.

3.10 Pay hospitals for the care they deliver. Hospitals have no financial incentive to provide better access or a more comfortable environment to attract more patients. Hospital administrators see empty operating rooms as savings and suffer no loss if patients decide they will be better cared for at another facility. The result: fewer services and a lower standard of patient care.

3.11 Free Canada's medical schools to train the doctors Canadians need. Much of the current shortage of physicians in Canada is the direct result of provincial intervention. Merely relaxing the existing restrictions on medical school admissions, as is now taking place, will not resolve the problem in the long term. Instead such restrictions should be abandoned entirely, freeing medical schools themselves to determine their level of admissions. At the same time, permitting medical schools to price their training at its actual cost will allow students themselves to decide whether a career in medicine is profitable, given open supply to the marketplace.

AN AGEING POPULATION: THE IMPACT ON SOCIAL PROGRAMS

As is the case in all industrialized countries, Canada's population is aging. The greying of our society will have profound consequences on our social programs. Unfortunately, the consequences of this greying have been known for years but little has been done to prepare for it or to mitigate the negative affects of an aging population.

A GREYING SOCIETY

There is no question that Canada's population as a whole has been getting, and will continue to get, older. In 1966, the median age in Canada was 25.4 years of age (Statistics Canada, 2006c). By 2006, the median age had increased to 38.8 years. Statistics Canada projects that the median age will increase to 44.3 years by 2031. In other words, the median age in Canada will have increased by an astounding 74.4% between 1996 and 2031.

Similarly, the proportion of the population over 65 years of age is increasing while the portion under 20 years of age is decreasing. In 1966, the proportion of the Canadian population under 20 years of age was 42.1% while the proportion of those over 65 was 7.7% (Statistics Canada, 2006c). By 2006, the ratio of those under 20 years old to the total population had decreased to 24.0% and the ratio of those over 65 had increased to 13.2%. Statistics Canada projects that the ratio of those younger than 20 years old to the total population will continue to decrease to 19.9% by 2031 while the ratio of those over 65 will continue to increase to 23.4%.

Perhaps most indicative of the strains of a greying society is the ratio of young people to retirees. In 1966, there were 5.5 Canadians under 20 years of age for every Canadian over 65. That number decreased to 1.8 in 2006 and by 2031 Statistics Canada expects there to be 0.85 Canadians under 20 years of age for every Canadian over 65. In other words, there will soon be fewer young people than retirees in Canada.

As well, life expectancy has increased dramatically, from 71 years in 1960 to about 80 years now, with future increases expected. This means that retirees collect pensions for an increased period of time and that their working years form a proportionately smaller part of their lives. In other words, the proportion of contributing years to recipient years has declined substantially. Given this demographic change, the retirement age should be reconsidered.

STRESS ON CANADA'S SOCIAL PROGRAMS

The aging of our society has put increasing stress upon Canada's social programs because most government programs are designed to transfer income from current workers to current retirees. At their inception, public pension programs like Old Age Security and

Canada's health-care system were based on the assumption that the demographics prevailing in the 1960s would persist. It was considered reasonable social and economic policy to transfer a small amount of money from a large group of younger workers to benefit a small group of retirees. Unfortunately, in this century that demographic assumption is being stood on its head. (This fact should stand as a warning to present policy makers that the sustainability of Canada's social programs requires that we get our demographic assumptions "right.") Faced with this new demographic reality, the programs of the 1960s clearly cannot be expected to deliver their anticipated benefits.

Consider the Old Age Security (OAS) program, the "cornerstone" of Canada's retirement-income system. Old Age Security pensions are available to all Canadian citizens and legal residents 65 years of age and over, providing they have lived in Canada for a minimum of 10 years of their adult lives. Current Old Age Security benefits (including the Guaranteed Income Supplement and Survivors Allowance) are paid for out of federal tax revenue. In 2005, these benefits accounted for 16.3% of total federal program spending, up from 13.1% 20 years ago. The change in Canada's demographic makeup will continue to increase the portion of federal revenues needed to fund OAS benefits. Yet, the maximum OAS payment has declined from 16.1% of average industrial wage in 1970 to 14% in 2003.

Canada's health-care obligations suffer the same problems. In 2005/06, publicly insured health care consumed 19.3% of total federal, provincial and local government revenue. As the portion of the population over 65 years of age increases, health care will consume an ever great portion of revenues because the years after age 65 are by far the most costly (Esmail et al., 2005). In fact, the average annual health spending for those between the ages of 15 and 44 is $1,314 per year and $2,050 for those between 44 and 65. It increases significantly for those aged 65 to 74, for whom average health spending is $5,192 per year. Average health spending increases to $9,494 a year for those between 75 and 84, and to $17,756 for those over age 85 (Esmail et al., 2005).

Given the current structure of Canada's social programs and the aging population, we simply do not have the resources to pay for the promises that have been made in the form of public pensions and medical services without increasing taxes, altering benefits, incurring debt, or some combination of the three. According to the latest data, without the necessary resources Canada has made promises to its citizens that total $1.54 trillion (2003). (**For more information, see Palacios and Veldhuis, 2006.**)

WHERE NEXT?

First and foremost, Canadian governments must acknowledge the impact that an ageing population will have on Canada's social programs and must justify any new spending in light of the fact that we do not know how we are going to pay for the programs to which we have already committed. Further, fundamental reform of government programs such as health care and OAS is required to reduce the future burden of these government programs. A greater use of the private sector is one way governments can slow increases in health spending and reduce the unfunded liability of the health-care system (Harris and Manning, 2005b).

Canadians must also rethink the structure of "pay-as-you-go" systems where current contributions finance current benefits. A more prudent approach would be to accumulate funds in individual accounts for future payment. For example, McMahon and Zelder (2002) and Ramsay (1998) propose Medical Savings Accounts (MSA) to reform the functioning of health care in Canada. Government contributions to individual MSAs would replace direct government funding of health services. International experience replacing pay-as-you-go public pension systems with pension savings accounts would also be instructive for Canada. For example, almost 25 years ago Chile replaced its pay-as-you-go public pension system with a privately administered national system of Pension Savings Accounts (PSA) (see Pinera, 1998 for more information). Singapore also finances its social security system through a mandatory program of private saving (see Asher, 1995, 1999).

Finally, changes to the public retirement system must be paralleled by changes to incentives for private savings, in order to allow more Canadians to save more money independently. There are a host of potential changes that could be implemented without seriously affecting government revenues, such as eliminating the limits to savings in tax deferred accounts (RRSPs and pensions), implementing new pre-paid savings accounts (**Kesselman and Poschmann 2001a, 2001b**), altering the tax treatment of withdrawals from RRSPs,[1] and lowering taxes on savings such as dividends and capital gains outside of tax deferred accounts (Harris and Manning, 2005b).

CONCLUSION

The choice is inescapable: either Canada must change how it prepares to fund the post-retirement years of an aging population, or those years for many will be decades of worry, fear, inadequate care, and decreasing life quality. The strategy of "pay-as-you-go" funding for pensions cannot be sustained. The alternatives we suggest can be effective in helping Canadians' enjoy more prosperity and security in retirement. In a virtuous side-effect, they would also help create capital for investment.

RECOMMENDATION

❀ Increase the retirement age and undertake the required investigation to determine the appropriate age.

---

1   Currently, all withdrawals from RRSPs are taxed as normal personal income. In other words, the withdrawals from RRSPs do not reflect the nature of the income earned within the account.

CHAPTER 4

SUPPORTING PARENTS AND CHILDREN

CHILD-CARE POLICY IN CANADA

We envision a Canada that is the best place in the world for children to grow up—where every child experiences the love, care, and opportunity essential to their development. We envision a Canada where every parent has the freedom to bring up their children as they consider best—as well as child-care choices that suit their unique needs. In short: a Canada where both parents and government policy "put children first."

But what is the reality? Governments increasingly coerce parental choice, subsidizing some child-care options and not others. Thousands of Canadian children are being funnelled into formalized daycare, though this is far from their preferred option. Our government continues to divert resources to some of Canada's most prosperous families—those with two wage earners—away from single-earner families that often struggle financially to raise their children. This is particularly unfair to poorer Canadians, without the means to make other choices.

THE NEED: HELPING PARENTS BE PARENTS

Childhood is a special time of life. It is when we form the attachments, habits, attitudes, personalities, and fundamental personal skills that will carry us through the rest of our lives. It is not too much to suggest that almost everything truly vital to our success or failure as adults we learn as children. Canadian children deserve the best possible foundation for later success: an environment that provides the full measure of all these emotional, social, intellectual, and spiritual necessities. Families, not governments, are in the best position to determine what environment will best ensure that their children flourish into happy, secure, and productive adults.

Canadian parents deserve the freedom to make their own decisions about what is best for their children. Every family, particularly those with fewest resources, should be able to count on the help they need to put those choices into effect. None should fear the state's interfering hand in how their children are best raised. Canadian families deserve to have available to them the option that best fits their children's needs. This includes parenting at home or with a relative; it includes informal daycare, including services run by friends and relatives. And it includes formal daycare. But Canadian children should never be trapped in a one-size-fits-all system, determined and sanctioned by government policy. Each child is unique; one size will never fit all.

WHAT IS BEING DONE? BUILDING THE NANNY STATE

The past decade has witnessed a surge of government activism in the area of child-care policy—culminating in the five-year, $5-billion, national child-care initiative modeled after the Quebec system of universal daycare, which the federal government announced in its February 2005 budget. The election of a new government in January 2006 shelved the national daycare plan. It may have new life in the form of a private member's bill (Bill C-303), which secured parliamentary committee approval in May 2007, and awaited its third and final reading.

This activism has been justified by social and economic trends that show women joining the work force in record numbers and a growing number of families headed by single mothers. In 2005, 71.8% of women with children under the age of six were in the paid workforce, up from 67.6% in 1999 (Roy, 2006). Over roughly the same period, the percentage of families headed by single parents (the vast majority of them women) grew from 9.4% in 1971 to 16% in 2004 (Statistics Canada, 2005a). Child care has assumed additional significance in light of provincial reforms intended to encourage welfare recipients, including single parents, to make the transition from dependency to employment (Schafer et al., 2001; Gabel, Clemens, and LeRoy, 2004).

WHO'S MINDING BABY? PATTERNS OF CHILD CARE USE

More families where both parents work and more working single parents, have inevitably meant that more Canadian children are being entrusted to someone other than their parents. In 2002/2003 (the most recent year for which data are available), 54% of children between the ages of six months and five years received care from someone other than a parent or guardian, up from 42% in 1994/1995 (Bushnik, 2006). The vast majority (72%) of these children are cared for outside of formal daycare. Almost half (46%) are cared for in someone else's home by a relative or non-relative; about one in five (21%) are cared for in their own home by a family member or someone else (Table 4.1).

The most significant recent change has been an increased reliance on care by relatives—up 34% between 1994/1995 and 2002/2003 to nearly one child in three (29.4% of all children). Parents across Canada were also more likely to have a relative raise their child at home in 2002/2003 than in 1994/1995. National daycare use increased during this time period by 43%. On the other hand, care by non-family members outside a formal daycare fell by a third (33%).

While reliance on daycare appears to be growing nationally, it is important to note striking differences among provinces (Table 4.1). Daycare is used least in Saskatchewan (13.3% of children) and most heavily in Quebec (51.9%), where daycare is universally available to all parents at the nominal cost of $7 a day (Bushnik, 2006). This policy in Quebec, which priced daycare significantly below other child-care choices, contributed to a 85% increase in reliance on daycare there between 1994/1995 and 2002/2003, and a concomitant drop in care by relatives (down 14%) and other home-based care (22%). Because Quebec represents approximately one-quarter of Canada's population, this massive shift produces a statistical overstatement of the growth in formal daycare use nationally. Not every province saw a growing number of parents rely on formal daycare during the study period. In Alberta, Saskatchewan, Ontario, and Newfoundland, daycare use fell. At the same time, it increased substantially in British Columbia, Manitoba, and New Brunswick, even in the absence of universal or low-cost daycare programs in those provinces. These provincial variations highlight the importance of giving provinces the freedom to set policies that reflect the unique needs and preferences of their citizens.

RECENT DEVELOPMENTS

In the 2006 federal budget, the new Conservative government introduced its Universal Child Care Plan to support families with children. Starting in July 2006, the Universal Child Care Benefit of $100 per month per child under the age of six began flowing to all parents, regardless of their child-care choices. The government also announced new funding of $250 million per year to fund the creation of up to 25,000 new child-care spaces, beginning in 2007/08, while promising that the $850 million funding promised the provinces for early childhood development and early learning and care would also continue through to 2013/14.

Table 4.1: Distribution of children by type of main non-parental child-care

	Outside the home with non-relative		Outside the home with relative		In own home with non-relative	
	1994/95	2002/03	1994/95	2002/03	1994/95	2002/03
Canada	42.9	30.3	14.0	15.7	14.0	7.7
Newfoundland & Labrador	19.5	14.6	20.7	22	25.0	14.5
Prince Edward Island	40.8	34.6	18.3	24.4	13.9	4.3
Nova Scotia	31.0	27.3	12.6	25.1	25.5	8.0
New Brunswick	40.4	39.9	17.2	17.3	14.8	7.9
Quebec	42.7	25.8	15.1	9.2	13.1	6.0
Ontario	44.2	33.6	12.4	18.5	13.2	8.9
Manitoba	51.4	35.4	17.8	17.4	10.8	6.4
Saskatchewan	57.4	54.4	15.7	17.2	10.5	4.6
Alberta	46.0	39.2	11.9	17	12.3	8.2
British Columbia	40.2	26.4	17.7	22.1	20.9	10.8

Source: Bushnik, 2006; The Fraser Institute.

WHAT PARENTS WANT

When the Vanier Institute surveyed Canadians, asking them to rank seven child-care choices by their preference on a scale of one to five, on average, parents picked daycare dead last (Table 4.2). That was not surprising, considering that the study also found that 90% of mothers and 84% of fathers who were working full-time would prefer to work-part time and care for their child at home if they could afford it (Bibby, 2004). Interestingly, public opinion on this issue crosses party lines. In a 2003 COMPAS survey of Ontario voters, 67% of confirmed Conservative voters, 58% of Liberals, and 64% of NDP supporters preferred care by a relative as a second choice to a parent staying home to care for an infant or pre-school child (COMPAS, 2003). These polling data suggest that, absent policies that bias parents towards one specific form of care (as in the case of Quebec), actual patterns of child care in Canada roughly reflect parental preferences.

Nevertheless, proponents of legislation such as Bill C-303 seek to resurrect the blueprint for a national daycare system by putting strict conditions on new federal child-care dollars flowing to the provinces through an enriched Canada Social Transfer (CSF). Such legislation threatens to lead us onto the same road—since abandoned—that we once went down with respect to social assistance: heavy-handed, monolithic federal interventions that too often felt to recipients more like a trap than a helping hand. Moreover, it ignores the principles of freedom of choice, personal responsibility, and balanced federal-

arrangement

In own home with relative		Daycare centre		Change (%) in daycare use, 1994/05–2002/03	Change (%) in own-home care with relative, 1994/05–2002/03
1994/95	2002/03	1994/95	2002/03		
8.0	13.7	19.5	27.9	43%	71%
19.1	29.6	15.8	19.3	–8%	55%
9.3	8.2	17.7	28.5	59%	–12%
11.0	15.3	19.9	24.4	1%	39%
7.3	13.5	20.2	21.5	3%	85%
3.9	7.2	25.2	51.9	62%	85%
11.2	16.8	19.0	22.2	–1%	50%
6.4	13.7	13.6	27.1	66%	114%
4.4	10.5	12.1	13.3	–13%	139%
6.1	16.9	23.6	18.6	–10%	177%
8.4	20.9	12.9	19.8	53%	149%

ism that, as we have seen, underlie Canada's achievements in education and are so desperately needed as remedies to our ailing health-care system. Surely to organize two different but related services for children—child care and K-12 education—on contradictory principles heading in opposite directions is a formula for disaster. Yet, federal politicians are still comparing the daycare initiative to the development of Canadian health care. This is cause for alarm: Canadian parents do not deserve this failed model of policy-making.

This is not to say there is no role for government in supporting formal child-care settings. Considered as a part of programs designed to get people off social

Table 4.2: Canadian child-care preferences

	National	Women	Men	Ages 18–34	Ages 35–54	Ages 55+
Partner	1	1	1	1	1	1
Parent(s)	2	2	2	2	2	2
Other relative	3	3	3	3	3	3
Home day care	4	4	4	5	4	4
Day care centre	5	5	5	4	5	5

Source: Bibby, 2004: 55.

assistance and into the workforce, for example, and weighed against the human and financial cost of long-term welfare dependency, there is a legitimate case for providing required child-care support to low-income single parents. This underscores the importance of evaluating existing and proposed child-care policies in light of other programs intended to support families with children. In 2005/2006, federal assistance for families with children (including transfers to provinces) amounted to $14.8 billion (Tables 4.3a and 4.3b). With new child-care initiatives set to increase this figure considerably over the next few years, it is critical that we evaluate the effectiveness of this level of spending.

GROWTH SPURT: THE FEDERAL SPENDING RECORD

Conditional grants

The federal government has been using its spending power to finance a growing array of child-care services since 2000, when it signed an Early Childhood Development (ECD) agreement with provinces. That agreement promised to add $2.2 billion over five years to CHST transfers, which provinces were obliged to invest in new ECD programs. An additional $900 million (over five years)

Table 4.3a: Spending on Families With Children ($millions)

	2004/05	2005/06	2006/07	2007/08
Maternity Leave	980.0	941.4	*(data not available)*	
Parental Leave	2,117.0	2,186.9		
Adoption Expense Tax Credit (projected)	—	5.0	5.0	5.0
Child Care Expense Deduction (projected)	550.0	605.0	695.0	700.0
Eligible Dependent Credit (projected)	680.0	710.0	730.0	755.0
Children's Fitness Tax Credit (projected)	—	—	40.0	160.0
Canada Social Transfers (CST)				
Early Childhood Development (2000)	500.0	500.0	500.0	500.0
Early Learning and Child Care (2003)	150.0	225.0	300.0	350.0
Early Learning and Child Care Initiative (2005)	200.0	500.0		
Child Care Spaces Initiative	—	—	—	250.0
Canada Child Tax Benefit	8,688.0	9,145.0	9,530.0	9,460.0
Universal Child Benefit			1,610.0	2,335.0
New Child Tax Credit			1,500.0	1,500.0
TOTAL	13,865.0	14,818.3		

Department of Finance Canada, 2007; Government of Canada,2006a, 2006b, 2007; Human Resources and Skills Development Canada, 2007.

Table 4.3b: Spending on families with children, not incl. maternity/paternity leave ($millions)

	2004/05	2005/06	2006/07	2007/08
Adoption Expense Tax Credit (projected)	—	5.0	5.0	5.0
Child Care Expense Deduction (projected)	550.0	605.0	695.0	700.0
Eligible Dependent Credit (projected)	680.0	710.0	730.0	755.0
Children's Fitness Tax Credit (projected)	—	—	40.0	160.0
Canada Social Transfers (CST)				
Early Childhood Development (2000)	500.0	500.0	500.0	500.0
Early Learning and Child Care (2003)	150.0	225.0	300.0	350.0
Early Learning and Child Care Initiative (2005)	200.0	500.0		
Child Care Spaces Initiative	—	—	—	250.0
Canada Child Tax Benefit	8,688.0	9,145.0	9,530.0	9,460.0
Universal Child Benefit			1,610.0	2,335.0
New Child Tax Credit				1,400.0
TOTAL	10,768.0	11,690.0	13,410.0	14,515.0

Department of Finance Canada, 2007; Government of Canada,2006a, 2006b, 2007; Human Resources and Skills Development Canada, 2007.

was earmarked for early learning and child care in 2003. The 2007 federal budget promised to honour these commitments through to 2013/14, topping this $850 million in annual child-care funding with an additional $250 million per year for its Child Care Spaces initiative.

While the new funding is to be "notionally earmarked" for child care, the provinces retain final discretion in how to disburse these funds, and deliver child-care programs in their proper jurisdiction. Manitoba, for instance, agreed to subsidize only regulated, non-profit child-care providers but has made its first priority raising the wages and training levels of child-care workers (Government of Manitoba, 2005b). Ontario is taking a different approach. Based on European models, Ontario's Best Start program will expand in coming years to provide institutional child care during non-school hours for all four- and five-year-olds enrolled in junior and senior kindergarten—to be extended eventually to all children older than 30 months. Alberta has signalled a more flexible strategy, allowing for-profit as well as non-profit providers to be eligible for subsidies. Uniquely among the provinces, Alberta also provides a Kin Childcare program, which funds parents to pay a non-resident, blood relative to care for their children.

While the federal transfers do afford flexibility, they also threaten to distort provincial priorities that might better reflect their citizens' preferences.

Requiring that federal funds be spent only on non-parental child care, for example, disadvantages families that choose to sacrifice income by having one parent stay home to take care of their children. Provinces that accept the federal grants also become obligated to oversee services that families, neighbours, and the many charities and churches of the non-profit voluntary sector previously provided privately and informally. As well, by pressuring provinces to direct limited resources into child care, these grants constrain other options, such as tax cuts, that could make other choices more affordable for Canadian families. At heart, the federal child-care transfers once again give the federal government leverage to influence policy priorities in an area of exclusive provincial jurisdiction. This is the same discredited pattern of intervention that has led Canadian health care into a quagmire of mediocrity and the exact opposite of the balanced federalism that has lifted Canadian education to international excellence.

Tax deductions

The federal government also allows working parents to deduct from their annual federal income tax bill up to $7,000 of child-care expenses for children under the age of seven, and $4,000 for children between the ages of seven and 16. This Child Care Expense Deduction (CCED) covers formal daycare, day camps, and boarding school—but not care by a parent. This preferential tax break is projected to cost the federal government $695 million in 2007 and is directed to non-parental care arrangements, while discriminating against families who choose to care for their children at home. (Table 4.4 for a summary of Canada's tax bias.)

Seventy-one percent of respondents to a 2002 Strategic Council survey either "strongly agreed" (40%) or "somewhat agreed" (31%) that "the current tax system makes it more difficult for families to choose to have one parent stay at home with younger children" (Strategic Council, 2002). This view crossed all party lines, although supporters of what was then the Canadian Alliance were somewhat more likely (78%) than Liberal supporters (68%) to agree that the tax system impeded parental choice.

Universal Child Benefit

The most significant child-care policy reversal since the election of a Conservative government in January 2006, was the introduction of a $1,200 cash allowance allocated annually to parents regardless of whether they chose to have their children cared for by a parent, a nanny, a neighbour, or formal daycare. Similar to the universal Family Allowance or "baby bonus," by 2007/08 this Universal Child Benefit (UCB) is expected to flow to 1.5 million families with

Table 4.4: Canada's income tax bias

	SCENARIO 1			SCENARIO 2		
	Mom	Dad	Total	Mom	Dad	Total
Income	$40,000	$40,000	$80,000	$80,000		$80,000
personal exemption	$7,756	$7,756		$7,756		
spousal exemption				$6,586		
child care deduction		$11,000				
Taxable income	$32,244	$21,244		$65,658		
@ 16 percent	$24,427	$21,244		$17,841		
@ 22 percent	$7,817			$32,185		
@ 26 percent				$15,632		
Total tax paid	$5,628	$3,399	$9,027	$14,000		$14,000
Tax Bias						$4,973

Source: Veldhuis and Clemens, 2004.

over two million children at a total cost of nearly $2.4 billion. By putting child-care cash directly in the hands of parents, the UCB responds to the concerns of families who are prevented from choosing parental or other informal care arrangements for financial reasons. Unfortunately, the UCB also creates a new multi-billion dollar entitlement that must ultimately be financed by taxpayers. In essence, this redistributive policy has the government taxing money out of one pocket, only to put some of it back into the other, at the cost of much bureaucratic inefficiency.

Other new tax credits

Recent federal budgets have also seen the introduction of a growing number of new tax credits targeted towards families in children. Budget 2005 introduced a non-refundable Adoption Expense Tax Credit, recognizing specific adoption expenses up to a maximum of $10,000. Budget 2006 introduced a Children's Fitness Tax Credit for up to $500 in eligible fees for physical fitness programs for each child under the age of six. Finally, Budget 2007 introduced a new $2,000 Child Tax Credit the government estimated will provide up to $310 per child in tax relief to more than three million families. After these new tax credits, the UCB, and an ever-growing CST are added up, by 2007/08 the Conservative government will be spending approximately one third more on Canadian families and children than the Liberal government did in its last complete fiscal year in office (2004/05).

Parental leave benefits

Government support for child care also includes increasingly generous parental leave benefits funded by Employment Insurance (EI). First included in the Employment Insurance system in 1971, maternity leave benefits were extended to adoptive parents in 1984; parental leave benefits for either parent were added to those previously reserved for mothers in 1989. In the intervening years, both eligibility for, and the duration of, benefits have been extended. Eligible new parents now receive a combined total of 50 weeks of leave at 55% of their insured income (up to a maximum annual gross income of $39,000). In 2005/06, these benefits were worth an estimated $3.1 billion—an increase of 172% since 1998 (not adjusting for inflation).

These growing costs are directly related to relaxed eligibility requirements and extended benefits. In 2004, nearly two thirds (65.9%) of all mothers received parental leave benefits at some point during their pregnancy or after the birth of their child, up from 54.9% in 2000. Over the same period, the length of the average leave increased from seven to 11 months (Statistics Canada, 2005c). Most new parents surely welcome assistance that reduces the cost of staying at home in the crucial first months of a child's life. Indeed, a 1998 COMPAS survey found that 89% of parents would prefer to care for their children at home beyond the subsidized leave period if they could afford to (COMPAS, 1998). A 2002 Strategic Council survey similarly found that three-quarters (76%) of respondents would rather have one parent stay home with their children than place them in some other form of care, if money were not a consideration.

Unfortunately, there is one significant problem with the current parental leave program provided through EI: its sharply unequal treatment of self-employed families that falls especially heavily on women in the workforce. While self-employment has grown rapidly over the past 25 years, especially amongst women, the self-employed (with the exception of fishers, hairdressers, and taxi and other drivers) do not contribute to the EI system. Nor do they qualify for parental leave benefits. As a consequence, nearly one in three self-employed women is back at work three months after giving birth, compared to just 3% of paid workers (Statistics Canada, 2004b).

LIVING UP TO OUR POTENTIAL

While there are legitimate reasons to include child-care help in the overall mix of social programs, many publicly funded child-care benefits violate the principles of balanced federalism, parental choice, and, by limiting parental options, the freedom of Canadian families. The lessons we have stood by in education, are at last learning in welfare, and have not yet applied to health care, must be heeded in child care: provincial governments are closer to the people they serve than Ottawa and thus in a better position to develop social programs. Ottawa must respect the constitutional role of the provinces in managing child-care policy instead of using its fiscal clout to force choices on provincial policy and thereby onto parents. In addition to distorting priorities, this blurs accountability as the roles of the two levels of government become hopelessly confused. Ottawa must respect the constitutional role of the provinces in managing child-care policy.

If provincial jurisdiction is respected, diversity and excellence will flourish in our care of Canada's children outside of school hours just as it has inside the classroom. Canadians can learn from what has proven successful in other parts of the country, avoid what has failed, and develop new initiatives that best reflect their own priorities. Help for parents should discriminate against none. Assistance should not benefit the rich at the expense of the poor or struggling, as government-funded daycare programs all too often do by favouring two-income families over those that sacrifice to allow one parent to stay at home.

Most importantly, our vision for child care is centered on the family. Families, not state bureaucrats or politicians, should make the choices that best suit their needs. This key principle has two sides: families should have the freedom, means, and responsibility for raising children—and government should not interfere in these choices, except in truly exceptional circumstances.

Perhaps most significantly of all, most parents put government-supported child care last on their list of preferred choices. According to an Ekos poll conducted in the summer of 2004, just 30% of Canadians favoured more and better child-care programs. Nearly twice that number favoured parent-centered assistance: either direct financial subsidies (28% of respondents), tax breaks (21%) or simply information to help parents meet their own needs (18%) (*Windsor Star*, 2005: A9). Similarly, when Ontarians were asked in 2003 to choose whether they would rather have government give money to daycares to reduce costs or give money to parents so they can better afford whatever care they think is best, only slightly more than one in three (35%) indicated that money should be allocated to daycare (COMPAS, 2003). In other historical analyses of preference, Canadian women agreed most frequently and strongly on policies that supported choice in how they care for children (Michalski, 1999).

WHAT SHOULD BE DONE

Governments in Canada should stop penalizing child-care choices with biased tax breaks. Government policy should not privilege formal, paid daycare over care by a parent or another family member. Families should have the freedom to choose the child-care arrangement that is right for them without being penalized through the tax code. To that end, a Universal Child Expense Deduction (UCED) should replace the Child Care Expense Deduction that now covers only the cost of formal, institutional care.

Sixty-five percent of Canadians surveyed by COMPAS in 1998 felt that "changing the tax law to make it easier for parents with young children to afford to have one parent at home," should be a high or very high priority (COMPAS, 1998). Accordingly, the current Child Care Expense Deduction should be phased out over a five-year period. Over the same time, the Dependent Deduction currently provided to all tax-paying families with children should be gradually increased. While this change will have a neutral effect on federal revenue, the bias towards non-parental child care would be eliminated.

Under this new system, families would face the same tax burden and receive the same amount of federal support (in terms of tax-exempt income) regardless of whether they choose to have their children cared for by an unpaid caregiver within the home or in a formal daycare environment. This universal deduction will give parents greater freedom and personal resources to care for their children in the way that best suits their needs, values, and family circumstances.

The federal-provincial balance in childcare should be restored by eliminating conditional grants. Canada is a large and diverse country, a diversity reflected in the different choices that parents in different provinces make for the care of their children. A Canada that believes in strong and free families must respect these differences. As we have seen repeatedly, the government that is closest to the citizens it serves is most likely to make the best choices on their behalf. Accordingly, the federal government should abandon any attempt to dictate social policy choices through conditional transfers and instead vacate tax room to provinces to pursue their own priorities. This respect for the proper balance of Confederation will have the additional benefit of promoting more responsive, accountable programs.

In the same spirit, provinces fashioning their own distinctive child-care policies should adopt a "bottom-up" or demand-driven approach, directing subsidies to parents, not selected care providers. This can be done either through a system of tax credits, deductions, or child-care vouchers. Bottom-up solutions put decision-making power in the hands of consumers and are vastly more efficient.

Self-employed parents should be treated fairly and government should not create a disadvantage for them as compared to regularly employed parents. Canadian parents clearly value the opportunity to remain at home in the crucial weeks and months before and after a child's birth. Parental leave programs can assist them by reducing the cost of leaving the labour force temporarily to care for their children. Yet the existing EI-based, federal leave-benefits program clearly fails our growing number of self-employed parents. They deserve better.

A recent survey by the University of Guelph's Centre for Families, Work and Well-Being found that, while most self-employed women (82% of professionals and 96% of those in lower-earning fields) want access to maternity leave benefits, they would prefer a voluntary scheme to a mandatory, EI-type program (Rooney et al., 2003: 36). Interestingly, this preference persisted even if a voluntary model was more expensive than a mandatory scheme. Put another way, Quebec's mandatory new program for self-employed workers is neither what most self-employed Canadians want nor the most cost-effective option. Instead, the federal government should allow self-employed individuals to fund their own parental leave by borrowing from their own tax-sheltered retirement savings. Funds withdrawn to support parental leave should be exempt from income tax as long as they were repaid over a period of 10 to 15 years. This voluntary Parental Savings Plan (PSP) would be modeled after the existing First Time Home Buyers Plan, which allows individuals to borrow up to $20,000 from their RRSP towards the purchase of their first home and Life-Long Learning Plans that permit similar borrowing to pay for post-secondary education.

CONCLUSIONS: PARENTS KNOW BEST

Our child-care objectives for Canada respect parental preferences and reaffirm the pre-eminent role of the family in providing and caring for children. Our recommendations would also reduce unnecessary inefficiencies that drive up the costs of child care. By putting more resources and decision-making power in the hands of parents, the policies we propose will respond to the unique needs and values of every Canadian family. By trusting parents, rather than a distant government, with the responsibility for their children's care, growth, and early development, these policies reflect the principles of a strong and free Canada.

RECOMMENDATIONS

The following policy proposals reflect the preferences that Canadians have repeatedly expressed—but political leaders have consistently disregarded.

4.1 Stop penalizing child-care choices with biased tax breaks. Government policy should not privilege formal, paid daycare over care by a parent or another family member.

4.2   Restore federal-provincial balance by eliminating conditional grants. Canada is a large and diverse country, a diversity reflected in the different choices that parents in different provinces make for the care of their children. A Canada that believes in strong and free families must respect these differences.

4.3   Support self-employed parents as well as the employed. The existing EI-based, federal leave-benefits program clearly fails our growing number of self-employed parents. They deserve better. Legislation should be enacted to allow these parents to fund their own parental leave by using their RRSP savings, in the same way that individuals can borrow these funds for home purchases or life-long education.

A MORE DYNAMIC ECONOMY
UNLEASHING PROSPERITY

We envision a Canada that leads the world in economic vigour and individual prosperity.

This may seem an ambitious goal, but we do not think it is unrealistic. In a time of rising economies in Asia, mounting demand and global competition for resources, and a growing premium on knowledge-intensive, innovative industries, Canada has everything it needs to lead the world: a talented and skilled population, a well-developed resource sector, sophisticated technical and financial sectors, and top-tier research institutions. We already have much to be proud of. But "good" is a long way from "best." We have too often settled for less. We have it in our hands to do very much better.

The key to acquiring the resources that will provide Canadians with the goods and the services they aspire to lies in a powerful dynamic: the virtuous effects of economic freedom. Empirical evidence demonstrates in case after case that no better predictor exists of a nation's prosperity and its citizen's quality of life than the degree of economic freedom they enjoy. In truth, economic freedom is much more than that: economic freedom is also inextricably tied to civil liberty. Absent economic freedom, no nation has maintained a stable democracy; with it, no nation has failed to expand freedom in other dimensions over time.

The same evidence-based indices offer a reliable guide to the steps Canadians can take to liberate the full potential of our natural and human assets. In the chapters ahead, we explore the indicators of economic freedom—the tools of wealth creation—more fully. As perhaps should not surprise, they both reinforce and reflect the principles that inform our whole body of analysis here: placing choice and resources directly in the hands of individuals wherever possible, and where it is not, reposing them in the level of government closest to those who will be affected by its decisions.

Central to realizing our vision for Canada as the world's most prosperous and socially advanced country, is achieving a scale of government in proportion to the sum of national economic activity that maximizes growth and social progress: the size of government that is "just right." Research into the experience of other nations, as well as our own, provides compelling evidence that in Canada, government in recent decades has consumed far more of our national wealth than is optimal. We discuss the evidence, and propose a national target of reducing overall government activity in Canada to approximately one-third of GDP from its present level of nearly 40%. One manifestation of excessive government is over-regulation: we analyze the symptoms of this burden on Canadians' potential prosperity and suggest remedies.

Canadians' present prosperity is a testament to the powerfully beneficial effects of one particular expression of economic freedom: trade. Indeed, it is not too much to say that open, transparent markets are the mechanism by which economic freedom works its magic. Yet we have frustrated the intent of our constitutional framers by erecting thickets of regulatory barriers to trade in goods or services amongst our own citizens when provincial borders intervene. We address practical steps to remove these obstacles to prosperity.

If our recommendations are put into practice, Canadians can expect to see their national prosperity surge forward, as innovation and investment unleash the full potential of our rich endowments of human and natural assets. Individual Canadians can expect their own prosperity to increase as market-based choices direct the development of these assets toward the most efficient, productive, and rewarding purposes. Our internal and external trade will grow, encouraging competitiveness among Canadian businesses, rewarding the best with larger markets and providing Canadian consumers with the widest possible choice of the world's best goods and services at the lowest price.

The following pages also contain

❧ a Monograph on economic freedom's role in enhancing Canadian productivity;

❧ two Monographs on the application of market-based principles to long-standing and emerging challenges for aboriginal economic development and environmental conservation.

In each of these areas, we believe that the expansion of economic freedom and the application of market-based principles will contribute significantly to the realization of our vision of a Canada that leads the world in individual and collective prosperity and well-being.

CHAPTER 5

FREE TO PROSPER

ECONOMIC FREEDOM

Economic freedom is the key to prosperity. In empirical studies in the world's top, peer-reviewed, academic journals, economic freedom has consistently been shown to create investment, increase prosperity, enhance competitiveness, and advance numerous other positive social outcomes. By contrast, customs, institutions, laws, policies, and practices in business and government that constrain economic freedom also constrain growth and reduce the prospect of prosperity.[1] No nation that lacks economic freedom has ever consistently improved the material lives of its citizens. Nor, for that matter, has any such nation ever established a stable democracy that respected other freedoms. Freedom is not easily subdivided. Canada owes much—including our stable democracy and enviable prosperity—to a generally high degree of economic freedom. Canada is consistently in the top ten of the world's economically freest nations, as measured by The Fraser Institute's annual report, *Economic Freedom of the World*.

But once again, "good" is a long way from "best." Indeed, Canada ranks just in the middle of the top ten in the measure of the economic freedom we provide to people and enterprises. We can do better. Canada can and must strive to give its citizens the greatest degree of economic freedom in the world. That measure of freedom is an essential prerequisite to achieving both the world's highest levels of economic performance and its most democratic governance.

---

1 See, for example, Easton and Walker, 1997; Farr, Lord, and Wolfenbarger, 1998; Grubel, 1998a; and Gartzke, 2005. For a summary of the literature, see Doucouliagos and Ulubasoglu, 2006.

What does economic freedom require and how is it constrained?

Economic freedom means liberating citizens to make more of their own economic decisions. The idea necessarily implies a limited government: over-sized governments, those that over-tax or substitute their decision-making for individual initiative and choice, are a major constraint on economic freedom.

Economic freedom requires an incorruptible rule of law, one that protects both persons and rightfully acquired property and applies equally to the powerful and the weak. More exactly: "Individuals have economic freedom when property they acquire without the use of force, fraud, or theft is protected from physical invasions by others and they are free to use, exchange, or give their property as long as their actions do not violate the identical rights of others" (Gwartney, Lawson, and Block, 1996). Where rule of law is weak or corrupted, where property rights are weak or denied, economic freedom is not only constrained—it can scarcely exist.

Economic freedom requires sound money. Inflation is a form of silent expropriation, eroding the value of wages, savings, and property. When inflation is not only high but also volatile and unpredictable, individuals and enterprises cannot plan for the future; they are thus effectively denied the exercise of economic freedom. An unsound money supply or erratic and confiscatory monetary policy is therefore another major constraint on economic freedom.

Economic freedom is expressed in the freedom to trade, in its broadest sense: to buy, sell, exchange, and transport resources, goods, services, and information freely across domestic and international borders, and to make contracts concerning these transactions. Limits on trade, whether domestic or international, are a further serious constraint on the exercise of economic freedom.

Economic freedom requires that government regulation of credit, labour, and business be minimized rather than maximized. Governments not only limit domestic and international exchange, they may also develop onerous regulations that limit the right to gain credit, to hire or work for whom you wish, or to operate commercial enterprises freely. Excessive regulation of this kind once again constrains economic freedom.

Most importantly, economic freedom is not readily divisible. Nations that respect economic freedom in just one area, while constraining it in others, do not enjoy its great advantages. Conditions and policies that enhance economic freedom must be considered in total, as an overall package. To attain the full prosperity of which we are capable, Canadians require the greatest possible degree of freedom across the board.

Measuring the economic freedom of Canadians

Canadians are justly proud of our political freedoms. But what is our record when it comes to economic freedom? The Fraser Institute's annual report, *Economic Freedom of the World*, measures this equally important quality across 42 distinct variables in five different areas. Table 5.1 provides a summary of the latest outcomes of these measurements, revealing Canada's over-all rank compared to other OECD nations as well as the non-OECD economies of Hong Kong and Singapore. The result is unequivocal: on a scale where first place should be the goal, Canada's performance should be improved for the benefit of all Canadians.

1   *Size of government*

Overall, out of 32 economies considered, Canada comes in at eighth place in appropriate size of government. We have the eleventh highest marginal income-tax rate, and the share of our economy consumed by government is closer to the bottom of the stack than the top: in 21st place out of 32 jurisdictions. In other words, Canada is far from the top of the class. In fact, we are relatively heavy taxers compared to other developed nations. This unnecessarily decreases Canadians' economic freedom, reducing our ability to make our own decisions with our own money and putting those decisions in the hands of politicians and bureaucrats.

This over-sized governmental sector, compared to our leading competitors and trading partners, constitutes a major constraint on our ability to achieve superior economic performance. If we are to attain the quality of life we aspire to, we must liberate more of our economy to create prosperity. This will require striking a better balance between the public and private sectors without damaging social services. The analysis and recommendations of Chapters 7 and 8 describe steps we can take to achieve this critical goal.

2   *Legal structure and security of property rights*

An impartial legal system and secure property rights are essential to economic freedom. But Canada's ranking in this crucial area shows alarming decline. As recently as 2000, Canada ranked fifth best internationally on legal institutions and secure property rights, tied with Austria, Switzerland, and the United Kingdom with a score of 9.3 out of 10. By 2005, our ranking had plummeted to fourteenth among the 32 nations considered here and our score to 8.6.

For lack of military interference in politics and for the integrity of the legal system, Canada received perfect scores in both years; as did many other developed nations. However, Canada ranked twentieth in protection of intellectual property, down from twelfth in 2004. This decline is due to improved performance in other nations. Canada's score actually rose from 8.0 in 2000 to 8.2 in 2004.

Table 5.1: Canada's ranking for economic freedom compared to that of other

1 Size of Government		2 Legal System & Property Rights		3 Sound Money	
Hong Kong	9.2	Denmark	9.4	United States	9.8
Singapore	8.1	Norway	9.3	Singapore	9.8
Mexico	7.9	New Zealand	9.3	Sweden	9.7
United States	7.6	Iceland	9.2	Luxembourg	9.7
Switzerland	7.4	Netherlands	9.2	**Canada**	**9.7**
Turkey	7.3	Switzerland	9.0	Switzerland	9.7
Iceland	6.9	Finland	9.0	Ireland	9.7
Canada	**6.8**	Germany	8.9	New Zealand	9.6
New Zealand	6.7	Sweden	8.9	Finland	9.6
United Kingdom	6.7	Australia	8.8	Greece	9.6
South Korea	6.4	Luxembourg	8.7	France	9.6
Australia	6.4	United Kingdom	8.7	Spain	9.6
Hungary	6.3	Austria	8.7	Austria	9.5
Japan	6.2	**Canada**	**8.6**	Italy	9.5
Greece	6.1	Singapore	8.4	Belgium	9.5
Ireland	6.1	Japan	8.3	South Korea	9.5
Italy	5.9	Ireland	8.3	Hong Kong	9.5
Poland	5.9	Hong Kong	8.0	Japan	9.5
Germany	5.7	United States	7.7	Germany	9.5
Portugal	5.7	France	7.5	Denmark	9.5
Luxembourg	5.3	Belgium	7.5	Netherlands	9.5
Austria	5.2	Portugal	7.4	Portugal	9.5
Spain	5.2	South Korea	7.2	United Kingdom	9.4
Slovak Republic	5.0	Spain	7.1	Australia	9.4
Finland	5.0	Czech Republic	6.8	Hungary	9.4
Netherlands	4.9	Greece	6.7	Norway	9.3
Norway	4.7	Hungary	6.7	Poland	9.3
Czech Republic	4.5	Slovak Republic	6.7	Slovak Republic	9.2
Belgium	4.3	Turkey	6.6	Czech Republic	9.1
Sweden	4.2	Italy	6.4	Iceland	8.7
Denmark	4.0	Poland	5.8	Mexico	8.1
France	3.7	Mexico	5.7	Turkey	4.9

Source: Gwartney and Lawson, 2007. Note the data is for 2005.

OECD nations, Hong Kong, and Singapore

4 Freedom to Trade Internationally		5 Regulation		Summary index (rounded)	
Hong Kong	9.4	New Zealand	8.8	Hong Kong	8.9
Singapore	9.3	Hong Kong	8.6	Singapore	8.8
Ireland	8.4	Singapore	8.3	New Zealand	8.5
Slovak Republic	8.2	Iceland	8.3	Switzerland	8.3
Netherlands	8.1	Denmark	8.1	**Canada**	**8.1**
Belgium	8.1	Finland	8.0	United Kingdom	8.1
Czech Republic	8.0	United States	8.0	United States	8.1
Luxembourg	7.9	United Kingdom	7.9	Australia	7.9
Hungary	7.9	Switzerland	7.9	Ireland	7.9
New Zealand	7.9	**Canada**	**7.8**	Finland	7.8
Germany	7.8	Australia	7.6	Iceland	7.8
Denmark	7.7	Norway	7.6	Luxembourg	7.8
Sweden	7.7	Luxembourg	7.4	Denmark	7.7
Austria	7.7	Slovak Republic	7.4	Netherlands	7.7
United Kingdom	7.7	Hungary	7.3	Austria	7.6
Canada	**7.5**	Ireland	7.3	Germany	7.6
Finland	7.5	Sweden	7.0	Hungary	7.5
United States	7.5	Japan	7.0	Japan	7.5
Switzerland	7.3	South Korea	7.0	Norway	7.5
France	7.2	Netherlands	6.9	Sweden	7.5
Spain	7.2	Czech Republic	6.8	Slovak Republic	7.3
Mexico	7.2	Austria	6.7	South Korea	7.3
Australia	7.1	France	6.7	Belgium	7.2
Italy	7.1	Spain	6.7	Portugal	7.2
Portugal	7.0	Mexico	6.7	Mexico	7.1
Poland	6.7	Poland	6.6	Spain	7.1
Turkey	6.7	Belgium	6.5	Czech Republic	7.0
Norway	6.6	Germany	6.2	France	7.0
South Korea	6.5	Portugal	6.2	Italy	7.0
Japan	6.4	Italy	6.1	Greece	6.9
Greece	6.3	Greece	5.8	Poland	6.9
Iceland	5.8	Turkey	5.6	Turkey	6.2

In two other sub-indexes, our nation suffered serious declines in both score and ranking. In 2000, the independence of Canada's judiciary scored 9.2 out of ten, earning a rank of sixth, tied with New Zealand; five years later, our score had fallen to 7.9 and our ranking to fifteenth place. For impartial courts, we had a score of 9.2 in 2000, placing Canada in a four-way tie for fourth spot with Germany, Ireland, and New Zealand. By 2005, our score had declined to 7.4—tying us for fifteenth spot. Both these falls are extremely troubling. We focus here on economic policy. A full discussion of our legal system would require a separate study. Nonetheless, the integrity and overall effectiveness of our legal system are essential not only to our economic well-being but also to many other aspects of our lives. Canada's decline in this area should raise a national alarm. We call for a thorough investigation into why the reputation of Canada's legal system is slipping.

3   Access to sound money

Canada has solved (at least for the time being) what was once a dangerous problem that threatened our economic security: the erosion of sound money through inflation. Canada is in a five-way tie for third spot on sound money, with a score of 9.7 out of 10. This is our highest score in any area of the index by more than a full point. Moreover, the 0.1 point by which we trail the world leaders, Singapore and the United States, is the closest we come to top spot in any area of economic freedom.

We approve of, and support, the overall monetary course Canada is following to preserve its sound currency and, thus, will make no recommendations in this area other than to stay the course. It must be noted, however, that our good performance on sound money is hardly superlative: virtually all other developed nations have scores about as good as Canada's. In short, Canada's competence in this area, while important, confers no special advantage against the nations that are our main competitors.

4   Freedom to trade

As a trading nation whose prosperity is strongly linked to international commerce, Canada's score in this area is especially disappointing. In 2005, Canada tied for sixteenth place in freedom to trade, with a score of 7.5 out of 10. That was a drop of 0.8 point—and four places—from 2000, when Canada was in a three-way tie for twelfth spot with Denmark, Spain, and Sweden, scoring 8.3.

Canada's opportunity to trade is immense. In an era of relatively inexpensive global transportation, we sit between the great markets of Europe and Asia. We share an open border with the world's largest economy, that of the United States. Canadians should lead the world in our freedom to trade internationally. Instead, our ranking over the last four years is dismal—and declining. Canada's first problem in this area, despite our professed commitment to trade liberalization, is our high and variable tariff wall. Overall, Canada's tariff barriers rank us 26th, very close to the bottom of the 32 nations considered here, tied with Australia. Our regulatory barriers to trade are also relatively high, placing us in a tie for the eighteenth spot with the United Kingdom.

Chapter 9 will discuss a dimension of trade not directly measured by the Economic Freedom index but significant nonetheless to a large federation like ours, with distinctive regional economies and numerous provincial boundaries: restrictions on internal trade. Canada cannot achieve the world's best economic growth unless it first accomplishes greater freedom of exchange within our own country. Chapter 13 will offer concrete ideas for improving Canada's international trade.

5 *Regulation of credit, labour, and business*

Excessive government regulation of economic activity represents yet another serious constraint on economic performance. Again Canada's rank, as measured by the Economic Freedom index, is decidedly second rate. Among OECD nations plus Singapore and Hong Kong, Canada ranks tenth overall. Very worrisome is Canada's poor score in "extra payments or bribes" required to secure regulatory approvals—in other words, corruption. In this sub-index, Canada ties for seventeenth place with Ireland, in the bottom half of nations compared. This is particularly troubling considering Canada's poor score in the legal area.

These data are based on a survey; they lack the kind of detail that might support a judgement about the real extent of the problem. A full inquiry into the international perception of the need for "extra payments" in Canada is beyond the scope of this report. But once again, the evidence of our low standing raises a flag. We note that further investigation is required.

CONCLUSION AND RECOMMENDATION: MAXIMIZE ECONOMIC FREEDOM

In this chapter, we have described the vitally important role that economic freedom plays in achieving economic prosperity. We have measured the extent to which Canadians enjoy economic freedom by international comparison and found that, in the league of developed countries with whom we compete most directly, our performance is only middling. We conclude that Canadians must be as economically free as the top jurisdictions in order to achieve world-leading levels of economic performance. This conclusion leads us to a single but vitally important recommendation:

5.1 Maximize, at all levels of government, the economic freedom of Canadians.

In the following chapters, we examine in more detail the key constraints on economic freedom in Canada and recommend steps to reduce or remove them altogether.

CHAPTER 6

A MORE MODEST STATE

OPTIMAL GOVERNMENT

The size of government, defined as the level of government spending compared to the size of the economy, has an impact on Canada's ability to achieve high rates of economic growth and social progress. Most Canadians correctly view government as a positive force in the economy. On the other hand, most Canadians would also agree that governments can become too big. Indeed, history has proven that a completely government-controlled economy is not conducive to economic and social well-being. Somewhere between the two extremes of zero government involvement and a completely government-controlled economy exists a point at which economic growth and prosperity are maximized; this is what economists refer to as the optimal size of government.

The notion of an optimal size of government raises several questions: How can we know what size of government is optimal or "just right" for a country, in terms of maximizing economic growth and social progress? How big is government in Canada—and is its spending below or above the optimal level? If not, how should we go about reaching the optimal level? We attempt to answer all of these questions below.

How much a government spends in any country is, of course, a political compromise. Most countries are made up of citizens with different preferences. Some voters will want to keep government spending to a minimum while others favour more government involvement. Regardless of differences over the degree of government involvement, however, we believe most Canadians agree in desiring the highest level of economic and social progress attainable. To that end, Canada needs an open, honest, and vigorous debate about the optimal size of government (Harris and Manning, 2005). That debate, moreover, should be conducted on the basis of sound empirical research.

THE "U" CURVE

Economists often use an upside down "U" curve to explain the notion of the optimal size of government. In Figure 6.1, the vertical axis measures the rate of economic growth or any other socioeconomic value we wish to maximize. The horizontal axis measures the level of government spending as a percentage of gross domestic product (GDP), the value of all the goods and services produced by an economy.

The shape of the curve can best be explained using a simple analogy (Walker, 1997). Think of government spending as a factor of production, like the use of fertilizer in agriculture. The initial use of fertilizer on a piece of land increases its agricultural output. As more fertilizer is added, agricultural output continues to increase but at a decreasing rate. At some point, the amount of fertilizer applied is optimal: any increase or decrease will lower agricultural output. Eventually, if enough fertilizer is applied, the excess will poison the field and nothing will grow. Likewise, with zero government involvement in the economy, the level of basic public services is insufficient to sustain prosperity: economic growth and social progress are low. Initial government spending tends to finance services that promote economic freedoms: the maintenance of a legal system, protection of persons and property, a sound currency, essential transportation infrastructure, and basic education. These lead to greater economic growth and social progress. As the size of government continues to increase, rates of growth and progress also rise, albeit more slowly. At the top of the inverted "U" curve, government spending is optimal: beyond this point, more government spending will actually reduce the rate of economic growth and may impede rather than impel social progress. The tax revenues being collected to support that excess government spending would be more productive if the money were left in the hands of individuals and business to spend or invest as they see fit.[1]

SIZE OF GOVERNMENT AND ECONOMIC GROWTH

That is the theory. But where, exactly, is the top of the "U" curve? A growing body of empirical research into the impact of government spending on economic growth is illuminating the answer.

Studies tend to focus primarily on the United States. For example, Richard Vedder and Lowell Gallaway (1998) investigated the size of the US government

---

1   The composition of government spending is also important: for example, spending to ensure access and efficiency in the judiciary and the proper protection of people and property is highly effective. Spending on business subsidies and other grants to business may not be efficient.

Figure 6.1: Optimal size of government

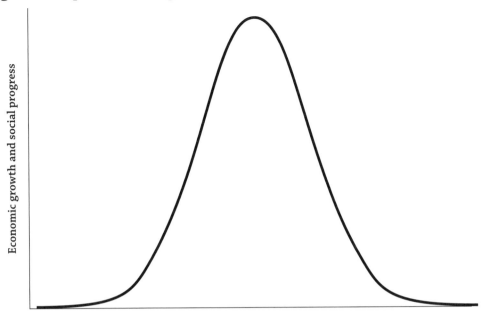

Government spending as a percentage of GDP

(y-axis label: Economic growth and social progress)

and its effect on economic growth for the Joint Economic Committee of the US Congress. Among their many findings was that moderate down-sizing of the federal government between 1991 and 1997 increased economic growth. They concluded that down-sizing government further still would also be growth-enhancing (Vedder and Gallaway, 1998). In the view of these researchers, cutting the size of the US government to 17.45% of GDP would produce sizable and permanent increases in GDP. Gerald Scully of the University of Texas (Dallas) reviewed six decades of historical data to investigate what level of aggregate tax burden maximized the rate of economic growth in the United States. Using data for the years from 1929 to 1989, Scully concluded that the growth-maximizing tax rate was between 21.5% and 22.9% of gross national product (Scully, 1995).

Two studies have examined the size of government in Canada. Economists Herbert Grubel and Johnny C.P. Chao compared the size of government in Canada to economic growth rates between 1929 and 1996. They concluded that economic growth was maximized when governments consumed approximately 34% of GDP (Chao and Grubel, 1998). Using a different methodology, William Mackness examined spending and growth between 1926 and 1996; he concluded that economic growth was greatest when total government spending was in the area of 20% to 30% of GDP (Mackness, 1999).

In addition to these single-nation studies, a number of scholars have analyzed data for multiple countries. For example, Harvard economist Robert

Barro investigated a wide range of variables in an attempt to determine their effect on economic growth in different jurisdictions. When investment in such services as education and defence was excluded from government spending, he found a "significantly negative association" between the share of a nation's economy represented by government consumption and GDP growth (Barro 1991: 430). Gerald Scully explored the relationship between tax rates, tax revenues, and economic growth for 103 countries. He found, in general, that economic growth was maximized when governments took no more than 19.3% of GDP (Scully, 1991). Stefan Folster and Magnus Henrekson (2001) examined the growth effects of taxation and government spending in "rich" countries and again found a strongly negative relationship. In fact, they found that for every 10% increase in government's consumption of GDP, economic growth fell by 0.7 to 0.8 percentage points (Folster and Henrekson, 2001). Most recently, Afonso, Schucknecht, and Tanzi (2005) analyzed the performance and efficiency of the public sectors in 23 industrialized countries. They found that "countries with small public sectors report the 'best' economic performance." When government spending exceeds 30% of GDP, economic growth declines. Strikingly, the researchers also concluded that "spending by big governments could be, on average, about 35% lower to attain the same [public sector performance]" (Afonso, Schucknecht, and Tanzi, 2005: 337).

SIZE OF GOVERNMENT AND SOCIAL PROGRESS

The foregoing studies confirm that more government spending does not necessarily lead to greater economic growth. In fact, spending beyond the optimal level lowers economic growth. Many people argue, however, that societies trade off a small amount of economic growth in order to achieve greater social progress. But empirical studies do not confirm this relationship.

"Social progress" may, of course, mean different things to different people. But one important study by Gerald Scully attempted to aggregate many views by examining 16 different indicators from 112 countries including literacy, infant mortality, life expectancy, caloric consumption, access to health care, infrastructure, political freedom, civil liberties, and economic freedom. Using data for 1995, Scully compared countries whose governments spent less than 40% of GDP to those whose governments spent more than 50% of GDP; he found little or no difference in social outcomes (Scully, 2000). Indeed, for advanced countries on average, Scully could find no meaningful progress on these 16 social indicators for government spending that rose above 18.6% of GDP (Scully, 2000). There is some variance among countries. For instance, the rate at which government spending ceases to provide any marginal benefits in Canada is 19.5% of GDP.

Likewise, Vito Tanzi and Ludger Schuknecht studied social progress in 17 industrialized nations. They also found that governments spending more than 50% of GDP did not significantly outperform those spending less than 40%. In fact, not only did "large government" countries fail to progress faster than "small government" countries, but countries with "medium"-sized governments (spending between 40% and 50% of GDP) also did no better (Tanzi, 1995; Tanzi and Schuknecht, 1997a, 1997b, 1998a, 1998b).

THE "RIGHT SIZE" OF GOVERNMENT FOR CANADA

On the basis of these independent studies, we conclude that there is in fact such a thing as an "optimal" size for government, beyond which any increase or decrease in spending reduces economic growth. In addition, there is considerable evidence that this "optimal" point is at the smaller end of the scale of government size rather than the larger. That is, "small" governments that still provide critical public services achieve social progress that is the same as, or greater than, that of "large" or even "medium"-sized governments. The foregoing studies suggest that the optimal range for government spending is likely between 20% and 35% of GDP. While this "right size" will vary from country to country and even vary over time, the estimates suggest that the optimal scale for government in Canada is at the upper end of this range.

Government spending in Canada
relative to competing countries

The OECD estimates that Canada's governments spent 39.5% of our GDP in 2006. Figure 6.2 ranks this percentage with that of 27 other industrialized countries. The comparison reveals that Canada maintained the ninth smallest government, spending slightly below the OECD average of 40.6% of GDP. However, Canada spends more on government than its chief trading partner, the United States, where governments consume only 36.5 % of GDP. Likewise, Canada's government sector is substantially larger than that of Australia (34.0%), an economy that shares many characteristics with Canada's. Other notable comparisons include Ireland (34.6%) and Japan (36.3%).

Figure 6.3 presents an historical perspective on government spending relative to the economy in both Canada and the United States. It reveals that government in Canada has historically been much smaller than it is today. From 1930 to 1965, apart from the period of the World War II, our government spending fell within 20% to 30% of GDP. Interestingly, Canadian and American governments during this period were roughly the same size in terms of percentage of GDP. Beginning in 1965, however, Canada experienced a dramatic growth in government that continued until recent years, opening up a significant gap

Figure 6.2: General government total outlays as a percentage of GDP, 2006

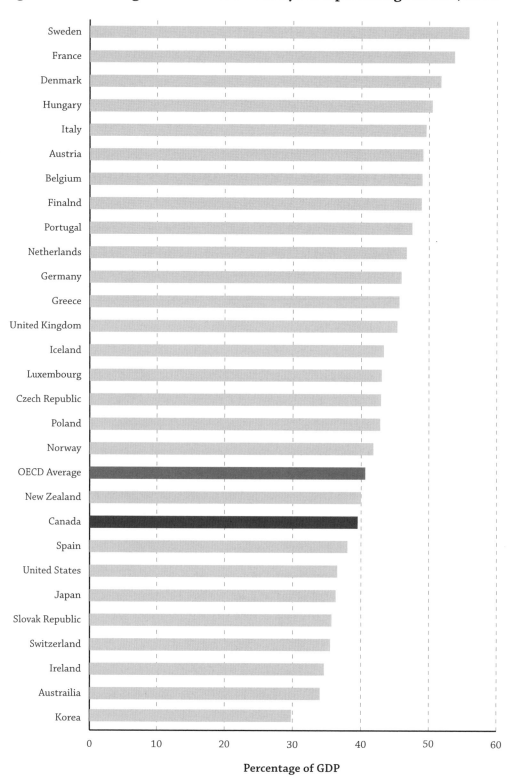

Percentage of GDP

Source: OECD, 2006a; data are estimates.

Figure 6.3: Size of government in Canada & the United States, 1929–2008 (2007 & 2008 are projections)

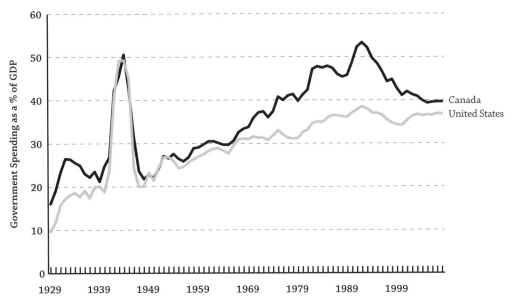

Source: OECD, 2006a; Statistics Canada, Public Institutions Division, 2007; US Department of Commerce, Bureau of Economic Analysis, 2007.

relative to the United States. By 1992, that gap had reached 14.8 percentage points. Since then, Canada has reduced the size of its government from 53.3% to 39.6% of GDP; the gap with the United States has narrowed but not closed.

The most important comparison, however, is not the size of government in Canada relative to other countries, or even over time, but rather to empirical estimates of the scale of government that would optimize increases in our prosperity. The studies referred to above put this scale in the range of 20% to 35% of GDP. Taking the upper end of this range as a fairly conservative figure, government in Canada today is at least 13% larger than it need be to maximize economic growth and social progress.

BENEFITS OF REDUCING THE SIZE OF GOVERNMENT

The trend in the size of Canada's government from the 1960s onward is not unique. Indeed, from 1960 to the mid-1980s, government spending as a percent of GDP increased dramatically in most industrialized countries (Tanzi, 2005). In fact, most countries' governments continued to grow well into the 1990s, albeit more slowly. However, a recent study published by the International Monetary Fund (Schuknecht and Tanzi, 2005) found that the governments of most industrialized countries stopped growing sometime between 1982 and

2002. Many then began to shrink quite dramatically. This study, in particular, provides us with good evidence of what happens to economies and societies when governments retrench. Schuknecht and Tanzi determined that most OECD nations had reduced the size of their governments between 1982 and 2002. For instance, government spending as a percentage of GDP in Ireland decreased by 16.4 percentage points from its 1982 peak to 2002. The GDP share of Canada's governments dropped from a high of 52.8% in 1992 to 41.4% ten years later—a decline of 11.4 percentage points. All told, six countries cut their government spending by more than 10% of GDP. Six more cut spending by 5% to 10% of GDP (Schuknecht and Tanzi, 2005).

Tanzi and Schuknecht sorted these countries into two general groups: "ambitious" reformers and "timid" reformers. Countries were considered "ambitious" if the reduction in their government spending exceeded 5% of GDP. Reformers were also split into "early" actors (countries whose spending peaked by the early to mid-1980s) and "late" actors (those whose spending continued to rise into the early to mid-1990s). Canada was classified as an "ambitious" but "late" reformer; our government spending reached a maximum of 52.8% of GDP in 1992, decreasing to 41.4% by 2002.

Schuknecht and Tanzi then examined the impact of reduced government spending on a host of indicators. Contrary to the fears of many, these did not include declines in economic growth. To the contrary, in most cases economic growth actually improved after reforms. In addition, economic growth rose twice as fast among ambitious reformers as it did among timid ones. Employment displayed similar results, with ambitious reformers again enjoying greater improvement than timid nations. Examining socioeconomic indicators, the authors found that the negative effect on income distribution from reduced government spending was small and, in fact, was largely mitigated by higher rates of economic growth and more targeted public spending.

Another important study, "Public Sector Efficiency: An International Comparison" (Afonso, Schuknecht, and Tanzi, 2005), measured the performance and efficiency of the public sectors in 23 industrialized countries in 1990 and 2000. The authors calculated indexes for two indicators: Public Sector Performance (PSP) and Public Sector Efficiency (PSE). For the first of these, the authors used seven sub-indicators, covering administrative, educational, health, and public infrastructure outcomes, as well as income distribution, an indicator of economic stability, and another for economic performance. They found "notable but not extremely large differences in PSP across countries" (Afonso, Schuknecht, and Tanzi, 2005: 326). In general, "small" governments (spending less than 40% of GDP) performed better on the index than either "medium" (40% to 50% of GDP) or "large" governments (those consuming more than half their nations' GDP). Canada's Public Service Performance rating for 2000 was the same as that of the United States—a tie for twelfth place among the 23 countries studied. Both nations scored slightly above the group average.

The authors next used government spending as a percentage of GDP to calculate different countries' cost of achieving their measured Public Sector Performance. Using both total spending and spending for specific purposes (goods and services, education, health, public investment) as a basis, this produced their second index—Public Sector Efficiency. Here, the authors find more significant differences. Canada, for instance, ranked tenth among the 23 countries for its Public Sector Efficiency, just above the average but much lower than the United States (fifth). Once more, "small" governments scored higher in Public Sector Efficiency than "large" or "medium" ones did.

Finally, the authors measured "wastefulness" in public spending. In keeping with the other findings, small governments were much less wasteful than larger ones. Canada ranked twelfth in this calculation, with an input efficiency score of 0.75—meaning that Canada could attain the same public-sector performance using only 75% of its current government spending.

Conclusion: Less can be more

Smaller public sectors, Tanzi and Schuknecht have found, generally perform better than medium-sized or big governments. Their evidence indicates that Canada could attain the same public service performance it does today with significantly less government. Marked reductions in government spending as a share of GDP in many OECD countries have significantly improved fiscal, economic, human-development, and institutional performance indicators. We conclude that Canadians would benefit economically and socially from rebalancing the size of our government sector to an optimal level. In 2006, Canada's federal, provincial, and local governments consumed 39.5% of our national income, according to OECD estimates. While this is the ninth-smallest government among 28 industrialized countries, it remains proportionately larger than those of the United States, Australia, Ireland, and Japan. More importantly, it is well beyond the level that maximizes economic growth and social progress.

RECOMMENDATION: THE 33% SOLUTION

Empirical estimates put the optimal size of government for maximizing economic performance in Canada at somewhere between 20% and 35% of GDP. As a reasonable initial objective toward right-sizing government, Canada should:

6.1 Adopt spending and taxation policies at all levels of government that would move the total government share of GDP to 33%[2] or less within five years.

In the next chapter, we recommend the specific changes in public spending and taxation required to achieve this target and give Canadians the increase in prosperity that optimizing the size of government makes possible.

---

2 A target roughly in line with the estimate by Herbert Grubel and Johnny C.P. Chao (Chao and Grubel, 1998).

DATA USED TO ESTIMATE GOVERNMENT SPENDING IN CHAPTERS 6 AND 7

To avoid confusion, it is important to note an important distinction between the source of data referenced in Chapters 6 and 7. In Chapter 6, we used data derived primarily from the OECD in order to provide international comparisons. Chapter 7 deals primarily with Canada alone. Hence, we use data drawn from Statistics Canada's Financial Management System to estimate spending more accurately.

This results in a slightly different estimate of the size of government. In 2006/07, the latest year for which Statistics Canada data is available, Canadian federal, provincial, and local governments spent a combined $574.6 billion. This amounted to 41.7% of GDP (compared to the figure of 40.3% that appeared in the Chapter 6).

As a basis for our analysis in Chapter 7, we also estimate a "status quo" level of growth in government spending from 2006/07 to 2011/12. We base this estimate on Statistics Canada's data for 2005/06 and assume that no major changes in spending are enacted. Specifically, we grow federal spending going forward by the average rate of growth from 2005/06 to 2007/08, as provided by the federal Department of Finance (Canada, Department of Finance, 2006). Growth in provincial and local government spending to 2011/12 is estimated using the average growth rate experienced over the past five years.

Our baseline calculations estimate consolidated federal, provincial, and local government spending at $575.0 billion in 2006/07, growing to $734.5 billion by 2011/12. Using this estimate, the size of government is expected to be 40.4% of GDP at the end of the five-year period (2011/12).

CHAPTER 7

"RIGHT SIZING" GOVERNMENT

ACHIEVING THE 33% SOLUTION

Reducing government's share of the Canadian economy from 39% to 33% will require adjustments. But these adjustments need not be wrenching. And it must be borne constantly in mind that the main objective of the adjustments is to attain for Canadians the highest standard of living and quality of life in the world.

What policies would move us toward this goal? The changes we recommend apply to both sides of the fiscal ledger, to spending as well as taxation, and to all levels of government. Our target for achieving the necessary adjustment is the 2012/13 budget year—a five-year time horizon.

We also note that the overall rate of taxation, as reflected in government's share of the national economy, is only part of the picture. The type of taxes employed to capture that share also matters. Therefore, we examine the current structure of government revenues in Canada and propose that reductions coincide with a rebalancing of taxation toward revenue sources that we believe would be most efficient.

Constraining public spending
and reducing taxes

The goal outlined above is to rebalance the division of the Canadian economy so that more resources are left to private companies and individuals to spend or invest productively as they choose. This objective stands against a recent record in which total government revenues at all levels have continued to increase, despite a number of important tax-rate reductions. Total government revenues in Canada have never been higher and are now over one-half trillion dollars. Happily, a relatively strong economy over the last decade has meant that these revenues represent a declining share of GDP. Stronger measures are needed, however, to reduce the total size of government permanently and thus increase the share of the economy held in private hands. Specifically, our objective requires a real reduction in the growth of government spending coupled with continued economic growth. Government spending need not be reduced in absolute terms but its growth needs to be slowed.

There are many ways governments might reduce their overall spending to 33% of GDP but all demand some measurable restraint in public spending. We outlined a plan to achieve this over five years in our 2006 publication, *Building Prosperity in a Canada Strong and Free*. We proposed that growth in consolidated federal, provincial, and local government spending be constrained to about 1% per year for the next five years.[1] Under this scenario, government spending would grow from $575.0 billion in 2006/07 to $599.9 billion by 2011/12.

Table 7.1 presents the size of government from 2006/07 to 2011/12 under two different scenarios: growing spending using the "status quo" assumptions, and growing spending at about 1% per year. An interesting calculation is the cumulative difference between the "status quo" level of government spending and the "constrained" level. This difference increases from $23.9 billion in 2007/08 to $134.7 billion in 2011/12. Over the five-year period, the cumulative difference amounts to $388.2 billion. In other words, reducing the size of government to 33% of GDP by 2011/12 would shift $388 billion in spending away from government and back into the hands of individuals, families, and wealth-creating, job-creating businesses.

Unfortunately, governments are rapidly moving in the wrong direction, with large increases in spending instead of spending restraint (Table 7.2). The average increase among the provinces in the last fiscal year was 5.1%, increasing to 5.7% if the territories are included. The smallest increase, though still too large, was 3.0% in Prince Edward Island; Alberta's increase, at 9.2%, was very worrisome and threatens to throw the province off its successful economic track. The longer this continues, and the larger the increases, the more Canada will move away from a growth-enhancing size of government and the harder it will be to achieve it. Now in 2007, the recent burst of government spending will already require greater restraint in future years to achieve the 33% solution than we estimated in 2006. Ultimately, we are moving away from, rather than towards, greater prosperity for Canadians.

---

1   The precise number used in this volume was 0.9%. In an earlier volume, we estimated that government spending would have to be constrained to 1.6% increases annually. The reduced level of increase reflected in the new estimate is due to recent and significant spending increases by the federal government and several provinces.

Table 7.1: Restraining the size of government in Canada

	2006/07	2007/08	2008/09	2009/10	2010/11	2011/12	Totals
(1) Size of government: "status quo" growth rates							
Total Spending (millions of dollars)	575,012	603,759	634,020	665,845	699,311	734,524	3,912,471
Percent of GDP	39.6%	39.8%	39.9%	40.1%	40.3%	40.4%	
(2) Size of government: constrained growth rates							
Total Spending (millions of dollars)		579,900	584,829	589,800	594,813	599,869	2,949,212
Percent of GDP		38.2%	36.8%	35.5%	34.2%	33.0%	
Difference in spending: (1) – (2)							
		23,859	49,191	76,045	104,497	134,654	388,246

Note: To calculate a baseline for overall federal, provincial, and local spending from 2006/07 to 2011/12 we use "status quo" growth rates. That is, federal spending is estimated using growth rates provided by the federal Department of Finance (2006 Budget) and provincial and local government spending is estimated using the average growth rate of spending from 2000/01 to 2005/06. In other words, the basis for our analysis assumes that federal spending grows in line with the federal government's own estimates and that provincial and local governments increase spending at the average rate experienced over the past five years.

Sources: Statistics Canada, Public Institutions Division, 2006; Canada, Department of Finance, 2006.

Table 7.2: Consolidated Provincial-Local Government Spending ($millions)

	2005/06	2006/07	Increase
Canada	335,738	353,031	5.2%
Newfoundland	5,628	5,836	3.7%
Prince Edward Island	1,400	1,442	3.0%
Nova Scotia	9,094	9,483	4.3%
New Brunswick	7,325	7,635	4.2%
Quebec (adjusted for abatements)	82,662	87,175	5.5%
Ontario	124,335	128,977	3.7%
Manitoba	12,102	12,778	5.6%
Saskatchewan	11,352	11,944	5.2%
Alberta	35,014	38,250	9.2%
British Columbia	40,345	42,830	6.2%
Yukon	773	849	9.8%
Northwest Territories	1,290	1,428	10.7%
Nunavut	152	156	2.6%

Source: Statistics Canada, Financial Management System, 2006; The Fraser Institute.

EXAMINING THE STRUCTURE
OF GOVERNMENT REVENUES

The adjustments we propose could shift more than one-third of a trillion dollars from the hands of bureaucrats and politicians to the private sector over five years. How that shift is accomplished is also significant. A reduction in the size of government on this scale provides an extraordinary opportunity not only to reduce taxation levels but also to reform the tax system.

In order to identify the most efficient mix of tax changes, we first examine how government revenues are presently structured across federal, provincial, and local levels—both in absolute terms and relative to national income. Next, we discuss the nature of taxation in Canada and review the literature on which types of taxes are least damaging to economic growth. We also compare the tax mix in Canada to that employed by our chief competitor nations. This analysis will set the context for the recommendations that follow.

CRITICAL DISTINCTIONS
Rates versus revenue: The still-rising cost of government

Tax cuts have been much discussed and widely promised in Canada over the last few years. Certainly, the previous federal government's professed commitment to a $100-billion tax cut, combined with major reductions in tax rates in Ontario, Alberta, and British Columbia, have led to a popular impression that taxes have been reduced in Canada. In absolute terms, this impression is wrong. While there have been important reductions in tax rates at both the federal and provincial levels, the amount of revenue collected has reached record highs.

Figure 7.1 illustrates the historic growth of total revenues at all levels of government in Canada combined, since the 1990/91 fiscal year.[2] Revenues are depicted in both nominal and inflation-adjusted (real) terms. Clearly, despite tax-relief measures enacted at various levels of government, revenues have continued their upward trend. Total government revenues increased at an average rate of 4.5% a year on a nominal basis, reaching $603.2 billion in 2006/07. When inflation is accounted for, the real growth rate is only somewhat less: still an average of 2.4% a year. Even more alarming is the fact that recent increases are even larger. Since 2001/02, nominal spending has averaged a 5.2% annual increase, an annual increase of 2.9% when inflation is taken into account.

Figure 7.2 breaks down this overall growth in government revenue over the same period by level of government: federal, provincial, and local. Canada Pension Plan revenues, which consist primarily of compulsory contributions,

---

2   Revenue figures are consolidated and include the Canada Pension Plan (CPP) and Quebec Pension Plan (QPP).

Figure 7.1: Total federal, provincial, and local revenues, 1990/91–2006/07

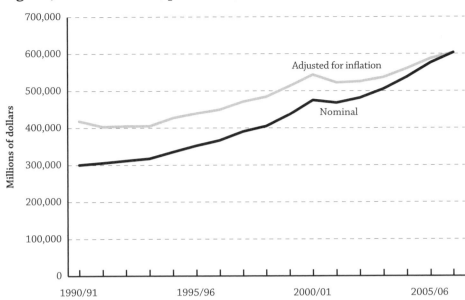

Source: Statistics Canada, Financial Management System, 2003, 2004, 2005, 2006, 2007.

are displayed separately. Plainly, very little has changed. In 1990/91, the federal government collected 42.0% of total tax revenues (47.2% including CPP/QPP revenues). Provincial governments collected 41.3%. Local governments collected only 11.5%. By 2006/07, the federal government collected a slightly smaller share directly, 39.4%, while collecting 46.8% if CPP/QPP payments are included. Provincial governments collected slightly more, 42.9%, mostly at the expense of local governments, whose share dropped to 10.3%.

More significant than dollar increases, however, is the share of the economy (GDP) drawn off by governments (Figure 7.3). Even though revenues increased in both nominal and inflation-adjusted terms over this period, consistent growth[3] meant that by the end, government consumed a smaller share of the economy. Specifically, total government revenues as a share of GDP peaked in 1998 at 44.9%. They have since declined to an estimated 41.0% of GDP in 2005, a decrease of 3.9 percentage points.[4] Once again, however, this decrease reflected strong economic growth rather than any actual decline in government revenues.

---

3 Between 1990 and 2005, real GDP grew at an average annual rate of 2.6%. Since 2000, real GDP has experienced an annual growth rate of 3.0%.

4 Represents an 8.7% decrease in total government revenues as a share of GDP. It is important to note that Canada as a whole has moved from a marked position of deficit in 1990 of 5.8% of GDP to a surplus of 1.7% of GDP in 2005 (OECD, 2006).

Figure 7.2: Nominal revenues by level of government, 1990/91–2006/07

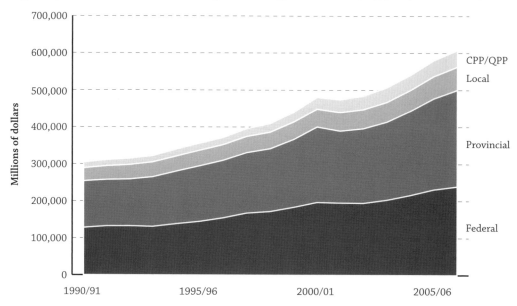

Source: Statistics Canada, Public Institutions Division, 2003, 2004, 2005 and 2006; The Fraser Institute.

Figure 7.3: General government revenues as a percentage of GDP, 1989–2008 (2007 & 2008 are projections)

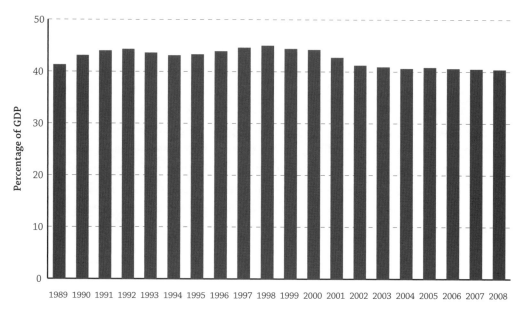

Source: Organisation for Economic Co-operation and Development, 2007b: Annex Table 26.

Not every dollar alike: How taxes differ

It is not only the overall burden of taxation that may constrain Canada's prosperity. Equally important is the structure of the tax burden, often called the
"tax mix." Not all forms of taxation are equally efficient; that is, different taxes
will have different costs for each dollar of revenue raised, when all costs are
considered, including impact on economic growth and collection costs. Similarly, not every tax reduction may be equally effective at stimulating growth.
Most studies on the subject quantify this difference as the "marginal efficiency
cost" (MEC) of a particular tax. Every tax imposes some economic cost, distorting the behaviour of individuals and businesses. Taxes on investment income
(interest, dividends, and capital gains) for instance, decrease the after-tax rate
of return; this leads to less saving and investment than would otherwise occur.
Likewise, taxes on capital (corporate income and capital taxes) reduce the rate
of capital accumulation so that, again, fewer resources are available for investment. Sales taxes distort consumption decisions. Taxes on labour incomes
reduce take-home wages, discouraging effort and diminishing the number of
hours worked. Research has consistently found that business or capital-based
taxes impose significantly higher costs on an economy than do sales, payroll,
or personal income taxes.[5]

These differences mean that reductions in various types of taxes also produce uneven effects. The federal Department of Finance, for instance, recently
calculated the "welfare gain"—the increase in economic well-being—that
would result from each dollar of reduction in various taxes (Baylor and Beausejour, 2004).[6] Differences were dramatic, as can be seen in Table 7.3. Each $1 cut
from personal income taxes on capital (dividends, capital gains, and interest
income), offset by a $1 increase in lump-sum tax revenues, led to a welfare gain
of $1.30. At the other end of the scale, $1 cut from consumption taxes, similarly
offset, produced the smallest benefit, a mere 10¢ welfare gain.[7]

Similarly, the economic cost of raising a dollar of revenue from one kind of
tax may be different from that of raising a dollar from another. Estimates of
the MEC for Canadian taxes, based on another study from the Finance Depart-

---

5 For further information on the effects and costs of capital-based taxes, please see
   Auerbach, 1983, 1996; Beaulieu et al., 2004; Chirinko and Meyer, 1997; Chirinko et al.,
   1999; Cummins et al., 1996; Fazzari et al., 1988; Goolsbee, 1998, 2004a, 2004b; Razin
   and Yuen, 1996.

6 Benefits of different types of tax cuts were calculated by assuming that any revenue
   loss was offset by a non-distortionary "lump-sum" tax increase.

7 A number of other studies examine the economic or welfare costs of specific taxes in
   the United States: Feldstein, 1999; Gravelle, 2004, 1989; Gravelle and Kotlikoff, 1993;
   Cai and Gokhale, 1997; Liu and Rettenmaier, 2004; and Holtz-Eakin and Marples,
   2001a, 2001b. For a summary of these studies, see US GAO, 2005.

Table 7.3: Welfare gains from tax reductions[1]

Capital Cost Allowance	$1.40 [2]
Sales Tax on Capital Goods	$1.30
Personal Capital Income Tax	$1.30
Capital Tax	$0.90
Corporate Income Tax	$0.40
Average Personal Income Tax	$0.30
Wage Tax	$0.20
Consumption Tax	$0.10

Note 1: Revenue loss is assumed to be recovered through "lump-sum" taxation. Welfare gains are calculated as the gain in economic well-being per dollar of tax reduction.

Note 2: The estimate for an increase in capital cost allowances (CCA) is for new capital only. Increasing CCA is not a tax reduction per se but rather an increase in a deduction against corporate income taxes.

Source: Baylor and Beausejour, 2004.

ment, are shown in Table 7.4.[8] Corporate income taxes are found to carry a much higher MEC ($1.55) than more efficient types, such as sales ($0.17) and payroll ($0.27) taxes. Both these studies concluded that consumption and payroll (wage) taxes impose lower economic costs than do capital-based taxes.

Canada's tax mix compared to that of our chief competitors

The share of Canada's economy taken up by government ranks in the low mid-range of OECD countries (Figure 7.4). At 39.9 % of GDP, however, it is higher than the OCED average of 38.7 %. In addition to collecting more taxes than the OECD average, Canada is among the most reliant in the OECD on the most economically damaging types of taxes. Table 7.5 breaks down how much revenue, as a percentage of the total, various industrialized countries collect from five different groups of revenue sources: income and profit, social security, payroll, property, goods and services, and other revenues. The comparison reveals that Canada is the fourth-highest user of the most damaging type of taxes, those on income and profit. Canadian governments collected 46.5% of their total revenue from those damaging tax types in 2004, more than one-third higher than the OECD average of 34.4%.

8   Among the most widely cited calculations of marginal efficiency costs are those by Harvard professor Dale Jorgensen and his colleague Kun-Young Yun (1991). Jorgensen and Yun's estimates of the MEC of select US taxes indicate a significant difference in the economic costs of different taxes. Corporate income taxes ($0.84) were shown to impose much higher costs than other, more efficient, types of taxes such as sales ($0.26). In other words, it costs the economy $0.26 to raise an additional dollar of revenue using consumption taxes and $0.84 to raise an additional dollar of tax revenue using corporate income taxes.

Table 7.4: Estimates of marginal efficiency costs (MECs) for selected Canadian taxes

	MEC ($CDN)
Corporate Income Tax	$1.55
Personal Income Tax	$0.56
Payroll Tax	$0.27
Sales Tax	$0.17

Source: OECD, 1997.

Figure 7.4: General government revenues as a percentage of GDP, 2007 (projected)

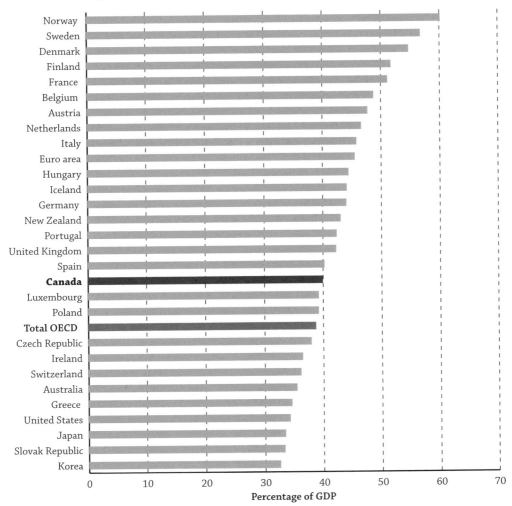

Source: OECD, 2007, <http://www.oecd.org/dataoecd/5/51/2483816.xls>.

Table 7.5: Revenue, as a percentage of the total, collected from different categories of taxes (2003)

	Income and profit	Social security	Payroll	Property	Goods and services	Other
Canada	**46.5**	**15.2**	**2**	**10.2**	**25.9**	**0.3**
Mexico	24.6	16.5	1.2	1.6	55.5	0.6
United States	43.4	26.3	—	12.0	18.3	—
Australia	58.4	—	4.4	8.7	28.5	—
Japan	32.0	37.7	—	10.0	20.0	0.3
Korea	27.9	20.7	0.2	11.3	36.3	3.5
New Zealand	61.1	—	—	5.0	33.8	—
Austria	29.4	33.9	6.1	1.3	28.2	0.9
Belgium	38.6	31.3	—	3.9	25.0	—
Czech Republic	25.1	42.3	—	1.1	31.2	—
Denmark	60.3	2.4	0.4	3.8	32.7	—
Finalnd	38.6	26.8	—	2.6	31.7	0.1
France	23.3	37.1	2.6	7.6	25.6	3.6
Germany	27.3	40.7	—	2.5	29.2	—
Greece	23.5	34.7	—	4.4	37.1	—
Hungary	23.6	30.1	2.3	2.3	40.8	0.8
Iceland	44.0	8.3	—	6.3	41.1	0.2
Ireland	39.3	15.0	0.6	6.9	37.8	—
Italy	31.4	30.3	—	6.1	26.4	5.5
Luxembourg	33.2	28.3	—	7.8	30.4	0.2
Netherlands	24.6	36.9	—	5.3	32.0	0.4
Norway	46.2	21.6	—	2.6	29.7	—
Poland	17.9	40.9	0.7	3.8	36.0	—
Portugal	24.2	31.8	—	4.6	38.6	0.5
Slovak Republic	18.8	39.4	—	1.8	39.8	—
Spain	28.2	34.8	—	8.1	28.0	0.4
Sweden	37.7	28.4	4.7	3.1	25.8	0.1
Switzerland	43.4	24.4	—	8.5	23.7	—
Turkey	22.1	23.9	—	3.1	47.7	3.2
United Kingdon	36.8	18.8	—	12.0	32.0	—
OECD Average	34.4	25.9	0.9	5.6	32.3	0.7

Note: Categories may not add to 100.0 due to rounding.

Source: Organisation for Economic Co-operation and Development, 2006b: Table 7: Tax Revenue of Main Categories as Percentage of Total Taxation (2004).

At the same time, Canada makes relatively little use of more efficient revenue sources such as consumption taxes (referred to in Table 7.5 as taxes on "Goods and services"). Governments in Canada collected only 25.9% of their revenues from efficient consumption taxes in 2004, compared to an OECD average of 32.3%. In addition, the recent decision by the federal government to reduce the federal sales tax (GST) and a commitment for a further reduction in the future will lessen Canada's reliance on this relatively efficient form of revenue collection and create greater dependency on income and profit taxes, which are far more costly and damaging to the Canadian economy and Canadian workers.

CONCLUSION: THE RIGHT TAXES FOR A GOVERNMENT OF THE "RIGHT-SIZE"

The size of Canada's government sector is clearly greater than the optimal point for increasing prosperity. In the previous chapter, we identified a practical target for rebalancing government closer to roughly one-third of the Canadian GDP, which the research shows is closer to the optimal size of government than where we are now. In this chapter, we call for tax reductions sufficient to achieve this target within five years.

In particular, we call for the reduction of those taxes that most heavily penalize work, savings, investment, and entrepreneurship. The foregoing evidence is unequivocal. The difference in the economic impact of different types of taxes is striking: as much as $1.20 in economic welfare gained or foregone for each $1 tax cut, depending on which type of tax is reduced. At the same time, Canada stands dramatically apart from its OECD peers in relying disproportionately on the least efficient tax types. Unfortunately, once again governments are moving in the wrong direction with cuts to the GST, a highly efficient tax, rather than equally substantial reductions in inefficient taxes.

Clearly, Canadians can choose to do better. As we observed at the outset of this chapter, Canada has an opportunity to improve its economic performance dramatically by changing its tax system in two ways. The first is to capture the increased prosperity that would flow from rebalancing our economy toward a more optimal size of government involvement through substantive reductions in the overall level of taxation. The second is to accomplish that reduction by cutting first and most those taxes that are most damaging to economic growth. As indicated by Monograph 3, "Doing More: Improving Canada's Productivity" (page 139), these are precisely the tax cuts required to improve Canada's productivity and our ability to compete more effectively internationally.

RECOMMENDATIONS TO ACHIEVE THE OPTIMAL SIZE OF GOVERNMENT

To reduce the tax load on Canadian business[9] and allow Canadians to achieve our full economic potential:[10]

7.1 Accelerate the complete elimination of all corporate capital taxes.[11] This is largely a provincial issue, as the federal government has already committed itself to rapidly eliminate capital taxes.

7.2 Reduce corporate income-tax rates. Specifically, the federal government should reduce its rate to 12.0% from 21.0% over the next five years.[12] The provinces are encouraged to reduce their corporate income-tax rates by a minimum of 30%, with a target rate of 8%. The cost of these reductions will vary dramatically by province since some (notably British Columbia, Alberta, and Saskatchewan) are already approaching the target rate.

7.3 Increase aggressively the amount of income eligible for the "preferential" federal and provincial small-business tax rate. Over time, this "preference" should be eliminated entirely, not by raising the small-business tax rate but rather by reducing the general corporate income-tax rate.[13]

7.4 End the practice of applying sales tax to business inputs in the five provinces that have maintained it, namely British Columbia, Saskatchewan, Manitoba,

---

9 For a thorough discussion of business taxes and the rationale for their reduction, please see Veldhuis and Clemens, 2006.

10 Jack Mintz, the eminent Canadian tax economist who headed up the influential federal Technical Committee on Business Taxation, has calculated that Canada has the second highest effective tax rate on capital investment among industrial countries (Mintz et al., 2005).

11 A recent study (Veldhuis and Clemens, 2006) estimated that all governments in Canada would collect a total of $3.9 billion in corporate capital taxes in 2006/07. The total cost of eliminating corporate capital taxes over the five-year period was estimated at $12.0 billion.

12 The federal corporate income-tax reduction was estimated to cost $28.8 billion over five years (Veldhuis and Clemens, 2006). The provincial reductions were calculated to cost roughly $18.3 billion over the same five-year period (Veldhuis and Clemens, 2006). Veldhuis and Clemens (2006) provide a number of suggestions (such as closing preferential tax loopholes) to reduce the net cost of the suggested tax relief. The annual savings from these suggestions was estimated to be $6.2 billion in 2005/06 alone.

13 For further information on the small-business income-tax rate and the problems associated with large marginal increases as firms lose their eligibility for the lower rate, please see Hendricks et al., 1997 and Clemens and Veldhuis, 2005.

Ontario, and Prince Edward Island. These provinces are further encouraged to harmonize their provincial sales taxes with the federal goods and services tax (GST), which already exempts business inputs. This would provide a double benefit by also reducing by one half the paperwork required for businesses to collect and remit sales taxes. Provinces that implement exemptions without harmonization will not benefit from reduced administration and compliance costs and could actually increase these costs.[14]

To reduce personal income taxes and harness the productive energies of workers, business owners, and entrepreneurs across country:

7.5 Move toward a single-rate personal income tax on both the federal and provincial levels. Removing the disincentives for work, saving, investment, and entrepreneurship inherent in increasing tax rates as incomes rise, will encourage productive activity and make the Canadian economy more efficient.

7.6 Raise the thresholds at which higher rates apply for jurisdictions that retain multiple tax rates. One of the problems in the current Canadian personal income-tax system is that "middle" and "upper" income-tax rates are applied at relatively low levels of real income.

To encourage savings and investment:

7.7 Eliminate capital gains taxes.[15] As a small, open economy struggling to compete for business capital, it is critical that Canada create and maintain a strongly attractive investment climate. Eliminating levies on capital gains would not only remove one of the most economically costly of tax types but also send a strong pro-development and investment signal to potential investors.

7.8 Retain taxes on investment income at competitive rates. The ideal would be to move toward a single-rate, integrated, tax system.[16] Failing that more fundamental reform, however, it is critical that Canada and its provinces ensure that our treatment of savings, dividend, and interest income remains strongly competitive internationally, especially with the United States.

---

14 For an excellent discussion of this problem, see Veldhuis, 2006.

15 For further information on the benefits of eliminating capital gains taxes, please see Grubel, 2000, 2001, and 2003; Veldhuis, Godin, and Clemens, 2007.

16 For further information on integrated flat tax systems, please see Emes and Clemens, 2001; Hall and Rabushka, 1995.

7.9   Eliminate contribution limits for RRSPs and RPPs. The majority of Canadians save exclusively in tax-deferred accounts such as RRSPs. Greater flexibility in their use would have beneficial economic effects.

7.10   Introduce tax-pre-paid savings accounts. These are essentially the reverse of RRSPs, in that the tax is pre-paid but earnings are tax-exempt, as are any withdrawals.[17]

---

17   For further information, please see Kesselman and Poschmann, 2001a.

DOING MORE: IMPROVING CANADA'S PRODUCTIVITY

Productivity growth is one of the most important determinants of increased living standards. Unfortunately, growth in Canada's productivity has decreased significantly in recent years and is now among the lowest in the industrialized world. More worrying is the fact that little has been done to address the problem. To secure and improve upon our current standard of living, Canadian leaders must begin to address our poor productivity performance.

PRODUCTIVITY AND WHY IT MATTERS

Productivity is a measure of the ability of our economy to transform inputs like raw materials and labour into valuable goods and services. The most common and widely understood measure of productivity is labour productivity, the average value of output produced per hour worked. Workers who produce more goods and services for each hour worked are able to command higher wages. Increased productivity also makes Canadian companies more profitable and competitive. Lastly, a more productive economy provides greater economic output from which governments are able to extract revenue.

CANADA'S PRODUCTIVITY PERFORMANCE

On all accounts, Canada is facing a serious productivity problem. Internationally, Canada ranked nineteenth amongst 24 industrialized countries in terms of average labour productivity growth over the last ten years. Specifically, Canada's average annual labour productivity growth of 1.4% between 1996 and 2005 was less than one-third that of Ireland, the top ranked country with average annual labour productivity growth of 4.3%. Closer to home, average annual labour productivity growth from 1996 to 2005 in the United States (2.4%) was also substantially higher than Canada's.

As a result of Canada's disappointing productivity performance, Canadian incomes have fared poorly compared to the United States. Using a broad measure of living standards, the value of all goods and services produced in an economy on a per person basis (GDP per capita), indicates a marked decline between Canada and the United States over the last two decades. Canada's GDP per person was 87.0% of the US' value in 1986 and has since dropped to 84.9% in 2005. Narrower measures of living standards such as average after-tax income per person have experienced sharper declines: 78.4% of that in the United States in 1986, dropping to 68.0% in 2005. In other words, our inability to transform inputs into outputs has meant a marked decline in our standard of living.

The impact of Canada's poor productivity performance on Canadian incomes is perhaps best summarized by a recent report published by the Organisation for Economic Co-operation and Development: "Despite buoyant employment in recent years, the GDP-per-capita gap vis-à-vis the United States remains substantial, reflecting to a large extent lower productivity levels" (OECD, 2007). Productivity increases are a key driver in standard of living. We become more prosperous by producing the things and services we use and sell more efficiently. Canada's lagging productivity performance means that Canadians are poorer than we should be. Improving our productivity in the ways we recommend would increase the prosperity that individuals and families enjoy in Canada.

PENALIZING CAPITAL INVESTMENTS

One of the primary reasons for Canada's poor productivity growth is an economic environment that penalizes, rather than promotes, capital investment. Increasing the amount of capital workers have at their disposal is one of the principal drivers of productivity and increased living standards. In addition, technological advances are often embodied in new investments in machinery and equipment.

A review of the academic research indicates that business taxes significantly influence the incentives for capital investment.[1] Jurisdictions with high business taxes reduce the after-tax rate of return on investment. Lower returns reduce the incentives for investment and leave firms with less money to reinvest in new machinery, equipment, and technology. Accordingly, *Advantage Canada*, a recent report from the federal Department of Finance, proclaims, "Business investment is critical to our long-term prosperity. It yields innovation and growth, with more jobs and higher wages for Canadian workers. High business taxes are harmful because they reduce the returns from investment, thereby reducing the amount of investment that take place in Canada" (Department of Finance, 2006).

Unfortunately, Canada has one of the highest tax rates on incremental capital investment in the world: the effective tax rate on capital in Canada is 36.6%, the sixth highest out of 36 countries (Mintz, 2006).[2] In addition, Canada is an outlier in the industrialized world in terms of our heavy reliance on the most economically damaging taxes, personal and business income taxes (Clemens et al., 2007). Canadian governments collect 46% of their revenue in income and profit taxes compared to an average of 34% among industrialized countries.

IMPROVING CAPITAL PRODUCTIVITY

The most effective means of increasing productivity in Canada lies in creating an environment that is conducive to the accumulation of capital. In *Building Prosperity in a Canada Strong and Free*, volume IV in this series, we proposed numerous changes to

---

1   For a detailed literature review on the impact of taxes on investment, see Veldhuis and Clemens, 2006.

2   The marginal effective tax rate (METR) is the tax rate that firms pay on an additional dollar of return generated from a capital investment. Indeed METRs are the best indicator of the competitiveness of business taxes in that they are a comprehensive measure that includes income taxes, capital taxes, depreciation and inventory cost deductions, and sales taxes imposed on business inputs.

make Canada's taxes more competitive. Most importantly, Canada must reduce business taxes broadly defined. On the personal side, substantial reductions in middle and upper personal income-tax rates are necessary to harness the productive energies of workers, business owners, and entrepreneurs across the country. Most critically, the federal and provincial governments should follow the lead of Alberta by moving towards a single-rate personal income tax.

Not to be overlooked is the formation of human capital. It is key to increased labour productivity. Its foundation must be laid in the K-12 years, equipping young Canadians with numeracy, literacy, an understanding of science and civics, and the other elements of knowledge and personal skills necessary to undertake further preparation for the rapidly changing labour market. In an earlier volume, *Caring for Canadians in a Canada Strong and Free*, we showed how educational choice is related to improved K-12 performance in Canada and reviewed international evidence on this positive relationship.

CONCLUSION

The data are unambiguous and economists generally agree that Canada faces a serious productivity challenge that must be tackled immediately. To improve Canada's productivity, an economic environment that is conducive to investment must be created and steps must be taken to improve the productivity of human capital. To that end, Canadian governments must make their tax systems more competitive and increase freedom of choice and accountability in education.

RECOMMENDATIONS

✤ Eliminate all capital taxes to encourage increased capital investment.

✤ Reduce substantially overall business taxes to allow increased capital accumulation. In particular, reduce corporate income taxes and eliminate all corporate capital taxes.[3]

✤ Harmonize provincial sales taxes with the federal goods and services tax (GST) to ensure that business inputs are exempt from sales taxes.

✤ Reduce substantially middle and upper personal income-tax rates to harness the productive energies of workers, business owners, and entrepreneurs across the country.

✤ Move towards a single-rate personal income tax.

✤ Increase school choice in Canada to improve the foundations for improvements in human capital.

---

3   A recent study (Veldhuis and Clemens 2006) estimated that all governments in Canada would collect a total of $792 million in corporate capital taxes in 2006/07. The total cost of eliminating corporate capital taxes over the five-year period was estimated at $12.0 billion.

THE HIGH PRICE OF RED TAPE

GETTING REGULATION RIGHT TOO

A fundamental consideration in achieving our vision for Canada is the demonstrated fact that economic freedom is the most potent driver of prosperity. Where economic freedom is constrained, so too are prosperity, social progress, and quality of life. As we established in chapter 2, excessive government regulation constitutes a critical constraint on economic freedom and, hence, on Canada's economic performance. If we are to achieve the best-performing economy in the world, we must address and relieve this burden.

Regulation is the imposition by government of rules intended to modify economic behaviour (Jones and Graf, 2001: 7). These rules may be imposed on individuals, business and labour entities, activities, or markets. They are enforced by the threat or imposition of penalties. In addition to their goal of modifying behaviour, such regulations inevitably also create costs for those affected, costs that are ultimately borne by consumers and taxpayers.

The impact of regulation on business competitiveness cannot be emphasized enough. Regulations shape the environment in which firms operate at every turn. They affect an entrepreneur's decision to start a business, the size of the business, and how it operates. Regulations also condition the speed at which businesses are able to respond to market changes and new opportunities. In short, they decisively affect a firm's ability to innovate and compete in the constantly evolving global marketplace.

Measuring the impact of regulation on economic activity is quite different from—and harder than—determining the impacts of taxation and public spending (Jones and Graf, 2001: 3). These latter activities are highly visible, typically recorded in public accounts, and subject to intense scrutiny by political opponents, the Media, and citizens at large (Jones, 2002: 9). Regulation is less visible; it is generally far less subject to scrutiny and accountability. The economic impact of regulatory activity is also much more difficult to determine; the only fraction readily accessible is the impact of the administrative cost of enforcement (Jones and Graf, 2001: 3). Nonetheless, it is important to make the effort. As the following section shows, the results are illuminating.

THE COSTS OF REGULATION

Regulations impose two kinds of costs on business and society: direct and indirect (Jones and Graf, 2001: 3–4).

Direct costs

Direct regulatory costs can be broken down further into administrative and compliance costs. Administrative costs are those that government agencies incur in the course of overseeing and enforcing regulations. These costs appear in government budgets and are the only part of the regulatory footprint that is visible and easily measured (Jones and Graf, 2001: 3).

The second, and more significant, direct cost of regulation lies in compliance. These are costs that firms and individuals incur in order to abide by regulations. Unfortunately, governments are required neither to estimate nor to report these costs. Some call these kinds of costs "hidden taxation" (Jones and Graf, 2001: 3), since they act as an additional tax on doing business. The Fraser Institute has attempted to measure both components of regulatory cost in Canada. Jones and Graf (2001: 4) estimated that Canadians spend about $103 billion a year, or about $13,700 per family of four, on regulatory compliance. This represents a burden of "hidden" taxation equivalent to 43% of what such an average family already pays in recognized taxes. In other words, due to government regulation, an average family's real tax burden is actually 43% higher than it appears to be.[1] The estimate of compliance costs by Jones and Graf (2001) was based on previous research by Weidenbaum and DeFina (1976), which found that for every dollar government spends to administer regulation, the private sector spends $17 to $20 to comply with it.

Indirect costs

Indirect costs refer to the price paid by individuals and businesses as they amend the choices they would otherwise freely make, in order to accommodate regulatory requirements. Indirect costs include profits foregone when regulations force a business to postpone getting a product to market (for

---

1   Figures in this section from Jones and Graf, 2001 supplemented with unpublished data from The Fraser Institute for Tax Freedom Day, 1997.

example, to secure government approval for a drug). They include the cost of changing a product to respond to a regulatory mandate (as when labelling requirements are changed). Regulations impose additional unquantifiable costs when they prevent individuals from acting freely on their own preferences in choosing certain products or services (Jones and Graf, 2001: 4). These indirect costs multiply when excessive requirements for permits, licences, and regulatory approvals hinder innovation, delay development, and reduce both productivity and competitive flexibility.

Of course, the optimal level of regulation is not zero. Some regulations, such as those that directly protect persons, property, and the sanctity of contracts, provide important benefits. Distinguishing between "good" and "bad" regulation—determining which regulations yield a positive benefit-to-cost ratio and which do not—is at the heart of effective regulatory reform. The challenge is the same we encountered earlier when considering the size of government: to strike the right balance between free economic choice and regulation that truly carries a net benefit. As with the "optimal" size of government, that balance is critical to achieving for Canadians the best economic performance and quality of life.

It is beyond the scope of this study to determine the benefit/cost ratio of every category of regulation, let alone of the host of specific rules in force in Canada. What we propose instead is to examine the overall regulatory burden on Canada's citizens and their businesses in comparison with that imposed on their competitors in other OECD countries, Singapore, and Hong Kong. As proxies for this purpose, we will examine regulations that affect the start-up, operation, and termination of a business, and the property rights that are the foundations of all business.

WHERE WE STAND: INTERNATIONAL COMPARISONS

Our data for this inquiry come from two sources: The *Global Competitiveness Report*, published annually by the World Economic Forum;[2] and The World Bank's recently created database, *Doing Business: Benchmarking Business Regulations* (2007).

Global Competitiveness Report

The *Global Competitiveness Report* is based on a survey of business decision-makers in each country and ranks the countries it surveys on a number of indicators, including the following three aspects of business regulation:

---

2   Note that the data from the World Economic Forum used in this section were taken from Gwartney and Lawson, 2007.

1   *Burden of Regulations*: the burden imposed by such requirements as business permits, regulations, and reporting;

2   *Time with Government Bureaucracy*: an indication by senior managers who rate, on a scale of 1 to 7, whether they have to spend a substantial amount of time dealing with government bureaucracy;

3   *Irregular Payments*: an impression of the extent to which irregular payments must be made to secure such normal business requirements as import and export permits, business licences, currency exchange, tax assessments, police protection, or loan approvals.

As can be seen from Table 8.1:

1   Thirteen countries impose a lighter administrative burden on business enterprises than Canada. Canada ranks fourteenth (tied with United Kingdom) on this scale, out of 32 countries (30 from the OECD plus Hong Kong and Singapore).

2   In 12 countries, senior managers spend less time with bureaucracy than they do in Canada.

3   With respect to demands for irregular payments as conditions of regulatory approvals—an arbitrary practice that generates uncertainty and opens the door to corruption—Canada ranked eighteenth (tied with France and Portugal) in 2005. In other words, irregular payments were viewed as less frequent in 15 other countries.

Doing Business: Benchmarking Business Regulations

Doing Business: Benchmarking Business Regulations measures the actual requirements placed on businesses in various countries and their associated costs. It focuses on three areas of regulation: the requirements to start a business, to close a business, and licenses. Each of these is broken down further into components (Table 8.2). Components of "Starting a Business" measure the general requirements to start a business in each country: the number of procedures, their cost, the time needed to complete them, and minimal capital required. Canada ranks first, implying that Canada, of all OECD countries, is the easiest place to start a business. It takes only three days to complete the two principal procedures required and costs less than 1% of average per-capita income to start a business in Canada.

Table 8.1: Business regulations

	Burden of Regulations		Time with Government Bureaucracy		Irregular Payments	
	Score	Rank	Score	Rank	Score	Rank
Australia	3.1	19	4.2	27	6.4	9
Austria	3.6	10	4.3	25	6.4	9
Belgium	2.8	26	5.8	5	5.9	21
Canada	**3.3**	**14**	**4.8**	**13**	**6.0**	**18**
Czech Republic	2.3	31	4.3	25	4.9	27
Denmark	3.7	9	6.1	2	6.7	3
Finland	4.9	3	7.0	1	6.6	5
France	2.6	29	4.5	22	6.0	18
Germany	3.1	19	4.5	22	6.5	8
Greece	2.7	28	3.7	29	4.7	30
Hong Kong	4.8	4	3.7	29	6.3	14
Hungary	2.8	26	4.9	10	5.4	24
Iceland	5.3	1	6.1	2	6.8	1
Ireland	3.9	7	5.0	9	6.1	17
Italy	2.0	32	4.6	18	5.5	23
Japan	3.6	10	5.3	6	6.4	9
Luxembourg	4.0	6	5.1	8	6.3	14
Mexico	2.6	29	3.3	31	4.7	30
Netherlands	3.2	16	4.6	18	6.3	14
New Zealand	3.5	13	4.7	16	6.8	1
Norway	3.8	8	5.3	6	6.6	5
Poland	3.1	19	4.9	10	4.3	32
Portugal	3.2	16	3.1	32	6.0	18
Singapore	5.1	2	4.9	10	6.7	3
Slovak Republic	3.1	19	4.1	28	5.0	26
South Korea	3.1	19	4.8	13	4.9	27
Spain	2.9	25	4.8	13	5.8	22
Sweden	3.2	16	6.0	4	6.6	5
Switzerland	4.1	5	4.6	18	6.4	9
Turkey	3.0	24	4.7	16	4.8	29
United Kingdom	3.3	14	4.5	22	6.4	9
United States	3.6	10	4.6	18	5.3	25

Note: Scores are on a scale from 1 to 7 where higher scores indicate less regulation. Rank out of 32.

Source: World Economic Forum (various issues).

Table 8.2: Staring and closing a business and dealing with licenses

	Starting a Business				
	Procedures (number)	Duration (days)	Cost (% GNI per capita)	Minimum Capital (% GNI per capita)	Rank (out of 31)
Australia	2	2	1.8	0.0	2
Austria	9	29	5.6	59.6	25
Belgium	4	27	5.8	21.8	18
Canada	**2**	**3**	**0.9**	**0.0**	**1**
Czech Republic	10	24	8.9	36.8	25
Denmark	3	5	0.0	44.6	10
Finland	3	14	1.1	27.1	12
France	7	8	1.1	0.0	9
Germany	9	24	5.1	46.2	24
Greece	15	38	24.2	116.0	31
Hong Kong, China	5	11	3.3	0.0	5
Hungary	6	38	20.9	74.2	27
Iceland	5	5	3.1	15.9	11
Ireland	4	19	0.3	0.0	6
Italy	9	13	15.2	10.4	20
Japan	8	23	7.5	0.0	12
Korea	12	22	15.2	299.7	30
Mexico	8	27	14.2	12.5	22
Netherlands	6	10	7.2	62.3	19
New Zealand	2	12	0.2	0.0	3
Norway	4	13	2.5	25.1	15
Poland	10	31	21.4	204.4	29
Portugal	8	8	4.3	38.7	17
Singapore	6	6	0.8	0.0	8
Slovak Republic	9	25	4.8	39.1	23
Spain	10	47	16.2	14.6	28
Sweden	3	16	0.7	33.7	14
Switzerland	6	20	2.2	15.1	16
Turkey	8	9	26.8	18.7	21
United Kingdom	6	18	0.7	0.0	7
United States	5	5	0.7	0.0	3

Note 1: Luxembourg has been excluded.

Note 2: For details on how ranks are computed, see <http://www.doingbusiness.org/EconomyRankings/>.

Source: World Bank, Doing Business Dataset. <http://www.doingbusiness.org/> (as of June 5, 2007).

Closing a Business				Dealing with Licenses			
Time (years)	Cost (% of estate)	Recovery rate (cents on the dollar)	Rank (out of 31)	Procedures (number)	Time (days)	Cost (% of income per capita)	Rank (out of 31)
1.0	8.0	79.7	11	17	140	13.8	12
1.1	18.0	73.7	18	14	195	79.1	21
0.9	3.5	86.4	7	15	184	61.8	20
0.8	**3.5**	**89.3**	**4**	**15**	**77**	**117.9**	**15**
9.2	14.5	18.5	30	31	271	14.5	27
3.0	4.0	70.5	19	7	70	67.8	2
0.9	3.5	89.1	5	17	56	108.0	16
1.9	9.0	48.0	24	10	155	75.0	10
1.2	8.0	53.1	22	11	133	89.1	8
2.0	9.0	46.3	26	17	176	68.8	23
1.1	9.0	78.9	13	22	160	23.3	24
2.0	14.5	39.7	27	25	212	260.0	29
1.0	3.5	79.7	12	19	111	15.7	13
0.4	9.0	87.9	6	10	181	22.2	7
1.2	22.0	39.7	28	17	284	142.3	26
0.6	3.5	92.7	1	11	96	19.8	1
1.5	3.5	81.8	10	14	52	175.9	11
1.8	18.0	63.2	21	12	142	104.5	13
1.7	1.0	86.3	8	18	184	137.6	25
2.0	3.5	68.6	20	7	184	27.2	6
0.9	1.0	91.1	3	13	104	50.4	4
3.0	22.0	27.9	29	25	322	85.6	30
2.0	9.0	75.0	17	20	327	60.3	28
0.8	1.0	91.3	2	11	129	22.0	3
4.0	18.0	48.1	23	13	272	17.1	19
1.0	14.5	77.6	14	11	277	65.7	22
2.0	9.0	75.7	16	8	116	115.3	5
3.0	3.5	47.1	25	15	152	57.2	17
5.9	7.0	9.8	31	32	232	150.2	31
1.0	6.0	85.2	9	19	115	68.9	18
1.5	7.0	77.0	15	18	69	16.0	9

The area, "Closing a Business," measures both the cost and time required to terminate a business, and the recovery rate once a business fails. Here, Canada ranks fourth out of 31 countries (OECD plus Hong Kong and Singapore).[3] Only Japan (first), Singapore (second), and Norway (third) do relatively better. These data show that it takes almost ten months and 4% of the value of the business to close a business in Canada. By comparison, it takes just over seven months and 4% of the estate to close a business in Japan. It takes somewhat longer to close a business in Singapore (ten months) and Norway (11 months) but costs less (1% of the estate). The OECD countries where closing a business is most difficult are the Czech Republic and Turkey, where it takes nine and six years, respectively.

Canada scores poorly, however, in the area, "Dealing with Licenses." Compared on the time and expense of acquiring all the licences and permits needed to build a warehouse, Canada ranks fifteenth out of 31 countries (OECD plus Hong Kong and Singapore). It should be noted that the test case for Canada was Toronto, where it was determined to take 77 days on average to complete the 15 necessary procedures, at a cost of 118% of per-capita income—that is, the average income of each person in the nation. Experience may be different elsewhere in Canada.

WHEN LESS IS MORE: THE BENEFITS OF LIGHTER REGULATION

Both the direct and indirect costs of regulation make firms less efficient and thus less competitive. Regulations that are too restrictive make it difficult to reallocate capital and labour in a timely way to respond with agility to market changes. Either way these costs are ultimately paid by consumers, through higher prices, or by employees whose jobs are lost when their employers are forced out of business.

On the other hand, empirical research demonstrates that reducing business regulation leads to more business investment and higher productivity overall. Nicoletti and Scarpetta (2003), for example, looked at the effect of regulation on both manufacturing and service industries in 18 OECD countries over the last two decades. They found that lowering barriers to entry—such as restrictive licensing, limits on foreign firms, administrative burdens, and tariff and non-tariff barriers—resulted in productivity gains. Indeed, they found that if some European countries reduced their elevated barriers to entry in service industries to the OECD average over a ten-year period, they

---

3   *Doing Business* ranks 31, rather than 32, countries as it does not include Luxembourg.

could expect to see total factor productivity in that service sector increase by 0.1 to 0.2 percentage points.

Alesina et al. (2005) studied barriers to entry in seven utility, transportation, and telecommunications industries in 21 OECD countries from 1975 to 1998. They found that reductions in barriers to entry lead to higher levels of investment in the long run. Bassanini and Ernst (2002) investigated the impact of regulation and non-tariff trade barriers on innovation in 18 manufacturing industries, using data from 18 OECD countries. They found that non-tariff barriers and inward-oriented regulation both had an unambiguous negative relationship with research and development. On the other hand, "stronger protection of intellectual property rights [was] positively associated with higher R&D intensity" (2002: 6).

At the extreme, the cost of complying with excessive regulation may reach a point at which a firm is better off bribing officials in order to avoid their obligations or operating in a black market. Djankov et al. (2002) found exactly this when they examined the regulation of start-up firms in 85 countries in 1999. After looking at the number of procedures and forms, time, and cost required to operate legally, they found that countries with heavier regulatory burdens also had higher levels of corruption and larger unofficial economies.[4]

CONCLUSION: OVER-REGULATED AND UNDER-PERFORMING

Based on these studies and Canada's rank relative to its OECD competitors according to World Economic Forum and the World Bank, we must conclude that, in comparison with its industrialized peers, there are only two areas of business regulation in which Canada is a top performer: the requirements for starting and closing a business. If Canada places fourteenth on burden of regulation, thirteenth in the amount of time consumed with bureaucrats, and eighteenth on demands for irregular payments, there is obviously both scope and an urgent need for significant reform in each of these areas. Reducing regulation is essential to putting Canadian business enterprises in a better position to compete with those in other industrialized countries. In Monograph 4, "The Power of Choice: Let the Market Establish Energy Prices" (page 153), we consider the impact of deregulation and appropriate regulation of energy markets.

---

4   They also found that a higher level of regulation of entry is not associated with higher-quality products, lower levels of pollution, or better health outcomes.

RECOMMENDATIONS

Canada needs to clear away the regulatory jungle that currently hampers our ability to innovate, adapt, seek out new markets for our products, and attain the achievable goal of leading the world in prosperity and quality of life. We therefore urge a fundamental change in how Canada introduces, manages, and retires business regulation and recommend the following measures.

8.1 Follow up on the Smart Regulation Initiative. In March 2005, the Government of Canada launched the Smart Regulation Initiative (Canada, Privy Council Office, 2006). "Smart" stands for Specific, Measurable, Attainable, Realistic, and Timely. This initiative's goals were to improve the effectiveness and efficiency of regulation at all levels of government by eliminating overlaps among agencies and jurisdictions and to update old rules to reflect new realities. A key principle was to identify "best practices" in regulation both within Canada and around the world and to encourage their general adoption. The Smart Regulation Initiative should be continued. We are encouraged that the 2007 federal budget contains a pledge to finalize and extend the "smart regulation approach" under the new label of "Creating a Performance-Based Regulatory System."

8.2 Require government officials and interest groups proposing new regulations to submit detailed benefit/cost estimates, including estimates of compliance as well as administrative costs.

8.3 Require Parliament and legislatures, or their appropriate committees, to hold regular "de-legislation/deregulation" sessions where the only item of business is to strike obsolete, unnecessary, and overly restrictive laws and regulations from the books.

8.4 Enact compulsory "sunset" provisions with every new regulation. All new or renewed regulations should automatically expire in five years unless specifically extended for a similar term. This will oblige government to re-examine its regulatory structure regularly and determine whether individual rules still serve a useful purpose. Every level of government, as well as any public agency charged with regulatory oversight, should adopt this requirement.

THE POWER OF CHOICE: LET THE MARKET ESTABLISH ENERGY PRICES

In chapter 5, we enumerated some of the many benefits that flow from greater economic freedom and freedom of choice. Armed with those crucial freedoms in a competitive market, consumers generally benefit from lower product and service prices. Wider application of these same principles in the energy sector, along with full cost accounting for environmental responsibility, could dramatically redirect consumer choices of type and quality of energy to use. A reduced regulatory burden would benefit consumers through increased investment in new energy supplies, making energy available from a wider choice of sources, at lower costs. Integrating the cost of environmental protection into the energy-pricing process will provide consumers with greater incentives to use cleaner types of energy.

What would the necessary reforms and benefits look like in practice? Experiences from the electrical, transportation, and hydrocarbon sectors give us some idea of what to do—and not to do.

PRICING ELECTRICITY

Regulating electricity prices through lengthy public hearings to determine a provider's revenue requirement is costly and cumbersome. Instead, a number of countries, states, and provinces have established "open" markets where the wholesale price of electrical energy is determined by the meeting point between offers to supply and bids to purchase electricity. The market-price signals provide an indication as to whether and when additional generation capacity may be required. Generally, this will lead to investment in new capacity when risk takers believe that they can earn a sufficient rate of return. The price signals also provide consumers with information needed to decide whether electricity is a "good deal," or whether they should look to another source of energy, such as natural gas, to meet more of their energy needs.

In addition to the cost of the energy, electricity consumers must pay the "wire" cost, that is, the cost of delivering electrons from generating stations through high- and low-voltage transmission systems to their point of use. Because electricity transmission and distribution systems are natural monopolies (the presence of competing lines in the same territory would greatly increase costs for customers of both), the tariffs consumers must pay for electricity transportation are virtually everywhere determined by regulatory processes or government decree. That is, even where competitive markets in electricity providers have been established, the transportation component of consumers' total cost of electricity is generally regulated.

Only two provinces, Alberta and Ontario, have "open" wholesale markets in which electricity producers (operators of power plants of all types) and importers offer electricity for sale, and industrial consumers, distributors and exporters offer to purchase electricity. In the rest of Canada, the wholesale electricity price is determined by regulatory processes with the Crown-owned generators sometimes (as in British Columbia) meeting a portion of their requirements through purchases from privately owned electricity producers. In Alberta, retail electricity customers can also choose between regulated electricity prices based on expected prices (adjusted later to reflect their provider's actual costs) and fixed-term pricing plans offered by electricity marketers.

Ontario's case is instructive. The province set out to deregulate its wholesale electricity market in May 2002 but very soon intervened to protect consumers from high electricity prices (using a number of "rebates" for this purpose), with the result that market price signals soon lost their relevance. The province also returned to regulating the retail electricity prices that residential, institutional, and small commercial and industrial consumers pay for electricity. In addition, the Ontario government opted to determine the amount of new generation capacity that was to be built as well as the types of energy that were to be used (e.g. natural gas, coal, nuclear, hydro, or other renewable energy sources).

By embarking on de-regulation and then suddenly pulling back, Ontario gave the worst-possible signal to investors, who became very reluctant to move forward with, or even propose, plans for new generation facilities in an environment where the rules could so easily change. The result was similar to what California earlier experienced: limited generation capacity put upward pressure on electricity prices, and government responded with subsidies to assist consumers. The lesson for policy makers is simple: plan carefully before going ahead with deregulation but then stay the course.

Extending economic freedom and choice to Ontario's electricity supply arrangements would see all retail consumers pay prices based on competitive wholesale market prices; it would also see decisions to invest in new generating capacity based on market assessments. Applying these principles in the rest of Canada where they have been excluded until now from electricity supply, would allow the market price signals to guide both consumers' and investors' decisions. Through time, these reforms would result in more efficient allocation of resources to generate power, and consumer choices that reflect the relative costs of electricity and competing energy sources.

INFRASTRUCTURE APPROVAL PROCESS

Delays in the construction of natural gas pipelines and related infrastructure can substantially raise the cost of natural gas to consumers (CEPA, 2005). That is so in large part because of general escalation in gas prices, so that volumes contracted for later will be more expensive. But delays in construction can also result in inflated capital costs for infrastructure if, as in western Canada today, a shortage of skilled trade workers puts pressure on wages. For example, Imperial Oil Resources Ventures Ltd. and their co-venturers applied to the National Energy Board (NEB) in the fall of 2004 for a permit to construct the Mackenzie Valley Pipeline. The NEB has completed its hearings except for a wrap-up session planned for late 2007, following receipt of a report from the Joint Review Panel, which has been conducting parallel hearings to examine the environmental and social aspects of the project. The Board's decision is not expected before late 2007, at the earliest. Meanwhile, indications are that the estimated cost of the pipeline has risen sharply and that it will not be built (if at all) until 2014—three years later than planned.

Not only are regulatory processes such as those involved in the approval of the Mackenzie Valley Pipeline costly but the time they require can result in project proponents' missing the window of opportunity for low-cost construction or marketing opportunities and, ultimately, in their cancelling their planned investment. Such processes must be streamlined so that a review of the applicants' proposal, its economic, social and environmental impacts, and the issues raised by interveners, may be completed and a decision reached within relatively short and well-defined period of time.

LOCATING KEY FACILITIES

Economic freedom applies equally to consumers in choosing their energy provider and to investors deciding where to locate resource-processing physical capital. Alberta, for instance, has witnessed a great deal of discussion about the location of facilities to upgrade bitumen from the province's oil sands. Alberta's government has expressed its wish to have such facilities built in Alberta, rather than in the United States; it is in the latter, however, where the output of any new plant would be much closer to its eventual market, that construction costs have been rising less rapidly. The desire to have as much bitumen upgraded in Alberta as possible, in order to "maximize the value for Albertans and to create new business opportunities and long-term jobs," is understandable (Alberta Speech from the Throne, 2007). However, the provincial government must recognize that Albertans' longer-term interests lie in the benefits of economic freedom and choice, and that its most appropriate role is ensuring that the business environment is conducive to investment, letting market forces decide when and where upgraders are built.

Whether they are built in the United States or Alberta, additional upgraders will enable Alberta bitumen production and related employment and income to continue to grow. Letting market conditions determine where the upgraders are situated will ensure that investors benefit from the highest possible returns. Moreover, the increased upgrading capacity will provide a growing, stable, and secure source of oil for all North American energy consumers.[1]

RESPONDING TO ENVIRONMENTAL CONCERNS

Environmental considerations are not a secondary concern. Regulatory processes for approving energy projects must affirm the basic principle that consumers must have access to the "lowest-cost alternative," where cost also includes the cost of mitigating adverse environmental impacts. Environmental costs should therefore be built fully into the price consumers pay. For example, if policy changes require greenhouse-gas emissions to be reduced, then emitters of those gasses must be required to absorb the full cost. The prices of different energy products will necessarily also reflect such costs, creating price

---

1   If the government were to try to induce companies planning to invest south of the border to invest in Alberta through special fiscal regimes, this would contravene the spirit, if not the provisions, of the North American Free Trade Agreement.

incentives for consumers to use the most environmentally-friendly source of energy. Of course, this also requires that consumers be free to choose the most efficient option among the widest possible range of energy suppliers.

CONCLUSIONS

Informed free choice is the most powerful tool we know for creating a more prosperous, productive economy. In an era of tightening competition for energy resources and increasingly strict environmental constraints, this tool should be brought to bear on Canada's energy supply. Allowing competitive providers to determine market prices for wholesale and retail electricity supply, and permitting investors in all forms of energy to decide when (and where) market opportunity justifies new capacity, would make available energy from a wider choice of sources, at lower cost. When all environmental impact costs are included in prices for competing energy alternatives, consumers will have clearer incentives to choose those with less environmental impact.

RECOMMENDATIONS

✦ Deregulate the price-setting dynamic at both the wholesale and retail level where electricity demand and supply are large enough to ensure that electricity prices could be determined by competitive market forces. Examples of such policy are found in Alberta, Texas, the United Kingdom, and other jurisdictions. This requires adequate planning and preparation to ensure that the market rules are appropriate and well understood at the outset, and that the business environment is conducive to new generation investment.

✦ Embed the costs of environmental protection in the energy pricing process where possible,[2] so that consumers are receive incentives to use cleaner types of energy.

✦ Streamline regulatory processes, including those pertaining to environmental issues, to ensure that energy project applications are dealt with as efficiently and quickly as possible. Alternatives with promise for reducing "regulatory lag" and the cost of compliance must be examined and effective measures implemented. It may be necessary to impose time limits on some regulatory procedures to ensure that they do not cause plans that would eventually have passed all social and environmental hurdles to be abandoned due to a change in the business climate.

✦ Recognize as a matter of public policy that the most efficient allocation of capital, whether in relation to energy production facilities or any other investment, occurs when a project's location is decided by proponents who have the freedom to choose based on the economics of the particular situation (and their own investment to lose if they are wrong).

---

2 See Monograph 5, "The Environment: Nature and the Market Must Meet" (page 167).

CHAPTER 9

FREE TRADE AT HOME

BREAKING DOWN BARRIERS

Liberty to work, trade, and do business with whom we prefer is a central component of economic freedom. It is essential to our goal of attaining for Canadians the greatest possible prosperity and quality of life. Chapter 13 will offer concrete suggestions for improving our nation's position in international trade. Here, however, we draw attention to a type of restriction on trade that is not explicitly measured by the index published in Economic Freedom of the World but which nonetheless imposes very real costs upon a large federation like Canada, with our distinctive regional economies and numerous provincial boundaries. That is, restrictions on internal trade.

Canada cannot achieve the goal of leading the world in prosperity and economic growth without greater freedom of trade and exchange within our own country. In other words, Canada needs an open, efficient, and predictable domestic market in order to improve its productivity and competitiveness in an increasingly globalized world. There would be ancillary benefits: more open trade at home would strongly reinforce the integrity of our federation as a true economic union. The sadly balkanized state of Canada's domestic market, fragmented by persistent inter-provincial barriers to trade, is analyzed below. That discussion leads to recommendations for removing those barriers and achieving a freer domestic market.

BACKGROUND: A LEGACY OF RESTRICTION

Sir John A. Macdonald's "National Policy," while perhaps justifiable in 1879, created an economic environment that, in one form or another, dominated Canada for 80 years—until after the Second World War. This policy allowed Canadian business to develop behind high tariff walls. The immediate result was a high-cost manufacturing sector based almost exclusively in central

Canada. But the same policy had other negative consequences. It acted to discourage processing of natural resources in Canada, since products made by inefficient, tariff-protected manufacturers were seldom able to compete with foreign products. It led to the protection of certain farmers with "supply management" programs; these erected barriers to domestic trade and left a legacy of inefficient production that still demands protection. For Canadians, these policies have ultimately meant higher prices, lower wages, less consumer choice, and severely constrained productivity. Canada was not alone in following this protectionist strategy. Other countries did the same, including the United States. But it was a strategy that allowed our governments to ignore the impact their policy choices were having on the efficiency of Canada's domestic market and our overall competitiveness (Hart, 2004: 8; Statistics Canada, 2002: Introduction, p.3).

Happily, federal governments in more recent years have stepped away from this nineteenth-century strategic thinking—albeit only partially. But among the provinces it remains disturbingly robust, despite the clear intent of Confederation's founders. Section 121 of Canada's Constitution in effect prohibits the erection of tariff-based barriers to trade within Canada. In a crucial oversight, however, it does not provide a mechanism to eliminate non-tariff barriers.[1] Moreover, this section does not cover trade in services or intellectual property, or provide explicitly for free flows of capital and labour.

The federal government has constitutional authority to regulate some key aspects of interprovincial trade. It uses this authority in relation to drugs, some aspects of trade in agricultural and food products, and the labelling of goods traded interprovincially. But this federal authority cannot interfere with the right of provinces to regulate within their own areas of constitutional authority. Provincial governments, for example, have constitutional authority (sometimes shared with the federal government) to regulate workers, building standards, the environment, agricultural and food products sold within their borders, transportation, businesses, finance and securities, education, and alcoholic beverages. For nearly 130 years, provincial governments have exercised these powers to maintain barriers to interprovincial trade, investment, and labour mobility—all in the name of protecting local and provincial interests. The result is a mishmash of measures and standards that create resilient but virtually invisible non-tariff barriers in Canada's domestic market, with no effective incentive or mechanism to remove them. As one observer has said: "interprovincial barriers to trade create an interlock-

---

1   "All articles of the Growth, Produce, or Manufacture of any one of the Provinces shall, from and after the Union, be admitted free into each of the other Provinces" (*The Constitution Act*, 1867, Article 121).

ing, tangled and expensive web of vested interests. Together they slowly and steadily choke Canada's economic arteries, losing output, incomes and jobs for Canadians" (Parsons, 1994: 2).

Three practices in particular create most of these internal barriers to trade: (1) discriminatory rules, such as preferences based on provincial residency; (2) differential standards or regulations that, for example, require different qualifications for identical occupations; and (3) inequitable administrative practices, such as local worker requirements. These barriers harm both consumers and producers. The additional costs are mostly borne by consumers while producers sell less due to higher prices. They reduce the ability of Canadian firms to trade in other provincial markets and limit their international competitiveness. The result is a less efficient economy than we could have. The costs to the Canadian economy are difficult to estimate. Whatever the real cost to Canadians, it is measured in billions of dollars per year.[2]

LOOKING ABROAD: CHANGING PATTERNS OF INTERNATIONAL AND DOMESTIC TRADE

Numerous studies and commissions over the years have identified barriers to interprovincial trade as a major impediment to the Canadian economy. The Rowell Sirois Commission identified them as an issue in 1940.[3] So did the Macdonald Commission in 1985.[4] In constitutional negotiations in 1980 and again in 1990, Canadian governments tried without success to agree on steps to free the domestic market. By 1990, however, the pattern of Canada's overall trade began to change significantly. The tariffs that had protected Canada's domestic market for years, the residue of the old National Policy, were disappearing. This was particularly true for trade within North America, as a result of the Canada-US Trade Agreement (CUSTA) and the North American Free Trade Agreement (NAFTA). But it also followed from the introduction of the World Trade Organization (WTO). As the external tariff wall fell, internal barriers that reduce the productivity and the competitiveness of the domestic economy became correspondingly more important.

---

2 Beaulieu, Gaisford, and Higginson, 2003 provides a review of the literature on costs.

3 "The heart of the problem lies in the fact that the simplest requirements of provincial autonomy ... involve the use of powers which are capable of abuse ... The problem is to preclude or restrict abuses without interfering with legitimate and even necessary powers" (Canada, Royal Commission on Dominion-Provincial Relations, 1940).

4 "Federalism justifies variation among provinces in response to local preferences ... the need to accommodate diversity ... must be balanced against the objective of gains from trade" (Canada, Royal Commission on the Economic Union and Development Prospects for Canada [Macdonald Commission], 1985: vol. 3, pp. 135–40).

The change in trade that ensued was significant. In 1990, Canada's inter-provincial and international exports were almost identical in volume. By 1995, interprovincial exports were only 62% of international exports, and had fallen still further to 44% by 2000. The balance swung somewhat back by 2005, when interprovincial exports amounted to 53% of international exports. Viewed another way, international exports were 26.1% of GDP in 1989 and interpro-vincial exports, 22.1%. By 1997, international exports were 40.2% of GDP and inter-provincial exports, 19.7%. By 2005, the levels were 37% and 20%, respective-ly.[5] The increase in international exports has been driven by improved Canadian labour costs relative to the United States, reduced US tariffs, and the American appetite for imports (Grady and Macmillan, 1998: 26). The declining share of interprovincial exports in GDP is the result of lower Canadian tariffs (encourag-ing more international imports), slower growth in Canada than in the US market, and relatively small increases in the prices of goods traded inter-provincially.

Interprovincial trade remains more regional than national in Canada. Trade is concentrated within four regions: the Atlantic Provinces; central Canada, which is Québec and Ontario; the western provinces; and the North (Statistics Canada, 2002: 10). Domestically, the provinces and territories in these groupings trade mainly among themselves. Distance makes a difference; that is, the Atlantic region has the smallest trade with the western provinces and vice versa.

Despite the great distances of our geography and persistent internal non-tariff barriers, interprovincial trade remains a significant part of the Canadian economy. Studies in the 1990s determined that borders reduce trade between nations by more than would be expected on the basis of official barriers alone. This is because it is more expensive and difficult to trade internationally, where potential business partners may not be well known to each other, than it is to trade at home, where partners are more likely to share common values, under-standings, and circumstances (Helliwell and McCallum, 1995; Helliwell, 2002; McCallum, 1995). International trade contributes more to Canada's economy than ever. It could be more important still, if our domestic economy were more productive and efficient.

DASHED HOPES: EFFORTS TO FREE
CANADA'S DOMESTIC MARKET

The Charlottetown Accord to amend the Constitution, which was accepted unanimously by Canadian governments on August 28, 1992, committed leg-islatures to remove barriers to the movement of persons, goods, services,

---

5   Comparative analysis of international and domestic trade data can be found in several studies from Statistics Canada including: Statistics Canada, 1998; 2000; 2002; 2004c.

and capital.[6] The Accord was defeated by a referendum on October 26, 1992. Having failed to resolve the issue through constitutional change, Canadian governments turned to non-constitutional means (Knox, 1998). In December 1992, federal, provincial, and territorial trade ministers agreed to negotiate a comprehensive agreement to "promote an open, efficient and stable domestic market for long-term job creation, economic growth and stability." This was to be accomplished by reducing and eliminating "to the extent possible, barriers to the free movement of persons, goods, services and investments within Canada" ([Committee on Internal Trade], 1995): "Preamble," p. 1). First ministers signed the Agreement on Internal Trade (AIT) on July 18, 1994. It came into force on July 1, 1995.

The Agreement on Internal Trade includes general rules that establish reasonable principles for an open domestic market. Unfortunately, these apply only to specific sectors in a manner laced with qualifications, exclusions, and exceptions. Disputes under the agreement can only be directed to a complicated, time-consuming, and ultimately unenforceable resolution process. AIT has changed some things but governments have ignored many of its obligations, particularly those intended to extend its coverage. Ten years after it came into force, the agreement has proven to be ineffective. It is now being reviewed and revised by governments under the leadership of the Council of the Federation.[7]

The failure of AIT to eliminate remaining inter-provincial barriers within Canada led the British Columbia and Alberta provincial governments to resort to a bilateral trade agreement. On April 28, 2006, the Premiers of British Columbia and Alberta ratified a Trade, Investment and Labour Mobility Agreement (TILMA) (British Columbia, Ministry of Economic Development, 2006), an extension of AIT that aims to eliminate or reduce many of the interprovincial barriers between British Columbia and Alberta left out by AIT. TILMA is an improvement over AIT for several reasons. For example, it is more comprehensive and broader, mainly due to its architecture. In TILMA, all sectors are covered except those explicitly exempted; AIT, in contrast, aims to eliminate or reduce barriers to trade only in those industries and sectors that are included in the agreement. Furthermore, TILMA allows broader access to government

---

6 "Reducing Internal Trade Barriers. Forging an economic union today means moving beyond a simple prohibition against inter-provincial tariffs on goods towards free internal movement of persons, goods, services and capital. A new provision would reflect the commitment of governments to this objective. First Ministers have agreed to discuss how best to implement the principles of a stronger internal common market" (Canada, Intergovernmental Affairs, Privy Council Office, 2001).

7 The Council was established in December 2003 and is made up of the leaders of all of Canada's provincial and territorial governments.

procurement to businesses and eliminates duplicate business registration and reporting requirements so that businesses registered in one province are automatically recognized in the other.

In addition, TILMA addresses the two main shortcomings of AIT, its inadequate treatment of labour mobility and its lack of an effective dispute-resolution mechanism. AIT was supposed to eliminate or reduce barriers to labour mobility within Canada by requiring jurisdictions to mutually recognize occupational qualifications from other jurisdictions and to agree on a process to harmonize occupational standards (Conference Board of Canada 2005: 17–18). However, implementation of the section in AIT on labour mobility has been slow and incomplete. It was only in February of 1999 that all governments, except Quebec, signed A Framework to Improve the Social Union for Canadians in which they committed to full compliance with the Labour Chapter of AIT by July 1, 2001 (Labour Mobility Coordination Group, 2001: 1). The Labour Mobility Coordination Group, reporting on the progress of the Labour Chapter of AIT, noted that by the 2001 deadline, governments and regulators had substantially met their labour mobility obligations or were well underway to doing so for 42 of 51 regulated professional occupations covered by AIT.[8] However, very few of the occupations were fully mutually recognized by the 2001 deadline. For example, as of April 1, 2007, 27 of those 42 occupations had yet to be fully reconciled or mutually recognized between Alberta and British Columbia (Labour Mobility Coordination Group, 2001; Government of British Columbia, 2007). This means that 27 of those 42 occupations cannot freely practice in both British Columbia and Alberta without going through additional assessments, training, or testing.

One of the most cited complaints against AIT is the inadequacy of its dispute-resolution mechanism, which allows private persons and businesses to bring complaints against other parties but cannot enforce compliance (Conference Board of Canada, 2005: 24–25).[9] That is, AIT panels cannot enforce its rulings if a disputing party disagrees with their decisions (Conference Board of Canada 2005: 25). Once the panel's decision is issued, the panel relies on the good will of the parties in dispute to comply with its findings. The panel has no power or authority to enforce its decision by issuing fines or through some other formal channel if one of the parties disagrees with the panel's decision.

---

8   Professional occupations are usually regulated by non-government bodies which were delegated regulatory authority by governments (Labour Mobility Coordination Group, 2001: 5). Trades, in contrast, are regulated directly by provincial and territorial governments.

9   Note that NAFTA allows a business to bring a complaint against other party under Chapter 11 on Investment whereas under WTO only governments can bring a case against another government (Conference Board of Canada, 2005: 24–25).

The lacks a mechanism to enforce the panel's decision makes the entire dispute resolution process ineffective.[10]

TILMA, in contrast, has given the two provincial governments a two year deadline to mutual recognition of remaining professional occupations and trades that are not yet mutually recognized. The deadline, in effect, prevents provinces from slowing down or postponing the mutual recognition process. Furthermore, TILMA also clearly outlines a dispute-resolution process that is enforceable. The most important difference between the dispute settlement mechanisms of TILMA and AIT is that, under TILMA, the non-complying party can be fined up to $5 million. It is important to mention that the monetary award is not available for economic damages incurred by the complainant before the panel's findings. Instead, the monetary fine is issued only for non-compliance with the panel's recommendations. That is, even if the panel found that a party violated the Agreement, no penalty can be awarded with the initial ruling by the panel. Only if one of the disputants fails to comply with the panel's ruling within a period specified by the panel, which cannot exceed one year, and the other disputant files a complaint, can the panel issue a monetary award. One of the factors determining the monetary award is the economic damages incurred by the complainant caused by non-compliance of the other party after the panel issued its initial findings. If the disputants are both parties, then the panel may either issue a monetary award or authorize retaliatory measure of equivalent economic impact or both.

TILMA is clearly an improvement over the AIT and thus it would be a step in the right direction if other provinces join the TILMA. This would take the provinces further along the path to free trade within Canada. Article 20.1 of TILMA states that any Canadian province or territory or the federal government may accede to the Agreement given they accept its terms. Rights of Canadian jurisdictions to join additional interprovincial trade-enhancing agreements are spelled out in Article 1800 of the AIT.

The governments of British Columbia and Alberta might want to finalize TILMA before accepting additional provinces. For instance, by April 1, 2009, the two provinces will negotiate the extent to which the TILMA applies to Crown Corporations, government-owned commercial enterprises; regional, local, district and municipal governments; school boards, publicly-funded academic, health and social service entities; and non-governmental bodies that exercise authority delegated by law (Government of British Columbia, 2006a). It might be easier to achieve a consensus when only two provinces are involved. Once finalized, the other provinces would be able to accede to TILMA by fully accepting its terms.

---

10 The AIT dispute resolution process is also complicated and time consuming, further reducing its effectiveness (see, for example, Beaulieu, Gaisford, and Higginson, 2003: 32–33).

It is important to mention that TILMA is an improvement over AIT but it is not a perfect solution to interprovincial barriers within Canada. TILMA has many exceptions such as taxation and social policy (including labour standards and codes, minimum wages, employment insurance, social assistance benefits, and worker's compensation) as well as regulated marketing and supply management of poultry, dairy, and eggs in Alberta.

CONCLUSION: UNSEEN BARRIERS MATTER

Past and present efforts to liberalize internal trade in Canada, and the studies referred to above, suggest the following conclusions. Canada has a significant domestic market that operates reasonably well, given our relatively small economy and large geographical size. But our domestic market is neither as open nor as flexible as it ought and needs to be. This is because of significant and complex non-tariff trade barriers between provinces that are a product of Canada's federal structure and the legacy of more than 100 years of protective trade policy. These barriers are not uniform but rather a mix of measures. Some are intended to protect local or special interests. Some result from differences among jurisdictions in standards and regulations. Still others arise from duplicative and protective administrative practices, at both the federal and provincial levels. Some barriers are obvious; others are almost invisible, embedded in long-standing and accepted interprovincial practice. Many of these seem intractable, protected by a culture of entitlement and a tradition of applying constitutional authority unilaterally rather than cooperatively. These attitudes may be rooted in historic regional differences and mistrust.

These barriers, whatever their characteristics, continue to limit Canada's economic productivity and competitiveness. They reduce the ability of our businesses to adapt creatively and quickly to changes in world economic conditions, and to the needs of our main trading partners, particularly the United States.

Canada lacks effective constitutional means to strike down barriers to trade in our domestic market. There is no constitutional obligation for Canadian governments to apply their authority in a way that does not create such barriers or to avoid compromising the integrity and productivity of the national economy. Two attempts to strengthen the economic union and deal with non-tariff barriers, in 1980 and 1990, failed. Non-constitutional initiatives to eliminate domestic trade barriers, notably the 1995 Agreement on Internal Trade (AIT) and ongoing efforts to establish some form of national regulation of financial securities, have met with very limited success. The Alberta/BC Trade, Investment and Labour Mobility Agreement (TILMA) is a step in the right direction.

RECOMMENDATIONS

The abolition of costly and unproductive barriers to internal trade would significantly enhance the performance of the Canadian economy, both at home and in its international competitiveness. To that end, we recommend the following measures.

9.1 Accept the principle of an open domestic market. The purpose of such acceptance by all provincial and territorial governments and the federal government would be to establish that all Canadian governments accept that measures they undertake must not operate as barriers to trade, investment, and worker mobility.

9.2 Agree to:
  * establish rules to define what would be considered a barrier; these might be similar to those in the current AIT;
  * define under what circumstances a measure presenting a barrier to trade might be permitted; this could be based on the "legitimate objective" provision in the AIT;
  * remove or change any measures, policies, or practices that create an unjustifiable barrier;
  * support the creation of a quasi-judicial Canada Internal Trade Tribunal to enforce the foregoing trade rules;
  * take the necessary legislative steps to ensure that these rules can be enforced in relation to measures in their jurisdiction.

9.3 Establish a Canada Internal Trade Tribunal. The purpose of the Tribunal would be to enforce the trade rules established under the principle of an open domestic market. It would be a standing tribunal that would hear complaints from individuals, businesses, or governments against measures that may be barriers to trade, investment, and worker mobility. It is assumed that governments will continue to enter into multilateral and bilateral agreements on matters such as public-sector procurement. The Tribunal could also provide an enforceable dispute-resolution mechanism for these agreements. Ideally an existing body, such as the Canadian International Trade Tribunal, could serve as the Internal Trade Tribunal. A legal basis for the Tribunal we propose might be found under the federal power to legislate in relation to inter-provincial trade. If not, it should be established by inter-provincial agreement under the auspices of the Council of the Federation.

9.4 Establish a Canada Internal Trade Council. The purpose of the Internal Trade Council would be to provide an advisory and political forum for issues not covered by the general agreement referred to in Recommendation 1 above. As such, it should be made up of ministerial representatives from all governments. Not all impediments to trade will be susceptible to challenge before the Internal Trade Tribunal. Issues such as public-sector procurement, business registration, and disclosure requirements affect the domestic market but will require a separate specific agreement to resolve. The same applies to many regulatory regimes that are better reconciled by agreement than through challenge before a panel. The role of the Internal Trade Council would be to monitor the performance of Canada's internal market, identify issues and impediments that need to be resolved, sponsor initiatives including multilateral and bilateral agreements, and resolve these issues. The Council would issue annual public reports to governments and to the Council of the Federation.

9.5 Investigate federal constitutional powers to free internal trade. Elsewhere, we have vigorously argued that Ottawa should respect the division of powers in Canada's Constitution and stop interfering in areas of provincial jurisdiction. In internal trade, on the other hand, Ottawa has declined to vigorously employ its own constitutional powers, which are admittedly unclear, to remove inter-provincial trade barriers. Unfortunately, the use of this power involves a more difficult question than may first appear. Few trade barriers are erected specifically as "trade barriers," even if that is their intent. Instead, they are typically enacted under the guise of consumer protection or some other provincial power. Removing such barriers could thus be interpreted as an intrusion on provincial responsibility. We recommend a federal reference to the Supreme Court asking it to clarify, first, the extent of the present federal commerce power (i.e., the power of the federal government under the present Constitution to strike down inter-provincial barriers to trade) and, second, what kind of amendment would be required, if necessary, to give the federal government that power.

9.6 Negotiate the geographic extension of TILMA between governments in Canada. While TILMA is not a perfect agreement, it is a step in the right direction. In the future negotiation of such agreements, no measure that can operate as a barrier to domestic trade should be excluded; any measure that constitutes such a barrier should be changed or removed unless it can be demonstrated that it is necessary to an essential public policy, and that it accomplishes this purpose in the least trade-restrictive way possible; and penalties for maintaining proscribed barriers, as assessed by any tribunal established under such agreements, should not be limited and should apply until the barrier is removed.

THE ENVIRONMENT: NATURE AND THE MARKET MUST MEET

The preceding chapters argue for stimulating stronger economic growth in Canada by enhancing economic freedom and the operation of free markets. But "stimulating stronger economic growth" must mean more than simply increasing Canada's per-capita production of goods and services. If the quality of our natural environment is a fundamental dimension of quality of life—as we believe it is—then economic performance must be pursued in ways that are compatible with environmental conservation, not at the expense of either nature or future generations.

Most of the economic activity that sustains our standard of living is organized not by governments but by markets, in which consumers, business, and industry are the principal actors. But for every good and service we produce, we also produce a stream of waste, pollution, and environmental stress. There is therefore no real solution to the challenge of environmental protection without full-fledged participation by business and industry.

The instinctive reaction of politicians of all stripes to a problem that appears to be created by business is to propose some new form of regulation. This has been the conventional response to the problem of environmental degradation from international protocols like Kyoto to a myriad of national, provincial, and local environmental regulations. These are inherently slow to respond to the dynamic market circumstances under which environmental threats occur and change, have high transaction costs, and are frequently oriented more to micromanage process than to secure positive outcomes. While regulation clearly retains a place in the portfolio of responses to environmental challenges, the integration of market principles into public environmental stewardship could achieve many important goals far more responsively, while putting permanent downward pressure on the cost of protecting natural assets.

In its purest form, a "market" is simply a mechanism for bringing supply to demand, using financial incentives and pricing signals to do so. If the demand is for oil, flour, or health care, the proper combination of pricing signals and financial incentives will stimulate a supply to meet that demand. It follows that if the demand is for cleaner water, air, or energy, or sustainable soil, wildlife, and forests, the discovery and application of the appropriate pricing and profit signals can just as readily satisfy those demands.

Business and industry respond minute by minute to the price signals and financial incentives that generate economic activity. The most urgent priority for effective environmental protection must therefore be to devise appropriate signals and incentives to close the market gap between demands for environmental protection, and the businesses in a position to provide that protection. Pioneering efforts in this direction, as well as economic theory, indicate that the three core principles of successful policy will be personal responsibility exercised through property rights and freedom of choice; markets in a variety of forms; and full-cost accounting and pricing in the use of environmental resources.

Property rights are already extensive and deeply rooted in our Common Law tradition. They could be far more energetically asserted than at present (and better respected by courts and legislatures) to motivate and empower individual landowners to better protect their property's environment against pollution originating from beyond it. As desirable as it might be to enshrine property rights in the Canadian Charter of Rights and Freedoms, that is not imminent. Meanwhile more vigorous assertion of property rights can significantly advance the care we give the environment.

Markets are the arenas where demand meets supply and they come in many forms. In respect to the environment, creative environmental policy-makers and entrepreneurs in Canada and abroad have innovated markets in environmental resources themselves (wetlands), natural services (water retention in soils), trade in emission credits (air pollutants), and ecosystem stewardship (bio-diversity markets). This plainly does not exhaust the range of opportunities to bring self-correcting, self-funding, choice-of-provider market supply to the demand for sustainable environmental quality.

For pricing signals and financial incentives to produce the desired outcome, however, there must be no dishonesty in pricing and no free-riders. This cannot be accomplished for environmental protection unless the costs of the environmental impacts of producing a good or service, as well as those of mitigating or eliminating these impacts, are measured and fully internalized into the price of the good or service being produced. Equally, the principle of "user pays" in the use of environmental services should apply as far as social equity allows.

Examples of these principles' effectiveness in addressing pressing environmental challenges are multiplying in Canada and abroad. Opportunities to extend market thinking to additional environmental challenges range widely. At institutional scale, they suggest making much wider use of the talents and commitment of non-governmental organizations in environmental stewardship, perhaps through a market in stewardship contracts for publicly owned land. At street level, they suggest charging householders by the garbage can for solid-waste disposal rather than a flat fee that gives no incentive to reduce waste.

We illustrate the scope for this approach through placing one especially salient environmental issue in close focus. Politically sensitive, essential for all other environmental processes to flourish, vital to industry and human life, water poses a particularly critical component of our environmental challenge. In the balance of this Monograph, we therefore look more closely at the application and implementation of market principles to the protection of Canada's water.

FOCUS: WATER

"Some would say that water cannot be entrusted to markets because it is a necessity of life. To the contrary, because it is a necessity of life, it is so precious that it must be entrusted to the discipline of the markets that encourage conservation and innovation."

—Terry Anderson (Anderson, 1998)

While alternatives exist or may be developed for resources such as oil, there is no substitute for water. Around the world, many countries are already experiencing water crises. Thirty-six American states anticipate water shortages before 2015 (Glennon, 2006). And Canada, despite its vaunted possession of close to one-fifth of the world's fresh surface water, is not as immune to the same danger as many Canadians might think. Only a small part of Canada's water is annually renewed (1% of the contents of the Great Lakes, for example). Most of our water flows into the Arctic Ocean or Hudson Bay while 90% of Canadians live within 300 km of the border with the United States. Human demand for water peaks at different times than does precipitation. The result is that several regions are at high risk of severe imbalances between available water supply and the expectations of consumers and industry.

In Canada, the risk is most acute in Alberta. A fast-growing population, roughly half the country's irrigated agriculture, and rapidly expanding but water-intensive development of oil-sand deposits, are running up against a declining flow in the province's major rivers. In some, summer levels have dropped as much as 30% over the past century (Schindler and Donahue, 2006). British Columbia's Okanagan region is also forecast to encounter seasonal shortages of water within the next decade (Cohen and Neale, 2006); Vancouver Island, the Gulf Islands and other areas are also vulnerable. Southern Ontario may be surrounded by the Great Lakes but its heavy concentration of population, industry, and agriculture presents mounting challenges both to maintain water quality and allocate constrained supplies. Coastal areas in the Maritimes face a different risk: sea levels that have risen by as much as a metre in some areas over the last century threaten critical freshwater aquifers with salt contamination.

WHAT'S "BAD" ABOUT A "PUBLIC GOOD"?

Canadian governments have traditionally framed water policies within a "public good" concept of the resource, relying on bureaucratic direct management, patchwork regulation, and allocation based on political judgment. As a result, most of Canada's water is treated legally and economically as an open-access "common good," quite differently from how other natural resources, notably minerals or petroleum, are treated. In those cases, while the state retains ownership of the resource it relies on the private sector—disciplined by market competition that rewards the most efficient, productive operators—to develop specified assets in return for a license or royalty fee paid to the public account. By contrast, most Canadian governments jealously protect (and frequently subsidize heavily) a state monopoly over public water supply. In this system, (a) supply is frequently over-subscribed, (b) there is a reliance on *fiat* decisions to allocate the resource among competing users, (c) large—even unlimited—withdrawals of water are allowed without any return to the public account, and (d) with the exception of Alberta, markets are not used to direct water to its highest-value use.

As regional and seasonal shortages become more common, these policies have increasingly negative effects. Open access to subsidized supply invites a "tragedy of the commons" for Canada's water. When shortages occur, the existing policy framework offers governments few options other than to rely on supposedly "equitable" across-the-board cuts to all users, selective cutbacks determined politically, or some combination of the two. None of these is efficient from an economic standpoint, in the sense of lowering overall water use at the least cost to Canada's wealth and social welfare. Central decision-making by government is, moreover, inherently cumbersome, unresponsive and slow.

A CHANGE OF COURSE

There is a better option. Market principles of transparency in cost (no subsidies), choice (freedom to decide where the resource can be used most productively), and individual responsibility are useful in maximizing the value of Canada's water while protecting the resource for the future. In the Canadian context, a full restoration of the constitutional allocation of powers would free the provinces to extend these market principles to water policy. The principle of subsidiarity, meanwhile, strongly supports the contention of most water-management experts, that allocation decisions are best made almost literally at "ground-level" by jurisdictions like watershed councils or irrigation districts, or transacted freely among willing buyers and sellers.

Experience abroad and at home confirms the advantages of greater reliance on market principles in the management of water. Australia's decision to allow farmers in the Murray-Darling River basin to buy and sell irrigation water beginning in the early 1980s increased net farm incomes by as much as $17 million US in some subsequent dry seasons (Anderson and Snyder, 1997; Sturgess and Wright, 1993). Similarly, since Chile introduced markets for bulk water a "dramatic increase in agricultural production and employment has been accomplished without the need for new hydraulic infrastructure" (Anderson, 1998; Schleyer, 1994). After Alberta allowed water rights for the South Saskatchewan River to be traded (subject to provincial approval) at the beginning of this century, studies found that "water moved to higher-value production, increasing productivity, [and] from relatively low- to high-efficiency irrigation equipment," improving conservation of the resource (Nicol, 2005). In eastern Ontario, a pilot program initiated under a Conservative government in 2000 created a novel market in water-pollution reduction credits; phosphorus released to the South Nation River has since been reduced at one-sixth the cost of a regulatory regime (O'Grady, 2002).

Similar market-based strategies could be employed to allocate, conserve, and protect Canada's water far more effectively than centralized state decision-making, at much lower cost. The potential for markets to allocate available water to the highest-value use on a real-time basis, while protecting environmental and social values, should be explored in more settings. Australia's "cap-and-trade" system, which sets a permissible maximum for total withdrawals from a given watershed and allows trading within that amount, is one model. Another, establishing a variable-volume, equal-share structure akin to the "individual transferable quota" for fish stocks, has proven successful in the Colorado-Big Thompson system in the United States. In densely industrialized southern Ontario, there is untapped potential to slash demand for new water by enabling the re-sale of waste water among industrial, commercial, and institutional users on the model conceptualized as Natural Capitalism by Paul Hawken and Amory and Hunter Lovins (2000). While economic theory suggests strongly that judicious exports of unpackaged water might also deliver significant benefits to Canada, such international trade in water remains—for the present—politically unacceptable to a majority of Canadians, and for this reason we do not pursue the topic here.

THE PRICE HAS TO BE RIGHT

By contrast, a wide range of interest groups might be expected to support (or at least find it difficult to oppose) a move to full-cost pricing of water, where those costs include not just the price of the "pipes" but also of ensuring a perpetual supply of the resource itself. At present, public subsidies and the absence of any substantial price constraint encourage individual Canadians to think of water as virtually free; the same is true for industry. The result is gratuitous waste and disincentive for innovations in efficiency that might delay future shortages.

To send a clear signal of the true value of water to every Canadian dozens of times a day—whenever one of us turns on a tap or a business sticks a pipe into a river, aquifer, or reservoir—there is absolutely no substitute for a pricing system based on a full accounting of costs. Comprehensive full-cost pricing for water should be introduced for all users, including agriculture and water-consuming industries as well as the commercial, institutional, and residential sectors (with appropriate safeguards to ensure that no Canadian is denied a sufficient supply of clean water for their personal needs). The Canada West Foundation, the Canadian Boreal Initiative, and others are evolving new techniques to quantify the cost of maintaining land uses that protect water supply. Their efforts should be encouraged, with the goal of developing a rigorous and transparent standard similar to the Generally Accepted Accounting Principles for determining the "full cost" of water. In France, raising the price of water closer to its true cost reduced waste by as much as 55% (Anderson, 1998); Canadians can anticipate comparable savings.

CONCLUSION

Water is a subject of extraordinary sensitivity. In Canada, anti-market voices have misinformed the public and biased opinion against available market-based policy options. Those alternatives nonetheless present a promising path toward integrating the full environmental implications of our choices into every investment and purchase decision, a necessary condition to arrest ecological degradation of all kinds. Well-formulated property rights and market principles offer the best response to looming water shortages—not only from the standpoint of economic security but equally from that of ecological security.

RECOMMENDATIONS

❦ Implement policies to require universal water metering and progressive volume pricing, based on the full cost (capital, plus operation and maintenance) of delivery from source and research-based estimates of the cost of ensuring an adequate supply of water into the future. Water withdrawn directly from natural sources such as aquifers or rivers should also be priced at a level sufficient to protect future supply. This recommendation applies at the provincial level, where the constitution places jurisdiction for water along with other natural resources.

🍁 Phase out all subsidies for water delivered for agricultural or industrial purposes under existing arrangements and shift water charges, over time, to a "full-cost" basis.

🍁 Give local governments the authority to create markets in "secondary" water, where the density of industrial presence justifies it, together with appropriate funding to provide the infrastructure connections that such a market would require.

REBALANCED AND REVITALIZED
RESPONSIVE DEMOCRACY

The Canada we envision is the world's most responsive democracy, accountable to the world's most active, informed, and satisfied citizenry.

That is hardly the case today. In recent national elections, fewer than two eligible voters in three have cast ballots, and governments have taken power with the support of less than one Canadian in four. A disturbing number of our citizens feel that politics in general has become the preserve of charlatans and scoundrels; those Canadians' withdrawal from involvement in the exercise of democratic self-government risks turning that as yet overly pessimistic judgment into a self-fulfilling prophecy.

We believe that restoring the vitality of our nation's democracy is an imperative not only of political principle but of pragmatic self-interest for every Canadian. Vibrant functioning democracies, deeply sensitive to the interests and priorities of their voters, simply serve their citizens better than regimes that are insulated from responsibility to their constituents.

The keys to democratic vitality seem evident to us. The primacy of the individual citizen must not only be recognized in rhetoric but reflected in practical mechanisms to ensure that government answers to Canadians—not the other way around. Canadians must have effective means to direct their governments in terms more nuanced and thoughtful than a quasi-quadrennial up-down vote at the ballot box. And as we have urged before, the constitutional balance of responsibility for government between Ottawa and the provinces must be restored, wherever possible, with a devolution of decision-making and resources to the level of public authority closest to the Canadians that will be affected by government's actions.

Accordingly, the following chapters begin by exploring effective measures to check, expunge, and prevent from recurring the drift, the disconnect from popular opinion, the demonstrable incompetence, partisanship, and outright public-sector corruption of some recent years. We next present a menu of reforms and innovations that would invigorate Canada's democratic culture by increasing the involvement of ordinary citizens in public governance and strengthening the "infrastructure" of policy formation. Lastly, we address a fundamental dysfunction in Canada's political condition whose remedy, as we have seen here repeatedly, would trigger advantages well beyond a better functioning democracy: the costly imbalance between the federal and provincial voices of government in resources and activity.

Transparent, accountable government is more responsive government; it has no shadows in which to conceal violations of the public trust. If the steps we recommend are taken, public officials will have greatly enhanced incentives to give you good value for your tax dollars. When public services fall short of your expectations, you will know clearly which government or agency to hold accountable. At the same time, you could find yourself making a direct contribution to Canada's next-generation democratic "infrastructure." At school, your children would be learning how to make the levers of daily democracy answer to their priorities. New ideas would enrich your understanding of the choices we face as a great nation and in our local communities. A more balanced federation would bring better health care, education, and social services at lower cost, as provincial governments free themselves from federal shackles and respond to their own citizens' priorities. As our democracy is strengthened and all of Canada's governments perform better, you will be able to enjoy greater confidence in our federation's future.

Perhaps for no Canadians has the reality fallen shorter of these ambitions to date than for our aboriginal citizens. From exclusion and disenfranchisement early in our history to the heavy-handed paternalism of the present Indian Act, the "service" that aboriginal Canadians have received from government presents an abject record of failure, waste, alienation, and even abuse. Similarly, the apparent conundrum of persistent regional economic disparities, despite the commitment over the years of billion of dollars, has bedevilled federal governments for decades. In this section, therefore, Monographs spotlight how the powerful effects of citizen-led democratic principles and economic freedom might begin to break the log-jam on these stubborn problems. Canada will achieve our vision as the world's best-governed democracy only when every citizen enjoys and feels invited to express an effective voice in public decisions that affect them directly or represent the national consensus.

CHAPTER 10

RESTORING TRANSPARENCY AND ACCOUNTABILITY

We envision a future in which every Canadian has the tools necessary to exercise the most important right a democracy can confer on its citizens: the right to evaluate and judge those who govern, to correct laws that limit freedom, to check the waste of public monies, to discipline those who abuse power, and to sustain those who use it wisely and justly. But for Canadians to exercise these critical responsibilities, there must first be transparency and accountability in government. These goals may seem abstract; they are not. Transparency, in essence, means that governments must give us the information that we, as citizens, need to form a fair judgment of their performance. Accountability means that when errors do occur, someone—a minister, a senior deputy, or an entire administration—takes responsibility for that error. The two ideas go hand in hand. Without transparency, citizens and their representatives in Parliament have no way of knowing when officials or ministers depart from their wishes. Without some legal means to hold governments accountable, transparent access to information about their activities is useless. For Canadians to exercise the essential democratic role of evaluating their governments' performance, those who govern must act in a manner that is simultaneously both transparent and accountable.

Those who resist steps to improve transparency and accountability argue that respect for these values will constrain the ability of governments to act rapidly and decisively. Doubtless, a government with unchecked power can act faster than one subject to internal and external controls. But in a democracy such as ours, where government wields power only by consent of the people, the demands of efficiency can never be allowed to trump accountability to Canadians.

This principle is not merely ethical or ideological. Accountability and transparency are intimately linked to how well government performs. This might seem like simple common sense: a government that knows its citizens are watching will be more likely to tailor its behaviour to their interests. But there is empirical evidence for this link as well. One recent study found that free access to information was the single most powerful factor driving economic growth (Siegle, 2001). Other research shows that international investors consistently favour countries whose governments demonstrate high levels of transparency (OECD, 2003). This is hardly a surprise: the more open a government is, the less likely it is to make arbitrary and unexpected decisions; and the fewer opportunities it has for corruption. Still other findings suggest that more transparent government can reduce a country's risk of external conflict (Ritter, 2000). Presumably, when countries negotiate with ample information about one another, discussions are less likely to collapse and lead to confrontation.

But transparency and accountability make their most vital contribution to the functioning of a responsive democracy. Citizens with transparent access to information about their governments are able to hold public administrations to account for their acts and decisions. Only then is democracy's promise fulfilled: a government in service to the people, rather than a people in servitude to the powerful.

THE NEED: STOP THE ROT

We might complacently assume that Canada compares well to other democracies on this score. But we would be wrong. Transparency International, a non-governmental watchdog against corruption based in Berlin, ranks nations around the world for their openness and accountability. Its annual "Corruption Perception Index" (Transparency International, 2005) is compiled by asking country experts, citizens, visitors, and both resident and non-resident business leaders to assess the extent of corruption in each country evaluated. By this ranking, Canada has slipped from being the seventh least corrupt country in the world as recently as 2001 to placing a dismal fourteenth in 2005. While our standard has slipped, other countries like Australia, Austria, Norway, the United Kingdom, and Switzerland have moved ahead of Canada in this ranking.

But Canadians hardly need to look abroad for evidence that transparency and accountability have been in decline in our government. The Gomery Inquiry ("Gomery Commission," 2005, 2006) catalogued a disheartening accumulation of lapses in administrative ethics and responsibility: secretive partisan awards of federal sponsorship contracts, gross overspending, confusion and misdirection regarding the goals of the Sponsorship Program, scandalous flouting of applicable rules and guidelines, multiple conflicts of interest, evidence of criminal culpability, and a breathtaking refusal by those making flawed decisions to accept responsibility for their actions.

Yet even this sordid account ought not to have surprised us. The Auditor General of Canada foreshadowed Justice Gomery's conclusions as early as 2003.

In her report that year she wrote: "From 1997 until 31 August 2001, the federal government ran the Sponsorship Program in a way that showed little regard for Parliament, the Financial Administration Act, contracting rules and regulations, transparency, and value for money" (Canada, OAG, 2003/November: 3.1). This obliviousness, unhappily, was neither unique nor exceptional. As the Auditor General continued: "The pattern we saw of non-compliance with the rules was not the result of isolated errors. It was consistent and pervasive. This was how the government ran the program. Canadians have a right to expect greater diligence in the use of public funds" (3.122).

That expectation remained unmet. In 2005, the Auditor General identified still more trouble spots. She found these to be especially rife in programs involving more than one level or department of government, or which included participation by the private and voluntary sectors, non-governmental organizations (NGOs), or individuals. Such "horizontal" initiatives are naturally complicated. Jurisdictions overlap. Responsibility for attaining goals becomes blurred (Canada, OAG, 2005/November: 4). Even when individual participants are subject to appropriate audit guidelines (not always the case), these may not capture the whole picture of what is being achieved—and at what cost. When something goes wrong it is difficult or even impossible for Parliament, let alone the public, to assign responsibility.

These are avoidable problems. Remedies exist to redress the imbalance between sprawling, unaccountable, and unresponsive governments and the citizens they exist to serve. The proposals that follow would do much to restore transparency and accountability in federal affairs to a standard in which Canadians could take confidence and pride. The current government has made substantial progress towards this end since this report was initially published. In response to the rot uncovered by the Gomery Inquiry, the Harper government passed the Federal Accountability Act in December 2006. The Act has made considerable changes, and progress made by the current government will be dutifully acknowledged in this report.

GETTING THE GOODS: IMPROVE GOVERNMENT REPORTING
Sound information is critical to good decisions and to accountability. Sadly, much of the information about government activity that reaches Parliament and Canadians at large is difficult to use. This is partly a legacy of reporting systems developed originally on a department-by-department basis—fragmented, disconnected, and rarely consistent. From these it is difficult to identify trends, compare effectiveness across departments, or grasp the government's overall performance. What is lacking is any integrated system to draw the spending and accomplishments of all departments into a single, useable report.

One Canadian province has been nationally recognized for its success in addressing this problem. Over the last several years, Ontario has deployed state-of-the-art information technology, replacing disparate financial systems in ministries and agencies throughout the province with a single, integrated system. This was no small task. Ambitious, expensive, and time-consuming, it took five years to accomplish. Since its completion in October, 2004, however, Ontario's Integrated Financial Information System (IFIS) has provided public-service managers with timely, comprehensive, and comparable financial data from across the range of provincial operations. Better informed managers are far better equipped to ensure that subordinates stay on task and costs are kept under control.

While costs would be significant, such an initiative at the federal level could significantly improve government performance, transparency, and account-ability. Consistent and comparable reports from operations across the range of government activities would inherently improve monitoring. It should also enhance transparency, simplify evaluation, and promote better planning.

In *Rebalanced and Revitalized: A Canada Strong and Free* (Volume III in our series), we recommended that the Federal Government consider developing an integrated, government-wide, financial reporting system. Since our initial report, The Federal Accountability Act has established the position of Parliamentary Budget Officer. This does not establish a complete information system, but it works towards a standard system and is a step in the right direction.

The right to know what our governments are up to in our name is basic to a responsive democracy. It underlies deeply rooted democratic values: freedom of the press, free elections, and ministerial responsibility. So important is this right, in fact, that it compels a key presumption: that when a citizen asks his or her government for information, that information should be forthcoming as a matter of right, unless there is good reason for it to be withheld. There may be such good reason: the protection of another citizen's privacy or the security of the nation. But the citizen requesting the information should not have the burden of justifying the request and explaining its purpose. Government, in short, must disclose whatever information the public requests or provide a reasonable explanation as to why it may not be disclosed.

It was in this pro-user spirit that Canada's Access to Information Act 1985 was originally designed. However, during the 20 years since the Act came into force, the federal government has continually whittled away its scope through arbitrary exclusions and exemptions. These often directly violate the Act's explicit standard that "necessary exceptions to the right of access should be limited and specific, and that decisions on the disclosure of government information should be reviewed independently of government" (Access to Information Act 1985 [Can]: s 2).

The Act established an authority to conduct such independent reviews. Appointed by, and reporting directly to, Parliament, the Information Commissioner is further empowered to investigate complaints from citizens that information to which they are entitled is being arbitrarily withheld. The Information Commissioner's Annual Report 2004-2005 (Reid, 2005: 9) notes that many federal officials distrust and resist the Act. In defiance of its principles, they continue to control what information is disclosed and when, denying the right of Canadian citizens to the fullest possible information about the conduct of their government. Apparently not satisfied with violating the spirit of the existing law, the previous government assembled an internal Task Force in 2001 to reform the Act (Canada, Access to Information Review Task Force, 2002). Its recommendations would, if implemented, actually increase the potential for government secrecy rather than reduce it, the Commissioner warned (Reid, 2002: 11–14).

This is worrisome. It invites the conclusion that governments cannot be trusted to uphold our right to know what they are doing in our name, on our behalf, and with our money. As citizens, we must insist on better answers. In the "Blueprint for Reform" (Reid, 2001), the Information Commissioner made specific recommendations as to how better to meet the original intentions of the Act. The previous government, in its response, "A Comprehensive Framework for Access to Information Reform" (Canada, DoJ, 2005/Apr), rejected most of these. More recently, however, the Federal Accountability Act has introduced a duty to assist those seeking access to information. In our earlier report, we argued that several reforms proposed by the previous Information Commissioner deserved another look. In particular, we argued that the Access to Information Act should be extended to cover all crown corporations, offices of Parliament, and organizations that spend taxpayers' money or perform public functions. We are happy to report in this volume that The Federal Accountability Act does exactly that.

Government delegates many activities to Crown Corporations and other arm's-length bodies. Yet these organizations still spend taxpayers' money in pursuit of a public objective. It follows that they should also be accountable under the Act. To bring all of government into the light, any entity that meets any one of a broad list of criteria should be subject to the Act. The criteria might include the following. Is it funded by taxpayers' money? Does the government own it or its parent entity? Does it perform a service essential to the public interest in a federal jurisdiction?

Although progress has been made, we believe more has to be done. Public officials should be required to document their actions and decisions and preserve the public's right to access these records. Before we can hold individuals entrusted with authority to account for government's performance, we must first be able to know, clearly and with confidence, who did what. For that, citizens must have access to some record of officials' decisions and actions. Notebooks, correspondence, and file systems represent the primary source for this type of information. The previous government's 2001 Task Force recommended that these sources be excluded from public access—hidden.

We agree with former Information Commissioner Reid that this would severely threaten citizens' access to information they are entitled to and need. The newly enacted Federal Accountability Act and Mr. Justice Gomery's second report, *Restoring Accountability* ("Gomery Commission," 2006), confirm and preserve the public right of access to such records. Beyond that, they would require officials to document all activities and decisions. Enacting these reforms establishes a higher, yet still reasonable, standard of accountability for public officials.

The health and safety of Canadians should be put before the secrecy of government with a public-interest override of all exemptions. Few would argue that government should have a higher priority than protecting public health and safety. Yet federal law today sometimes places government secrecy ahead of these public interests. That has to change.

Secrecy could override health and safety. If, for example, information about an imminent threat to Canadians' health were revealed during a private Cabinet meeting, not only does current legislation not compel the release of such information but custom effectively forbids it. Cabinet deliberations, including briefings, are excluded from the Act and presumed to be confidential. Even in the face of public demands, this information would not—and arguably could not—be released. That is intolerable: Canadians deserve to be informed unconditionally of threats to their health or environment.

Two provinces, Alberta and British Columbia, have instituted a public-interest override in their Freedom of Information legislation. In British Columbia, this stipulates that "despite any other provision in the Act, the head of a public body must disclose any information about a risk of significant harm to the environment, to the health and safety of the public or to a group of people, or the disclosure of which is otherwise clearly in the public interest" (Freedom of Information and Privacy Act R.S.B.C. 1996 [BC]: c 165, s 25). A similar override is long overdue in federal legislation governing access to information.

The exclusion of Cabinet confidences should not be an absolute but should instead be transformed into an exemption subject to review by the Information Commissioner. Clearly, Cabinet ministers need to be able to speak freely and frankly with one another in order to come to a consensus over policy. They argue and cajole. Horse-trading is done. For these exchanges to be effective, a degree of secrecy is required. But governments have chosen to interpret this requirement with an uncalled-for absolutism, excluding Cabinet confidences entirely from public access (Access to Information Act 1985 [Can]: s 69). This directly contradicts the presumption that should apply, as stated in the Act and restated above, in favour of the public's right to information.

Mandatory exclusion of Cabinet confidences from the right of request under the Access to Information Act should end. These confidences should instead receive a presumption of exclusion, subject to independent review. A non-partisan outside authority, likely the Information Commissioner, should decide whether disclosing any requested material would breach a Cabinet's requirements for confidentiality or not. Cabinets need their privacy. But it need not extend to every document that comes before them. Case-by-case determination of exemption is preferable to an absolute exclusion.

In the current Parliamentary Session, the House of Commons Standing Committee on Access to Information, Privacy, and Ethics has discussed further changes to improve access to information legislation, though discussions are still at an early stage.

CLEAR EXPECTATIONS: SARBANES-OXLEY FOR GOVERNMENT

Citizens are sometimes likened to "shareholders" in government. Their counterparts in the private sector have weathered a parallel series of governance scandals in the behaviour of companies like Enron, WorldCom, HealthSouth, and Tyco. In response, shareholders in public companies are also demanding higher standards of disclosure, transparency, and executive accountability. In the United States, Congress answered these demands with the Sarbanes-Oxley Act 2002, which requires American public companies and their auditors to meet clear and extensive standards in their accounting, financial reporting, and disclosure practices. Some key Sarbanes provisions insist on complete independence for auditors and annual outside reviews of internal financial controls. Corporate executives who knowingly and wilfully misstate financial information now face larger fines and stiffer jail sentences.

Canadians have seen the results of slipshod financial controls, poor accountability and miserly disclosure over many years. In 1997 and 1998—just when the government of Canada was moving from a deficit to a surplus position— the Auditor General of Canada refused to give what is called a "clean" opinion of the government's financial statements. Instead, he gave a "qualified" opinion, stating that the government misstated its bottom line by $800 million in 1997 and by $3 billion in 1998 (Canada, OAG, 1998/Apr). Few Canadians ever became aware of these serious misstatements of facts. No repercussions whatsoever befell the officials and politicians responsible for them.

Evidence has since emerged of numerous management failures in the federal government: the so-called "billion dollar boondoggle" at Human Resources Development (Manning, 2002: 219–22), another billion-dollar fiasco in attempting to create a gun registry (*Toronto Star*, 2004: A6) and, capping all, the Sponsorship Scandal. It is especially telling that the malodorous and possibly criminal activities involved in the last of these were successfully concealed from the public for years; this despite, according to testimony given to the Gomery Inquiry, their being known to hundreds of people, many of them public servants (Mullins, 2005). It is high time that Canadians held government to legally enforceable standards of disclosure, transparency, and accountability at least as high as those required of public corporations.

Since our initial report, the Federal Accountability Act did introduce three measures that address these concerns. The Act introduced fraud involving public funds as a new offence, it strengthened the role of internal departmental audit committees, and further clarified the managerial responsibilities of deputy heads.

Fiscal responsibility in New Zealand

We could learn from New Zealand's example. Through the early 1990s, the government of that nation had accumulated an irresponsibly large debt (almost 50% of GDP), using creative accounting to obscure the reality and seriousness of the situation from the public. In 1994, the citizens of New Zealand, through their representatives, drew the line. To encourage government to manage its finances more responsibly and transparently, New Zealand's Parliament enacted the Fiscal Responsibility Act 1994. It established principles of responsible fiscal management and financial reporting and required government to operate in accordance with those principles.

The Fiscal Responsibility Act asked several things of New Zealand's government, none of them radical. It asked the government to reduce the spiralling public debt to prudent levels and maintain a net worth sufficient to buffer future economic shocks and demographic changes. It asked that government manage fiscal risks prudently and choose policies likely to preserve a predictable and stable tax rate. Beyond adopting these principles, government was asked to demonstrate adherence to them by issuing regular and comprehensive reports on its short- and long-term fiscal outlook. These must conform to Generally Accepted Accounting Practices (GAAP) (Fiscal Responsibility Act 1994 [NZ]: s 4).

New Zealand's Fiscal Responsibility Act, like the Sarbanes-Oxley Act, holds those in charge to account. In that country a "chief executive," equivalent to a Canadian deputy minister, leads each government department. The chief executive is held responsible for the financial management and performance of the department; for establishing internal accounting controls and making sure that they produce reliable information; and, for ensuring that the department complies with legislative reporting requirements. Importantly, there is a separation created between the creation and execution of policy. Accountability is enhanced by holding the minister and deputy separately responsible for their tasks. We believe Canada should adopt a system of responsibility similar to that in New Zealand.

In the United States, executives in public companies know the standard of disclosure they are expected to meet and the penalty for failing to do so. In New Zealand, it is clear who is mandated to accept responsibility for the actions of each government department. Canadians should require no less from our public officials. In our previous volume, we called on the government to enact legislation that set out acceptable principles for responsible fiscal management and reporting, and obliges government to act in accordance with them. Canadians must hold our governments to standards of disclosure, transparency, and accountability at least as high as those expected of publicly listed private companies. This involves regular reporting of financial and performance results in detail according to a standardized and easily understood accounting scheme. Good management is not a question of politics. Policy objectives may change; fiscal rectitude should never deviate from the highest standards. We are again happy to note that the government has moved forward in this direction through the Federal Accountability Act.

Setting out in clear terms the management principles and reporting standards that officials are expected to meet will give citizens and Parliament a powerful tool for evaluating government performance. Legislation that clearly identifies those office-holders who are mandated to accept responsibility for meeting these expectations will make accountability possible. Public officials who fail to comply with accountability legislation should face clear consequences like those that corporate executives face under the Sarbanes-Oxley Act. In his first report, *Who is Responsible?*, Mr. Justice Gomery criticized a system that shies away from punishing wrongdoers. During the scandalous heyday of federal sponsorships, employees who failed to certify that any work was done in exchange for public payments, a certification required of them by the Financial Administration Act, were not asked to resign. They were merely reassigned. Such feeble "consequences" are hardly adequate ("Gomery Commission," 2005). *Restoring Accountability*, Mr. Justice Gomery's second report, addressed this inadequacy. It urged that such a breach be treated as it would in the private sector—as grounds for dismissal ("Gomery Commission," 2006).

Canada's Financial Administration Act 1985 sets out clear consequences for office holders who violate standards when collecting or managing public funds. It prohibits officials from receiving compensation for performance of non-official duties, conspiring or colluding to defraud Her Majesty, permitting any contravention of the law by any other person, wilfully making or signing any false entry, failing to report knowledge of a contravention of law to a superior officer, demanding or accepting or attempting to collect payment for the compromise, adjustment or settlement of any charge or complaint for any contravention or alleged contravention of law. (Financial Administration Act 1985 [Can]: s 80)

Breaches of the Act invite penalties ranging from written warnings through suspensions or demotions all the way to termination or, in extremely rare cases, criminal prosecution. Conviction of the offences itemized above exposes an official to a fine of no more than five thousand dollars, as well as possible imprisonment with a maximum term of five years.

By contrast, Sarbanes-Oxley punishes any corporate officer who knowingly or willfully defrauds shareholders of a publicly traded company with fines of up to five million dollars, imprisonment for as long as 20 years, or both (Sarbanes-Oxley Act 2002 [US]: s 1106). Canadians should hold those who manage our taxes to the standard of accountability that we demand of corporate managers. Penalties for officials who mismanage public money should reflect those faced by corporate managers who commit similar offences. Here again we have seen significant progress under the Federal Accountability Act, which creates a Director of Public Prosecutions and new offences involving fraud with public funds.

Another area that cries out for improvement is protection for "whistle-blowers." This helps promote accountability in two ways. It empowers employees to take action when they encounter evidence of fraud. It also acts as an incentive for managers to conduct their affairs properly. On November 25, 2005, the first federal legislation for the protection of whistle-blowers in the public service was given Royal Assent. The Public Servants Disclosure Protection Act (Bill C-11) was introduced to establish a procedure for disclosing wrongdoing in the public sector. In protecting those who reveal misconduct from retaliation, it measures up well to Sarbanes' safeguards for private-sector whistleblowers. But, while this is surely a step in the right direction, we must agree with Mr. Justice Gomery that improvement is still in order ("Gomery Commission," 2006: 186). Alan Cutler, one of those who brought attention to the Sponsorship scandal, described Bill C-11 as "fatally and fundamentally flawed" because it would require a whistleblower to prove that any subsequent discipline was in reprisal for his action (Harris, 2005: 31). This burden of proof, Cutler argued, serves only to deter potential whistle-blowers. We agree. We believe the burden of proof should fall instead on the employer, who must demonstrate that actions directed at a whistle-blower were not a reprisal.

The legislation also amended the Access to Information Act and the Privacy Act to exclude from access any information gathered as a result of a whistle-blower's disclosure. Finally, Bill C-11 stripped both a whistle-blower and those they accuse of the right to read and correct even personal information about themselves that was collected under its provisions. Government justifies all these constraints by citing the need to protect whistle-blowers' identities. We agree instead with the Information Commissioner: such constraints are unnecessary. Both the Privacy Act and the Access to Information Act already protect identities during an investigation and allow information to be withheld if its disclosure might impede investigators or hamper law enforcement. Both Acts prohibit whistle-blowers and accused persons from being identified to the Media and the public. Further constraints on the right of access to information should be withdrawn as unjustifiable.

A STRONGER WATCHDOG: ENHANCE THE POWER OF THE AUDITOR GENERAL

As an impartial observer of spending and performance, the Auditor General (AG) provides Parliament and Canadian citizens with information they need to hold government accountable. But the Auditor General's office is not as independent from government as it could be. Like most federal departments and agencies, the Office of the Auditor General must negotiate its budget annually with the Treasury Board. In her 2002 report, Auditor General Sheila Fraser acknowledged that this reliance on government for funding poses a threat to the independence of her role. It leaves open the possibility, whether real or perceived, for government to withhold funds in order to influence the Auditor General's judgment. This should be corrected. The Office of the Auditor General should apply directly to Parliament—not the government—for its appropriation. This would preserve the independence of this critical function of accountability and transparency that has served Canadians so well in the past.

Once again the Federal Accountability Act has moved in the right direction. According to the FAA website,

> The Auditor General is one of five Agents of Parliament currently participating in a two-year pilot project in which an all-party Parliamentary Advisory Panel considers the funding requests of Agents prior to a final Treasury Board decision on their budgets. This process gives Parliament a greater role and respects the independence of Agents of Parliament, while allowing the Treasury Board of Canada Secretariat to provide input on panel recommendations. <http://www.faa-lfi.gc.ca/docs/ap-pa/ap-pa12_e.asp>

More is also needed. Under existing legislation, the Auditor General lacks authority to force the government to respond to her findings. In May 2002, the Auditor General alerted Jean Chrétien, then Prime Minister, to serious problems within the Sponsorship Program. Despite this warning, the wasteful program was not officially cancelled until December 2003 ("Gomery Commission," 2005: 14). Had she possessed the authority to temporarily suspend programs displaying "consistent and pervasive ... non-compliance with the rules" (Canada, OAG, 2003/November: 3.122), the Auditor General could have saved significant amounts of the taxpayers' dollars and prompted a review of the program 17 months sooner.

We therefore believe it important for Parliament to fund the Auditor General's budget directly through a special appropriation for that purpose. As well, in order to increase the capacity of the Auditor General to compel compliance with his or her recommendations, the office should be given the power to freeze funding to programs temporarily, pending their demonstration of compliance or further investigation, and to impose penalties for non-compliance or ineffective compliance..

In *Rebalanced and Revitalized: A Canada Strong and Free* we recommended that the Auditor General should be provided with statutory authority to audit, at his or her discretion, any organization or individual that performs a service for the government. We are glad to report that the Federal Accountability Act

> require[s] that the Government include in funding agreements with recipients provisions that support Auditor General audits ... that recipients maintain records with respect to federal funding provided; create a contractual right for the Auditor General to inquire into the use of funding provided; and require that recipients provide information and records to the Auditor General on request. <http://www.faa-lfi.gc.ca/docs/ap-pa/ap-pa12_e.asp.>

"IF IT MATTERS, MEASURE IT": A REPORT CARD ON GOVERNMENT PERFORMANCE

Economic freedom matters, so researchers at The Fraser Institute, working with others around the world, developed the Economic Freedom index to measure how free individuals in various countries are to make their own economic decisions. The fiscal performance of government matters; so The Fraser Institute's researchers developed an index to score how Canada's federal and provincial governments compare in performance of fiscal policy. School and hospital performance matter, and so these researchers, with others, developed the *Report Cards* on Canadian schools and the Hospital Report Card, which rank the performance of these institutions on the basis of measurable outcomes, providing an objective basis on which citizens can exercise their freedom of choice in education and health care. (See "How The Fraser Institute Does It," pages 190–191, for more on these reports.)

Plainly, the overall performance of government matters, especially since governments are largely responsible for the conditions that either expand or restrict economic freedom, as well as for policies that govern schools, hospitals, courts, and many other services that directly affect Canadian lives. In order to provide an objective measure of progress toward our goal of making Canada the best-governed federal democracy in the world, we therefore propose what may be the world's most ambitious grading exercise: a report card on government performance in Canada.

We suggest that this initiative first measure the performance of the federal government—a report card on Ottawa. It could then be extended gradually until there were annual reports measuring the performance of every provincial, territorial, aboriginal, and municipal government as well. Implementing this proposal will clearly be a large and complex task. Canadians from different regions of the country, from varying socio-economic circumstances, and from a spectrum of cultural backgrounds and political persuasions will obviously have a wide range of views on what constitutes "good" and "bad" performance by government. Arriving at criteria for evaluation on which all can agree, and that can be measured objectively, will be a major undertaking. So too will be the collection of the necessary data, the statistical analysis, and the publication and distribution of the results. It is, nevertheless, a task well worth pursuing. As a first step towards its accomplishment, we recommend a national conference on evaluating the performance of the government of Canada.

CONCLUSIONS: PROTECTING THE CITIZEN'S RIGHT TO KNOW

We are all familiar with the phrase, "garbage in, garbage out." The quality of Canadians' judgments about our government can only ever be as good as the quality of information available to us. Yet we have identified numerous ways in which existing policy is designed to conceal the facts of government from the public and insulate key decisions and decision-makers from scrutiny.

This cannot lead to better government or more responsive democracy. For transparency and accountability to be meaningful, Canadians must not only know what government is doing on their behalf, but also who is responsible for critical decisions, the information on which those decisions are based, and the outcomes they produced. Similarly, Canadians have a right to expect their public servants to meet clear standards of performance—and to enforce career and personal consequences on any who fail to meet or who breach those standards.

The individual citizen comes first in a democracy. Practical mechanisms will ensure this principle is respected so that government answers to Canadians—not the other way around.

RECOMMENDATIONS

10.1 Bring all of government into the light by broadening the scope of Canada's Access to Information Act 1985 to include any entity that meets a broad list of criteria that might include: Is it funded by taxpayers' money? Does the government own, or partially own, it or its parent entity? Does it perform a service essential to the public interest in a federal jurisdiction?

10.2 Ensure that Canadians know, clearly and with confidence, who did what, by requiring public officials to document their actions and decisions and preserve the public's right to access these records.

10.3 Put the health and safety of Canadians before the secrecy of government, by requiring (subject to limited exceptions) that public bodies disclose any information about a risk of significant harm to the environment, to the health and safety of the public or a group of people, or where the disclosure is clearly in the public interest.

10.4 End mandatory exclusion of Cabinet confidences from the right of request under the Access to Information Act; instead these confidences should receive a presumption of exclusion, subject to independent review by the Information Commissioner.

10.5 Enact legislation (taking Sarbanes-Oxley and New Zealand's Fiscal Responsibility Act as models) empowering Canadian citizens to hold government to legally enforceable standards of disclosure, transparency, and accountability at least as high as those required of public corporations, and holds those in charge to account.

10.6 Require deputy-ministers to sign contracts of employment making them personally responsible for the department's performance.

10.7 Increase protection of "whistle-blowers" but without putting further constraints, beyond those already contained in the Privacy and Access to Information Acts, on public access to information or the right of whistle-blowers (and those accused) of seeing and correcting the appropriate files.

10.8 Fund the Auditor General's budget independently of the government of the day, through a special Parliamentary appropriation for that purpose.

10.9 Increase the capacity of the Auditor General to compel compliance with his or her recommendations by giving the office the power to freeze funding to programs temporarily, pending their demonstration of compliance or further investigation, and to impose penalties for non-compliance or ineffective compliance.

10.10 Convene a national conference to outline the measures necessary to create a credible and objective report card on government performance in Canada, modeled on the report cards on individual aspects of government performance pioneered by The Fraser Institute.

HOW THE FRASER INSTITUTE DOES IT

SCHOOL REPORT CARDS

The Fraser Institute's *Report Cards* on elementary and secondary schools collect relevant, objective indicators of school performance into one public document so that anyone can easily analyze and compare individual schools. Typical indicators are: student performance on province-wide tests; rates of failure on the same tests; differences in the performance of male and female students on these tests; grade-to-grade transition rates; and participation rates in core subject areas. Where parents can choose among several schools for their children, the *Report Card* provides an objective basis for that decision. It further equips parents to ask more relevant questions when they speak with teachers and provides a measure that shows whether schools are improving over time. This in turn encourages schools to achieve better results—or see enrolment fall.

FISCAL PERFORMANCE INDEX

The *Fiscal Performance Index* reports how well Canadian federal and provincial governments manage their taxpayers' money. Based on 20 indicators, the *Index* focuses on three key areas of fiscal performance: (1) Government Spending, (2) Tax Rates and Revenues, and (3) Debt and Deficit. The first measures public-sector consumption relative to the economy in each jurisdiction, revealing how well governments control spending. Tax Rates and Revenues compares tax rates currently and over time, as well as the portion of revenue received in transfers from the other levels of government. Debt and Deficits tracks deficit financing and the relative burden of accumulated debt. The fiscal policy a government pursues can be a critical determinant of a provincial or national economy's long-term success. The *Fiscal Performance Index* is an independent measure by which taxpayers can hold their governments accountable.

HOW THE FRASER INSTITUTE DOES IT

ECONOMIC FREEDOM

Economic Freedom of the World measures how free individuals in 141 nations are to make their own economic decisions. These annual reports on economic freedom focus on the protection of property, respect for contracts, and the extent to which individuals engage in fully voluntary transactions. The index uses 42 variables from objective third-party sources grouped into five key areas: Size of Government, to determine how much of a citizen's wealth is expropriated by the state; Legal Structure, to determine how well property rights and contracts are protected; Sound Money, to determine whether government uses inflation to expropriate property; Freedom to Trade; and Regulation of Credit, Business and Labour, to determine how freely individuals engage in voluntary agreements in these areas. Canada typically places in the bottom half of the top 10 nations, behind leaders such as Hong Kong, Singapore, and New Zealand. In *Economic Freedom of North America*, a measure of economic freedom in Canadian provinces and US states, all but one of the provinces rate in, or close to, the bottom 10 jurisdictions. Alberta, the exception, rates in, or close to, the top 10. Indexes of economic freedom provide both a description of each economy and a prescription of how the economic freedom of citizens can be increased.

HOSPITAL REPORT CARD

The *Hospital Report Card* ranks acute-care hospitals in Canada in order of their outcome performance. It employs some 60 indicators of patient safety and in-patient care developed by the US Department of Health and Human Services' Agency for Healthcare Research and Quality. These indicators are used to measure hospital performance in 12 US states including New York, Texas, and Colorado. Indicators of in-patient care include mortality rates, the appropriate use of procedures, and the volume of procedures for which evidence shows that greater volume is associated with lower mortality. Indicators of patient safety focus on preventable complications and adverse events following surgeries, procedures, and childbirth. The indicators analyze data from the Canadian Institute for Health Information for the period from 1997 to 2004. Of Ontario's 136 acute-care facilities, 46 hospitals, representing 40% of in-patient records in the province, voluntarily agreed to participate in the first report.

CHAPTER 11

A MENU OF DEMOCRATIC REFORMS

In Chapter 10, we addressed the need to restore transparency and accountability to the structures and operations of the Canadian government today. In Chapter 12, we shall come to grips with the most serious imbalances within our system of government, defects that demand our urgent attention if we are to be any better governed in the future than we have been in the past. But, neither restoring transparency to government operations today nor rebalancing its parts tomorrow will durably preserve the relationship at the very heart of any vibrant democracy. In that relationship, the people must always outrank those they elect or engage to serve them. As Canadian society continues to grow in size and complexity, however, as technologies advance and governments respond to new threats and challenges, the ways we ensure citizen oversight will continue to evolve.

Here, we examine ways to improve the functioning of our Canadian democracy. Independent audits and accountable bureaucrats cannot keep the relationship in balance on their own. It takes informed, confident citizens, equipped with the tools they need to exercise their democratic rights and responsibilities. We need, as well, a flourishing culture of democracy: institutions that empower citizens to make their priorities known, support for citizens who seek to influence the public discourse, investment in the democratic "software" of policy ideas, and exploration of the best ways to choose representatives that reflect the diversity of Canadian views.

These requirements face us for the long term. In the end, whether we accomplish our goal of making Canada the best governed, most democratic, most productive country on earth may be determined by how well we Canadians meet these challenges. Many different courses have been suggested for advancing democratic reform. In this chapter, we offer of menu of 12 proposals for strengthening our democratic processes and institutions. Most are not exclusive; they could be pursued without ruling out other options. Some involve considerable investments of time and political capital, others little more than a decision by cabinet.

We do not put forward the ideas in the following pages as recommendations but as options worth considering. We invite readers to review this menu of democratic reforms for themselves, to consult the references for further information, and to make their own decisions as to which of them Canadians should pursue. At the conclusion of the chapter, however, the authors and The Fraser Institute recommend the reforms that we believe deserve the most immediate attention of our fellow citizens.

1 CIVIC EDUCATION

Civic education is essential to meaningful democratic government. It is the vital knowledge of the idea of democracy itself and how government actually works that equips children and adults to exercise their political freedoms and participate effectively in democratic decisions.

Civic education is like "driver's ed" that qualifies citizens to take the keys of the country. And it is largely missing from Canadian curricula. The extent of "civ-ed" in Canadian elementary and secondary schools runs from non-existent to spotty. Only four Canadian provinces require students to complete courses dedicated solely to civics before they can graduate from high school (Griffiths and Lyle, 2005). Comparable education for new Canadians and adults in general is even more limited.

It is worth doing more. In a poll conducted during the 2004 election by the Dominion Institute and the *National Post*, 69% of students between 14 and 18 years felt civic education helped them follow politics and make informed decisions. The degree of civic education also seems to increase political participation: in the same poll, those who had studied politics and government were 10% to 15% more likely to say they would vote if given the opportunity and twice as likely to indicate support for a specific party (Griffiths and Lyle, 2005). Of course, school-based civic education must be focused on the essentials of democratic citizenship and be as free as possible from the political biases of provincial governments, school boards, school administrators, and teachers' unions. To ensure this, parents should be directly involved and consulted in the development of provincial civics curricula and permitted to audit in-school delivery.

Given limited resources and classroom time, efforts to inculcate such basic civic habits as reading, voting, and communicating with public representatives should target students from 16 to 18 years (Milner, 2001: 22). An initiative by the Dominion Institute called the Democracy Project has had some success engaging youth through national surveys, town-hall meetings, and a "democracy in the news" module (www.thedemocracyproject. ca). Employing new technologies such as SMS text messaging, the national surveys encourage youth to voice their opinions on the future of democracy in Canada.

The non-partisan, non-profit, organization, Student Vote (www.studentvote. ca), which is supported by Elections Canada among many others, has developed a program to give Canadian students a parallel election experience during an official election period. Registered schools receive learning materials to complement a series of participatory activities that help students learn about the democratic process, party platforms, and local candidates. Events are organized to encourage critical thinking among students who might represent their chosen parties in a debate. On a day chosen by the school, students assume the duties of Deputy Returning Officers and Poll Clerks to conduct a school-wide vote whose results are released to the public, shared with the Media, and compiled by Student Vote.

During the 2006 Canadian general election, more than 450,000 students took part in Student Vote programs at more than 2,450 schools from all provinces and territories. In a survey completed by some participating students after the 2004 election, 88% said they would vote in the future, 87% said they believed voting is an important responsibility, and 45% discussed politics with family or friends during the campaign (Student Vote, 2004).

2   CITIZENS' ASSEMBLIES

In 2003, the Government of British Columbia embarked upon a unique and innovative process to recommend changes in the province's electoral system: it convened The Citizens' Assembly on Electoral Reform. The Citizens' Assembly comprised 159 members, two selected at random from the list of voters from every electoral district in the province, along with the chair. No current politician or anyone who had recently run for or held a public office was included in the Assembly. The citizens set their own governance and procedures and were given a budget of $5.5 million, but were required to report no later than December 2004. The Assembly could recommend only one electoral system. If it chose to recommend something other than the current single-member riding, first-past-the-post model, its proposal would go to the people in a referendum held at the same time as the next provincial election, May 17, 2005. To be adopted, the proposal for reform would require the approval of at least 60% of validly cast ballots and a simple majority in

48 of the 79 electoral districts. Ultimately, the multimember riding, transferable-vote system proposed by the Citizens' Assembly received significant public support but did not meet this threshold.

The accomplishment of the Citizens' Assembly was nonetheless remarkable. It was a unique exercise in deliberative democracy, capable of being both plenary and conclusive. More often, the approach to potential democratic reform relies on some sort of advisory body—a Royal Commission perhaps—or on elected bodies that have a vested interest in the outcome. The Citizens' Assembly separated the process of developing institutional and systemic reforms from the politicians and interest groups that might benefit from the reform. At the same time, legislation required that any proposal flowing from the Citizens' Assembly be considered through a referendum— both putting the decision to citizens at large and providing finality (Gibson, 2002: 7–8). Ontario has since employed a similar Citizens' Assembly on Electoral Reform. The Assembly has proposed a mixed-member, proportional electoral system for the province, which will be the subject of a referendum in October 2007.

A 1996 experiment in deliberative democracy by the Canada West Foundation concluded that ordinary Canadians were amply capable of grasping complex policy issues. The conclusions these assemblies of citizens reached were often very similar to those of government hearings and policy conferences. For the citizens involved, the exercise proved highly educational; surveys before and after indicate that the opinions of many underwent significant change during the assembly (Vander Ploeg, 1996: 1).

To advance public understanding and acceptance of complex proposals, the citizens' assembly offers a valuable tool. Likewise, proposals for electoral or constitutional reform are likely to be more credible and acceptable to citizens in general if they have been developed through public deliberation. To be credible, the assembly must be representative, not just in terms of geography but also of demography. The body must be small enough to deliberate the question at hand effectively with appropriate support.

The challenge is in the details of the assembly: it is difficult to balance representation, effectiveness, and affordability. Beyond the costs to convene a sizeable body across a sizable geography over a long period of time, any effort to increase the transparency and educational effect of the exercise will cost additional money. British Columbia's Citizens' Assembly, held over 18 months, cost $5.5 million. By comparison, the Royal Commission Citizens Forum on Canada's Future met for eight months in 1990 and 1991 and cost $22 million. The Royal Commission on Aboriginal Peoples, which cost $60 million and met from August 1991 to November 1996, was the longest and most expensive such effort in Canadian history (*CBC News Online*, 2004).

3 FIXED ELECTION DATES

Elections are currently required at least every five years in Canada though historically they occur roughly once every four. In most provinces, they occur on dates picked by the party in power before the writs are dropped. Legislation has been proposed to require fixed election dates every four years, except when a government loses the confidence of Parliament or its legislature. The principal benefit claimed for fixed election dates is that they reduce the ability of governments and governing parties to manipulate the timing of elections with an eye to the polls solely for partisan advantage.

Fixed election dates already exist for some municipal and local elections. Ontario's Municipal Elections Act requires that municipal elections be held on the second Monday of November, every three years. In Alberta, the Local Authorities Election Act sets the date for local elections as the third Monday of October, every three years beginning in 1983. Legislation fixing most election dates at every four years has been put into effect in British Columbia, where provincial legislation now provides for provincial elections on the second Tuesday in May in the fourth calendar year following the previous general election. The first election held on this timetable was on May 17, 2005; the next will be on May 12, 2009. In Ontario, the Election Act affirms the Lieutenant Governor's power to dissolve the Legislature in the event of a vote of non-confidence. The first fixed election date for Ontario will be October 10, 2007; subsequent elections will be on the first Thursday in October in the fourth calendar year following the most recent provincial election. Legislation modeled on the British Columbia and Ontario examples has been passed at the Federal level. The law sets October 19, 2009 as the date for the next general election provided the Government maintains the confidence of the House of Commons.

Fixed election dates have been criticized on the grounds that flexible election timing is a necessary element of the Westminster parliamentary system. It is true that a key component of the responsible government tradition is the principle that, if a government loses the confidence of Parliament, then Parliament ought to be dissolved and an election called immediately. Legislation in both British Columbia and Ontario allows for this possibility.

The cost of elections is a concern of those who oppose fixed election dates. Fixed election dates extend the campaign period beyond the current writ period, in which campaign spending and advocacy group participation are tightly regulated. Rules governing election spending might become effectively obsolete. On the other hand, there is a possibility that fixed dates for elections will reduce their administrative costs, since election officials will be able to start work well in advance of polling dates. Likewise, government bureaucrats and parliamentary committees will be able to plan their agendas better without interruption from unexpected elections (Milner, 2005: 20–21).

4 REFORM OF THE ELECTORAL SYSTEM

It is frequently complained that Canada's one-member-riding, first-past-the-post system of electing representatives to Parliament and provincial legislatures produces skewed results. In the 1997 general election, the Liberals won 155 seats or 51.5% of the House of Commons with only 38.45% of the popular vote (Chief Electoral Officer of Canada, 1997: 70). A little more than three years later in the 2000 general election, Jean Chrétien led the Liberals to a third successive majority government securing 57.1% of the House of Commons with only 40.8% of the popular vote (Chief Electoral Officer of Canada, 2000: 18). In the 2004 and 2006 general elections, the disparity between votes received and seats allocated has not been as drastic. Even so, as Table 11.1 shows, the Bloc Québécois continues to elect more MPs than its popular vote would suggest it should, while the NDP and Green parties find themselves at a disadvantage. This discrepancy arises because our simple plurality, first-past-the-post system of selecting "winners" requires only that a candidate receive more votes than any other in the riding to be elected. The result tends to favour front-runners and regionally popular parties while under-representing parties whose support is spread relatively thinly across the country.

The current system often produces large majorities in the House of Commons that are little more than an artefact of the process (the last two elections being more the exception than the rule). The system also serves to exaggerate regional strengths and weaknesses, producing a House with strong regional overtones. This has exacerbated tensions and conflict as parties cater to their regional bases of support rather than to a broader national audience. Finally, many votes are "wasted," since a candidate can win with as little as 30% of

Table 11.1: 2004 and 2006 general elections—disparity between votes received and seats allocated

Political party	2004			2006		
	Number of seats	Percentage of seats	Percentage of popular vote	Number of seats	Percentage of seats	Percentage of popular vote
Bloc Québécois	54	17.5%	12.4%	51	16.6%	10.5%
Conservative	99	32.1%	29.6%	124	40.3%	36.3%
Green	0	0.0%	4.3%	0	0.0%	4.5%
Liberal	135	43.8%	36.7%	103	33.4%	30.2%
New Democratic	19	6.2%	15.7%	29	9.4%	17.5%

Source: Elections Canada, <www.elections.ca>.

the vote. Indeed, in the last federal election there would seem to have been little point in voting for a Liberal candidate in Calgary or for a Conservative in downtown Toronto.

For all these reasons, many Canadians see a case for considering alternatives. The main objective in reforming the electoral system is to make representation in Parliament and the legislatures more genuinely representative of the views of Canadians at large. It is argued that doing so will also increase public confidence and participation in elections.

Still, Canadians are understandably cautious about embracing an unfamiliar system of electing their representatives. The current system may work to the disadvantage of small or new parties but in so doing it usually generates a strong majority government capable of advancing its platform. Parties that aspire to govern are forced to build broad coalitions, engaging diverse groups across regional and social divides. Extremist groups are seldom able to win seats unless their support is geographically concentrated. As a result, strong majorities are generally accompanied and held in check by a coherent opposition. The existing system is also straightforward and easy to understand. A valid ballot requires only a mark next to the name of one of the candidates and the count is simple to administer. There is a clear link between votes received and seats won. Elected members represent a defined geographic region, which facilitates a strong association between representatives and their constituents. Voters can make their choice for a preferred party or an individual. And, while it happens infrequently, popular independent candidates are sometimes elected (Reynolds, 1998).

At the same time, alternative systems are not without unintended consequences of their own. One problem is that an electoral system designed to improve the representativeness of an assembly may not, under the British parliamentary system, be best at producing an effective executive capable of making decisions and taking action. Instead, an assembly that closely reflects the range of voters' views may have no party in a clear majority equipped to form a cabinet and advance legislation. The more "proportional" the electoral system adopted, the greater the demands on the coalition-building skills of elected members, if good decisions are to be made.

That said, ongoing concerns with the existing system have prompted some to seek electoral reform. The alternative most often proposed is some form of proportional representation. The goal of this approach is to distribute seats in the assembly in close proportion to the support that voters give each competing party. In theory, this would give a party that attracted a certain percentage of the popular vote something close to the same portion of seats in a legislature. Desirable as this goal may appear, accomplishing it in practice is not necessarily simple or straightforward. It may require voters to sacrifice some degree of choice (as in the first option described below) or subject vote tallies to the application of mathematical formulae in order to determine a "winner" (as in the other options described). Advocates of alternative approaches argue that these are modest difficulties in light of the more nuanced assembly that proportional representation achieves.

Principal variants of proportional representation

List systems

Most people associate proportional representation with list systems. Typically in these systems, parties submit a list of candidates. Voters cast ballots in support of the party of their choice. When the ballots are counted, seats are awarded to parties based on the total number of votes they attract. The parties then fill their seats from the candidates named on their lists, sometimes, though not always, starting with the first name on the list and working down.

Different jurisdictions take different approaches, however, to calculating the number of seats to be awarded to each party from the total number of ballots cast. One such approach establishes a "quota" of votes that signifies that a party has won a seat; depending on the chosen formula, this could be the number of votes cast divided by the number of available seats. A party wins a seat for each "quota" of ballots cast in its favour. Austria, Belgium, Greece, and Iceland all use some form of this "largest remainder" system (O'Neal, 1993: section B-1–A-a; Farrell, 2001: 71–73). In a variant known as the "highest average" system, each party's votes are divided by a series of divisors to produce an average vote. The party with the highest average vote after each round of the process is allocated a seat. Its votes are then divided by the next divisor (O'Neal, 1993: section B-1–A-b&c). Israel, Norway, and Sweden all use some form of the highest average system (Farrell, 2001: 73–74).

Both these systems achieve very proportional results, to the advantage of smaller parties. But it is difficult to win a majority government under them, often necessitating complex and fractious coalitions. Representatives have no territorial affiliation. This weakens elected members' bonds with their constituents and reinforces party affiliation, especially where party officials choose candidates' ranking on the electoral list. For these reasons, list systems tend to be more popular among smaller countries or lower levels of government.

Single transferable vote (STV)

The Citizens' Assembly on Electoral Reform recommended this type of system for British Columbia. Had the so-called BCSTV system been approved, the province would still have 79 MLAs. But rather than 79 ridings with one representative each, many ridings would have been combined and represented by as many as seven MLAs, while still preserving the existing ratio of voters to representatives. In an election, each party could field as many candidates in a riding as there were seats to win. At the polls, voters could rank as many or as few candidates as they wished, in order of their preference, on a single ballot. A weighting system and threshold formula using a quota designed for this purpose in 1868 by English mathematician and lawyer, Henry Droop, would then be used to allocate seats for a particular riding (BC Citizen's Assembly on Electoral Reform, 2004). A similar STV system is employed in Ireland and for Senate elections in Australia.

The STV achieves greater proportionality as the number of representatives per riding increases. But a greater number of representatives also weakens the relationship between electors and elected. The system is also somewhat complicated, which means that there is no simple correlation between the number of votes cast for a party or candidate, and the seats allocated. Finally, since candidates from the same party compete for the same votes in their riding, there is increased factionalism within political parties (Farrell, 2001: 144).

Mixed member proportional (MMP)

The Commission on Prince Edward Island's Electoral Future proposed this electoral model for that province. The Commission's proposal maintained 27 seats in the Prince Edward Island's provincial legislature but each voter would have cast two ballots in order to allocate them. In the first, citizens in 17 districts would vote for their choice of local representatives through the current first-past-the-post system. But each party would also field a slate of ten additional candidates. The second ballot would allocate the remaining ten seats in Prince Edward Island's Assembly to these candidates on a province-wide proportional basis, using the highest-average method. The proposal was put to a plebiscite in November 2005 and failed by an overwhelming margin. The Ontario Citizens' Assembly on Electoral Reform has proposed a MMP electoral system for the province; iy will be put to a referendum in October 2007.

New Zealand adopted a MMP system in 1996. The first coalition government elected under this system operated much as previous majority governments elected under the old system had. The speaker and deputy speaker, along with 14 of 17 committee chairs, came from the governing parties. The difference was evident, however, when the coalition government collapsed after 19 months. A new minority government was able to fill the vacuum and navigate the government through until the end of the normal three-year term (Shugart, 2001: 321).

While an MMP system is generally very proportional, the reliance on lists of candidates can favour party executives over local candidates. It also creates two classes of representatives, those representing geographic regions and those representing their parties (Reynolds and Reilly, 1997).

Alternative vote

The alternative vote, or preferential ballot, has been used in Australia to elect members of the House of Representatives (their equivalent of the Canadian House of Commons) since 1918. The system preserves the single-member riding while allowing voters to rank candidates in order of preference. It can be employed without increasing the number of seats in a legislature and does not create two classes of representative.

Australian political parties field candidates for the lower house on a riding basis, as in Canada. But rather than vote only for their first choice of candidate, Australian voters must rank every candidate on the ballot according to their preference. If they do not, the ballot is considered spoiled. When ballots are counted, any candidate who receives a simple majority is immediately elected. When no candidate wins a majority, the winner is the candidate who receives the highest number of first, second, and other vote preferences, using votes transferred from successively eliminated candidates with the least support (Farrell, 2001: 56). The system minimizes "wasted" votes because voters are afforded the opportunity to vote for a number of candidates with similar platforms, making their intentions relatively clear.

The alternative vote has been used historically in Canada. Provincial elections between 1926 and 1955 in Alberta used the system as did provincial elections in Manitoba from 1927 to 1957, and in British Columbia in 1952 and 1953. The Reform Party of Canada and the Alberta and Ontario Progressive Conservatives have all used the alternative vote for party elections and a growing number of parties employ it, rather than more expensive run-offs, to nominate local candidates.

The alternative vote does not necessarily produce more proportional results. It does, however, facilitate coalition building across partisan lines without forcing formal coalitions or mergers. This has been the case in Australia, where the National and Liberal parties together have managed to compete with the Labour party (Flanagan, 1998).

Proportional representation in summary

Each of the foregoing variants of proportional representation—List System, Single-Transferable Vote, Mixed Member Proportional, and Alternative Vote—as well as our existing first-past-the-post system has advantages and shortcomings. It is well to remember that political parties and interest groups have distinct partisan interests in any proposed reform to the current electoral system. The most credible proposal for any electoral reform is likely to be developed by an independent body, such as Ontario or British Columbia's Citizens' Assemblies and should only be adopted by carrying the judgement of a clear majority of the electors in a referendum. Elections are the defining exercise of a democracy. The public must have confidence in whatever system is adopted and must therefore be the final arbiter of its acceptance. Any referendum on electoral reform must be accompanied by effective educational campaigns that explore the nature and implications of any proposed reform thoroughly.

5   REFERENDUMS

Referendums are a way to refer an issue or series of questions to the electorate directly rather than leave the matter to elected representatives alone. They are especially attractive when the issue is one that bears directly on the interests of the representatives: the adoption of a new constitution, a constitutional amendment, or the recall of an elected official. But they have also been used to determine citizens' views on a proposed law or a specific government policy. Referendums also serve educational ends.

The term "referendum" generally refers to circumstances in which the expressed will of the majority of the electorate is binding on the government. A "plebiscite" is generally consultative or advisory but not binding on a government, although the government might have a moral obligation to respect its result. That said, the terms are often used interchangeably.

There is no serious argument that "direct democracy" measures like referendums are a substitute for representative democracy but such measures can serve as an important and even necessary complement. The use of referendum mechanisms varies widely among democratic states, the most extensive use being made by countries like Switzerland (Fossedal, 2002).

National referendums have been used in Canada on prohibition (1898), conscription (1942), and the Charlottetown Accord (1992). Referendums have been used more often at the provincial level: in the 1990s alone, there were referendums in Quebec (1995 on sovereignty), Newfoundland (1995 and 1997 on denominational schools), Saskatchewan (1991 on public funding for abortion, balanced budget legislation, and constitutional amendments), British Columbia (1991 on direct democracy), Northwest Territories (1992 on division of the territory), and Nunavut (1997 on the composition of the new legislature) (Mendelsohn and Parkin, 2001: 3). On May 17, 2005, British Columbia held a binding referendum asking citizens if the province should adopt the single-transferable-vote (STV) electoral system. The measure received majority support in at least 48 of 79 electoral districts but only 57.69% of total valid ballots were cast in favour, short of the 60% threshold (Elections BC, 2005: 9). Prince Edward Island held a plebiscite November 28, 2005 asking if the province ought to adopt a mixed-member-proportional system. That measure did not meet either of its thresholds; in only two districts did the measure receive majority support and, province-wide, only 36.42% of ballots were cast in favour (Elections PEI, 2005).

The principal benefit of properly run referendums is the opportunity they provide for citizens to participate directly in policy decisions. This is particularly true if referendum campaigns are accompanied by adequately funded educational campaigns on all sides of the issue, so that the public is thoroughly informed and engaged in the process before casting their ballots.

A criticism raised against referendums is that they invite a "tyranny of the majority." While constitutional guarantees of minority rights reduce this risk, it nevertheless exists. Consequently protection of minority interests must be an important consideration in the undertaking of any referendum. Experience has shown, however, that properly framed approaches need not exclude minority interests (Mendelsohn and Parkin, 2001: 6). The cost and timing of referendums can sometimes be deterrents. British Columbia met this challenge by holding its referendum on electoral reform at the same time as a provincial election.

6   CITIZENS' INITIATIVES AND RECALL

Referendums and deliberative bodies like the B.C. Citizens' Assembly rely on the government's initiative. Citizens' initiatives allow the people to lead. Various jurisdictions employ one or more of three general types of these mechanisms: "direct" initiatives, whose binding force bypasses legislatures; "indirect" initiatives, which include a role for legislatures; and "recall" initiatives, which allow citizens to dismiss a previously elected representative. A principal criticism of top-down referendums is that governments employ them only when they are relatively certain of the outcome. Initiatives in the forms described below provide a counter-balance, allowing citizens themselves to effect legislative change.

There is reason for concern that citizens' initiatives might become frivolous and expensive exercises, manipulated by partisan or special interests to advance a specific agenda with little or no public support. Likewise, there is concern that initiatives, like referendums, may become tools used by the majority to over-ride the interests of the minority. These risks are real. Avoiding them requires careful consideration of how initiatives are approved for wider public consideration, how their financing is regulated, and what threshold levels for adoption are appropriate.

Principal variants of citizens' initiatives

Direct initiatives

Direct initiatives allow citizens who can muster sufficient support for a proposition to give it legal effect without the consent of the legislature. Typically, if enough signatures are collected on a petition in the allotted time, the proposed measure is placed before the electorate through a referendum. If enough voters approve the measure, it becomes law. California uses such a system, though it has sometimes proved troublesome. Even though established political parties are usually not involved in the process, it tends to be dominated by advocacy groups and professional associations. Furthermore, legislation passed by initiative in California requires another initiative to be amended. While this protects the direct wishes of the electorate, in practice most legislation requires some amendment over time and the requirement for a further referendum becomes unwieldy (Mendelsohn and Parkin, 2001: 10; Piott, 2003).

Indirect initiatives

Indirect citizens' initiatives involve the legislature. Its role is usually to frame the proposal or draft and pass any statute that may result from the people's vote. In British Columbia, for example, the Recall and Initiative Act (R.S.B.C. 1996, c. 398, <www.qp.gov.bc.ca/statreg/stat/R/96398_00.htm>) allows any registered voter to ask the Chief Electoral Officer to issue a petition on a legislative proposal. The proposal may cover any area within the jurisdiction of the provincial legislature. If the Chief Electoral Officer approves the request, the applicant has 90 days to collect signatures from at least 10% of the electorate in each electoral district. If that is accomplished, the petition and a draft bill are submitted to the Select Standing Committee of the legislature, which has 90 days either to recommend the bill's consideration by the legislature or to refer it back to the Chief Electoral Officer for a vote by the public at large. To be approved, more than 50% of registered voters must favour the measure, along with a majority in at least two thirds of the electoral districts in the province. If the threshold is met, the Government is required to introduce the bill at the earliest possible opportunity. Readings or amendments proceed as with any other bill and there is no guarantee the measure will be passed (Elections BC, 2002: 4–5). That said, there is a certain moral and political obligation on elected representatives to respect the wishes of the electorate.

In Saskatchewan, the Referendum and Plebiscite Act (S.S. 1990–91, c. R-8.01, <www.canlii.org/sk/laws/sta/r8.01/20051216/whole.html>) requires a plebiscite under certain conditions. If a petition respecting a matter under provincial jurisdiction is submitted to the Minister of Justice bearing the signatures of at least 15% of Saskatchewan's electors, the Minister is required to initiate a plebiscite (Saskatchewan Justice, 2005). While not legally binding on the government, there is a moral and political obligation to act if the plebiscite is approved.

Recall initiatives

"Recall" refers to a mechanism that allows voters to dismiss—or "recall"— an elected official for cause. Recall measures are generally grouped among citizens' initiatives because they require citizens to collect signatures in support of a petition. They may also trigger a new election. In Canada, a strong populist movement after the First World War sought recall mechanisms for Members of Parliament. Many constituency associations of the Progressive Party responded by requiring their candidates elected in 1921 to prepare undated resignation letters, so that constituents could later force their removal by dating and publishing the letters. The practice was later prohibited by the Dominion Elections Act. The Social Credit Party came to power in Alberta in 1935 and the next year passed the Alberta Recall Act. Liberal opponents of the government promptly initiated a recall petition against Premier William Aberhart. The Recall Act was repealed in 1937 and the petition against the Premier was not completed (Lortie, 1991: vol. 2, 243–44).

More recently, British Columbia has taken up the recall mechanism. No member of the Legislative Assembly can be recalled for 18 months following their election. But after that period, any registered voter can apply for a petition to recall their representative. The application must include a 200-word statement indicating why, in the opinion of the applicant, the member ought to be recalled. If the application is approved, the proponent has 60 days to collect signatures from at least 40% of voters registered in the particular electoral district in the last election. If that is accomplished (and the proponent has complied with financial regulations), the member is removed. A by-election must be called within 90 days to replace the recalled member, who is permitted to run again (Elections BC, 2003: 4).

7 "THIRD PARTY" ADVOCACY AND ELECTORAL FINANCING

There are many "third parties" in the Canadian public conversation. The term refers to any person or group other than a registered political party or candidate. "Third parties" include professional and trade associations, charitable groups, public-policy organizations, and interest groups of every persuasion. Under existing law, the broad collection of viewpoints these groups represent is severely restricted in expression, especially at election time.

"Issue campaigns" seek to bring a subject forward on the political agenda. They typically muster public support for some particular policy proposal, creating pressure on political parties and elected representatives to respond by adopting it. As political parties have withdrawn from issue campaigns, this tool has become more available to third parties.

Efforts to restrict free expression by third parties have a long history in Canada. The 1966 Barbeau Committee on Election Expenses first recommended that candidates' spending on print and broadcast media be limited. The committee also observed that such limits could be circumvented by third parties, spending on behalf of a specific candidate. The 1971 Chappell Committee on Election Expenses recommended both political parties and candidates be subject to spending limits during elections. The 1974 Election Expenses Act, therefore, prohibited anyone but candidates and political parties from incurring election expenses. There was, however, an exception: it permitted third parties to incur expenses to advance issues of public policy. The Liberal government of the day removed this exception in 1983 but the courts restored it. As a result, no limits applied to third-party spending during the 1984 and 1988 federal elections (Harper v. Canada (A.G.), 2001 ABQB 558, <www.alberta-courts.ab.ca/jdb/19982003/qb/Civil/2001/2001abqb0558.pdf>).

After the 1988 election, the Royal Commission on Electoral Reform and Party Financing (the Lortie Commission) reviewed this subject once again. In its final report, the Commission argued that spending limits on candidates, registered parties, and third parties were necessary to guarantee some measure of fairness between those with access to significant financial resources and those without (Lortie, 1991: vol. 1, 339–40). The Commission further recommended that third parties be limited to $1,000 in partisan election expenses. The number was chosen because it was more than the average individual contribution and would allow any individual or group to engage in significant political activity (Lortie, 1991: vol. 1, 352–53). Reflecting Lortie's recommendations, the Elections Act was amended to limit third-party election expenditure to $1,000, ban it outright as polling day approached, and prohibit third parties from pooling resources to defeat these constraints. Again, the courts overturned these limits.

Parliament next introduced Bill C-2, which became the new Canada Elections Act (2000, c. 9, <laws.justice.gc.ca/en/E2.01/14253.html>) in 2000. The new legislation limits third-party election advertising expenses to $168,900 during a general election and to not more than $3,378 in any given electoral district to promote or oppose a particular candidate or candidates, indexed for inflation. Third parties must also disclose their financial contributors for the period from six months before the writ is dropped through to election day (Elections Canada, 2004). The current law has twice been struck down by Alberta courts but was upheld by the Supreme Court in 2004 in the decision Harper v. Canada (2004, <www.lexum.umontreal.ca/cscscc/en/pub/2004/vol1/html/2004scr1_0827.html>).

In a dissenting opinion, however, Chief Justice Beverley McLachlin, Mr. Justice John Major, and Mr. Justice Ian Binnie argued that the law set spending limits so low that third parties were unable to communicate effectively on election issues during an election campaign. Their dissent noted that the Chief Electoral Officer had testified that to run a full-page advertisement in major Canadian newspapers on a single occasion would cost $425,000—in excess of the national limit. The Canada Post bulk mailing rate for a single mail-out, roughly $7,500 in some electoral districts, likewise exceeded the local spending limit. The national spending cap further diminishes the local one, being set at a level that precludes spending to the local limit in all 308 electoral districts.

Federal law further restricts charitable organizations. Political activities are permitted, including public calls to political action, or communications urging government to adopt, change, or retain any policy or law. But the Canada Revenue Agency allows a charitable organization to devote no more than 10% of its resources in any year to such "political" activities (Canada Revenue Agency, 2003).

It is important to prevent abuses of third-party advocacy. At the same time, freedoms of speech and association are of central importance to a functioning, responsive democracy. That would seem to argue strongly for rules that encourage, rather than restrict, participation by third-party interest groups and advocates.

8 THE COURT CHALLENGES PROGRAM

In *Rebalanced and Revitalized: A Canada Strong and Free* we recommended changes to the Court Challenges Program. The program did not create interest-group litigation. Business interests and francophone, women's, and religious groups had all brought issues to Canadian courts before. Government support has instead equipped many small or marginalized groups for long court cases. Over the years, the Court Challenges Program nourished a network of such interest groups. These came together in 1992 to thwart an attempt to cancel the program altogether (Brodie, 2001: 358). The most recent iteration of the Court Challenges Program was established in 1994. It provided financial assistance to advance language and equality rights through court cases. In the decade afterwards, the program committed almost $19 million, funded by Heritage Canada, to support litigation (Court Challenges Program of Canada, 2005: 19).

The principal benefit of the Court Challenges Program was in defraying the costs of court action by groups or citizens seeking the protection of the Constitution and the Charter of Rights and Freedoms. Such support is not inherently troublesome. But when government intervenes on behalf of a social interest against some government interest, it incurs a conflict. By supporting both sides in such cases, government exhibits what Professor Ian Brodie describes as the embedded state at war with itself in court (Brodie, 2001: 376). In addition to the problem of conflicted interest, there is also the danger that the Court Challenges Program becomes a tool to advance government policy through proxy cases in the courts rather than a bulwark for the rights of under-resourced plaintiffs. Because of these problems, the current government has cancelled the programme.

9 FREER VOTING IN PARLIAMENT AND LEGISLATURES

Convention in the name of party "discipline" demands strict obedience among backbenchers in Canada's Parliament. Governments tend to interpret the defeat of any measure they introduce, or the passage of any substantive opposition measure, as a loss of Parliament's confidence. This interpretation is used to coerce government members into supporting measures they may disagree with, lest their vote topple the government of which they are a part. Other factors also contribute to what has been called, derisively, the "trained-seal" effect. Though specifics vary, Canadian political parties choose their leaders in party-wide procedures; while their parliamentary caucus is important, the leader ultimately does not answer to it, but to party members. Further, the "perks" of a government MP's life—committee chairmanships, parliamentary secretary appointments, and cabinet positions—are in the hands of the leader, who may use them to reward loyalty and punish dissent. Likewise, the Prime Minister and Cabinet have little incentive to emancipate the back benches. They wish to advance their parliamentary agenda and protect the interests of their ministries. A compliant House facilitates both objectives.

It is difficult to shake off the shackles of party affiliation. First, it is tough to get elected as an independent. Even such a high-profile candidate as John Nunziata was unable to get re-elected after his expulsion from the Liberal caucus for criticizing the government's failure to rescind the GST as it had promised. Rare exceptions include the late Chuck Cadman, who was an incumbent when he ran as an independent, and Quebec radio personality, André Arthur. Second, once elected, independents do not enjoy the parliamentary resources or procedural prerogatives available to party members. As a result, they find it difficult, not to say impossible, to pursue an independent parliamentary agenda effectively.

In provinces where one party consistently wins strong majorities, some efforts have been made to engage back-bench members' participation through caucus. In Alberta, for instance, every bill is reviewed by caucus; as many as one in four get sent back to ministers for revision. Once caucus deliberations conclude, however, all are expected to support the government in the legislature. This practice effectively relocates the debate, deliberation, and compromise of the legislative function to caucus, reducing debate in the legislative assembly to a mere formality—and sharply diminishing the role of the vestigial Opposition (Dobell, 2003: 93).

These coercive tensions would be lessened, the effectiveness of Parliament and legislatures improved, and a better balance achieved between the front and back benches, by a more limited interpretation of non-confidence. The Conservative Party of Canada promised in the federal election of January, 2006 to make nearly all votes free votes for back-benchers, conferring "confidence" status only on measures such as the budget and main estimates (Conservative Party of Canada, 2006: 44). Another practice worth considering for Canada is that used by the British House of Commons. There, the government employs a symbolic signalling system to designate the significance it attaches to votes. In addition to free votes, three levels of "whipping" signal whether the confidence of the government is at stake (a three-line whip) or the vote is of a lower grade that will not necessarily trigger the government's defeat (two- and one-line whips) (Dobell, 2003: 90).

The principal benefit of freer voting in Parliament and legislatures would be to empower individual members to represent their constituents' wishes and their own consciences more effectively. This has the further benefit of strengthening Parliament's representative function, and restoring the importance of debate and persuasion in the House and its committees.

10   RESPONSIBLE GOVERNMENT FOR ABORIGINALS

In Canadian law, convention, and public opinion, there is a general consensus that aboriginal peoples are entitled to some form of self-government. There is at least as broad a consensus that the mechanisms put in place to realize that right have seldom worked well. From early encounters on, colonial powers recognized aboriginals as self-governing. The principle was enshrined, rather than surrendered, in treaties negotiated with aboriginal representatives and in the Royal Proclamation of 1763. The Canadian Constitution protects an aboriginal right to self-government and international law further entitles aboriginal peoples to self-government within existing states (Indian and Northern Affairs Canada, 2004). What form this right should best take, however, and how it should relate to other orders of government, remain uncertain.

Jean Allard, a long-time Métis activist, has criticized the current reserve system for its lack of accountability and balance (Allard, 2002). He argues that an elite exercise complete control on most reserves, ruling over a voiceless and impoverished underclass. This system has emerged while federal spending for aboriginals has grown from $262 million in 1969 to more than $6.3 billion in 1999 (Owens, 2002). Historically, responsible government proved elusive until people elected a legislature that derived its revenues from the people it represented and controlled its own expenditures. "No taxation without representation" may have been the watchword of the American Revolution but the reverse is also true: there can be no accountable representation without taxation. When a legislative body collects money, it is obliged to be responsible to those from whom it collects, namely the electors. In the current structure, however, federal transfers flow directly to aboriginal governments, bypassing their constituents and severing this critical link.

Allard has proposed the radical idea that aboriginal spending be redirected from reserve and band executives directly into the hands of individuals (Owens, 2002). This would require amending numerous well-established arrangements to allow aboriginals to receive their share of treaty money or land-claims settlements directly. Coordinated amendments would be necessary to permit aboriginal governments to tax their constituents, restoring a link that compels a certain level of accountability (Owens, 2000).

Efforts to develop a democratic model for aboriginal self-government and "get it right" have not, to date, been crowned with success. While a dramatic departure, Allard's proposal, along with other reforms to increase accountability and responsibility in aboriginal government, deserve serious consideration. For further elaboration of this important subject, see Monograph 6, "Aboriginal Governance: When All Else Fails, Try a Little Freedom" (page 217).

11 REFORM OF PARTY FINANCING AND PROCESSES

Money is as necessary to politics as air is to life. Since the birth of democracy, however, it has also been the root of scandal, undue influence, and—as disclosures in both Canada and the United States have recently driven home—temptations to criminal conduct. Canada has wrestled with this dilemma for several decades but defects, gaps, and unintended consequences from policy persist.

Canada recently overhauled the rules that govern political financing (An Act to Amend the Canada Elections Act and the Income Tax Act (political financing), 2002 [Can]). New regulations came into force on January 1, 2004, that limited individual political contributions to $5,000 per year to each registered party and its affiliated entities, including nomination contests; $5,000 per leadership contest for a registered party, in aggregate to all candidates; and $5,000 per election to a candidate with no party affiliation. Corporations, trade unions, and unincorporated associations are limited to $1,000 to each registered political party and its affiliated entities, as well as $1,000 per election to candidates with no party affiliation. (These caps were indexed to inflation and have since been raised.) The new rules raised the amount registered political parties are allowed to spend in a campaign (from $0.62 to $0.70 per voter) but included the cost of election surveys and research in the definition of "election expenses." Spending limits were extended to nomination campaigns, at 20% of the spending limit in the most recent election for the electoral district at stake.

The Federal Accountability Act has again lowered the limits on contributions. Effective January 2007, contributions by corporations, unions, and organizations are banned; the annual limit an individual can contribute to a particular registered party is now $1,000; and there is a different $1,000 annual limit on contributions to local entities of a particular registered party including candidates, nomination contestants, and district associations. All limits are indexed to inflation, and have already been raised accordingly (<http://www.faa-lfi.gc.ca/fs-fi/16/01fs-fi_e.asp>; <http://www.elections.ca/content.asp?section=gen&document=ec90557&dir=bkg&lang=e&textonly=false>).

The reach of mandatory disclosure of political contributors was extended in the 2002 reforms. Reporting requirements now capture all registered electoral-district associations, as well as leadership and nomination contestants. Leadership campaigns must submit weekly reports of contributions for the last four weeks of the contest. Nomination campaigns are required to submit a financial report if they collect more than $1,000 in contributions or spend more than that on expenses. The current government has also recently introduced Bill C-54, An Act to amend the Canada Elections Act (accountability with respect to loans), to eliminate a campaign-loans loophole, banning loans from unions, associations, or corporations, while limiting total individual loans, loan guarantees, and donations to the contribution limits set by the Federal Accountability Act. The Bill has not yet passed.

The most significant changes, however, affect the public funding of registered political parties. Parties that received at least 2% of the national vote in the last election (or 5% in ridings where they fielded candidates) are now eligible to receive an allowance, paid quarterly, of $1.75 per year for each of those valid votes. The amount is again indexed to inflation and has already been raised (Elections Canada, 2003). The immediate effect of these changes has been to increase the total funds available to parties, despite the extraordinarily low contribution limits on corporations and trade unions. The total amount awarded from the public purse to all parties in 2004, excluding election expenses, was roughly $22 million, more than double the $10 million the parties expected to lose to the new contribution limits (Sayers and Young, 2004: 2).

These reforms have clearly been to the benefit of party bank accounts. And with the Federal Accountability Act, all corporate and union contributions have been removed from the political process. But they have also severed an important link between political parties and the electorate. When a party is able to, indeed must, collect donations from a large number of people, its success or lack thereof reflects the strength of its organization and policy appeal. Parties have an incentive to appeal to the broadest possible group of voters and donors. A party out of favour with the general public will have thin support and be forced to reorganize or re-evaluate its positions. No longer is this the case in Canada. Rather, a party's financial fortunes are now based on past performance; its current appeal carries no financial consequences.

Parties should be encouraged to build broad coalitions, engaging as many people as possible, rather than to represent narrow interests. Reduced public financing, in conjunction with other reforms, could encourage small contributions from large numbers of donors rather than either large donations from small numbers of wealthy contributors or, just as worrisome, an unconditional allowance from a single donor—government.

Party nomination and leadership contests are now subject to contribution limits and reporting requirements. But consideration must be given to other aspects of these contests. The controversy surrounding recent nomination battles involving such prominent politicians as Sheila Copps, Michael Ignatieff, and Chuck Cadman calls into question the credibility of these processes. Top-down political influences have appeared to compromise democratic due process. It is worth considering whether Elections Canada should take an interest in the administration of nomination and leadership contests, or whether registered parties should be required to subordinate their internal processes to legally enforceable standards.

12 DEVELOPMENT OF POLITICAL INFRASTRUCTURE

Political parties—maligned as they often are—play a vital role in the organization and performance of our democratic system. When political parties decline in capability and public respect, democracy itself suffers. It has been argued by one of the authors that a principal reason for the decline in the effectiveness of, and respect for, political parties in Canada is the lack of adequate "democratic infrastructure" below the party level (Manning, 2005). He had in mind in particular the lack of numerous, well-funded, substantive think-tanks and strong links to academia to generate ideas in a host of public-policy areas but the term also embraces other deficits.

Linkages with activists to carry those ideas forward into the political arena are fragmentary. "Political investors" willing to make significant contributions to the democratic process itself rather than simply to support an election campaign are scarce. Practical political education and training for the "human capital" of democracy—everyone from poll captains to constituency executives to candidates to political aides to cabinet ministers—are woefully deficient. Channels of political communication, from political publishing houses to credible journals of different political stripes to substantial web-sites, are few. So too are large forums, conventions, or trade shows that bring together partisan participants in the political process from across this vast country for broader and less contentious purposes than those served by party conventions.

Canadian political parties and their supporters need to pay greater attention to the development of this democratic infrastructure—organizations and programs that generate and re-generate the intellectual, financial, and human capital of politics and policy. It is essential to the renewal and continued vitality of the democratic process.

CONCLUSIONS: BUILDING A BETTER DEMOCRACY

Democracy places the citizen first; this is its value. But too often, in the face of government bureaucracies and institutional imperatives, the interests of the citizen are secondary. The purpose of democratic reform is to restore the balance, to give citizens effective tools for participation and clear reasons for confidence in the democratic process. That goal demands that Canadians of every age and region, interest and background, be fully aware of the nature and implications of any proposed reforms. They must be fully consulted, informed, and engaged in the debate over "pros" and "cons" of the available choices. Most importantly, the choice must be theirs. Canadian democracy is no pet project of political activists or policy elites. It belongs to the people.

The preceding pages have presented a menu of proposed reforms of democratic processes and institutions. Each one—from electoral reform to citizens' initiatives to party financing reform—deserves consideration. We commend them all to our readers' attention. For our own part, however, we are persuaded that some items on the menu deserve to be made Canadians' highest priority. These will, we believe, have the greatest impact in encouraging Canadians to take their freedoms seriously, engage their governments and demand responses, and make their voices heard effectively in every decision that affects their interests.

RECOMMENDATIONS

To advance democratic reform in Canada, therefore, we urge the following.

11.1 Encourage citizens, interest groups, and political parties interested in democratic reform to review, debate, and decide on those reforms most deserving of their support from a menu of democratic reforms which includes: civic education, citizens' assemblies, fixed election dates, reform of the electoral system, referendums, citizens' initiatives and recall, "third party" advocacy and electoral financing, the court challenges program, freer voting in Parliament and legislatures, responsible government for aboriginals, reform of party financing and processes, development of political infrastructure.

11.2   Strengthen non-partisan and non-ideological civic education in Canada (menu item # 1).

11.3   Call together Citizens' Assemblies to consider other reform options, investing in referendums supported by educational campaigns to let informed voters decide whether or not a particular reform should be adopted (menu items 2 and 5).

11.4   Implement freer voting in legislatures and in Parliament, particularly on measures directed at advancing democratic processes and institutions (menu item 9).

ABORIGINAL GOVERNANCE: WHEN ALL ELSE FAILS, TRY A LITTLE FREEDOM

Everyone agrees: the estate of aboriginal peoples in Canada is unacceptable. Why does so little seem to happen? The indicators are well known: poor health, poverty, suicide, substance abuse, welfare dependency, and so on. All of these measures tie back to economic development. There is simply no doubt that prosperous, employed populations are healthier and happier than poor, unemployed ones. Everyone agrees with that too and still nothing happens.

A PARALLEL REALITY

The conventional wisdom is that this question should be met by the elaboration of a parallel society for aboriginals, as recommended by the Royal Commission on Aboriginal Peoples (1996), a policy given support by the actions and words of most national aboriginal leaders and the federal and provincial governments. This parallel society (and a "Third Order of Government") is to reflect and preserve traditional values, and provide for the economic development of Aboriginal people. A central feature of those traditional values is said to be collectivism, to a significant degree rejecting private ownership and the market economy. Historical evidence, however, does not support the myth that pre-contact aboriginal societies were inherently collectivist. The property arrangements of the time varied according to the economics of each band. Hunter-gatherer groupings obviously had customs different from those of agricultural tribes. But all respected property in their own way (Anderson et al., 2006).

As a first observation on whether collectivism has worked for Canada's aboriginals, it is notable that individuals who have opted out of the Reserve system and "gone to town," joining the market economy, do significantly better in indicators of health, education, and employment than their peers who stayed on the Reserve.[1] This applies to roughly half of all status Indians. The urban outcomes are still not good enough but they are much better than they were—and improving. This shows that aboriginals can do well in the mainstream world, as anyone who believes in equality would expect. This is not by itself proof that the "parallel society" idea is flawed, but there is other evidence.

Under the direction pointed by the Assembly of First Nations, government policy, and such formal constitutional documents as the Nisga'a Treaty, the parallel-society model looks forward to a number of self-governing aboriginal nations based on self-sufficiency, democratic

---

1   For example, on-reserve median incomes are about 42% of the mainstream while off-reserve attain 72% (Richards, 2006).

governance, and collective ownership. The "self-sufficiency" usually presumes extended, major subsidy, but the following discussion will focus more on governance and ownership.

THE "MARKET" IN GOVERNANCE

Governments have their own "markets" for discipline. The American Revolution was based in part on the memorable slogan, "No taxation without representation!" Canadian scholar Tom Flanagan has described the logical corollary, which is "no effective representation without taxation" (Flanagan, 2000). In other words, as long as a government is perceived to be using "other people's money," the voters care much less about the efficiency of the spending. The fact that band councils receive the vast majority of their revenues from a source (the federal government) other than the people of their own community, itself profoundly limits accountability. Band members have no effective mechanism to enforce accountability since they cannot cut off the flow of funds. Control of the money by an elite will appear to have legitimacy since the funds are transferred to bodies the elite runs. If the elite were forced to rely on contributions from band members, members would be considerably more motivated and have considerably greater ability to insist on accountability.[2]

Where the "other people's money" comes from the outside, the point is obvious. But the saying is equally true when the resources employed by a government are owned in common rather than privately. People just care less. That is one of the main lessons of the huge, real-world twentieth-century experiment with collective ownership and governance, then generally known as "communism." The consequences are not merely economic. The fact is, when a government owns the wealth and means of production, it also has the means of controlling the voters. This is dangerous for democracy. Private property is central not merely to wealth, but to freedom.

Setting aside the Canadian scene for a moment, it is instructive to look at the research of Stephen Cornell and Joseph Kalt in the "Harvard Project."[3] This long-running look at Indians in the United States, where arrangements vary much more from one tribe to another than is the case in Canada, amounts to a "natural experiment" not available here. One unambiguous conclusion was that tribes that rigorously insulated administration from politics were the most successful. This requires a distinct administrative structure with hiring, firing, and other management decisions undertaken according to normal professional standards, shielded from political interference. Our "parallel society" model makes little provision for this. Typically the opposite is true: politicians are in charge of administration. That this results in bad outcomes is not surprising. Quite independently of culture around the world, when governments run everything, as they do in collective societies, the "ins" and their friends do better than the "outs."

MISSING PIECES

We know from an overwhelming quantity of research and experience, summarized in this series and available everywhere, that free markets are absolutely essential to prosperous economies. Voluntary transactions, within a competitive and transparent market framework

---

2 The same lack of accountability occurs in the Atlantic Provinces, where much government expenditure is paid for by money raised in other parts of the country (McMahon, 2000b).

3 For a summary, see <www.ksg.harvard.edu/hpaided/overview>.

ruled by law, lead to the best economic outcomes. For individuals to engage in voluntary transactions of course, they must have private property. Under our current views of a parallel aboriginal society, this is not the case. Even private homes are not privately owned on many reserves and the land underneath is never privately owned, though it may be occupied under a "Certificate of Possession," which is a much lesser estate than fee simple. And for individuals to engage in enterprise, they must have available both risk and reward. Our current law, and any contemplated, makes it impossible for aboriginals to pledge what is currently their main asset, namely land, or even many moveable assets that are situated on reserve.

Of course, there are many obstacles preventing individual aboriginals from entering the mainstream economy and prospering. These include both real and potential prejudice from the mainstream community and resentment, which may take violent form, from the aboriginal community. Yet, many have entered the mainstream economy and done well. It is difficult to do this from a non-urban Reserve, however. And Reserve life itself, with what amounts to a guaranteed annual income and benefits, is often a competing and easier alternative. This is an ongoing recipe for the status quo.

OFFERING CHOICE

The combination of Chiefs and Councils and politically correct federal governments is tough for individuals to overcome. And it can be argued that the public has a duty to honour century-old contracts with those aboriginals who wish that. But we have a greater duty to afford individual choice and to respect the individual rights of aboriginals, even if the elites wish to limit them. "Choice" is the key word. No one should be forced. Rather we should do all we can to widen choices. First and foremost, that means education. Of course, people have been saying that for years. Some progress has been made but it remains an area of shocking underperformance. This is especially so in Reserve schools and will continue to be so until Bands and provincial governments allow scholastic measurement of aboriginal children.[4] There are few better illustrations, in the negative, of the Fraser Institute's credo, "If it matters, measure it."

Even more importantly, to give real meaning to performance measurements and individual choice, parents should be issued with education vouchers for their children, useable in any provincial school district and with whatever necessary additional assistance might be required for transportation and so on. Charter schools should also be permitted to provide further choice specifically tailored to the needs of reserve children. This is the application of "markets" to education, and it works.

Legislative and financial provisions should be changed to make genuine home ownership much easier for aboriginal families on Reserve. Progress is being made in this direction. It should be applauded and accelerated.

THE POWER OF THE WALLET

Far more controversial, because far more disruptive, is the idea of redirecting most of the money the federal government currently spends on aboriginals from a collective grab-bag delivered to the control of band elites, into private individual entitlements. Consideration

---

4   This is perfectly feasible, and already done by British Columbia; see Cowley and Easton, 2004, 2006.

should be given to sending a large portion of the over $5 billion per annum now sent to Chiefs and Councils for governmental purposes instead directly to Band members (the school voucher is one way to do this), with the Councils free to tax some of that money back if their voters will allow that. That policy will give life to "representation with taxation," and end the "other people's money" syndrome (see, for example, Allard, 2002).

CONCLUSION

The general proposition is clear. Markets amount to choice. By virtue of our laws and financial schemes, the choices available to aboriginals have been restricted or (more often) seriously distorted in favour of collective and non-market activity since the Indian Act of 1876. If the collective, non-market approach continues to be chosen by many, that in itself is a market decision. But the choice should be available. The Tools of Wealth Creation (TWC)—property rights, access to capital, and human capital development—are applicable in aboriginal policy. The TWC are typically available to the vast majority of the population in developed nations but are lacking among the poor in developing ones. Sadly, our reserve-based aboriginal population often lacks them as well. We noted above that full property rights are often absent on reserves. This limits access to capital, since aboriginals are unable to borrow against property. The state of education (human capital) on reserves is also very low. Our recommendations below are meant to redress these disadvantages.

The record of non-aboriginal "solutions" to the "Indian problem" that have been imposed on resistant beneficiaries leading to disastrous consequences is highly cautionary. We also need to acknowledge that one solution will not fit all situations. A commonsense way to proceed with reforms is to allow bands voluntarily to accept or decline a reform package, or individual elements of it. The impact of the reforms should also be reviewed on a regular basis; success will encourage other bands to join. While no band ought to be obliged to give up existing arrangements, it may in some cases be appropriate to insist that referendums be held, to allow band members to determine in a free vote whether their reserve adopts reforms.

RECOMMENDATIONS

* Separate administration of program funds from their political structure in aboriginal bands.

* Give parents and students a choice in education, provided through school vouchers and a legal framework supportive to the establishment of charter schools.

* Encourage private property ownership on reserves; in particular, home ownership should be ceded to individuals and families.

* Send to individuals and families the $5 billion now sent by government to chiefs and councils, with a concurrent provision to allow bands to tax back some of this money to fund their activities.

CHAPTER 12

REBALANCING THE FEDERATION

"OTTAWA VERSUS THE PROVINCES"

Democracy is a balancing act. It seeks to reconcile a myriad of competing views, perspectives, and ideas. It demands a dynamic balance between loyalty and dissent, competition and consensus, citizens and the machinery of government. Over time, every complex system tends to run out of adjustment, to lose its balance; and government is the most complex human system we know. Well into its second century, Canada's democracy has run seriously out of balance in several respects. Some of these, we believe, are critical.

Chapters 10 and 11 addressed a profound and fundamental imbalance that has developed between the institutions of government and Canada's citizens, and suggested both immediate and long-term counter-measures. But once the most pressing defects in the balance of citizen-government relations are addressed, and while we are still weighing our longer-term options for reform, an equally threatening imbalance in the federal structure demands our attention. It is the yawning mismatch between the responsibilities and resources of the federal and provincial governments. Rivalry between the two orders of government may be as old as the federation but the present imbalance is one Canadians can ill afford. We offer several observations and recommendations aimed at "rebalancing" the federation.

Fix the federal-provincial imbalance and Canada will be in a position to fix much else. Relieved of unproductive tensions generated by federal intrusions into their areas of jurisdiction, and sustained by tax-points conceded by Ottawa, provinces would be freed to innovate and respond more directly to their citizens' priorities. The pay offs are likely to be most dramatic in the areas of social services, where there is exclusive provincial jurisdiction. We shall argue that the benefits of democratic "rebalancing," with the emphasis placed on pushing the locus of choice down ever closer to the citizen, will soon commend the same philosophy to other arenas.

That said, serious imbalances remain within the central federal structure itself. One of these is of long standing: the impaired legitimacy of the appointed Senate as a house of regional representation. Another is of more recent currency: the so-called "activist" jurists and legislation "enacted from the bench." We see, however, that these concerns are rooted in a deeper malaise: the dwindling of the legislative function of government against the other two legs of the classic triad of constitutional democracy, the executive and the judiciary. In the concluding section of this chapter, we examine in detail how this relationship has fallen out of alignment and how it can be restored.

We urge efforts to rebalance the Canadian federation not for theoretical or ideological reasons. We do so because we believe that to do so opens the door to a democratic evolution that will expand Canadians' freedom of choice and embrace of responsibility, that will enrich the quality of our lives, boost our productivity and prosperity, and increase Canada's capacity for international leadership.

BACK TO THE CONSTITUTION: REBALANCING FEDERAL AND PROVINCIAL CAPACITY

The most serious imbalance affecting the performance of Canada's governments—both federal and provincial—has been created through continued federal intrusion into areas of social service such as health care, which our Constitution clearly assigns to the provinces. For decades, the federal government has intruded into these areas of provincial responsibility through the arbitrary exercise of the federal spending power. This violates the spirit of the Constitution. More materially, it creates needless strains in federal-provincial relations. It runs counter to the principle that essential social services are best delivered by the government closest to those served. By dividing responsibility for the consequences of social policy, it diminishes Canadians' ability to hold any one level of government accountable when policies fail.

Stronger provincial governments

The first step in rebalancing Canadian federalism should be, therefore, a devolution of power, responsibility, and revenue capacity from the federal government to the provinces in areas that the Constitution clearly and proper assigns to provinces. Provinces, in turn, should take the opportunity to consider a rebalancing and devolution of some provincial capacity to municipal authorities.

We urge this rebalancing primarily for its immediate effect on the improvement of government performance in Canada. But there are other good reasons to respect Canada's constitutional division of powers. Firstly, it is the Constitution, the foundational law on which all other statutes rest. The federal government should not be free to amend it *de facto* through the power to spend the taxpayer's money. That it has done so has played an important role in creating Canada's democratic deficit. People in provinces that voted strongly against the party in power in Ottawa found that the federal government, with little or no democratic representation from their province, would impose its unwanted policies in areas that the Constitution said were the province's to decide. The practice in effect disenfranchises provincial voters in areas of great significance to them—health and social services.

But perhaps the most powerful argument for rebalancing the Canadian federation is that it works. In first part of this volume, "Caring for Canadians: Quality of Life," we showed that policy success relates negatively to federal intrusion into areas of provincial responsibility. Where provinces are masters of their constitutional house, Canada outperforms most other nations. Where the federal government intrudes on areas the Constitution wisely placed in provincial jurisdiction, Canada has some of the worst policy results in the developed world. And when Ottawa reverses course and withdraws from provincial jurisdictions into which it once intruded, policy performance again picks up.

A stronger, more focused, national government

Thus far we have mainly discussed the need to rebalance the Canadian federation by devolving responsibility and funding capacity downward, to the levels of government closest to the people to be served. Some will argue that this will weaken the central government—reducing its importance and effectiveness, even weakening the ties that hold our federation together. "Not so," we reply. To us, "rebalancing the federation" also means strengthening the national government in key areas of its responsibility—areas where no one disputes the need for a strong federal government. Coincidentally, these are often areas where the performance of the federal government has been less than stellar in recent years.

Because its attention has been distracted from key federal duties, the federal Parliament should increase its focus on strengthening the performance of the national government with respect to

- Canada's foreign policy;
- its defence and military capability;
- the settlement of favourable external trade arrangements and the elimination of trade barriers within Canada;
- a sound currency and monetary policy;
- intellectual property law;
- the criminal law and provision for public safety;
- the discharge of federal responsibilities toward aboriginal peoples.

Note that we do not say there is no role whatsoever for the federal government in protecting Canadians' health, only that it is not to finance or prescribe the delivery of core services. Federal support for health care should focus on areas where it can do the most good without compromising provincial jurisdiction: support for health science and research, equalization payments to enable have-not provinces to meet national standards, the collection and dissemination of performance data on the health-care system, and coordination of a response to public-health hazards such as pandemics, which require a national response.

Unity in numbers: inter-provincial agreements to strengthen the federation

Some Canadians may worry that implementing our rebalancing proposals, particularly those that strengthen the provinces, must by definition weaken national unity. We reject that zero-sum formulation. In our view, the maintenance of national unity is not a monopoly of the federal government. Rather, it is a responsibility in which every Canadian, and every level of government, shares. Beyond that statement of principle, we envision an expanded role for the provinces and territories in strengthening the ties that bind our country together.

In the past, Canadians have relied heavily—excessively so—on the federal government to maintain Confederation's mortar. National initiatives like employment insurance, the Canada Pension Plan, equalization, regional development programs, government ownership of a radio and television network, and the Canada Health Act were all supposed to bind the nation more tightly together. To some extent, they have. But the arbitrary use of the federal spending power that accompanied many of these initiatives also provoked many of the dis-unifying tensions that afflict Confederation today, including chronic fiscal imbalances between the federal and provincial governments.

Other federal initiatives have been even more damaging to national unity. The Trudeau government's insistence that it, not the Quebec government, should be the guardian and promoter of the French language and culture in Canada, angered not only that province but also much of the rest of the country. The tactics employed by the same government to repatriate the Constitution so further alienated Quebec that its provincial government has still not officially accepted it. The National Energy Program, which arbitrarily transferred $100 billion in wealth from petroleum-producing provinces to the federal treasury and to consuming provinces, fanned the embers of Western alienation.

In more recent times, near-exclusive reliance on the federal government to preserve the federal union has had even more disastrous consequences. The top-down road to constitution-making taken by the Mulroney government's failed Meech and Charlottetown Accords set in train a reaction that prompted Quebec to hold a vote on rupturing Confederation's ties. The Chrétien government's subsequent mismanagement of the federalist side in the 1995 referendum campaign brought us to within 28,000 votes out of 4.67 million of a full-blown secession crisis. And then, when the chief symbol and voice for Confederation in Quebec—the federal government—became tainted with corruption exposed by the Auditor General and Mr. Justice Gomery's inquiry, support for separatism was once again dangerously re-energized.

Is there an alternative to relying so exclusively on Ottawa to keep the country together? Yes, there is! "Memorandums of Understanding" (MOUs) among the provinces and territories, initiated by premiers and territorial leaders, and facilitated by the recently formed Council of the Federation, have ample potential in this regard. Such "bridge-building" MOUs commit signatory provinces and territories to working together in concrete ways to pursue common goals—jointly required infrastructure perhaps, or shared trade interests. Such memorandums already exist among a number of the provinces and territories, covering everything from energy development to French language instruction (Table 12.1). But their use could profitably be deepened and expanded, particularly between Quebec and provinces like Ontario, New Brunswick, Newfoundland, and perhaps Alberta, with which it shares significant interests.

Canadians have relied too long on a single anchor—the federal government—to keep our federal ship secure during separatist gales. Mismanagement and corruption have, at least temporarily, dangerously weakened this anchor. But there are alternatives. New, flexible bonds woven among the provinces and territories—especially between Quebec and its immediate neighbours— may well hold us more securely than even a repaired federal anchor. We therefore believe that all provinces and territories, supported by the Council of the Federation, should make greater use of Memorandums of Understanding to pursue common objectives and interests. As well, we call for the negotiation of an increasing number of Trade Investment and Labour Mobility Agreements (TILMAs) among provinces.

Do provinces and territories need inspiration to put their energy into agreements to strengthen the cause of national unity? Let them look no further than the greatest such effort in our history: the forging of Confederation itself. When the idea of Canada was born in the nineteenth century, there was no federal government. The distant "Mother Parliament" in Britain was only mildly interested. It was the leaders of the disparate colonies, predecessors of today's provinces, who rose to the occasion and made history. They embraced the vision of a new nation commensurate in scale and spirit with the land that inspired it. And it was they who agreed upon practical designs for its implementation, proposals to create a national market, a federal constitution, and the longest railway in the world. If those earlier "provincial" statesmen could have such vision, what cannot their present-day successors do?

Table 12.1: Sample memorandums of understanding among provinces

Alberta and British Columbia

Memorandum of Understanding: Alberta/British Columbia Partnership on Child Welfare—October 8, 2003
(Alberta, International and Intergovernmental Relations, 2003, <www.iir.gov.ab.ca/canadian_intergovernmental_relations/pdfs/(4.2.1.5)%20AB-BC%20Child_Welfare_MOU.pdf>)

Alberta-British Columbia Memorandum of Understanding: Environmental Cooperation and Harmonization—May 26, 2004
(Alberta, International and Intergovernmental Relations, 2004, <www.iir.gov.ab.ca/canadian_intergovernmental_relations/documents/Environmental_Cooperation_MOU.pdf>)

British Columbia-Alberta Memorandum of Understanding: Bilateral Water Management Agreement Negotiations—March 18, 2005
(Alberta, International and Intergovernmental Relations, 2005, <www.iir.gov.ab.ca/canadian_intergovernmental_relations/documents/WaterManagementNegotiatingMOU_March22005_FINAL.pdf>)

Manitoba and New Brunswick

Manitoba and New Brunswick Sign Co-operation Agreement [news release]—January 23, 2003
(Manitoba, Information Services, 2002, <www.gov.mb.ca/chc/press/top/2002/01/2002-01-23-02.html>)

Northwest Territories and Alberta

Northwest Territories-Alberta Memorandum of Understanding for Cooperation and Development [in trade, transportation, tourism, and resource development]—October 17, 2003
(Northwest Territories, Department of Executive, 2003, <www.executive.gov.nt.ca/documents/AlbertaMOU-2003.pdf>)

Quebec and British Columbia*

Quebec and British Columbia Sign Agreement on Francophone Affairs [news release]—November 23, 2005
(British Columbia, Ministry of State for Intergovernmental Relations, 2005, <www2.news.gov.bc.ca/news_releases_2005-2009/2005OTP0135-001080.htm>)

Nova Scotia, Newfoundland, New Brunswick, and Prince Edward island

Memorandum of Understanding on Atlantic Canada Cooperation [establishing the Council of Atlantic Premiers]—May 15, 2000
(Council of Atlantic Premiers, 2000, <www.cap-cpma.ca/images/pdf/eng/capmou.pdf>)

The Atlantic Procurement Agreement: A Memorandum of Agreement on the Reduction of Interprovincial Trade Barriers Relating to Public Procurement—April 17, 1996
(Council of Atlantic Premiers,1996, <www.cap-cpma.ca/images/pdf/eng/APAEnglish.pdf>)

* This is not a unique agreement. Quebec has signed similar agreements with Nova Scotia, New Brunswick, Prince Edward Island, Yukon, Saskatchewan, and Alberta.

BALANCING THE BRANCHES: RESTORING THE LEGISLATURE TO EQUAL PARTNERSHIP WITH THE EXECUTIVE AND JUDICIARY

In liberal democratic systems of government, legislatures are said to make laws, executives to implement them, and the judiciary to interpret them in the context of concrete legal controversies (Dickerson and Flanagan, 2006: 297). This formal distinction among government functions is more or less reflected in the government institutions that are charged with putting it into practice. This does not, however, mean that the three branches of government are water-tight compartments, limited exclusively to their nominal functions. Nor were they ever intended to be. John Locke, an acknowledged founder of the modern "separation of powers," was quite clear that the executive has a "double trust" in the sense of having both "a part in the legislative and the supreme execution of the law" (Locke, [1690] 1980: 112). Or, as James Madison famously put it in the Federalist Papers, the checks and balances needed to generate moderate and decent government depend on at least some degree of "partial agency" of the formally separate branches in each other's affairs (Hamilton, Madison, and Jay, [1787] 2003: 294).

Accordingly, it comes as no surprise that even in the United States, which has a starker "separation of powers" than is found in Westminster-style parliamentary systems, such powers as the presidential veto make the chief executive a major law-maker, not just an executor of legislative will. At the same time, the American Senate's power to confirm treaties and major appointments gives the legislature a role in traditionally executive functions. Such "partial agency" or "double trust" is even more obvious in parliamentary systems of responsible government, where the political executive (the prime minister and cabinet) sits as a committee of the legislature and generally controls the legislative agenda. In both presidential and parliamentary systems, moreover—indeed, in all rule-of-law democracies—courts inevitably "legislate" as they adjudicate competing interpretations of ambiguous law. The real issue, in short, is not whether there is a mixture of functions among the three branches of government—there inevitably is, and a good thing too—but whether we have the right set of inter- and intra-branch checks and balances. In Canada, a rebalancing of inter-branch relationships is needed as much as the rebalancing of federalism discussed above.

The need for checks and balances

Nearly every competent observer, whatever their political allegiance, nowadays agrees that the executive and the judiciary have grown substantially in power and stature at the expense of the legislature. Indeed some, such as Donald Savoie (1999), have argued that under the relentless bureaucratization of power from Trudeau through Mulroney to Chrétien and Martin, cabinet itself has become little more than a focus group, with real or effective power lodged in the central agencies, especially the Prime Minister's Office (PMO). As Justice Gomery put it in his report on the Sponsorship Scandal, "[t]he concentration of power in the PMO makes it progressively more difficult for counter-balancing forces in Cabinet, in the public service, and in Parliament to modify or to oppose measures advocated by the Prime Minister" ("Gomery Commission," 2006: 128). Indeed, so powerful have prime ministers become that according to some commentators, except in situations of minority government, we would be subject to "dictatorship" (though perhaps of a "friendly" sort) (Simpson, 2001) were it not for the increase in judicial power brought by the 1982 Charter of Rights and Freedoms (Greene et al., 1998: 6; Allan, 1993: 8). Because opposition and backbench legislators no longer constrain executives in any meaningful sense, our newly empowered courts can and do. In F.L. Morton's words, as "executive-dominated legislatures have fallen into disrepute, courts and judges have filled the vacuum." Certainly public opinion surveys show that "many Canadians trust judges more than they do politicians" (Morton, 2003: 28).

The image of an executive "dictatorship" checked only by ermine-clad judicial guardians is exaggerated, however, notwithstanding the undoubted predominance of the executive. For one thing, real dictators who are unfettered by significant legislative constraints do not generally accept constraints from robed judges, who lack the power of either sword or purse (Hamilton, Madison, and Jay, [1787] 2003: 472). If judicial constraints work in Canada, as they clearly do, it is at least in part because political executives remain subject to other constraints, including legislative ones. Understanding full well that the so-called "trained seals" sitting on the government's back benches can be pushed only so far, no prime minister wants to test the limits of his allegedly dictatorial power (J. Smith 2003: 157). As Dawson and Ward put it, any sensible prime minister will be "sufficiently wise and far-seeing to limit his demands ... to those which will gain the general acceptance of his followers," or at least to those that will not provoke their outright rebellion (Dawson, Dawson, and Ward, 1989: 47).

A better house: strengthening the legislature

Still, even if the claims of executive dictatorship are exaggerated, it remains true that the legislature has become the weakling among the three branches and that it needs to be strengthened. For the healthy system of checks and balances contemplated by liberal democratic theory, Canadian legislatures need to play a more vigorous role in counter-balancing the power of both executives and courts. As Justice Gomery has rightly noted, the infamous "sponsorship scandal" arose in part because Parliament, which ought to be "the front-line guardian of the public interest" ("Gomery Commission," 2006: 4), had been unable "to exercise its traditional role as watchdog of the public purse" (7). He concludes that an institutional "rebalancing" (4, 6) is essential if the legislature is to regain its capacity effectively to "counter-balance ... the power of the executive in Canadian government" (8).

The weakness of legislatures stems from the fact that the first minister, whether premier or prime minister, has come to be the overwhelming source of legitimacy and authority for the entire cabinet and government. This symbolic as well as the effective centralization of power certainly imparts energy to the executive. At the same time, however, it brings with it considerable opacity and secrecy, and thus the avoidance of responsibility. To pose the problem of twenty-first-century governance in Canada in these terms invites a response, not so much in terms of solving a problem as of mitigating some unfortunate consequences. Specifically, transparency and responsibility in government require sources of legitimacy and authority independent of the first minister and his or her secretariat. The following are some ways in which this might be achieved.

The "other place": strengthening the Senate by the ballot box

A revitalized bicameralism is the most obvious way of breaking the stranglehold of executive power over the legislature. Ironically, the executive's need for the "confidence" of the Commons is precisely what sustains its dominance of that house. Within limits—and as we have noted, those limits remain important—government back-benchers in the Commons are loathe to risk the electoral consequences of defeating their own cabinet. Pressures for party discipline are lighter in the Senate because it is not a "confidence chamber." On the other hand, the Senate often (though not always) is reluctant to flex its considerable formal muscle because, being an appointed body, it lacks democratic legitimacy. Electing senators would remedy this defect and create a locus of significant constraint on the executive-dominated Commons.

While election has traditionally been part of the agenda for reforming the Senate, that agenda has often emphasized giving provincial electorates equal representation in the federal upper house, a reform requiring the kind of formal constitutional amendment to which Canadians have become allergic since the debacles of Meech Lake and the Charlottetown Accord. Making the Senate a more effective legislative constraint on executive power through election, by contrast, can be achieved without formal amendment by allowing provincial electorates to signify their preferred candidates for "appointment" to the upper house, leaving the number of senators from each province untouched. Formal appointment by the prime minister would eventually become, by convention, simply the conduit for electoral processes, much as the appointment by the Governor General of a prime minister has become the formal implementation of underlying electoral processes that democratically send members to the lower house.

Alberta has pioneered such "Senate elections" and in 1990 Prime Minister Mulroney reluctantly, as a concession to Don Getty, then Alberta Premier, in order to maintain his support of the Meech Lake Accord, appointed Stan Waters, a Reform Party candidate, who had been elected in this way. Although several other Albertans have been elected to the status of "senator in waiting," until recently Waters remained the only one actually appointed to the Upper House. Prime Minister Harper, whose political roots are in Alberta, committed his party to Senate reform in its 2006 election platform (Conservative Party of Canada, 2006: 44) and has just recently appointed Alberta's longest-standing "Senator-elect," Bert Brown, to the Upper House.

Critics of this approach to Senate reform argue that infusing the substantial formal power of the Senate with democratic legitimacy risks the kind of deadlock between the two branches that occurred in Australia in 1975, when an opposition-controlled elected Senate refused supply to a government that enjoyed the confidence of the lower house, thus threatening to bring essential government operations and activities to a standstill (Saunders, 2003; also D. Smith, 2003: 22–30). The Governor General had to step in and resolve the crisis by calling on the leader of the opposition to form a government, which then precipitated a new election. While the prospect of such deadlock is indeed a concern, it has happened only once in Australia and has not recurred since 1975, partly because an increase in the number of senators per state, in the context of a single-transferable-vote electoral system, has made it rare for either of Australia's major parties fully to control the upper chamber. Some smaller parties always secure enough seats to leaven the process and prevent inter-chamber gridlock (Bach, 2003: 183–88).

In Canada, something similar could be achieved if Alberta's precedent of electing candidates for senatorial appointment in conjunction with provincial elections is followed. New Brunswick has already offered to replicate the Alberta model (Laghi, 2004: A1) and a private member's bill advocating it has been introduced in Ontario (Mackie, 2004: A7). Once the process started, other provinces would certainly follow suit. Selected at different times, in different partisan contexts, and subject to different timetables for re-election (with none coinciding precisely with the election of members to the House of Commons), Senators would be unlikely to fall into the kind of disciplined partisan alignment that would produce deadlock between the House and Senate, especially if freer voting is permitted in both houses. No doubt there are other ways of achieving the same end, such as devising an appropriate electoral system for national Senate elections. And new mechanisms for negotiation and accommodation between the two houses would have to evolve. But, if the goal is to constrain what everyone agrees to be an overly powerful executive, this is all to the good and the recent steps taken by Stephen Harper's government in this direction are to be welcomed. Are there risks? Of course. But given the Australian example of an elected and effective upper chamber working well in a parliamentary system of responsible government, the risk is worth taking.

There have been two bills introduced by the current Harper Government that, if passed, would substantially reform the Senate. Bill C-43 An Act to Provide for Consultations with Electors on their Preferences for Appointment to the Senate, would formalize the "consultative" process used by Alberta to "elect" senators. Bill S-4 An Act to Amend the Constitution Act, 1867 (Senate Tenure), which would limit Senators to 8-year terms, has been effectively blocked by the Senate, and will not proceed any further until the Supreme Court rules with respect to the constitutionality of the proposed legislation. We believe both bills should be passed.

Working in groups: strengthening committees

The business of Parliament is ordered by various rules, procedures, and conventions. There are special and standing committees with distinct powers determined by the House and by its standing orders. Justice Gomery correctly identifies the strengthening of committees as a key component of "rebalancing" the relationships between executive and legislature. His report focuses particularly on the Public Accounts committee and we do not propose to repeat his many valuable recommendations here ("Gomery Commission," 2006: 75–80). More generally, we draw attention to the valuable innovation of the House of Commons in 2002 of choosing committee chairs and vice chairs through secret ballot among committee members (Docherty, 2004: 298). Generally, only government members may be elected chairs and opposition members as vice-chairs though, in some cases, such as the Public Accounts Committee, this is reversed so that the chair must come from the opposition benches (Canada, House of Commons, 2005: XIII, s. 106(2) [online]). In principle, this reform gives the committee leadership somewhat greater independence from the party leadership. An important side benefit is that it promotes parliamentary civility at the expense of overly aggressive partisanship; ambitious parliamentarians, in short, are no doubt more careful in how they frame partisan challenges to those whose respect (and thus votes) they might need to attain a committee leadership position.

However, the beneficial effects of electing committee leaderships are undermined by the fact that party leaders retain the right to remove members of their caucus, including committee chairs or vice-chairs, from their committees and reassign them (Docherty and White, 2004: 623). Not only does this power weaken the independence of committee leadership, it can also weaken the policy expertise that comes with experience on a committee if members are moved around too frequently. Simply put, the expectation in Standing

Order 114 that a committee's "membership shall continue from session to session within a Parliament" (Canada, House of Commons, 2005: XIII, s. 114(1) [online]) is in tension with the power of party leaders to move people around. This should be changed, so that committee members and their elected leaders have greater security of tenure during a legislative term. In Quebec, for example, committee memberships are fixed for two years (Canadian Parliamentary Review, 1996: 27).

Reforming the tenure and selection of committees and their leadership is worth the effort, of course, only if committees have real and important work to do and the resources to carry it out effectively. The importance of their work increases in proportion to how early in the legislative process they can begin to contribute to its outcomes. Most powerful is a committee that can initiate and formulate legislation with some expectation that it will be taken seriously. In Ontario, committees can initiate bills that are treated like private member's bills but with enhanced time for second reading during the regular "orders of the day" (Sterling, 2000 :7). Similarly, a committee that receives government legislation early in the process has greater influence than a committee that receives fairly complete legislation. In Ontario, legislation can be sent to committee right after first reading (7) and, at the federal level, it has been possible since 1994 to send bills to committee right at the start of second reading. Docherty and White (2004) note, however, that the federal provision has rarely been exploited. Perhaps a move to more free votes, as has been proposed by the Harper government (Conservative Party of Canada, 2006: 44), will create a legislative atmosphere in which earlier resort to committees will become a more attractive strategy. The need to work out compromises between the Commons and a more powerful and independent elected Senate would also raise the profile and importance of committee work, especially that of joint committees.

As for resources to do the work, the imbalance between those available to government and the committees expected to hold them to account is a perennial issue. Justice Gomery's report notes that, while some important improvements have been made, the committees still lack the staff and research capacity needed to perform well ("Gomery Commission," 2006: 80). Here we note and welcome the Harper government's promise to "[i]ncrease the power of Parliament and parliamentary committees to review the spending estimates of departments and hold ministers to account" (Conservative Party of Canada, 2006: 44).

We believe that Parliamentary committees —including joint committees of the Commons and an elected Senate—need to have an earlier role in the legislative process, be better structured, with more security of tenure for members and the chair, and be provided appropriate resources for the task. These measures can add value to our public life in many ways, not least by providing oversight or confirmation of appointments to some of the more important boards and commissions. We pay special attention in the next section to judicial appointments, because they involve the balance between the executive, the legislature, and the "third" branch of government.

A LEVEL BENCH: BALANCING THE JUDICIARY

Legislative reform should be seen as a way not only of reining in an overly powerful executive but also of balancing the growing power of the courts. Like executives, judges have an important role to play in the overall system but they, too, can become too powerful. Among other things, revitalizing legislatures makes it more difficult to present the courts as the only viable check on otherwise unlimited executive power and thus opens the door to a more healthy balance among the three branches. Certainly, under the Charter of Rights and Freedoms, judges are expected to protect citizens from the arbitrary infringement of their rights and freedoms by executive or legislative actions. But if such infringements are to be made less likely by healthy checks and balances within and between the executive and legislative branches, then Charter cases will generally raise policy questions of reasonable disagreement rather than outrageous violations of rights (Knopff and Morton, 1992: 144–51; Morton and Knopff, 2000: 34–37). Indeed, many leading commentators believe this has been the case even in the era of excessive domination by the executive (Hiebert, 2004: esp. ch. 2; Roach, 2001: esp. ch. 12; Russell, 1983: 43–44). After all, judges themselves often reflect and reproduce the very disagreements found outside the courtroom. Our judicial policy-makers act as valuable checks on their counterparts in the other branches but, if the overall system is to be properly balanced, they need (and deserve) to be checked and monitored in return. Two areas of oversight and constraint deserve particular attention: judicial appointments and the Charter's "notwithstanding clause."

Reforming judicial appointments

No one doubts that the Supreme Court of Canada, our final court of appeal, is fundamentally a policy-making body. Given that the actual parties before the court have already had an initial trial and at least one level of appeal, this additional and final appeal is needed less to determine which party wins the case than to resolve important issues of legal ambiguity—that is, to "legislate" by authoritatively choosing between competing interpretations of the relevant law (Archer et al., 1999: 326–90). This is why the Court refuses to hear cases that raise no substantial interpretive issue regardless of how large the personal stakes of the parties may be and why it will hear apparently picayune cases when the issues of legal policy loom large (330–32). When the legal issues before the Court involve choosing between plausible interpretations of constitutional law, which is more difficult for legislatures to change, the judicial role in policymaking becomes even more substantial (336–38).

Canada is hardly alone in experiencing an increasing judicialization of public policy; high courts the world over have gained significantly in constitutionally based policy-making power in recent decades (Hirshl, 2004; Ginsburg, 2003; Stone-Sweet, 2004, 2000; Morton and Knopff, 2000; Epp, 1998). However, Canada lags behind the many other countries whose method of appointing high court judges better reflects their substantial policy-making power. In the United States and many European countries, for example, authority to appoint is shared between the executive and one or more legislative chambers (Morton, 2004: 2). In federal regimes, the involvement of a federally organized upper house ensures some degree of regional input into the appointments process (2). In even more dramatic recognition of the judicial policy-making role, appointments to some constitutional courts include both government and opposition nominees (2). In Canada, by contrast, appointments to the Supreme Court are effectively in the hands of one individual, the already too-powerful prime minister.

Chief Justice McLachlin recently repeated her view that prime-ministerial appointment is the best way to prevent the "politicization" of the judicial appointments (Cordon, 2006 [online]). As many observers have pointed out, however, prime-ministerial appointment is already thoroughly politicized, with significant lobbying occurring in the backrooms (Morton, 2004: 3). The question is not whether politics will intrude into the appointments process but whether it will take place in an appropriately designed public process or out of public sight. Even retired Supreme Court judges (Ziegel, 1999: 3) have in recent years joined what Jacob Ziegel, one of our leading students of judicial appointments, calls the "near unanimous chorus of opinion among scholars reinforced by many publicly-sponsored reports that the existing system of appointments is incompatible with a modern federal democratic constitution governed by the rule of law and incorporating one of the most powerful bills of rights in the Western hemisphere" (19). In 2004, the federal Justice Committee examined proposals for reforming the appointments process but (over dissenting reports filed by all opposition parties) recommended only that a multipartisan nominating committee propose candidates for prime ministerial appointment and that the Justice Minister or Chair of the nominating committee defend the appointments before a House of Commons committee after the fact (Morton, 2006). Candidates themselves would not be subject to public confirmation hearings or a public interview like that in South Africa.

Significantly, even Prime Minister Paul Martin, whose Liberal majority on the Justice committee produced these pallid 2004 recommendations, considered them "too timid and intimated that he favoured greater input from Parliament" (Morton, 2006). We agree. The valuable work begun by the Justice

Committee in 2004 should be continued to bring Canada into line with the emerging norms and practices of other advanced liberal democracies with powerful, policy-relevant high courts. Some kind of pre-appointment hearing or confirmation process by an appropriate parliamentary committee (perhaps a joint Senate-Commons committee) should be given priority attention.

Even so, the process initiated by the Martin Government was employed most recently to select Supreme Court Justice Marshall Rothstein in 2006. Potential candidates were reviewed by an Advisory Committee initiated by the previous Martin Government, and then the Harper Government selected Justice Rothstein from among those short-listed. But Justice Rothstein did face additional questions from an ad-hoc all-party committee in a televised hearing, which marked the first time in Canadian history that a Supreme Court nominee faced questions from Members of Parliament.

We might also reconsider how we appoint judges of the provincial courts of appeal. Although these provincial high courts are "established" by the provinces, their judges are currently appointed by the federal government. Canada is one of only four federations whose central government appoints provincial or state judges in this way (Morton, 2006). Shifting the appointment power for these courts to the provinces would almost certainly diversify this crucial "talent pool" for Supreme Court appointments. This reform would require the more difficult and politically risky process of constitutional amendment but, if the federal government were prepared to relinquish this power, the provinces would no doubt accept it.

The Harper Government has undertaken a limited initiative to change the composition of Judicial Advisory Committees (JACs). The JACs are part of an appointments process that has been in place since 1988, intended as independent bodies to assess the qualifications of lawyers who apply to be appointed to provincial and territorial superior courts, the Federal Court of Appeal, the Federal Court and the Tax Court of Canada. Previously, the JACs consisted of seven members, four representing the province, bar, and bench, and three appointed by the Federal government to represent the general public. The Harper Government added an eighth member to the JAC, a nominee of the law enforcement community to be appointed by the Federal Government.

DETRACTORS NOTWITHSTANDING:
USING THE "N-CLAUSE"

The "notwithstanding clause" is part of the Charter of Rights and Freedoms (s. 33). It was integral to the compromises that made the constitutional reforms of 1982 possible. Without it, there would be no Charter. It was supported by provincial premiers on both the left (e.g., Saskatchewan's NDP premier Blakeney) and the right (e.g., Alberta's Progressive Conservative premier Lougheed). The provision's purpose was to prevent "public policy [from] being dictated or determined by non-elected people" (Lougheed, quoted in Morton, 2003: 26), or having "the courts heavily involved in decisions which are essentially political" (Blakeney, in Morton: 26) or as a "safety valve" to ensure "that legislatures rather than judges would have the final say on important matters of public policy" (Federal Justice Minister Jean Chrétien, in Morton: 26). In short, the clause was based on the widespread recognition that the Charter rights would often involve the kinds of reasonable disagreements that amount to "policy" or "political" choices. The clause—which had precedents in the 1960 Canadian Bill of Rights and several provincial bills of rights—reflected the view that judges were human beings whose decisions were not infallible and who often disagreed among themselves in ways that reflected legislative disagreements. From this perspective, it is unclear why a legislative minority should necessarily win the day just because it gained the support of, say, one or two more judges than the legislative majority.

However reasonable these original views might be, we cannot ignore the fact that the notwithstanding clause has fallen somewhat into disuse and even disrepute during the intervening years (Manfredi, 2001: 4–5). The repair of our legislatures envisioned above is no doubt part of what is required to give renewed legitimacy to the occasional use of the notwithstanding clause as part of the on-going policy dialogue between the branches of government. But it is also worth considering the proposal initially developed by Conservative MP Scott Reid (Reid, 1996) and later championed by judicial scholar (and now Alberta legislator) Ted Morton (Morton, 2003). Reid and Morton propose democratizing the legislative override by subjecting its use to approval or rejection in a referendum. Even rehabilitating legislatures may not give them the degree of public legitimacy and trust enjoyed by the court, in other words, in which case the solution may be to transfer ultimate control of the notwithstanding clause to "the only institution that commands more popular respect than the court system—the popular will itself" (Reid, 1996: 186).

In this proposal, a "decision to use the notwithstanding clause would be put to a provincial referendum at the next practical date," often in conjunction with an election, asking the people "to choose between the court's policy and the government's policy, or perhaps a new compromise" (Morton, 2003: 29). The process would work best if legislatures avoided pre-emptive uses of the notwithstanding clause, employing it only if the courts struck down a policy as unconstitutional. In this scenario, the legislature acts first without a notwithstanding clause, giving the courts an unfettered opportunity to respond. If the judicial response is negative and if the government feels strongly enough, the legislation is re-enacted with a notwithstanding clause that is then subject to the ultimate decision of the people. Even if the clause is upheld, moreover, it remains subject to the existing five-year limit. This is neither legislative dominance nor judicial supremacy; nor is it unguided populist will (the people having to choose between policies carefully deliberated by the other institutions). It is, in fact, a very thorough and balanced form of public dialogue. Alberta came close to adopting this proposal in 1999 (Morton, 2003: 29). It is time that both levels of government gave it serious consideration.

Restoring checks-and-balances, responsibility, and dynamism to government requires steps to strengthen Parliament, and to limit and render more transparent the growing powers of the executive branch (Prime Minister's Office and Cabinet) and the federal judiciary. We believe the ideas above will go a long way to achieving these objectives.

CONCLUSIONS: BACK TO THE FUTURE

We believe the framers of Canada's original constitution, the British North America Act (now the Canada Act 1867), got it fundamentally right in distributing powers and authority between the federal and provincial governments. Much of what ails the Canadian body politic today can be traced to departures from that fundamental balance of responsibilities and action. Freed from the distraction and distortion of federal intrusions into their areas of jurisdiction, and sustained by tax-points conceded by Ottawa, provinces are best placed to innovate in response to their citizens' priorities. At the same time, imbalances have developed within the federal order of government that require attention. Rebalancing the relationship between the executive, judicial, and legislative arms in Canada requires that we strengthen Parliament and constrain the growing powers of both the executive and judiciary. Fix the current imbalances and Canada will be in a position to fix much else. For example, Monograph 7, "Have-not Provinces: Stop 'Helping' Already (page 241), explores the impact of "rebalanced federalism" on improving the economic position of Canada's Atlantic Provinces.

RECOMMENDATIONS

12.1   Remove the federal government from the fields of social assistance, child care, and health care, and all other areas of provincial responsibility. The key recommendations for this rebalancing, as they apply to specific policy areas like health care, are found in the first part of this volume, "Caring for Canadians: Quality of Life."

- Coordinate with this withdrawal a reduction in federal revenues by the current value of federal fiscal transfers to the provinces in support of these services, vacating the equivalent tax room to the provinces.
- Have the provinces assume in full their constitutional responsibility for providing essential social services (education, health care, child care, and social assistance) and for developing whatever national standards are desirable in these areas by means of inter-provincial agreements facilitated by the Council of the Federation.
- Amend the current equalization formula to provide additional revenues to lower-income provinces for which a "tax point" is worth less than for higher-income provinces, to the effect that no province be "worse off" after the transfer of tax points than under the current system.

12.2   Strengthen the national government in key areas by having the federal Parliament focus on

- Canada's foreign policy;
- its defence and military capability;
- the settlement of favourable external trade arrangements and the elimination of trade barriers within Canada;
- a sound currency and monetary policy;
- intellectual property law;
- the criminal law and provision for public safety;
- the discharge of federal responsibilities toward aboriginal peoples.

12.3   Increase the use of Memorandums of Understanding by all provinces and territories to pursue common objectives and interests, facilitated and supported by the Council of the Federation.

12.4   Negotiate an increasing number of Trade Investment and Labour Mobility Agreements (TILMAs) among provinces (as also recommended in Chapter 9).

12.5   Provide a stronger check on the executive by strengthening the bicameral nature of Parliament, in particular by democratizing (electing) the Senate; to this end Bills C-43 and S-4 should be passed.

12.6   Strengthen the powers of parliamentary and legislative committees by giving them an earlier role in the legislative process, giving their members (especially their elected chairs) more security of tenure, and giving them the resources (budgets, staffs, research capacity) required to exercise those powers effectively.

12.7 Establish a pre-appointment hearing or confirmation process for appointments to the Supreme Court by an appropriate parliamentary committee to improve the transparency and balance of those appointments.

12.8 Pursue a constitutional amendment to shift the power of appointing justices to provincial courts of appeal from the federal government to the provincial governments.

12.9 Recognize the notwithstanding clause as a legitimate and necessary part of our Constitution and encourage its proper use through refining and democratizing its application.

HAVE-NOT PROVINCES: STOP "HELPING" ALREADY!

The Canada Strong and Free series has called for increases in economic freedom, more open and free markets, and respect for Canada's constitutional division of powers to improve the well-being of Canadians. Nowhere in Canada have these principles been less respected than in Atlantic Canada and nowhere have Canadians suffered more as a consequence. Massive federal intrusion, disrespectful of the constitution, has disrupted labour markets, weakened businesses, slowed economic growth, and reduced individual economic freedom.

Atlantic Canada was on a fast track to catch up with the rest of Canada prior to the vast expansion of regional programs in the early 1970s. By 1970, investment in Atlantic Canada had reached the national per-capita average. Unemployment in the three Maritime Provinces was only a shade higher than in the rest of the nation; and only two or three percentage points higher in Newfoundland. Then, with a burst of federal spending, the wheels came off the train. Three sets of programs set up the problem. Regionally extended Unemployment Insurance (now Employment Insurance) was supposed to provide a cushion for the unemployed. Instead, it increased unemployment. Regional development programs were meant to spur economic growth. Instead, they dampened growth. Fiscal federalism, embodied in equalization, was supposed to provide equivalent services across the country. Instead, it bloated government in "have-not" provinces and turned spending into a political tool.

THE LABOUR MARKET

Prior to the introduction of highly generous, regionally extended Unemployment Insurance (UI) in the early 1970s, every Maritime province had spent at least one year below the national unemployment rate and regional and national unemployment were converging. Even Newfoundland's unemployment rate was close to the national average. After the introduction of regionally extended unemployment insurance, which provided generous benefits for relatively few weeks of work, unemployment in the region soared to about 50% higher than the national average. Unemployment insurance became such a disincentive to work that in some months more than twice as many people collected UI as were officially unemployed. They were not counted as officially unemployed because they stopped looking for work while collecting UI. With a real unemployment rate of around 20%, both Statistics Canada and the Atlantic Provinces Economic Council reported labour shortages throughout the region after the creation of regionally extended UI. Business growth was frustrated because business, small business in particular, could not compete against the benefits offered by the UI system. For the next 30 years, unemployment in Atlantic Canada remained, and remains still, substantially higher than in the rest of Canada. Only recently has it begun to decline relative to the national average (see McMahon, 2000, chapter 5, for a full discussion these issues. See also Riddell, Kuhn, Clemens, and Palacios, 2006.)

THE GOVERNMENT SECTOR

Many people believe that equalization is the main federal transfer to the have-not provinces. In fact, fiscal federalism contains many types of transfers to the provinces, particularly in social services such as health care, which are under provincial jurisdiction (Clemens and Veldhuis, 2007: Expert Panel, 2006.) As the Expert Panel on Equalization and Territorial Financing Formula noted: "As if the Equalization program isn't complicated enough on its own, other federal transfer programs, particularly the Canada Health Transfer and the Canada Social Transfer, also include an equalizing component" (Expert Panel, 2006: 47).

Combined with federal spending on its own programs, this results in unsustainably large governments in Atlantic Canada. Figure M7.1 shows federal spending per province while Figure M7.2 shows total government spending per province. As high as the numbers represented in the chart are, they were once much greater: at the beginning of the 1990s, government spending in the Atlantic Provinces ranged from about 70% of provincial GDP to over 80%, depending on the province.

Figure M7.1: Per-capita federal program spending, 2005/06

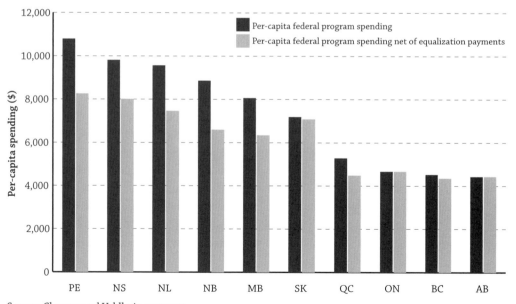

Source: Clemens and Veldhuis, 2007: 111.

Figure M7.2: Federal, provincial, and local government spending (% of GDP), 2005/06

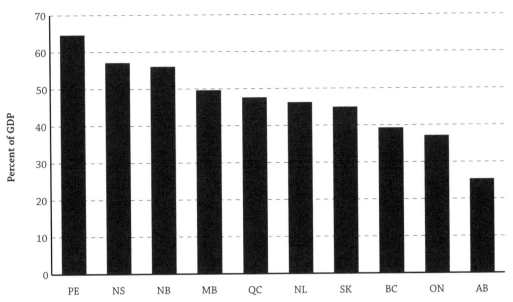

Source: Clemens and Veldhuis, 2007: 112.

"HELP" THAT HINDERED

Economic theory, backed by empirical analysis, shows that poorer regions grow more quickly than more advanced regions. This is called the rate of convergence and it occurs for at least two reasons. A lagging region need not invent new technology or more productive methods to grow more quickly. All it has to do is copy successful examples from more advanced regions. Poorer regions also typically have lower rates of pay than advanced regions. This labour advantage attracts employers and investment.

Atlantic Canada has lagged behind the rate of convergence of poorer regions in Europe, the United States, and Japan, where interregional transfers are much lower than in Canada (McMahon, 2000). The vast regional transfers of funds through fiscal federalism and "economic development" programs have actually hindered, not helped, regional growth in Canada. A study sponsored by the government of Nova Scotia and the Atlantic Canada Opportunities Agency, which was supposed to show that Nova Scotian businesses were competitive, instead found that the corrosive effects of government spending—both through sizeable government contracts and though economic development subsidies— was undermining competitiveness.

> [A] significant proportion of the Nova Scotia firms visited were partially dependent either directly upon provincial or other forms of public purchasing or indirectly through subcontracting to larger firms which are in turn reliant upon government spending for their survival and profitability ... *Public policy appears inadvertently to*

have reinforced market failure to some extent by cushioning profits via grants, subsidies and preferential purchasing thereby reducing the incentive to change ... The heavy reliance upon Federal transfers has indirectly promoted a dependency culture in the province ... a culture, as one owner manager said, of "a whole region being on the dole." (O'Farrell, 1990: 24–25; emphasis in the original)

THE FIGHT OVER EQUALIZATION

Although equalization is only one element in a whole menu of transfers to the region, the current controversy over equalization, especially as it relates to Atlantic Canada, reflects a clamour for more of what has ailed the region, not for effective remedy. The time and energy being spent on this dispute would be better invested in implementing long-term measures to address the economic disabilities that make equalization payments necessary in the first place. The key to moving Atlantic Canada forward is not to focus on maintaining its dependency on the federal government (and indirectly, the rest of Canada) but on measures, like those we suggest below, to place the region on a footing of durable prosperity that leaves no disparity to "equalize."

GETTING BACK ON TRACK

The magnitude of the fiscal flows to Atlantic Canada and the size of its government have declined somewhat in recent years. Employment Insurance has undergone some reform. This has produced some gains in growth, employment, and business competitiveness. It is now time to carry such reforms through to their logical conclusion so that the people of Atlantic Canada can receive their full benefit.

Respect the Constitution

Ottawa should remove itself from areas of provincial jurisdiction, end its fiscal transfers in these areas, and open an equivalent amount of tax room for the provinces. There are many reasons for this reform: respect for Canada's constitution; replacing federal-provincial finger-pointing with transparent accountability by one level of government with clear responsibility for programs like health care; freeing provinces to experiment and tailor programs to the unique needs of their people (see Harris and Manning, 2005a, 2005b for a fuller discussion of the need for these reforms.) At a stroke, this would end a large part of the over-equalization and government bloat in Atlantic Canada.

Equalization

The second key reform is to base equalization on the cost of providing services. Here it is important to remember the actual intent of the equalization program. The Constitution does not require that provinces receive equal revenues but rather that they be able to provide reasonably comparable services at reasonably comparable levels of taxation. And here, reality bites. It simply costs more to provide services, or build hospitals, in Toronto or Vancouver than in New Glasgow, Nova Scotia, or Saskatoon, Saskatchewan. Unless this is recognized in the equalization formula, then the intent of the Constitution will be violated in that poorer provinces, with a lower cost of living, will always be able to provide better services than rich provinces at the same level of expenditure.

Regionally extended Employment Insurance

It is simply unfair that an unemployed person facing identical circumstances should be treated differently by government depending on where they live. Regionally extended EI has proved a barrier to increasing employment in Atlantic Canada and should be removed.

Taxes

Government bloat eroded the competitiveness of the private sector in Atlantic Canada. Instead of taxing and spending, the provinces should reduce taxes. This has a proven track record in spurring growth, with Ireland serving as an outstanding example (Harris and Manning, 2006b)

Trade

Trade has a proven track record of boosting economic growth. Yet, too many trade barriers remain in place within Canada (Harris and Manning, 2006). Atlantic Canadian Provinces should adopt the Trade, Investment, and Labour Mobility Agreement (TILMA) struck between Alberta and British Columbia. This agreement has been shown to be a strong advance on the current agreements governing trade within Canada (Knox and Karabegović, forthcoming).

CONCLUSION

All Canadians would gain from the increased accountability that respect for the division of powers in our constitution would bring to key programs like health care. A reformed equalization program would, for the first time, actually meet the constitutional requirement for such a measure. The relief from government bloat and overspending in Atlantic Canada would increase economic freedom and allow Atlantic Canadians themselves to build their own prosperity, a process that was well advanced 35 years ago when federal spending suddenly intervened to knock the region off its path of increasing investment, declining unemployment, and strong growth.

RECOMMENDATIONS

❀ Factor into the calculation of inter-provincial equalization payments regional differences in the cost of providing comparable public services.

❀ End regionally extended entitlements to EI .

❀ Reduce taxes to spur citizen's productive potential in have-not provinces.

❀ Adopt in Atlantic Canada an agreement structured on the Trade, Investment, and Labour Mobility Agreement (TILMA) struck between Alberta and British Columbia.

A MODEL TO THE WORLD
INTERNATIONAL LEADERSHIP

Our vision for Canada does not end at our national shores and borders. We envisage as well a Canada that once again stands proudly on the world stage as a leader by its actions and example.

Realizing the other goals set out in preceding pages would go far toward achieving this one as well: any nation that demonstrates a superior quality of life, vibrant economy, and responsive, effective government will naturally evoke emulation by others. But there is ground to make up. Canada's reputation in the world has slipped badly in the past decade and a half, as our actions too often fell short of our word and our contributions to the wider global community became more rhetorical than real. Canada's military, once a source of justifiable national pride, was starved of funding, equipment, and personnel; our contribution to international peacekeeping, let alone peacemaking, became more rhetorical than substantive. Gratuitous anti-Americanism on the part of some of our leaders eroded relations with our closest neighbour and largest trading partner.

Against the backdrop of that evident deterioration, we began with a fundamental question: What should Canadian foreign policy in the 21st century seek to accomplish? In 1995, the Chrétien administration answered that question by undertaking to project Canadian values to the wider world. Historian Jack Granatstein, and others, argued a rival view, that Canada's foreign policy must promote Canadian interests (Stairs et al., 2005). We hold both perspectives. We believe that the Government of Canada should pursue clearly identified interests, that reflect long-established Canadian values, and that various dimensions of our foreign policy (for example, trade, defence, and aid) may be designed to advance different interests and values. For example, we value increased prosperity for ourselves and others; this value underlies our interest in trade liberalization and effective aid to those in need. We value security for

Canadians and others around the world; hence our interest in keeping North America safe, and in both making and keeping the peace abroad.

Let us avoid any semantic confusion of these two concepts. Or, worse yet, self-serving and vaporous rhetoric about the "superiority" of Canadian values. Talk is not enough. Canada's policies abroad must achieve what they set out to do. We can start by aiming for results, rather than proceeding out of ideology or in defence of political sacred cows. Accordingly, in this last part of the present book, we examine the three areas in which Canadians have most to gain—and to contribute—from revitalizing our international performance.

The first of these is international trade and the benefits to Canada of increasing the freedom of international trade. After making major advances in the closing decades of the last century, the momentum of efforts to extend the benefits of rules-based free trade more widely in the international arena has waned in the current decade. In Chapter 13, we discuss how Canada's governments can provide leadership in the promotion of international free trade in this new environment.

The second, examined in Chapter 14, is the unique relationship we share with the United States, based on geography, economy, history, culture, and deep-seated values. Canadians' self-interest in securing an open, strong, and mutually respectful continental relationship is evident; but it should not be overlooked that our ability to make a difference on the world stage is also directly proportional to our ability to influence the globe's most potent economic, political and military power.

Last, in Chapter 15, we turn to a foreign-policy objective that a majority of Canadians identify as a high priority: giving aid and assistance to the world's less fortunate. Applying the same evidence-based analysis that supports our earlier recommendations, we argue again that outcomes, not inputs, should guide our foreign-aid choices. Canadians wish to be generous; but they also deserve results for their generosity. Just as we pursue economic freedoms for ourselves, as the most powerful engines of wealth-creation that the world has ever known, so we should feel compelled to place the same empowering tools in the hands of the world's poor.

By putting into action the recommendations that follow, Canadians can look forward to both material and intangible rewards. Our economic prosperity will be enhanced by the further liberalization of international trade. Our security against hostile attack will be enhanced, as will the security of access to our most important commercial market. You will once again be able to take justifiable pride in Canada's real accomplishments abroad. You will have the satisfaction of knowing that the actions Canada's government takes in your name will make a real difference for the better in the lives of those facing adversity.

Canada is not among those nations that seek to make their mark on the globe through force of arms or treasure. But we can, and should, serve as a beacon to the world by championing freedom, practicing practical compassion and providing a model of that "peace, order and good government" to which we aspire for ourselves. To seek anything less is not only to shirk our duty to the world, but to fail in our responsibility to ourselves.

CHAPTER 13

LIBERALIZING INTERNATIONAL TRADE

PROSPERITY THROUGH TRADE

We envision a Canada in which Canadians strive to achieve standards of living, economic performance, and democratic governance that are the highest in the world and enable Canada to be a model of international leadership and citizenship. But Canadians will realize little of this vision without the enabling engine of a thriving economy. Put simply, the greater the prosperity Canadians enjoy, the greater our opportunity to do more for ourselves and for the world. And nothing breeds prosperity more efficiently than trade and free-market economies.

It has long been a truism that Canada is a trading nation. From our earliest days, Canadians relied on exports to bigger, wealthier markets for our livelihood. In exchange, we have benefited from a rich choice of imported goods, services, capital, and technologies. However, these benefits have masked an unhappy and less well-appreciated fact: the extent to which we have fallen short of the rewards we might have enjoyed. Too easily satisfied with the bronze medal, we have been unprepared to do what it takes to earn the gold. And the loss has been ours.

We think Canada can do better. We think Canadians are ready to take the steps necessary to make ours a gold-medal economy and Canada into the best place in the world from which to pursue global opportunity. We believe Canadians possess the confidence to strike down the obsolete policies and practices that hinder our productive resources—capital and labour—and that keep us from finding their most beneficial uses. Effective strategies and appropriate tactics are available. It is time to focus on the task.

POLICY EVOLUTION FROM "NATIONAL" TO "GLOBAL"

To begin, a little history may be in order. The North American colonies that ultimately joined together to become the Dominion of Canada in 1867 existed on the periphery of empire. For most colonists Britain, the "old country," was important as both a market and a source of manufactured goods. It remained so for many years. But Canadians were by no means averse to taking advantage of their proximity to the United States as well, either as a source of goods unavailable from local suppliers or as an outlet for some of their own exports. The new Dominion's very first government recognized this reality and tried to forge a trade relationship with our southern neighbours to develop this two-way trade further. Events, however, conspired against these early Canadians. With few exceptions, American lawmakers did not find freer trade with Canada attractive on any terms other than annexation. Canadians found this far too steep a price. As an alternative, Sir John A. Macdonald's second government adopted its National Policy in 1879—a decidedly second-best option.

Later historians emphasized the National Policy's virtues in building a Canadian nation. Perhaps, but for the first quarter-century following the adoption of the National Policy the effort to strengthen Canada's economy on east-west lines brought meagre results. The opening of the Prairies to dry-land wheat farming early in the twentieth century made the National Policy seem more successful. High tariffs and other protectionist devices did stimulate development of a thriving but high-cost manufacturing sector in Central Canada. But Canadians continued to pay a heavy price. Exporters of Canadian resource products to world markets found that the high cost of machinery and other inputs protected by the National Policy frequently undercut their ability to compete. Working Canadians paid the price in lower wages, higher prices, and less choice. The economy the National Policy fostered was larger than it was before but still less prosperous than it might have been (Dales, 1966a; 1966b).

AN AMAZING MACHINE

Imagine a spectacular invention: a machine that can convert corn into stereo equipment. When running at full capacity, this machine can turn fifty bushels of corn into a CD player. Or with one turn of the dial, it will convert fifteen hundred bushels of soybeans into a four-door sedan. But this machine is even more versatile than that; when properly programmed, it can turn Windows software into the finest French wines. Or a Boeing 747 into enough fresh fruit and vegetables to feed a city for months.

Indeed the most amazing thing about this invention is that it can be set up anywhere in the world and programmed to turn whatever is grown or produced there into things that are usually much harder to come by.

Remarkably, it works for poor countries too. Developing nations can put the things they manage to produce—commodities, cheap textiles, basic manufactured goods—into the machine and obtain goods that might otherwise be denied them: food, medicine, more advanced manufactured goods. Obviously poor countries that have access to this machine would grow faster than countries that did not. We would expect that making this machine accessible to poor countries would be part of our strategy for lifting billions of people around the globe out of dire poverty.

Amazingly, this machine already exists. It is called trade.

(from Wheelan, 2002: 187)

Forging an east-west economy also created tensions. Ontario and Quebec acquired most of the expensively protected manufacturing and thus became the National Policy's principal proponents. (Later on, even some agriculture in the two provinces came to depend on the peculiar Canadian institution of supply management, itself dependent on tight border restrictions.) Atlantic and the western provinces, on the other hand, came to rely largely on the export of resources—farm produce, fish, forest products, metals, and minerals. Western grain and cattle producers learned to live with the vagaries of international prices and competition. Even when demand for Canadian raw materials by the United States soared in the middle decades of the twentieth century, the federal government resisted easing protection for central Canada's manufacturers. Thus two sets of tensions developed: between export-oriented resource producers and import-competing manufacturers, and between the resource-rich periphery and the people-rich centre.

The structures created by these tensions proved difficult to alter. For much of the last century, Canadians clung to the illusion that a resource-based economy without secure markets for its products, yoked to inefficient manufacturers organized around import-substitution, could nonetheless sustain growth and prosperity. Facing stubborn barriers to their exports in the United States and Europe moreover, Canadians found it hard to resist their own manufacturers' calls for protection. Those manufacturers in turn became deeply attached to protection and even succeeded in convincing their fellow Canadians that higher prices and meagre choice were somehow important contributors to national identity (a view still held in some protected sectors).

But change did come. Bilateral agreements responding to the disaster of the Great Depression of the 1930s, and then multiparty negotiations after the even larger crisis of the Second World War, gradually chipped away at the familiar walls erected by the National Policy. Even so it took several generations before those walls were sufficiently low, and opportunities elsewhere sufficiently enticing, to convince cautious Canadian manufacturers to embrace a more open economy. Starting in the mid-1980s and with growing confidence in the 1990s, Canadians accepted that our prosperity depends on looking outward. The Canada-United States Free Trade Agreement, later extended to Mexico, and then the conversion of the post-war General Agreement on Tariffs and Trade (GATT) into the World Trade Organization (WTO) near the end of the century, dispelled much of the lingering legacy of the National Policy. They ushered in new policies geared to reap the full benefit of Canada's comparative advantages.

While Canada's east-west trade has barely changed in a generation, our north-south trade has doubled. As a result Canada is a more prosperous country. Consumers have more choices and pay less for them. Firms have more opportunities and service them more easily. Canadians have better-paying jobs and find them more satisfying. As Jan Tumlir, former chief economist at the GATT, observed: "It is depressing to think of all the effort wasted over generations, and the income foregone, because of the belief that an economy gains by protecting its industries" (Tumlir, 1985).

The 1990s thus witnessed a revolutionary change. Free trade became the default position; protection, the minority view. The transition however remains incomplete. Vestiges of the past remain, dragging down Canada's economic performance and the prosperity of individual Canadians.

THE EFFECTIVE BENEFITS OF TRADE AGREEMENTS

Canada now has one of the most open economies in the world, next door to the world's largest and most dynamic market. Just as the failure to secure open trade with the United States in the nineteenth century invited the National Policy, so successful agreements on freer trade in the late twentieth century have removed its rationale. Open trade has increasingly allowed Canadians to make the most of their comparative advantages, providing prosperity, jobs, and a choice of the best products in the global marketplace. Yet some Canadians continue to question whether freer trade is the most appropriate economic strategy for Canada.

There are Canadians who worry that trade agreements undermine our ability to pursue independent policy goals. It is true, of course, that all international compacts, whether their aims are economic, environmental, military, or civil, seek to curb national decision-making to a degree. States (and their citizens) make the reasonable calculation that their interests are better served if other states behave in a predictable and stable manner, subject to common rules, even at the cost of a measure of their own freedom of action. In this respect, trade agreements are no exception, nor very different from many other treaties, conventions, and declarations to which Canada is a party. As economist Ed Safarian notes, "enforceable rules on the way in which both governments and firms compete and how they collaborate ... provide the best guarantee that such competition and collaboration ultimately serve more than a parochial interest" (quoted in Hart, 1998, pg. 5). As citizens of a relatively small economy trading with larger, more powerful partners, Canadians have relied increasingly on the security of trade agreements in opening their market to international competition. Far from promoting unfettered market forces, these agreements have allowed trade and investment to grow on a sustainable basis according to clear rules.

Like most economic transactions, trade is fundamentally a private activity. Governments provide laws and institutions that facilitate these transactions but individuals determine the extent to which, and with whom, they trade. Increasingly, Canadian producers respond to the appetites of foreign, particularly American, customers while Canadian consumers choose foreign goods and services. As a result, Canadian exports of goods and services have expanded steadily over the past two decades to $520 billion in 2005, representing 37.9% of Canada's GDP. Imports were similarly robust, reaching $468 billion in 2005, or 34.1% of GDP. Our two-way trade is approaching the trillion-dollar mark (nominal terms) (Industry Canada, 2005).

A more complete picture emerges when we add the flow of capital to the exchange of goods and services. Foreign firms have a $415.6 billion stake in Canada. Canadians control assets abroad worth $465.1 billion. Canadian subsidiaries in the United States alone rang up $234 billion in sales in 2005, while American affiliates in Canada reported sales of $577 billion. "It is becoming increasingly meaningless, if not outright impossible," Howard Lewis and David Richardson point out, "to think of trade as something separate from cross-border investment, or of exporting as something separate from importing products and innovative ideas. All are tied together in the extended family of global commitment" (Lewis and Richardson, 2001: 11).

In this picture of Canada's trade, however, one partner eclipses all others. Trade with the United States amounts to an astounding $1.75 billion each day; service transactions add another quarter-billion dollars a day. To carry the trade more than 36,000 trucks cross the border every day, complementing the freight trains, ships, planes, buses, pipelines, and transmission lines that connect the two economies. Much of this is what economists call "integrative" trade; that is, exchanges among related parties or firms. Statistics Canada reports that about a third of what Canadian firms export was first imported. In the automotive sector, previously imported parts represented more than half the value of exports. Even food, agriculture, and forestry exports contained at least 10% imported content (Industry Canada, 2005, reporting Statistics Canada data).

The prosperity such trans-border trade generates benefits every region of Canada. Thousands of firms and their workers in every part of the country reach out to foreign markets either directly or as suppliers to other internationally competitive enterprises. Basic resources—grains, fish, forestry, metals, minerals, and energy—now account for less than a third of Canada's total exports. Fabricated resource products, machinery and equipment, automotive products, services, and consumer products make up more than two thirds (Industry Canada, 2005). Canadians are no longer just "hewers of wood and drawers of water." While basic resources continue to be important to our prosperity, Canada has become a knowledge-based industrial and service economy.

As well as we have done, we can do better. To put it bluntly, the policies of the last two decades have put Canadians in the race but they have not prepared us to win the gold medal. Others worked harder, have more advantages, are better prepared, or have otherwise placed themselves ahead of us. If Canadians want to do better, we must also do more. To that end, we must ask ourselves some basic questions. Are we ready to assign the last vestiges of the National Policy to the dustbin of history? Are we prepared to create a truly level playing field in Canada? Are we willing to pursue markets wherever they can be found? We think our fellow Canadian citizens are ready to answer "yes" to all of these questions. And in the pages that follow we outline what it will take to put that willingness into action.

DOING BETTER ABROAD BY DOING BETTER AT HOME

The key to economic growth is greater productivity, and the keys to productivity are innovation and adaptation. Robust trade is evidence of an economy that is innovating and adapting. Firms that trade internationally are more productive, pay higher wages, and earn greater profits (Lewis and Richardson, 2001: 11). But the reverse is also true. Whatever hinders innovation or slows down adaptation also robs Canadians of growth. The result is a weaker economy and less robust trade. A first task, therefore, is to identify what is inappropriate in our existing portfolio of policies and remove it.

In an earlier chapter, we showed how to identify what is inappropriate in our existing portfolio of policies and correct it by reducing the size of government, reforming the tax regime, and eliminating unnecessary regulations. What these reforms have in common is that they involve governments doing less, rather than more. This reflects the consensus of the past 20 years that governments do more for an economy when they forego efforts to shape its structure, and focus on creating a fiscal, monetary, and regulatory environment that sets producers and consumers free to pursue the transactions they believe to be in their own best interests. As the OECD notes,

> the efficiency benefits of an open trade and investment regime contribute to economic growth and hence rising incomes. By contrast, restrictions on trade and investment, in common with other economic distortions, shift an economy to a less efficient and sustainable mix of investment, production and consumption patterns, thus depressing economic growth prospects and reducing attendant benefits such as job creation and innovation. (OECD, 1998: 29)

As counter-intuitive as it may seem to some, reducing business subsidies, allowing weak firms to fail, eliminating remaining tariffs, and other "tough-love" measures will do more for the efficiency, productivity, and vigour (to say nothing of trade performance) of Canadian firms than virtually any other policy or program.

It is not that government has no appropriate role. Government activities from competition law to consumer protection enhance economic efficiency and contribute to prosperity. Governments also pursue valid non-economic objectives: policies that distort the market or affect trade may serve important goals, from national security to distributive justice. The challenge is to address society's most pressing priorities in balance with competing claims. Sound policies promote broad, national interests over narrow, special interests; they gain benefits for the many rather than the few. Proper instruments limit undesirable distortions.

Governments respond to squeaky wheels. This fact of political life is unlikely to change and, of course, the squeaky wheels of the past will not go quietly. As one American pundit put it: "The task of weaning various people and groups from the national nipple will not be easy. The sound of whines, bawls, screams, and invective will fill the air as the agony of withdrawal pangs finds voice" (Bowles, 1994: A16). But weaned these special interests must be, if our productivity and standard of living are to improve. And Canadians need not believe that every squeaky wheel represents a fibre of the national identity. The Wheat Board, agricultural supply management, ownership restrictions in financial services, transportation, energy, telecommunications, business subsidies, and tariffs, all may once have responded to perceptions of compelling public purpose. Today, they serve as little more than a drain on Canada's economic wealth.

A HARVEST OF INEFFICIENCY
FROM SUPPLY MANAGEMENT

Supply management in grain, dairy, and poultry farming offers a good example. Marketing boards were originally introduced in the 1920s and 1930s as voluntary organizations to strengthen the hand of farmers in dealing with customers. They proved useful. But then governments made them compulsory. Political considerations, not market forces, came to influence prices. The result was inevitable distortion. And when governments restricted imports of competing farm products to protect these schemes, the distortions multiplied.

As a result, today, almost every Canadian is worse off, while a very few continue to benefit. Consumers pay more than they should for milk, eggs, bread, and other products, leaving less to spend on other things. Efficient farmers earn less than they could in a free market. Inefficient farmers stay in business, even when the market would tell them they could earn a better living in another line of work. The value of production quotas inflates the price of farms, and deters owners from switching to products they might produce more efficiently. Farmers in other countries, including poor nations, lose the chance to serve Canadian customers and earn the income that would allow them to buy products from efficient Canadian exporters (Hart, April 2005).

Canada was not alone in attempting to stabilize farm incomes with measures that created as many problems as they solved. Many other countries did the same. The WTO Agriculture Agreement and the Canada-United States FTA eliminated some of the worst of these trade barriers. Many Canadian farmers and food producers responded well. They became more competitive and better integrated into world, and particularly North American, markets. Still, farm subsidies remain a major global problem.

Canada pays less than it once did in the way of direct cash subsidies to farmers Instead, our supply management system and high tariffs constitute indirect subsidies. The need to defend farm subsidies severely compromises the ability of Canadian negotiators to challenge egregious EU and US farm subsidies which are at roughly Canada's level. Phasing them out while mitigating the cost of adjustment for individual farmers would confer a triple benefit: clearing away a major inefficiency in our own economy, strengthening efforts to tackle subsidies elsewhere, and strengthening our foreign assistance efforts by opening up our markets to food exports from poor countries.

THE TRUE COST OF A "FREE" LUNCH

Agriculture is not the only sector that benefits from the largesse of government. The power of the state to coerce taxes from citizens is always prone to capture by groups who would like to benefit from this revenue. Much of what Canadians pay in tax goes to important public functions such as defence, social services, infrastructure, and justice. Tax revenue is also used to compensate for market inefficiencies and to redistribute income. Some also goes to prop up uncompetitive businesses.

Stalwart defenders of industrial policies and investment incentives, otherwise known as subsidies, insist that they either save or create jobs, or allow Canada to participate in industries that would otherwise be established elsewhere. There is no credible basis for such claims. It is hard to imagine circumstances in which politicians and bureaucrats are better placed to assess the viability of a particular activity than investors and entrepreneurs whose judgments are subject to market discipline. "Industrial policies" are no more than politicized redistribution schemes that penalize successful firms and reward laggards. For every job a subsidy "creates" or "saves," others are destroyed by the extra taxes needed to pay for the subsidy.

Canadian business leaders, arguing for lower taxes, frequently chastise government for providing subsidies to favoured sectors. Governments should take them at their word, ignore special pleading, and phase out all remaining business subsidies whether to aerospace, textiles and clothing, agriculture, or some other sector.

COVERT PROTECTIONISM

Restricting the foreign ownership of certain kinds of businesses is another form of protectionism that may not be obvious but nevertheless carries a price for Canadians. Limiting foreign participation in a sector devalues the capital invested there and reduces the incentive for firms to innovate and create new value. This type of "protection" in fact handicaps financial services, transportation, telecommunications, energy, and other sectors of the Canadian economy. Defenders of the policy argue that governments can enforce regulatory and other rules more effectively on Canadian than on foreign owners. Experience denies this. Numerous foreign-owned automotive and other firms operate in Canada in full compliance with our laws and regulations. There is no reason to think the same would not hold true in banking, air transport, communications, or energy.

If the issue is enforcement of Canadian laws, restricting the ownership of firms operating in Canada is simply not the appropriate way to accomplish this objective. Laws and policies of general application can do the job. For example, if Canada has a national interest in protecting its environment, that protection should be provided by laws that apply to all companies, regardless of who owns them. Likewise, if it is not in our strategic interest for an oil-sands operation to be owned by an agency of the communist government of China, or for a construction company owned by Bin Laden to be involved in building such plants, this can be prevented by policies that require any developer of strategic energy resources (regardless of ownership) to meet certain security tests.

There have been calls for the government to enact even stronger ownership restrictions against foreign takeovers. These must be resisted. Restricting to whom an entrepreneur may sell a business will, all other things being equal, reduce the value of that business by reducing the available market into which it can be sold. Therefore the return on that entrepreneur's capital and labour will be reduced, relative to freer economies. Given a choice, the entrepreneur will be more likely to found a new business somewhere other than a country that restricts the freedom to sell what she has for the highest value.

There is a better way to help Canadian companies: to empower our business firms to compete more effectively on the world stage, to better withstand adverse takeover attempts, and to conduct more takeovers of their own. Two major empowerment policies that we recommend are the following.

❧ Increase the financial strength of the private sector in Canada by major reductions in corporate tax levels (see chapters 6 and 7).

❧ Eliminate the remaining trade barriers between Canada and our biggest customer through establishing a North American customs union with a common, declining external tariff.

As well, Canadian competition policy should take the global marketplace into consideration, so that Canada does not prevent its companies from growing to a global scale. Subscale companies will otherwise inevitably be prone to being acquired in the course of consolidation that is a characteristic of mature industries.

In fact there are two options here. Either we let investors decide who should own what, or we let politicians and bureaucrats make those decisions. The last time politicians and bureaucrats involved themselves in trying to increase Canadian ownership of the energy sector (through the National Energy Program) it proved to be an unmitigated disaster. Our recommendation is, "let investors decide."

COSTLY HOLDOVERS FROM THE PAST

The Customs Tariff is a policy that continues to steal from Canadians on a daily basis. Most Canadians have long forgotten (if they ever knew) that the original purpose of the Tariff was to raise money for the colonial, and later, the federal government. In the nineteenth and early twentieth centuries, the Tariff often provided two thirds of federal revenue. That has not been true for at least six decades yet the Tariff lingers to protect a handful of manufacturers.

As a result of repeated rounds of negotiation over the years, tariff protection has been reduced until it represents less than 1% of government revenue and, spread across all imports, adds less than 2% to their cost. More than 80% of products now enter Canada free of duty as a result of the Canada-United States Free Trade Agreement (CUFTA), other tariff preferences, and concessions to developing countries. Indeed, the cost of collecting the tariff (and maintaining related programs such as rules of origin) are out of all proportion to the revenue it now raises.

Nevertheless, tariffs that remain do substantial damage. As Table 13.1 illustrates, tariffs of more than 200% effectively triple the price of dairy and poultry imports; imported textiles, clothing, and footwear are taxed at rates of up to 20%. Significant as such penalties are to Canadians who might use these products, they understate the full impact on the economy. They fail to capture the cost of a delayed movement of capital and labour from less productive activity into more productive endeavours.

Governments have simplified the Customs Tariff over the years and organized it around an internationally agreed schedule of products. But they have shied away from the simplest reform of all: eliminating the Tariff altogether. At one stroke, that would reduce 1,796 pages of customs law to a single sentence applying a statutory rate of "free" to every one of the more than 5,000 product lines now enumerated. The same stroke would eliminate hundreds of pages of regulations and administrative notices. It would achieve both freer trade and deregulation in one step.

As attractive as this looks, as long as the United States maintains its own Tariff it would complicate achievement of an even more important Canadian objective: a seamless North American market. A more practical goal is a Common External Tariff (CET) that would see the United States and Canada apply identical rates on the same product. In addition to lowering the tariff in both countries, a CET would eliminate the ruinous effect of rules-of-origin and sharply reduce the cost of cross-border trade. We will return to this issue later in our discussion of Canada-US relations.

Canadians claim to be generous and, in fact, have demonstrated a desire to help the world's least fortunate. But we could be much more helpful than we are. As long as we shelter industries such as textiles, clothing, and footwear behind high tariff walls and aggressive antidumping investigations, we hurt rather than help those foreigners who produce these products, most of whom live in countries much poorer than ours. Such protection is also unfair to us. It forces us to pay more for shoes, shirts, underwear, and other products than we would pay in a free global market. It is even unfair to the Canadians working in the protected industries, trapping them in low-wage jobs. In an economy that has added an average of more than 250,000 new jobs each year for the past four years, there is no justification for protecting the low pay and high prices that characterize such import-competing sectors.

Table 13.1: Some typical Canadian tariff rates in 2006

Product	Rate (%)	Product	Rate (%)
Wheat, durum	49.0%	Wheat, other	76.5%
Wheat, gluten	$397.30 per tonne, plus 14.5%	Barley	94.5%
		Ships	25.0%
Chicken	238.0%	Turkey	154.5%
Eggs	163.5%	Butter	298.5%
Milk	241.0%	Cream	292.5%
Cheese	245.5%	Yogurt	237.5%
Rivets	6.5%	Cotter pins	6.5%
Leaf springs	8.0%	Spices	3.0%
Cloth	14.0%	Yarns	8.0%
Carpets	12.5%	Footwear	20.0%
Knits	14.0%	Clothing	18.0%

Source: Canadian Border Services Agency, 2006.

Does this mean that Canada should close down its footwear and clothing factories? Not necessarily. Competitive Canadian firms exist in these industries. They would do well in a more open domestic market and could do even better if Canada's actions in retiring its tariffs persuaded other countries to drop their own barriers. Governments do not pick winners well. Markets do a much better job. To allow the market to do its job, governments should stop protecting the losers. If business subsidies, ownership restrictions, supply management, and other legacies of National-Policy thinking were eliminated, Canadians would liberate economic resources to migrate from areas of low return to areas of greater promise. The result would be a stronger, more productive, and wealthier Canada.

US economist Douglas Irwin has made an exhaustive study of all the arguments used to justify protection, demonstrating in each case the weak intellectual foundations upon which they all rest. He concludes: "About two hundred years ago, largely as a result of Adam Smith's *Wealth of Nations*, free trade achieved an intellectual status unrivalled by any other doctrine in the field of economics. Despite being subjected to intense scrutiny over the two centuries since that time, free trade has, by and large, succeeded in maintaining this special position" (Irwin, 1996: 217). Protection is a matter of politics, not economics. To an economist, the impact of protection is clear: it provides the illusion of benefit for a few but penalizes everyone else, often long after the original, short-term benefit has dissipated. As Adam Smith put it, "mercy to the guilty is cruelty to the innocent" (Smith, 1759).

Canadians can achieve many of the benefits of a more open economy on our own, without waiting for any other country to act with us. It is true that more might be achieved by acting together with others nations but here the perfect should not be made the enemy of the good. Removing trade barriers for the broad good of the nation will present a painful adjustment to those who have become dependent upon them. For example, the value of a dairy farmer's supply-managed milk quota may exceed the value of the cows and, for many, the quota system has become a retirement nest egg. To lose it or have its value diminished by freer trade in dairy products would be a devastating loss. Indeed, the difficulty of devising policies to ease such a transition is the main reason that trade agreements in Europe and North America have largely excluded agriculture. It is also why no Canadian government, regardless of its parliamentary majority, has been willing to tackle the high cost to our domestic economy of agricultural subsidies.

So, what to do? While drafting a detailed adjustment plan is beyond the scope of this study, we do propose three principles upon which such a policy should be based.

1 *Consultation*   Adjustment strategies, policies, and mechanisms must flow from full consultation with affected groups and individuals—both those who would suffer from eliminating protectionist measures and those who suffer from their continuation.

2 *Compensation*   Governments that created financial entitlements must accept the principle that those who will lose them are entitled to compensation.

3 *Limitation*   Neither consultation nor compensation can go on forever. The purpose of adjustment is to ease adaptation to a new economic environment, not to perpetuate a new form of dependence.

A SHRINKING RETURN FROM TRADE PROMOTION

Government has no place in the decision-making of Canadian consumers, importers, or exporters. For more than a century, Canadian officials have fanned out across the globe to promote our products. Today, Canadian trade commissioners can be found in over 150 cities around the world, backed by several hundred officials in the federal departments of Foreign Affairs, Trade, Industry, Agriculture, and Natural Resources. Provincial ministries operate their own parallel programs. All of these efforts assume that Canadian businesses depend on governments to find markets, promote exports, and unearth investment opportunities. But is this true? And is the benefit worth the significant effort expended?

At one time, distances seemed greater, foreign markets more remote, and the mix of Canadian exports more concentrated. In the early years of the last century, for example, when half of Canada's exports were grain products, government-to-government dealings were indeed critical to the success of exporters. But those days are long gone. Little of Canada's trade today takes place between unrelated firms operating in separate national markets. Most involves transactions within multinational firms or among firms closely allied in sophisticated production networks. A growing share is made up of parts for complex finished products. Many global firms would be hard-pressed even to identify which of their products are "Canadian." Bombardier's regional jets, for example, have more foreign content than Canadian. In these circumstances, the role of trade commissioners in promoting "Canadian" exports is marginal at best.

Foreign intelligence and international commercial and governmental contacts still serve a limited purpose. For example, officials should certainly be ready to help individuals and firms overcome specific problems encountered in entering new markets. They should seize every opportunity to negotiate better rules and terms of access. They should insist that other governments live up to their agreements and be equally prepared to ensure that Canadians do the same. They should use the dispute-settlement provisions in trade agreements to defend the rights of Canadians. They should build relations with emerging trade and investment partners.

Much of this, however, will have only a marginal impact on Canadian prosperity as a whole. Thanks to the sophisticated and mature global-trade regime that already exists, billions of dollars in international transactions now occur daily without the slightest government involvement. Weaning Canadian business off the government nipple, therefore, should extend to the trade and investment community.

Like other business subsidies, government trade promotion has vocal champions but, curiously, few opponents. The best way to determine whether a need exists is to put it on a user-pay business—as Australia has done. Private-sector market-intelligence and logistic services already compete in this area. Charging a fee for the services governments supply will soon determine how far Canadian firms value them—and at what price.

The Export Development Corporation and the banks

Among the most important export promotion programs the federal government offers are those of the Export Development Corporation (EDC). Its host of services include assessments of foreign markets and investment guarantees. Its most important program, however, is to extend credit to foreign purchasers of Canadian goods and services. Credit is largely offered on a commercial basis but also in the form of concessions; in effect, credit subsidies. Their extent is often difficult to gauge due to the credit power of the state. Global competition among governments in extending export credits in politically important sectors has become a major problem, preoccupying both the OECD and the WTO. Some sectors of the economy have become heavily reliant on this service.

Ostensibly, the EDC is a response to market failure: the inability or unwillingness of commercial banks to offer export credits, investment guarantees, and similar products at attractive rates. Perhaps, but there is also the suspicion that commercial banks find it hard to compete with a subsidized government "service." The quickest way to determine whether there is indeed a commercial need for government-supplied export credits and guarantees is for the EDC to charge clients the full cost of these services. Under these circumstances, commercial banks might well find it attractive to compete and offer a broader range of products for their commercial customers, including export financing and investment guarantees.

As with other business subsidies, the EDC has strong support from its constituency. That support would be more acceptable if the EDC services were not subsidized by the rest of us.

THE DIMINISHING ROLE OF "BIG TABLE" TRADE TALKS

Choosing what to negotiate and with whom is the essence of trade diplomacy. Unfortunately, over the past dozen or so years Canadians have been reluctant to finish what they started in the 1990s. The result has been a string of low-risk, low-gain negotiations. As Bill Dymond and Michael Hart point out: "The unpleasant reality is that the Harper government inherited a Canadian trade policy that is effectively bankrupt: there is no economic or commercial market in Canada for multilateral and regional trade agreements, and no political market for addressing pressing matters in the relationship with the United States" (Hart and Dymond, 2006). Clearly, the moment is ripe for new thinking about where Canadian trade policy can be effective and what its appropriate goals might be.

The World Trade Organization's Doha Development Round of trade negotiations offers a prime example. The round was suspended in July 2006 after participating governments agreed that none of the proposals then in play could bridge their differences. Only significant changes in view on the part of all the major players would justify re-starting talks. To date the table is empty and the prognosis pessimistic. In all of this, Canada played only a small role. Determined to protect a dwindling number of chicken and dairy farmers, our trade diplomats had little to contribute to the discussion. It was not always thus. In the not-too-distant past Canada, with the United States, the EU, and Japan, was a player, a member of the "Quad" that ran the World Trade Organization. Today India, Brazil, and Australia have displaced Canada at the centre of discussions.

It is tempting to blame this state of affairs entirely on the government's implacable defence of supply management in the barns of the nation. It is certainly bizarre that Canada, a major net exporter of farm products, remains rooted in the protectionist camp on this account. But that is not the only, or even the primary, reason for Canada's tepid engagement in the Doha Round. Put simply, Canada had little to gain or lose and no compelling stake in play. The truth is that Canada's most vital economic interests are now inextricably bound up with the United States; they can no longer be addressed multilaterally in the WTO.

The marginal importance to Canada of the Doha Round should not be confused with the WTO's continuing importance to us. Both the institution and the rules it administers continue to operate to Canada's advantage. The WTO is Canada's principal trade agreement with most of the world and provides a critical underpinning to the North American Free Trade Agreement (NAFTA). What has failed is not the WTO but only the consensus on expanding its purview. Governments have not rejected the need for global trade rules, for a global trade institution, or for transparent procedures to resolve disputes.

What they cannot agree on are the parameters for extending and strengthening those rules—and they are unlikely to do so any time soon.

This is no calamity for Canada. For this country, as for the United States and most of the rest of the industrialized world, the lion's share of what was desirable to accomplish in the multilateral arena has been achieved already. What remains unresolved is the more intractable residue of 70 years of negotiations. At the same time, established trading nations have resisted the efforts of emerging economies to recast the agenda in favour of development at the risk of diminishing the effectiveness of the current rules. There is potential benefit to expanding the global regime to include developing countries—including an expansion of trade in farm products. But, for developed economies, these advantages are small and outweighed by perceptions of the political pain that would flow from lowering the last of the protectionist walls. In any event, Canada has little leverage to alter either the dynamics or the direction of the conversation.

Multilateralism versus bilateralism: A false choice

Many Canadians may recoil from our questioning of the value of multilateral trade negotiations. They will see it as repudiating Canada's history. Even the first Director General of the WTO, Renato Ruggiero, observed that "Canadians have multilateralism in their DNA" (Ruggiero, 1996). True enough, but from the outset multilateralism was a choice, not a vocation, a means rather than an end.

The choice was pragmatic. Multilateralism offered Canadians sustainable benefits. But what is the purpose of the game? Governments enter into trade agreements to resolve conflicts and improve circumstances that they cannot resolve or improve on their own. Accomplishing this with as many partners at one time as possible is obviously desirable. When players in the multilateral game become hostage to the agenda of the most recalcitrant players, the desirability wanes. Canadians should always be ready to pursue our interests on a multilateral basis but we should never allow the ideology of multilateralism to stand in the way of our interests.

The lack of recent success in multilateral negotiations is in stark contrast to breakthroughs in regional and bilateral accords. Governments, particularly in developing countries, have been as eager to commit to liberalization under such narrower terms as they have been reluctant to conclude big-table accords. Canada has not been immune from this development. And, as it happens, Canada's most promising trade opportunities lie in exactly such bilateral discussions—with our closest neighbour, most strategic partner, and largest market, the United States.

THE FALSE ALLURE OF TRADE "DIVERSITY"

The manifestly apparent fact that the United States represents by far the most fertile field for Canadian business development meets a startling amount of resistance. Both inside and outside of government, policy entrepreneurs, vote-seeking politicians, academics, and activists are vocally committed to the idea that Canada needs to "diversify" its trade. They are confused.

It is not Canada but Canadians, as corporations and as individuals, who determine the pattern of trade and investment. Canada, the country, does not trade, despite frequent rhetorical assertions to the contrary. Trade flows from billions of discrete and seemingly unrelated daily choices by individuals about what to eat, wear, drive, read, and purchase. Markets and suppliers in the United States are now the overwhelming preference of Canadian firms and individuals, just as Canadian markets and suppliers have become more important in the United States. The pace of this growing economic interdependence accelerated perceptibly in the 1980s, to the benefit of both countries, and it has increased almost on a daily basis ever since. Calls to diversify Canada's trade relations fly in the face of this reality.

Ever since Prime Minister Trudeau pursued his failed "third option" in the 1970s, a small minority of Canadians has continued to worry about the "threat" of becoming integrated into the North American economy. The calamity they imagine looming over our southern border has, however, stubbornly declined to appear. As we noted earlier, the goods and services Canadians trade, mainly with the United States, are already highly diversified—and they are becoming more so. The range of products and suppliers vying for consumers' attention has increased dramatically over the past few decades, while Canadian producers now serve millions of customers. Most of these happen to be in North America because that is where the most profitable opportunities are to be found.

Are there profitable opportunities beyond North America that Canadian firms would prefer to service but cannot because of trade barriers? The evidence is not there. As a result of nearly seven decades of trade negotiations, the markets of the industrialized countries are, on the whole, open. The barriers that remain are of two types: those protecting the most sensitive—read politically potent—sectors, and regulatory and structural arrangements that are much more difficult to tackle. Multilateral and regional trade negotiations will continue to chip away at both. As we have said, Canadians should make every effort to eliminate such barriers both abroad and at home—not for some ephemeral and unachievable goal of diversification but because it just makes good economic sense.

To diversify Canadian trade to any measurable degree, however, our government would need to tell businesses where to trade, investors where to invest, and consumers what to buy. Other governments would have to do the same.

The United States, for example, would need to throw up obstacles to Canadian exports, while the Europeans, Japanese, Indians, Chinese, and others lowered theirs. The trade that resulted would certainly be more "diversified" but in diminished volumes that generate fewer good jobs and lower incomes. For the great mass of Canadians who work in the private economy, this would be the path of lunacy. Happily, it is a path that Canadians overwhelmingly reject and that has approximately a zero prospect of being pursued.

A generation ago, European markets represented the holy grail of diversification; today, it is India and China. Over the past two decades, these two Asian giants have taken steps to end years of economic isolation. As *The Economist* recently pointed out, they are again assuming their historic roles among the world's largest economies and most important traders (*The Economist*, 2006). China, in particular, has become an important exporter of consumer goods and a major importer of machinery and industrial inputs. Trade between Canada and China and, to a lesser extent, between Canada and India, has grown over this period. The total of this trade still amounts to less than the annual growth in our trade with the United States.

Typically for countries at their stage of development, India and China have become major exporters of low-cost, standard-technology, consumer goods, machinery, and parts for more sophisticated products. India, additionally, has become a major provider of professional and communication services. These exports compete largely with products from countries further along the development path, from Korea and Malaysia to Brazil and Eastern Europe. Canadians benefit from the downward pressure this competition puts on prices for these products. Both Asian giants are also major importers of resources, energy, and foodstuffs. Canada, to the extent it remains a supplier of such globally priced commodities, benefits from the increased demand for them, whether or not it ships any products to these countries. Thus, Canadians benefit and will continue to benefit from India and China's emergence as major traders, even if Canada itself does not become a major supplier to these markets.

There are benefits to strengthening commercial ties with India, China, and other emerging markets. But these flow from the real needs of Canadian business rather than from any ideological drive to diversify trade. Few barriers remain to the leading OECD markets; these present reliable, but mature, outlets for Canadian exports. India, China, and other emerging markets, by contrast, remain underdeveloped, their potential far from exhausted. That is in part because the risks of doing business there are great. Trade officials can reduce these risks by encouraging development of basic commercial instruments: foreign investment protection agreements, arrangements to avoid double taxation, and industrial cooperation accords. They can deepen relations through technical-assistance and capacity-building projects.

At the same time, an equal opportunity exists to pump up the other side of our trade balance sheet with these nations by taking the steps we have already identified at home: eliminating Canada's remaining tariffs, restraining over-zealous antidumping investigations, and abandoning ownership restrictions, supply management, and other inhibitors to imports of products and invest-ment from emerging economies.

Free-trade agreements with minor partners:
Much ado about too little

Effective diversification will not be accomplished by pursuing free-trade agree-ments with minor partners. While such agreements do little harm, they also do little good. They represent the increasing fondness in official Ottawa for activity over results. Negotiations with the European Free Trade Association, Singapore, Central America, the Dominican Republic, and Korea, efforts to conclude a Canada-EU Trade and Investment Enhancement Agreement or the Free Trade Agreement for the Americas (FTAA), the APEC talks, and Team Can-ada missions to every corner of the globe consume a disproportionate amount of time and energy. These efforts are marginal to Canada's primary interests, though they may have some utility in declaring Canada's commitment to free-ing trade, particularly with poorer nations, as discussed in chapter 15.

Nonetheless, realism is called for, particularly since few of these negotia-tions are going anywhere. Negotiations to establish an FTAA have run aground on the incompatibility of Brazilian interests with US political realities. Bra-zil's ambition for regional hegemony clashes with American designs for US-dominated hemispheric trade. American decision-makers meanwhile assign high costs and little gain to an agreement that opens the United States market further to competitive Latin American farm products. While some countries—Venezuela, Bolivia, and potentially Ecuador and Peru—are veering off on nationalist adventures uncongenial to trade liberalization, others are seeking and obtaining bilateral deals with the United States away from the FTAA table. The prospects of breathing life into the FTAA are, therefore, poor and Canada in any case is little more than a well-meaning bystander.

Similarly, the Asia-Pacific Economic Cooperation (APEC) free-trade nego-tiations effectively died with the Asian financial crisis in the late 1990s. Major countries—Australia, China, Malaysia, and Korea—are putting their effort into either intra-regional trade arrangements or bilateral deals with the United States. Whatever broader purposes the APEC may serve, free trade is not among them.

Canada's pursuit of bilateral free-trade agreements with the rump of the European Free Trade Association (Norway, Switzerland, Iceland, and Liech-tenstein) and the Central American Four (Guatemala, El Salvador, Nicaragua,

Honduras) likewise ran into problems in the face of small pockets of politically significant domestic opposition: shipbuilding in the former case and clothing in the latter. More recent negotiations with Korea face opposition from the well-organized auto sector. Canadians generally might benefit from these agreements but their prospects are slim so long as the potential gains are small and dispersed and opposition concentrated and well organized.

Finally, there is another hazard to proliferating FTAs with minor trade partners. They may actually complicate a more important goal: reducing the cost and complexity of administering our border with the United States. We believe that Canada should seek a common external tariff with the United States. Multiple FTAs, each with its own schedule of commitments on tariff concessions, make this harder. At this point, each FTA Canada has implemented has an American equivalent; some that are in negotiation do not. The United States itself has more FTAs than Canada and this alone will create enough difficulty. Canada does not need to add to it.

In short, it is a question of focus. Canada's government needs to guard against becoming captive to trade initiatives that bring us virtually no measurable benefit. There is no shortage of lobbyists and foreign leaders who would like a place on Canada's trade agenda. Many of their ideas may have some merit. But our government need not be their champion. There are bigger stakes on the horizon and they must be given priority, though Canada should remain informed and willing to participate when such ideas do not conflict with our larger interests or involve too great a diversion of resources.

CONCLUSIONS: TRADE DETERMINES OUR PROSPERITY

Canada's prosperity soars or stalls on the wings of trade. Our economy is substantial compared to some, but small by world standards. Without access to foreign markets, Canadian firms are unlikely to attain the scale required to finance innovation. And only through innovation can Canadians enjoy rising prosperity. The first priority of our foreign policy must therefore be to champion and practice freer trade.

Our approach in the past has, with few exceptions, been in keeping with our character: incremental, pragmatic, and cautious. More could have been done, or done more boldly. But those tasked with the responsibility have appreciated the realities: trade and investment are mainly private sector activities. Government can facilitate or frustrate these but seldom does it participate; and in those rare cases where it does—through, for example, crown corporations—the record offers little to suggest it can do better than the private sector. Slowly but steadily Canada has opened its economy and has become increasingly adroit at good trade practice. While there remain dissenters, support for free trade and open markets are now clearly the optimal position for Canadians. Domestically and internationally, the stage is set for Canada to reap the full benefits of the global economy.

At home, Canadians should sweep out the last vestiges of the National Policy and demand that markets be allowed to determine who will produce what for whom. From milk and poultry quotas to aerospace subsidies, from limiting telecom ownership to tariffs that coddle (and constrain) clothing and footwear firms, Canadians should pull the last props from beneath the uncompetitive and release the last curbs that hold back the strong. Government should stop trying to support losers and pick winners.

Abroad, Canada should pursue results rather than ideologies. Whether we act alone or with multiple partners, the rules of trade we adopt must reinforce rather than seek to replace market judgments. The goal must be a truly open, truly competitive global economy. This is a matter of fundamental freedom as much as economic efficacy. Governments that forbid their people to buy products from other countries or tax imports more heavily than domestic goods infringe their citizens' liberty. Only the strongest grounds justify such infringement. International free-trade agreements that deter trade barriers protect Canadians' freedom.

But our paramount focus must be the United States. Our relationship with America is unique. It is the only one we have that embraces every dimension of public policy, security, economic development, and human contact. Favoured by proximity, size, similarity of legal and popular cultures, and a common language, the United States has become the overwhelming first choice of both Canadian exporters and consumers—to the point that our two markets have become deeply integrated. Over time, Canadian firms will find additional opportunities in other markets, but only if they earn enough in North America to finance the effort. There is no other trading partner from whose growth, indeed from whose doubling or even trebling growth, we stand to gain as much as we do from merely incremental expansion of our trade with the United States. Deepening integration with the US economy must be on the agenda as the best way for Canadians to increase our trade, prosperity, and leadership potential. We discuss the opportunities to accomplish this in the next chapter.

RECOMMENDATIONS

Freer trade offers the most effective means to increase Canadian prosperity and empower our citizens. It offers a compelling focus for action. We believe the following steps are appropriate.

13.1 Eliminate the last vestiges of the National-Policy mindset, from supply management and business subsidies to ownership restrictions in transportation, telecommunications, and financial services to allow Canadian firms to become more productive and competitive in international markets.

13.2 Pursue a customs union and common external tariff with the United States, using the process to lower remaining tariffs and reduce cross-border transaction costs.

13.3 Institute full cost recovery from clients of government export promotion programs, including clients of the Export Development Corporation. The long-term goal should be to hand over such activities to private sector institutions.

13.4 Let markets decide with whom Canadians trade, either as exporters or as consumers. Ideologically driven efforts to diversify trade patterns substitute political and bureaucratic preference for market judgment and impoverish rather than enrich Canadians.

13.5 Continue to support Canadian exporters by working to expand market access, resolve specific trade problems where possible, and fully exercise Canada's rights under existing trade agreements. At the same time, Canada should live up to its own commitments and ensure that our domestic market is fully open to foreign competition.

13.6 Pursue free-trade agreements with minor partners only to the extent that they do not interfere with key Canadian trade goals.

CHAPTER 14

THE INDISPENSABLE PARTNER

"It is the ultimate irony, but one very reflective of our history, that our capacity to protect our own interests is enhanced when we engage even with the dominant power of the day; when we disengage, our influence diminishes."

—Hugh Segal (2003), Senator

"While there are differences, the commonality of our interests is overwhelming, though much less topical. In international fora the world over, from the G7 to NATO to the WTO, Canada and the United States agree more often than they disagree because for the most part our interests align. While we feel pride in our differences as a nation and a people, we fool ourselves and put our vital interests at risk if we fail to be conscious of our similarities."

—John Manley (2005), former Canadian Foreign Minister

We agree with both Hugh Segal and John Manley: Canada has much more in common with the United States than we have differences. Our capacity to promote Canadian interests and protect our vulnerabilities, moreover, is far more effective when we work with our American neighbours. Yet over the past decade and a half Canada's diplomatic focus has drifted away from our most important relationship.

Under Prime Minister Stephen Harper, Canada's government has devoted considerable attention to restoring that focus and undoing the damage of recent political indulgence. It has made an important start to returning the relationship to the close terms of a generation ago. But more is required. Canadians need to summon the intellectual discipline and care necessary to obtain mutual benefits on both the economic and security fronts; we cannot afford to ignore neither. Without such an effort, the relationship will continue to drift and Canada will move further down the list of countries the United States perceives as vital to its interests. Should that happen, our influence in both Washington and around the world will wane and Canadians will be the losers.

The time has come to embrace a mutually beneficial, ever deepening integration of our continental economy with new rules and institutions designed to render the border between our nations as invisible to commerce as possible while preserving valued differences of identity and social priority. The alternative—raising barriers to integration for the sole purpose of creating distance between ourselves and the United States while seeking to replace this vital relationship with other partnerships—is the route to a less prosperous and secure, more isolated future.

The ball is in our court. Dwight Mason, a former deputy chief of mission at the US embassy in Ottawa, describes US policy toward Canada as "fragmented, derivative and a function of the priorities of agencies and groups focused on particular US domestic issues" (Mason, 2005: 2). Canada, therefore, must supply the vision and initiative. To that end, Canadians must accept that our network of trade, security, environment, regulatory, and other cross-border arrangements has fallen behind the present realities of our relationship and the world. These networks and relationships worked well enough in the past. But in the face of terrorism and other threats, the issue today is how to strengthen joint security arrangements so that both countries can seize new economic opportunities and advance common interests.

While people in either country may at times celebrate our differences, reflection reveals our many similarities, common values, and shared goals. These are already driving the convergence of public policies, including security, immigration, food safety, the environment, and more. The remaining differences lie mostly in the choice of means rather than the ends themselves. The need is not for total harmonization—let alone homogenization—but for more sharing of information, cooperation, and coordination. What counts most is that the two governments share the same objectives and have confidence in each other.

Over the past two decades, as a result of policy choices and the evolution of technology and commerce, the Canadian and American economies have become deeply intermeshed. This has occurred through trade in goods and services, by way of mutual investment, cultural exchange, and the deepening of intercorporate and personal relationships. This integration can only deepen naturally wherever our two societies connect, resulting in an interdependence that is, as it has always been, asymmetrical—and thus of particular concern to Canadians. The question for Canada's government is whether to help or hinder the relationship, to manage it or let it drift.

We believe the choice is obvious. As historian Jack Granatstein concludes:

We share a continent, most values, many traditions, and much history. Ultimately, we share our bed with the Americans. After all, we Canadians helped make this bed, we lie in it, and we need to face up at last to the reality of our situation. Moral earnestness and the loud preaching of our values will not suffice to protect us in this new century. We have to put interests ahead of values, hard-headedness before wishful thinking. The alternative is too self-destructive to contemplate. (Granatstein, 2003: 27)

Two imperatives drive Canada's diplomacy toward the United States. One is unique to Canada; the other we share with most other countries. The first derives from Canada's geographic proximity, asymmetric interdependence, and deepening integration with the economy of the United States. The second flows from the sheer predominance of the United States in world affairs. Our goals will not be advanced by putting rhetorical or policy distance between Canada and the United States. The lifeblood of diplomacy is access, and nowhere more so than in Washington. Access is critical to influence and influence essential to persuade American decision-makers to be responsive to Canadian concerns. For Canada, therefore, access and influence must be the helix at the centre of our diplomacy toward the United States. To gain the confidence of the United States in Canada as a reliable partner requires sensitivity to security as the crucial American priority.

STUMBLING BLOCKS TO MORE PRODUCTIVE RELATIONS

It was perhaps inevitable that any relationship as important to Canadians as that with the United States should generate its share of myths and misconceptions. Some of these are relatively harmless. Others are deeply inappropriate adjuncts to the desire for a deeper and more mutually beneficial relationship. For some Canadians, relations with the United States are a matter of distance. They wish to hold America neither too far away nor too close. Distance, however, provides no guidance on any issue that may arise in the relationship. On many questions, from air transport safety to the prevention of disease, from promotion of cultural programs to refugee acceptance, Canada is best served by nourishing the highest degree of cooperation with the United States.

For its part, American policy toward Canada is driven purely by interest. We believe the same compass should guide our policy. The relationship will both "feel" and function best to the degree that we are guided by a clear sense of our interests, not distracted by subjective perceptions of intimacy or remoteness. As Canada's diplomatic sage, John Holmes, put it: "We should talk less about 'closer relations' between the two countries and more about 'better relations,' which are not necessarily the same thing. Nature has made us about as close as we could possibly be and this has made it all the more necessary that relations should be carefully structured" (Holmes, 1989: 314).

Some pundits believe that building a more productive relationship with the United States will come at the price of unacceptable sacrifices of sovereignty. Sovereignty, however, is not a goal but an instrument of national policy; a means, not an end. Canada has led the way in promoting, negotiating, and accepting a rules-based system for the conduct of international relations. The pursuit of more demanding forms of cooperation flows logically from those earlier efforts. Deepening bilateral integration with the United States, in particular, challenges us not to surrender but to exercise our sovereignty to achieve important national objectives.

Some Canadians also hold the view that Canadian and American assessments of the world around them are significantly different. In fact, they are not. Such differences as there may be do not flow from fundamentally different values or priorities but from different roles. The United States is the world's only superpower, with unique interests and responsibilities. Canada is its closest neighbour and, generally, closest ally. Issue by issue, our views usually coincide, even if the approach to them may differ.

Still other Canadians appear to believe that Canada's influence with the rest of the world is proportional to our ability to demonstrate independence from the United States. This is perverse. Experience shows that our ability to be a player on the world stage depends much more on the strength of our cards in Washington than the other way around. The rest of the world sees Canada as the "other" North American country, closely allied with the United States and deeply experienced in dealing with US officials but more accessible than the superpower. Canada's influence with the rest of the world thus derives directly from our ability to work with the United States and is diminished to the precise degree that we stand off. This does not require Canada's slavish acceptance of US policies and priorities. Addressing differences, however, does demand effective diplomacy and an ability to distinguish between issues of national interest and those of political convenience.

The prospect of further economic and security integration prompts some Canadian analysts to worry about the establishment of "Fortress North America." That fear is hard to find credible. Canada and the United States are among the most open countries in the world, welcoming goods, services, investment, ideas, immigrants, and refugees from around the planet. Our very desire to preserve our openness accentuates the need to guard against those who might take advantage of it to harm us or flout our laws. Both countries take protective measures, often on a cooperative basis. Updating arrangements to correspond to the threats of the 21st century is no more than good common sense. It need not, and is hardly likely to, undermine the historic openness of our societies.

There is also some fear that, facing reverses in the Middle East and criticism from abroad, America will withdraw into isolation. The siren song of isolationism has been a constant in American history but facts on the ground make it neither a credible nor a sustainable policy for any US administration. America's global interests preclude it. From Canada's perspective, the challenge is to ensure that we have influence in Washington, no matter which way the winds blow there.

Many more Canadians worry that the asymmetry between US and Canadian power leaves the United States no reason to accommodate Canadian interests, placing us in the position of supplicants. Asymmetry is a fact of life that we cannot change. The absolute values of each country's trade and investment accounts with the other are roughly equal. But because those values are relative to a US economy 14 times larger than Canada's—and because the United States' interests are dispersed more widely around the globe—our bilateral trade is about 18 times more important to Canadians than it is to Americans. The significance of each country's investments in the other similarly looms larger on Canada's radar screen than on America's. This imbalance is more pronounced today than a generation ago. But it does not necessarily follow that Canada lacks all influence. As Harvard's Joe Nye puts it: "The idea that Canada always loses or that Canada is the servant of the Americans just does not stand up to the historical test" (Nye, 2002: 7). With so much on their plates, however, US leaders will need to be convinced that vital American interests are put in peril by allowing deeper economic integration to become hostage to outdated rules, procedures, and institutions. We are most likely to get and hold their attention with a comprehensive initiative that addresses the full range of trade, investment, regulatory, and security issues on both sides.

Finally, there remain some Canadians who believe that the last major institutional advance in economic integration—NAFTA—failed. They contend that its trade-dispute settlement mechanism has not protected Canadian companies. The evidence is otherwise. Between 1994, when NAFTA came into effect, and the late 1990s (the period studied in the most recent available research) Canada faced few investigations for trade violations and won the majority. Over the same period, the European Union confronted five times as many investigations and seven times as many remedy orders as Canada. Japan's exports to the United States are much smaller than Canada's but it bore twice as many investigations and six times as many orders in the same period (Macrory, 2002; Rugman and Kirton, 2000). NAFTA has not only worked, it has worked well for Canada.

GOOD RELATIONS ARE KEY TO PRODUCTIVE RELATIONS

For Canada, good relations with our giant neighbour are a prerequisite to almost every other foreign-policy pursuit. For Canada to be effective with the rest of the world, it must first be more deliberate in its dealings with Washington. Our focus on the bilateral agenda must be clearly informed by political and economic priorities on both sides of the border. We will need to be far more attuned to coalition building. Only by forging effective alliances with bureaucratic, Congressional, and domestic constituencies in the United States will we advance our own agenda. At the same time, Canadians should acknowledge the strong cards we hold in pursuing our interests in Washington.

Our strongest card is a long, open border with the United States. Virtually every other country envies the benefits that flow from Canada's proximity to the world's most dynamic, energetic, and productive nation. To be sure, proximity brings friction. The United States is not always an easy neighbour. Power has its prerogatives and the United States is not shy about claiming them. Events in the United States can spill over into Canada, reasonably or not. On balance, however, few Canadians would trade the benefits of proximity for the disadvantages of distance. Proximity can also breed complacency and misunderstanding. Americans tend to be blithely ignorant of things Canadian, and Canadians, by contrast, are only too aware of the United States. At times, we can be suspicious and fall prey to misconceptions of our own. Both tend too easily to harbour stereotypes of the other. And both too readily assume

---

INSIDE THE BELTWAY

The United States is the world's most powerful and most democratic country. The combination of these two characteristics makes Washington a very challenging place in which to do business. Every domestic and foreign interest is represented in the world's most important capital and competes feverishly for favour and attention. As Allan Gotlieb observed after his seven-year tenure as Canada's ambassador there, "in Washington ... a foreign power is just another special interest, and not a very special one at that" (Gotlieb, 1991: 43).

Gaining attention and maintaining influence in Washington, therefore, is a highly developed art form. It starts with learning to work within the reality of the separation of powers. In fact, power is so finely divided and widely dispersed in Washington that it seems at times that no one is in charge. The president is by far the most important player in Washington, wielding both constitutional power and political influence. Unlike the prime minister in Canada, however, on many issues he has only the power to propose while Congress has the power to dispose—and the courts the power to disallow. Getting anything done in Washington, therefore, requires getting all the powers on your side. Gridlock is the default position. Bringing closure on a file, any file, is a major accomplishment.

Canadians have never warmed up to the highly adversarial and noisy way in which things get done in Washington. They prefer the more consensual and quiet way Ottawa operates. They also like a prime minister who gets things done without rubbing their faces in what it takes. The biggest problem for us, however, is confusing how the two capitals work. Whether they like it or not, Canadians need to be effective players in Washington. They must learn both the chutzpah and the patience that are needed to make a difference. And they need to be prepared to spend the resources required both in Washington and around the United States to gain access and ensure influence.

that proximity has bred similarity. Canadians and Americans do share many values and aspirations but we live in different societies with different politics and priorities. Viewed from afar those differences are minor; close up they loom large and invite missteps.

If Canada is to overcome these differences and engage America in pursuit of shared interests, it is critical that we focus on the object, purpose, and content of better relations. The inescapable factor here again is proximity: like it or not, Canada lies squarely within the US security and economic perimeter. Canadians may be more comfortable with the economic aspects of proximity, but we must accept that in the present climate it is security that appears on the US radar screen.

In fact the security perimeter has been in place at least since the late 1930s. At that time, US President Roosevelt made it clear to Prime Minister Mackenzie King that the United States viewed with grave disquiet the utter inadequacy of Canada's military. In the event of war, the United States was not prepared to tolerate Canada's becoming a launch pad for attacks upon it. The choice for Canada was clear, as King recognized: Canada could defend itself or the United States would do the job and, in so doing, serve its own interest. The creation of the Canada-United States Permanent Joint Board of Defence in 1940 institutionalized the two leaders' vision of a joint approach to North American security. Canada has ever since been an integral part of a continental security strategy defined, determined, and almost entirely implemented by the United States.

Canada is inescapably part of the North American economic sphere. As we noted in Chapter 13, three-quarters of Canada's international trade is conducted with the United States. A growing portion of this is intra-industry and even within companies. There is every reason to expect this integration of our economies to continue and no reason to imagine that Canada will suddenly choose to exchange the prosperity it has created for the quixotic pursuit of expanded trade with other countries. In these circumstances, the pre-eminent task of Canadian trade and foreign policy is to bring the architecture of the Canada-United States relationship into alignment with our deepening interdependence. Historically, the two countries have managed their complex relationship on an item-by-item basis. Governments have, in fact, typically taken great care to prevent sentiments surrounding one issue in the relationship from affecting the handling of others. This pragmatic approach may have served both countries well in the past but it is now out of date. Before September 11, 2001, bold initiatives on trade or the economy might have been considered on their merits. Today no initiative on the economy has any chance of gaining attention in the United States unless it also addresses security.

Enhancing our common security
for mutual benefit

The terror attacks on Washington and New York transformed America's view of the world. Fear for its physical security now overrides all other considerations. Until 9/11 an open Canada-United States border—and relatively free mobility of goods, services, and people across it—was taken for granted. Washington's response that day demonstrated how quickly it can seal the gates if it feels sufficiently threatened. Canada has a new role in the American consciousness that has little precedent. Within this new reality Canada can no longer free-load on America's commitment to continental and global security nor complicate those efforts merely because to do so seems politically attractive. Geography dictates that Canada and the United States work together for our mutual security.

Canada does not share a land border with any other country. At best, arrangements with third nations can complement our security cooperation with the United States; they cannot replace it. Fortunately, the foundations of cooperation are strong. The Canadian and US militaries enjoy deeply harmonious relations based on years of joint training, similar equipment, and shared attitudes. Americans do not need Canadian forces to get the job done, but they see value in Canadian moral and political support in a dangerous world. Increasing our defence spending, Canada's active service in Afghanistan, and our support elsewhere project a symbolic importance that should help restore US confidence in our ability and willingness to secure the northern front.

But Canadians must be ready to adjust our thinking as well. We must accept that the pressures of integration are as inescapable in the security realm as they are in the economy. And as with trade, the best way to manage these pressures is by strengthening formal and informal institutions that serve to reduce the asymmetry of power and level the playing field. Such institutions expose Americans to Canadian concerns and manage expectations through the adoption of shared norms, common procedures, and agreed standards of behaviour. They provide an arena in which both sides can plan for the future and in moments of crisis reduce the temptation to resort to ad hoc responses.

The Conservative government has brought a renewed sense of strategic vision and purpose to Canada's national security policy but there are three dimensions to our security relationship that require attention:

1   the evolution of cooperation with the United States on defence in a post-9/11 world;
2   border management and related issues of security, law enforcement, intelligence, and protection of infrastructure;
3   effects on Canadian foreign and defence policy from US action in the wider international security realm, especially in pursuit of its global war on terrorism.

These new challenges in the security relationship between Canada and the United States suggest that traditional assumptions and policy frameworks will need to be re-examined. Legacy institutions may no longer be appropriate to Canadians' present needs and future aspirations.

1   Continental defence

Historically, Canada's commitment to the defence of North America has been structured through NATO rather than bilateral institutions. Even so, from the Second World War on Canada has enjoyed a uniquely close defence relationship with the United States. It is reflected in the establishment of the Permanent Joint Board on Defence in 1940, the creation of NORAD in 1958, and the more recent establishment of the Bi-national Planning Group in 2003. In the current environment, it is clear that the tradition of subordinating bilateral cooperation with the United States to the broader North Atlantic Alliance is no longer sustainable.

In our view, Canada's interests will be better served by creating new bilateral institutions that respect national boundaries than by leaving ourselves open to unilateral US action if a sudden threat unexpectedly emerges. To that end, we believe Canadians should revisit two unfortunate decisions made by the Martin government, one dealing with the contours of a renewed NORAD to counter land, air, and marine threats to North America, and the other rejecting participation in the United States Ballistic Missile Defence program. In both cases, Canada's decisions reflected short-term political considerations rather than long-term strategic realities. And both undermined US confidence in Canada as a security partner. The result was a decline in access and influence without any compensating enhancement of Canadian security (indeed, rather the opposite) or of our standing in the rest of the world.

2   Border management and security

Security cooperation at the Canada-United States border has improved significantly since 9/11. But problems remain, especially in the treatment of individuals. Port-of-entry personnel remain preoccupied with the administration of customs and immigration regulations. The strategic focus remains on controlling points of entry and strengthening frontier patrols rather than on reinforcing the "virtual border" that resides in the two countries' traffic management and visa control systems (as well as those of third countries). To bring border management into line with the new security reality and deepening economic integration, a number of pressing challenges must be addressed.

Visa policies between the two countries are still sufficiently different to cause friction. There is growing pressure to harmonize visa policies (including visa standards, visa issuing practices, and relations with other states) but the complexities are significant and any initiative is likely to encounter stiff political and bureaucratic resistance. The "green border" (those thousands of kilometres of geography that separate formal ports of entry into the two countries) remains the "longest undefended border in the world," but this status is increasingly under challenge from new threats. Closer cooperation is needed to place the border under surveillance and to interdict not only terrorists but also conventional criminal elements that seek to exploit vulnerabilities.

Historically, neither Canada nor the United States has used "exit controls" to monitor aliens leaving their territory. Legislation in the United States (Section 110 of the Illegal Immigration Reform and Immigrant Responsibility Act) has now placed this option on the table. Canadians currently enjoy an exemption from US exit controls but that dispensation may prove temporary, raising the prospect of significant new friction in cross-border mobility.

Travelers embarking for North America from points outside the continent may represent a security risk. Countering this threat will require that Canada and the United States work together and with other nations. Pre-clearance measures offer a partial answer but visa requirements will also need to be addressed.

Canada and the United States share a great deal of critical infrastructure, notably oil and gas pipelines, electricity grids, and vital communication and transportation links. These are potentially vulnerable to terrorist attack in either country. Our mutual defence demands close cooperation, including intelligence-sharing, to reduce vulnerabilities.

3   Effects on Canada of US security policy and actions

If the relationship with the United States dominates our foreign policy options—as it must—and security dominates the US agenda—as it does—then Canada cannot afford to be any more indifferent to America's prosecution of its security mission internationally than we are to its priorities on North American soil. Whether the US "stays the course" in the Middle East and elsewhere, focuses aggressively on terrorism and other threats, withdraws into isolation, or pursues a middle course in cooperation with traditional allies, Canada will be affected. The Canadian public may well prefer the middle course, but the government must shape a response based on Canadian interests rather than sentiments. Our interests are poorly served by disdain for an American assessment of its threat environment that differs from what is popular in Canada. In fact, while Canada and the United States may disagree on tactics and emphasis, each country's perception of threats is generally indistinguishable from the other.

If Canadians wish to contribute to global peace and security they can only do so effectively as partners with the United States. Canada's capacity on its own can only, at the best of times, be small and symbolic. On the other hand Canadian efforts in concert with the United States can be transformative. As former Canadian ambassador to the United States Derek Burney points out, "if we establish a constructive relationship with the United States—asserting and defending key elements of our most vital relationship in a mature, focused manner—we will also be better able to advance other global objectives" (Burney, 2005).

ENRICHING ECONOMIC INTEGRATION

If the security of its citizens stands at the top of any government's responsibilities, prosperity is not far behind. Day-to-day, issues concerning bilateral trade, investment, and regulatory compliance dominate the days of thousands of officials and their political masters in both countries' capitals. Little of this is guided by any strategic view of priorities or direction. Canada's preference for compartmentalizing issues may have kept some potential conflicts in check while preserving the broader relationship. But it has also frustrated progress on major files and failed to keep up with changing realities. A global realignment of economic power, shifts in the US political landscape, and the two countries' deepening economic integration all compel a new and comprehensive Canadian strategy.

The 2005 Security and Prosperity Initiative adopted by Prime Minister Martin and President Bush and confirmed by the Harper government a year later laid a promising foundation. Both governments now receive regular status reports on its implementation. The earlier Smart Border Accord gave security and access to the United States a higher priority than before September 11. Both, however, operate within existing laws and policies and are therefore limited in scope. Extracting the full benefit of deeper integration requires a more ambitious initiative.

British economist David Henderson has defined integration of the kind that North America is experiencing "as a tendency for the economic significance of political boundaries to diminish" (Henderson, 1994: 179–80). The diminishing economic relevance of political boundaries disposes countries that are becoming more integrated to create common policies to regulate commerce, external trade, and investment. Canada and the United States, while formally committed to no more than a free-trade area, have in reality already implemented some aspects of a customs union and even of a common market. Based on broadly shared perspectives, the two governments have developed a dense network of consultative arrangements that ensure a high degree of convergence in their respective policies.

These manifestations of economic integration have now largely realized the benefits of traditional liberalization between Canada and the United States. The constraints on two-way trade and investment today are not the classic tariffs and quotas of old, but more subtle differences embedded in regulatory detail. Many of these may be enforced at the border but they will only be resolved by cooperation or coordination between the two national capitals.

Reducing the economic effect of the border

The international border has always been a critical presence in Canada's economic development. Efforts to either enhance or offset its impact have been a recurring theme in relations between Canada and the United States. It makes sense for an investor to serve the combined North American market from inside the larger market's territory. A constant goal of Canadian policy has been to offset this natural bias. Alleviating the burden created by border management is critical to this end. The current high level of trade reflects considerable success in the effort, but significant barriers remain, particularly in the treatment of cross-border traffic.

To realize the full benefit of deeper integration of their two markets, Canada and the United States should develop a customs union. To do this, the two nations must agree on a comprehensive program to reconcile remaining differences in regulatory practice and market governance. Reaching agreement on such a program will require that at least the following elements be included.

A common external tariff and related programs

As we noted earlier, Canada has much to gain from eliminating its tariff altogether. As a start, however, it can work with the United States to establish a common external tariff eliminating the need for cumbersome rules of origin in bilateral trade and reducing the need for border controls on the movement of goods. The easiest way to achieve a common external tariff is to adopt the lower duty applied by either country.

An agreed approach to non-tariff customs treatment of third-country goods

This should include non-commercial restrictions on third-country trade such as foreign policy and security-related sanctions.

Commitments to address remaining sectoral trade problems, particularly in agriculture

Both Canada and the United States maintain high levels of protection for certain agricultural commodities but the two lists of sensitive products are not the same. The private sector has already made good progress toward integrating the agri-food sector, making this task potentially less daunting than it proved during the Canada-United States Free Trade Agreement and NAFTA negotiations.

Formal and irrevocable commitment to a fully integrated, cross-border energy market

Canada and the United States took important steps in the Canada-United States Free Trade Agreement to facilitate the free flow of energy products between the two countries. Industry has since invested heavily in cross-border pipe and transmission lines and Canada is now the leading supplier of energy to the United States. A stronger treaty basis may be needed, however, to ensure full coordination of regulatory requirements, encourage further investment in new energy sources, and bolster American confidence in Canada as a secure supplier.

ENERGY AND SECURITY

Americans see a very close connection between energy and security. The United States relies on domestic supplies for much of its energy but the size of the United States economy is such that these resources are not enough. Even more critically, and whether or not the Europeans and Japanese appreciate it, the United States also worries about the energy security of its allies and trading partners. Any threat to global energy supply and distribution networks, therefore, gets immediate and full attention in Washington.

Most Americans do not realize that Canada is their most important supplier of energy. Fully 17% of the energy Americans consume every day originates in Canada, carried by a network of oil and gas pipelines and electricity transmission lines. The Midwest relies on Canada for half its energy needs. Canada is much more important to US energy security than all of the Middle East combined.

While Canada could be energy self-sufficient, the location of oil, gas, and electrical generating facilities is such that it makes sense to trade energy in both directions. Over the years, Canada and the United States have developed an integrated energy market with shared distribution networks. Governments in both countries have gradually accepted that the market should largely determine the future development and distribution of available energy.

This energy interdependence is now largely self-regulating and works to our mutual advantage. There are, however, gaps that would benefit from attention on both sides of the border. New facilities to bring energy from Alaska, the Mackenzie Delta, and the Alberta oil sands to consumers in Canada and the United States, for example, need to be developed together. Ensuring that integrated electricity grids work as intended cannot be done without close coordination.

In these circumstances, there is much to be said for Canada and the United States developing a North American energy security accord that looks at the best way to develop and distribute the continent's resources to the benefit of people on both sides of the border.

An agreed approach to trade remedies for each other's products and for third-country products

Despite a decade and a half of free trade, the application of trade remedies in a few sectors continues to affect the relationship. Intracorporate and other structural commercial integration has virtually eliminated pursuit of trade remedies by manufacturing and industrial firms. Problems persist in natural resources and agriculture, however. Many of these relate to different approaches to resource pricing. This suggests that addressing the differences that give rise to complaints may be more fruitful than further efforts to deter resorting to trade remedies.

Progressive access to government procurement markets

"Buy American" and "Buy Canadian" requirements continue to distort the sensible deployment of industrial resources and fail to reflect the integrated nature of North American producers. The time has come to move toward a fully integrated government procurement market.

Improving regulatory coordination, reducing overlap, and relying more on mutual recognition

Formal agreements and silent integration have accelerated regulatory convergence and narrowed differences. But they have neither eliminated existing inconsistencies (in design, objective, implementation, and compliance) nor discouraged new ones from emerging. These distort market efficiency and impose needless costs. In the past, governments attempted to reduce these consequences by agreeing to frameworks within which they would exercise their regulatory responsibilities. That approach is no longer sufficient. Instead, new institutions are required to achieve a much higher level of cooperation, coordination, and even joint decision-making. (See Hart, 2006 for a more complete discussion of what a more deliberate approach to cross-border regulatory cooperation would involve.)

A new approach to border administration

European governments have learned that well-functioning, integrated markets require mobility in all the factors of production and supply. Reducing, even eliminating, the effect of the border checkpoints on travel and most transactions is critical to ensuring that Canadians and Americans alike gain the full benefit from existing economic integration. Currently, border management requires the enormously costly administration of a dense array of laws, regulations, and procedures. The anticipated transaction and compliance costs, including the cost of unpredictable delays, grossly distort investment and trade decisions. Many procedures administered at the border involve either regulatory compliance (underlining the need for greater regulatory cooperation) or security (reinforcing the importance of greater attention to the "virtual" border). But Europe's Schengen Agreement, which allows for total mobility of people among 13 participating countries, has shown that it is possible to achieve a much less intrusive border among countries that have arrived at a high level of integration. A key there has been agreement on the treatment of third-country nationals.

FACTS ABOUT THE CANADA-US BORDER

About 70% of Canada's trade with the United States (by value) moves in or out of the United States by truck. About 13 million trucks crossed the border in 2005, or about 36,000 per day; the Ambassador Bridge between Windsor and Detroit alone handles some 7,000 trucks a day, or one every minute in each direction, 24 hours a day. On September 13, 2001, the line-up of trucks waiting to cross the bridge into the United States stretched 36 kilometres.

Industrial integration and the application of just-in-time production technologies have made an increasing number of plants on both sides of the border extremely vulnerable to delays. The automotive sector, for example, estimates that unexpected shutdowns due to the late arrival of parts can cost the industry up to $25,000 per minute, costs that will ultimately be reflected in the price consumers pay for vehicles.

About 75% of bilateral trade in goods moves through five border crossings: two at Windsor-Detroit, one at Fort Erie-Buffalo, one at Sarnia-Port Huron in Ontario, and one at White Rock-Blaine in British Columbia. These border crossings have reached their physical limit in processing both goods and people under current arrangements. Nearly 150 million individual crossings take place at the Canada-United States border each year, an average of close to half a million every day; 25 million cross in the Detroit-Windsor corridor; another 25 million use the Buffalo-Niagara corridor; and 15 million cross between British Columbia and Washington. In a typical year, up to 15 million Canadians travel to the United States for one day or more to break up the long winter, visit friends and relatives, conduct business, or pursue other objectives. Over the course of the winter, some 1.2 million Canadians spend one night or more in Florida.

On the Canadian side of the border, there are 135 land-border points, 140 inland offices, 203 airports (13 international), 187 commercial-vessel clearance points, and 313 marine entry points. Many of these are small and do not operate on a 24-hour basis. The United States similarly staffs the 135 Canada-US land-border points as well as pre-clearance facilities at eight Canadian airports but, given its much denser population, maintains many more inland offices, airport facilities, commercial vessel clearance points, and small marine ports of entry.

In addition to security and immigration responsibilities, customs officials at the border ensure compliance with numerous regulations governing the movement of goods and individuals. The Canadian Border Services Agency administers 96 statutory instruments on behalf of various federal departments and agencies; United States Customs administers some 400 statutory requirements.

The border between Canada and the United States is more than 5,500 miles long. Policing that border is a difficult task. Nevertheless, both Canadian and American officials agree that more than 99% of the people who cross the border are properly documented, do so for legitimate purposes, and pose no risk to either country.

TAKING ECONOMIC INTEGRATION TO THE NEXT LEVEL

In international relations, as in business or in life, standing pat is almost never an option. If Canada chooses not to manage our relationship with the United States toward a new level of seamless access and a common outlook to the world beyond the North American perimeter, if we are passive toward the progressive integration of our markets and neglect to address remaining incongruences, the inevitable drift will be backward. As the smaller player in the relationship, it is therefore imperative that Canada seize the initiative and propel the conversation.

Our values are not in danger, whatever the faint-hearted may imagine. Our interests are clear; we believe the foregoing sections identify the most salient. But our success in pursuing any of these objectives, however economically desirable they may be for both nations, will depend entirely on America's confidence in Canada as a partner in matters of international security. Progress on the security agenda is key to progress on the economic front. To manage the more ambitious features of an agreement on further economic integration, moreover, Canada and the United States will need to institute permanent new structures capable of continuous adaptation to the demands of a dynamic North American economy. As Allan Gotlieb has described it, one essential product of a deep integration initiative should be a jointly administered "community of law" in North America (Gotlieb, 2003).

FOCUSING ON DIFFERENCES THAT MATTER

The differences in objective, approach, and rationale of a wide range of Canadian and American laws and regulations are minor and, in most instances, unimportant. Those that do exist are usually matters of detail, the result of different histories, legislative practices, regulatory styles, and implementation experiences. In the final analysis, however, such differences are marginal in their impact. The need is not simply for harmonization, but for more sharing of information, cooperation, and coordination, both within each country and between Canada and the United States.

Officials on both sides of the border are aware of every detail of difference; many perceive their livelihoods to depend on these differences. It is not surprising, therefore, to find ministers being briefed about the importance of some of the differences and being told that addressing these differences is not a "simple" matter. That is true, insofar as it goes. Eradicating the differences that exist could, in many instances, prove a complex matter; it is also, in most instances, unimportant. What counts is that the two governments share objectives and have confidence in outcomes. That is a more important objective and much easier to attain.

Mutual Recognition Agreements, for example, offer a technique that falls short of the tyranny of harmonization to big-economy standards while meeting the political requirement of democratic governance of the market. Canada and the United States already have a number of such agreements and need to consider more.

This agenda will encounter materially less political difficulty if the Canadian government proceeds at the same time with the broader trade and domestic reforms we outlined in earlier chapters. Among Canada's economic partners, only the United States has sufficient presence in our market to find the impact of those reforms on its interests motivating. Pursuit of the two initiatives should thus complement each other.

Our two nations might identify a comprehensive agreement on deeper economic integration as their goal from the outset—or take a step-by-step approach, going as far as possible (or necessary) one issue at a time. There are good reasons to pursue the larger prize from the start. The United States political process, for one thing, more readily entertains a daring vision than a cautious one. "For any initiative to succeed," Allan Gotlieb has said, "it must meet a number of conditions. It must be bold, it must come from Canada and be espoused at the highest level. It must be comprehensive so as to allow trade-offs and broad constituencies to come into play. It must address the United States agenda as well as ours. Instrumentalism won't work" (Gotlieb, 2003: A16).

Those who watch the Canada-US relationship for a living have often quipped that for any initiative such as this to succeed, it needs to attract a high profile in the United States and keep a low one in Canada. They reason that in the American system any legislative project requires a lot of political oxygen to succeed, while in Canada that very same oxygen will be perceived as too threatening to allow the initiative that generates it to survive. While this conventional wisdom still holds true in Washington, we doubt whether Canadians are as hypersensitive as they may have been in the past. The fact that the dire effects predicted during the free trade debate of the 1980s failed to materialize seems to have exorcised some demons. We are inclined, as a result, to scepticism that raising the profile of any new Canada-US initiative will inevitably prove politically fatal. The substantial challenge lies at least as much in Washington as in Canada.

A word about Mexico

By signing NAFTA into law in 1993, Canada and the United States opened a new era in their relations with Mexico. NAFTA stands as a testament to the belief that North America involves three nations and that the destinies of all three are inextricably intertwined. A broad consensus is emerging, however, that for the moment Canada's challenge is to develop a bilateral, rather than a trilateral, agenda.

NAFTA's implementation raised expectations of closer relations among its three signatories. But the reality is that it provided a common framework of rules to govern two robust and rapidly evolving, but distinct, relationships:

one between the United States and Canada and another between the United States and Mexico. Canada's bilateral relationship with Mexico remains far less advanced. The issues that preoccupy Canada and the United States are not the same as those that arise between Mexico and the United States. There may be a place for trilateral rules and institutions in a few areas, such as surface transportation. In others, such as energy, parallel bilateral efforts will be more productive. To that end, the three governments may wish to consider inviting third-party observers to any two-way discussions they hold, and to encourage any success in bilateral negotiations ultimately to feed into trilateral negotiations. For Canada, however, Mexico's presence at the NAFTA table is no reason to avoid action on our urgent national interest in pursuing a formal structure to manage irreversible economic and security integration with the United States.

CONCLUSIONS: DESIGNING A NEW NORTH AMERICAN RELATIONSHIP

The end of the Cold War dissolved the comfortable certainties that guided Canadian foreign policy with considerable success for almost 50 years. Over much of that period, Canada came out of its colonial shell and played a mature and responsible role in global governance consistent with its power and national interests. During the last decade, Canadian foreign policy has been living off accumulated capital, substituting sentiment over interest and, with a few exceptions, ignoring the radical changes that have roiled global security and economic environment. Canadians expect and deserve a foreign policy that is effective, that achieves results and steps up to our responsibilities—to the international community and to us. Canada must chart a new course for a world in which conventional power is unipolar, dominated by the United States but in which security threats arise from the unpredictable behaviour of non-state actors and rogue states. It needs to structure a new relationship with the United States that captures the dynamics of silent integration.

The most important task that faces Canadians is to restore American confidence in Canada as a reliable partner. That is how most Canadians want to be seen, and it is how most Americans used to feel. Drift, neglect in our relationship, and a number of inappropriate choices have diminished the confidence we used to take for granted on both sides of the border. Building long-term trust will involve addressing our common security needs, strengthening our common border, and pursuing a common vision of a harmoniously integrated North American economy. We are not alone in calling for a major new initiative to strengthen the Canada-US relationship. The United States Council on Foreign Relations, for example, organized a task force of former political leaders and senior officials, academic specialists, and business leaders to look at emerging challenges in North America. It concluded, as we have, that there is an urgent need to address both security and economic issues on the basis of a bold vision of a "free, secure, just, and prosperous North America" (Council on Foreign Relations, 2005).[1] The American Assembly concluded at its 105th meeting that, "ultimately, the United States-Canada relationship will flourish, and the world will benefit, if our countries work together to address the most daunting global problems" (The 105th American Assembly, 2005). We agree. The time has come to conceive a new accommodation between Canada and the United States.

The issues raised in this section are challenging and move well beyond conventional approaches. We believe that we have presented a strong strategic plan for managing Canada-US relations for the benefit of Canada or, more accurately, for the benefit of Canadians. Its implementation will take work. It will demand creativity, not only from Canada's government but, even more, from Canada's academic, policy, and intellectual communities. But the alternative is to condemn Canadians to live in a less secure and less prosperous country. No Canadian would wish that for his or her fellow citizens. A future that relies on anything other than mutual confidence is too bleak to contemplate.

RECOMMENDATIONS

A good relationship with the United States is of central importance to Canada across virtually every domestic and international issue. The ability of Canada's government to advance the security and prosperity of all Canadians depends critically on working jointly with Americans, while Canada's place in, and contribution to, the world increasingly depend on its ability to gain and exert influence in Washington. In view of these facts, Canada should take the following steps.

14.1 Devote priority resources at the federal level to the management of our relationship with the United States.

14.2 Work with the United States to update the architecture of our relationship and develop a joint approach to the governance of our common economic and security space, working together to create both a more open and more secure common border for the movement of people and goods.

---

1   While tri-national in scope, the task force specifically recognizes the need to approach many of the issues on a two-speed basis, recognizing the differences in priorities and capacity in Canada, the United States, and Mexico.

14.3 Revisit the decisions not to participate in the Ballistic Missile Defence program and not to broaden the mandate of NORAD in order to place the Canada-US security relationship on the most mutually advantageous basis.

14.4 Negotiate with the United States to create a customs union involving a common external tariff, a joint approach to the treatment of third-country goods, a fully integrated energy market, a common approach to trade remedies, and an integrated government procurement regime, to encourage further integration of their two economies.

14.5 Work with the United States to promote regulatory convergence to obtain maximum advantage from economic integration.

14.6 Negotiate with the United States a comprehensive agreement embracing all of the foregoing to institutionalize measures to realize the greatest possible benefits from deeper economic and security integration for both our nations.

CHAPTER 15

REFORMING CANADIAN FOREIGN AID

GIVING THAT WORKS

Every year billions of dollars of foreign aid flows into developing countries with the goals of ending poverty and rebuilding societies shattered by conflict. Canadians overwhelmingly support the principle behind this assistance: doing what we can to help those less fortunate than ourselves. We wish to do our share. But the same weakness that crept into other areas of Canada's foreign policy in the last decade and a half—mistaking rhetoric and activity for results—has infected government's approach to foreign aid as well.

Canadians work hard for their money. They do not mind paying taxes for good purpose—and most would agree that alleviating poverty is such a purpose. But they do not appreciate having their money wasted on well-intentioned aid "activity" any more than anything else. It is time to put Canada's foreign aid practices to the test of the same criteria we have applied throughout our work, and which we believe Canadians want applied to every activity undertaken in their name: What is effective? Where should it be focused? What is appropriate? At the end of the day, will our assistance truly empower those we are trying to help?

As Figure 15.1 shows, Official Development Assistance (ODA) from OECD member countries totalled over $106 billion in 2005, a record high and an increase of 31% from the prior year. Canadian foreign aid has followed these global trends. In 2004/05, the Government of Canada allocated $3.7 billion to international assistance, a 21% increase over the prior year. Since 1960, Canada has spent over $60 billion on foreign aid.

There have been many trends in development aid since its birth in the 1960s but today the development community is almost exclusively focused on achieving the Millennium Development Goals (MDGs) (Table 15.1). The MDGs were designed to respond to the world's most pressing development challenges and

Figure 15.1: Trends in Official Development Assistance (ODA) from Canada and other OECD countries, 1960–2005

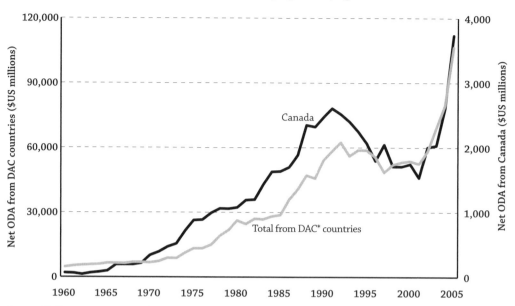

Source: OECD DAC Statistics on-line, <http://www.oecd.org/dataoecd/50/17/5037721.htm>.
*DAC is the Development Assistance Committee of the OECD and represents those nations giving development aid.

have been adopted by 189 nations, including Canada. They consist of eight specific goals that are associated with quantitative targets to be achieved by 2015. The funds needed to meet these goals are considerable. The UN Millennium Project estimates that $70 to $80 billion is needed each year at the start, in addition to current development spending, growing to $135 billion a year by 2015 (Sachs, 2005). This in turn requires that donor countries such as Canada approximately double the amount they give as a share of GNP. This "big push" to increase development aid might be worthwhile—if it did indeed reduce poverty in the developing world.[1] But will it? The burgeoning empirical literature on the topic is largely inconclusive (Burnside and Dollar, 2000; Collier and Dollar, 2002; Easterly, 2003; Sachs, 2005; Rajan and Subramanian, 2005; Hansen and Tarp, 2000). Both advocates and critics of aid have fallen into the habit of cherry picking statistics and studies to support their pre-existing views, while ignoring contradictory evidence. Perhaps the most accurate statement is that over $100 billion is spent annually on aid initiatives that cannot be proven to be effective in relieving poverty.

---

1   *The White Man's Burden* by Easterly (2006) provides an excellent overview of the history and failings of "big push" foreign aid initiatives. *The End of Poverty* by Sachs (2005) presents an opposite view, namely that "big push" aid efforts have failed simply because they have not been big enough.

Table 15.1: The Millennium Development Goals (MDGs)

1. Eradicate extreme poverty and hunger	5. Improve maternal health
2. Achieve universal primary education	6. Combat HIV/AIDS, malaria and other diseases
3. Promote gender equality & empower women	7. Ensure environmental sustainability
4. Reduce child mortality	8. Develop a Global partnership for Development

Source: United Nations, 2005.

Imagine if doctors spent $100 billion every year on treatment that was unproven to alleviate a patient's condition? This would be deemed completely unacceptable and vehemently challenged by the medical community as a tragic waste of valuable resources. Yet somehow the development community has met the same case with respect to poverty and social breakdown with tolerant apathy. This chapter analyses the current state of Canadian foreign aid and suggests more appropriate alternatives. We examine the traditional forms of aid and discuss why they have largely been unsuccessful. We suggest more promising alternatives, namely: (1) adopting a "Tools of Wealth Creation" (TWC) approach to aid disbursements; (2) pursuing Public-Private Partnerships (P3s) where they can be effective, for instance in building infrastructure and developing vaccines; (3) involving the international NGO sector more fully; and (4) transforming the Canadian International Development Agency (CIDA) to become a competitive, private-sector-like organization. We analyze the significant difference between humanitarian aid and development aid, and suggest ways to reform emergency and post-conflict aid to be both effective and more consistent with Canada's other foreign policy goals. And we conclude with a discussion of the fiscal and political implications of a new, better approach to Canadian foreign aid.

A TRADITION OF "AID" THAT DOESN'T HELP

Foreign aid generally falls into three main categories: Official Development Assistance (ODA), Official Assistance (OA), and Private Development Assistance (PDA).[2] Within the first category (ODA), there are two classes: multilateral aid, channelled through international organizations such as the World Bank, IMF, and UN Agencies, and bilateral aid, which donor countries give

---

2   Official Assistance includes grants to countries that are no longer considered developing, such as Israel and Singapore. Private Development Assistance includes funds from non-governmental organizations, religious groups, foundations, and private corporations (Radelet, 2006).

directly to recipients. It is the second of these—bilateral aid—that concerns us most. It also flows in two streams: ongoing development aid and humanitarian aid. The first, by and large, is meant to help its recipients escape chronic poverty; the second to alleviate acute suffering as a result of a temporary crisis or calamity (Figure 15.2. In this section, we focus exclusively on the first of these streams: development aid. Humanitarian aid will be addressed later.

Development aid is intended to help individuals, communities, and countries escape conditions of chronic poverty and "develop" toward conditions of self-supporting prosperity. Many criticisms are made of it, but here we focus on eight of the most common (Table 15.2).

Corruption is a heated topic in development aid. Its simplest form is what critics call "leakage": the large portion of aid money that fails to reach the impoverished and instead serves to entrench the ruling elite. A far worse criticism is that aid money actually causes corruption in developing countries by increasing the resources available for elites and factions to fight over (Svensson, 2005).

What is called "aid absorption" is another problem. A lack of "absorptive capacity" means that money given in aid raises demand for a resource that is already in short supply. For example, consider a country in Africa with a high prevalence of HIV/AIDS that also has a shortage of trained doctors and nurses. If this country receives hundreds of millions of dollars in aid for the treatment and care of HIV patients it may be difficult, given the shortage of skilled healthcare professionals, for the country to absorb the aid and use it as it was intended. What often happens instead is that aid money is either not spent (the country simply banks it, building up its foreign exchange reserves) or it drives up the price of certain domestic goods or services relative to others, at least in the short term. That may in turn appreciate the real exchange rate for the country's

Figure 15.2: Classification of foreign aid

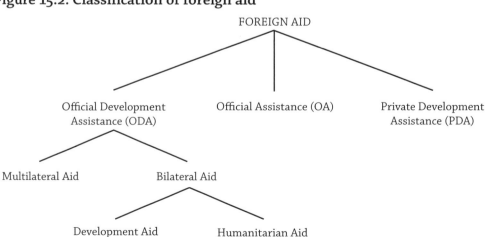

Table 15.2: Problems with traditional development aid

Recipient Countries	Donor Countries
Corruption	Principal-Agent Problem
Absorptive Capacity	Conditionality
Aid Dependency	Lack of Donor Co-ordination
Fiscal Distortion	Aid Volatility and Sustainability

currency, with damaging effects that ripple out across its economy. In addition, many studies indicate that there are diminishing marginal returns to aid, and that a saturation point exists after which additional aid does more harm than good. Different studies suggest that this point is anywhere between 15% and 45% of GDP (Lensink and White, 2001). Or, to put it another way, beyond the "saturation" point, the more aid a country receives, the less it can absorb—what has been termed the "aid-institutions paradox" (Moss et al., 2006).

Aid dependency is the country-scale version of the "welfare trap" familiar to citizens of countries wealthy enough to afford poorly designed social assistance programs. Entire nations may become reliant on perpetual aid flows. This corrodes the recipient country's sovereignty and may impede its development as well.

A further symptom of aid dependency is fiscal distortion, as the expectation of receiving large amounts of aid discourages national governments from developing a sustainable tax system. When some countries receive aid amounting to more than half of their entire economic activity (GNP), and a few governments actually receive more in aid than they spend (Table 15.3), the suspicion must be strong that both aid dependency and fiscal distortion are widespread pathologies.

We must emphasize that the blame for ineffective aid does not by any means lie exclusively with the countries that receive it. From the perspective of a donor country, a fundamental challenge is the principal-agent problem. This refers to the fact that the people providing aid money (taxpayers in developed countries) have no relationship with, and receive no feedback from, its intended beneficiaries (poor people in developing countries). This astonishing lack of accountability means that aid agencies have very little incentive to improve their effectiveness.

Conditionality is one of the most controversial aspects of foreign-development aid. It is also called "tied aid," in which a country like Canada provides aid money to a developing country with the explicit condition that it be spent on goods and services from Canada. For whom, then, is the aid really meant? The poor in the developed country? Or the Canadian provider of the goods and

Table 15.3: Aid dependency and fiscal distortion

Rank	Country	Aid as percent of GPD	Country	Aid as percent of government expenditure
1	Burundi	53%	Afghanistan	289%
2	Solomon Islands	47%	Nicaragua	137%
3	Timor-Leste	45%	Cambodia	107%
4	Liberia	42%	Ghana	73%
5	Afghanistan	37%	Uganda	71%
6	Sierra Leone	34%	El Salvador	69%
7	Madagascar	28%	Bhutan	65%
8	Guinea-Bissau	28%	Mongolia	63%
9	Eritrea	28%	Madagascar	45%
10	Democratic Rep. of Congo	28%	Bolivia	32%
11	Nicaragua	27%	Bangladesh	29%
12	Rwanda	25%	Lesotho	20%
13	Malawi	25%	Jordan	16%
14	Kiribati	23%	Maldives	13%
15	Mozambique	21%	Namibia	11%
16	Zambia	20%	Côte d'Ivoire	11%
17	Ethiopia	19%	Pakistan	10%
18	Guyana	18%	Republic of Congo	10%
19	Niger	18%		
20	Uganda	17%		
21	Mongolia	16%		
22	Gambia	16%		
23	Tanzania	15%		
24	Ghana	15%		
25	Cape Verde	15%		

Source: World Bank, 2005. Data on government expenditure is not available for all nations.

services? In their study "Who Gives Foreign Aid and Why?" Alesina and Dollar (2000) essentially answered that it is the second. They found that among OECD countries, internal political, economic, and strategic considerations drive the pattern of aid more than either humanitarian considerations or the likelihood of alleviating poverty.

Despite efforts to "untie" aid, about 20¢ of every dollar Canada donates continues to carry the condition that it be used to purchase Canadian goods or services. This damages Canada's humanitarian credentials. When the Development Assistance Committee (DAC) of the OECD conducted a peer review of Canada's aid practices in 2002, it specifically identified the high proportion of tied aid as a major shortcoming. In principle, there is nothing wrong with supporting Canadian interests abroad. The problem arises when this is done under the false pretence of providing development aid aimed at alleviating poverty.

Insufficient donor co-ordination and aid volatility further impede the effectiveness of aid. The first opens the door to duplication of effort among donor countries. The second can cause or exacerbate economic instability in recipient countries, especially those where aid constitutes a large share of GNP or government spending.

WHAT ARE THE ALTERNATIVES?

Given the widespread incidence of all of these problems, strong critics of development aid may be tempted to advocate abolishing it altogether. This would be both unrealistic and unwise. First of all, despite a wealth of literature on the problems with aid, there is also evidence that certain focused types of aid can indeed be effective in alleviating poverty. Clemens, Radelet, and Bhavnani (2004) broke aid down into different types, and found that assistance in developing infrastructure, in particular, does indeed have a robust positive relationship with economic growth.

Second, as we noted earlier, most developed countries engage in both bilateral and multilateral assistance, in the second case pooling their funds through major international institutions like the World Bank or United Nations. If Canada were to eliminate this second kind of aid, we would risk losing our place at the table in these institutions and with it an important voice in the global conversation. That would do nothing for, and could actively harm, Canada's interests in a rapidly globalizing world, particularly given the growing economic might of many developing countries.

Third, aid is an important arrow in Canada's foreign-policy quiver. The so-called "3-D" policy that Canada's 2005 International Policy Statement outlined requires a strong development-aid component to complement our efforts on the defence and diplomatic fronts (Canada, Foreign Affairs and International Trade, 2005). The 2006 Federal Budget outlined a plan to spend an additional $1.1 billion over two years on the armed forces and highlighted the government's commitment to strengthening Canada's role in the world. Effective development aid has a role to play.

Finally, from a democratic perspective, by far the majority of Canadians support foreign-aid programs. A survey by the Asia Pacific Foundation of Canada (2002) found that 71% of Canadians thought that foreign aid was either "very important" or "generally important." Among potential aid programs, poverty reduction elicited the strongest response; 64% of Canadians rated such initiatives "very important." Notably, this response was higher than for either promoting Canadian business interests abroad or promoting Canadian values. This suggests that there is broad public support for the idea of aid, although not necessarily for the ways governments have pursued it.

CANADIAN DEVELOPMENT AID THAT REALLY HELPS

If abolishing aid altogether is not the solution, then what is? We suggest that it can be found in refocusing Canada's aid effort, we should:

- promote economic freedom;
- adopt what we call the "Tools of Wealth Creation" (TWC) approach to development aid;
- channel aid less exclusively through governments and more through Public-Private Partnerships (P3s);
- strengthen and rely more heavily on the international NGO sector in Canada;
- transform the Canadian International Development Agency (CIDA) into a private-sector-like institution with particular attention to its accountability and efficiency, and the use of competition in its selection of projects and partners.

PROMOTE ECONOMIC FREEDOM

As we have already said, the evidence showing that development aid has any effect in alleviating poverty or producing prosperity is inconclusive at best. However, there is robust empirical evidence to show that something else does: economic freedom has a strong, positive, and unequivocal impact on a people's prosperity. The annual report, *Economic Freedom of the World*, published by The Fraser Institute in conjunction with members of the Economic Freedom Network, ranks countries based on their level of economic freedom (Gwartney and Lawson, 2006). Figure 15.3 illustrates in dramatic form the consistent and positive relationship between the degree of economic free-

Figure 15.3: The Economic Freedom Index and GDP per capita

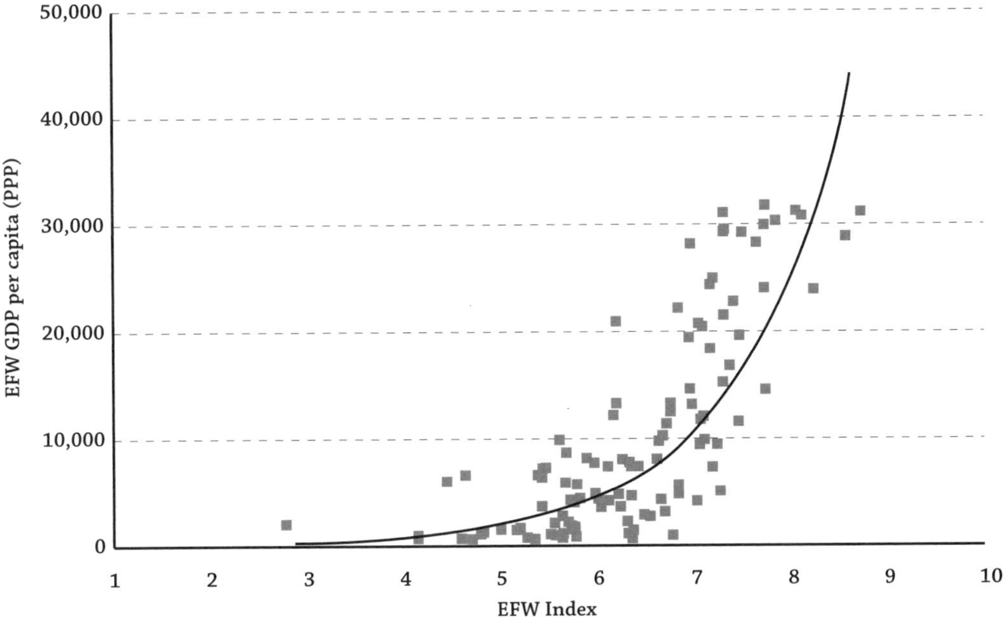

Source: Dataset from Gwartney and Lawson, 2006.

dom and a nation's prosperity as indicated by GDP per capita. This strongly suggests that development aid that focuses on creating environments of economic freedom rather than environments of economic dependence is a far more appropriate way to offer Canada's help to the world's poor. This insight provides the analytical basis of the sustained prosperity approach to development aid that we discuss next.

ADOPT A "TOOLS OF WEALTH CREATION" APPROACH TO DEVELOPMENT AID

Traditional development aid has largely looked to the redistribution of wealth from "haves" to "have-nots" as the way to alleviate poverty. This has yielded consistently disappointing results. The "Tools of Wealth Creation" (TWC) approach aims to better distribute the means to create wealth, rather than to redistribute wealth itself. The redistributive focus creates a fixed-pie mentality of permanent haves and have-nots in which poverty reduction is a matter of splitting the pie in a different way. The TWC alternative encourages developing countries to adopt the incentives that are essential to a well-functioning, productive economy while addressing the unacceptable levels of poverty present in the world today. It empowers recipient countries to begin to cure poverty, rather than merely treat its symptoms.

Too many academics, politicians, and (particularly) development practitioners are quick to dismiss the market economy as fundamentally flawed when in fact they may be reacting to a market economy that is simply insufficiently inclusive. We believe that it is not capitalism that has failed the world's poorer regions, but societies that have failed to provide their citizens with its powerful tools of wealth creation. This implies that rather than redistribute wealth from countries where those tools are put to use, aid should be designed to give people in developing countries access to the same tools that will allow them to reduce their own poverty. To accomplish this we focus on five fundamental tools of wealth creation: (1) property rights, (2) access to capital, (3) development of human capital, (4) access to technology and information, and (5) access to trade markets.

Property rights

A lack of property rights lies at the heart of many development problems. In his book, *The Mystery of Capital: Why Capitalism Triumphs in the West and Fails Everywhere Else* (2000), renowned Peruvian economist Hernando de Soto argues that while people in developing countries often have assets, they do not have the legal framework to use these assets as financial collateral and thereby turn them into productive capital. De Soto estimates that there is over $1.2 trillion of "dead capital" in Latin America alone. This is more than 10 times the total amount of foreign aid given annually around the entire world, an astonishing figure.

Development aid should therefore focus on creating an environment in which poor people can activate their own capital, rather than simply call for more aid money to be pumped into countries whose assets are inaccessible for lack of social, legal, and financial infrastructure. As a beginning, Canada could support initiatives such as the Urban Real Estate Rights Project in Peru (IPE, 2001) and help foster similar programs in other countries where none yet exist.

Access to capital

Without access to capital the other tools of wealth creation have little to work on. Where it is lacking, micro-credit is an obvious solution. Bangladeshi economist Muhammad Yunus has demonstrated its effectiveness through his Grameen Bank, winning the 2006 Nobel Peace Prize in recognition. His micro-lending bank's success shows that capitalism can indeed be a powerful weapon in the fight against poverty.

However, the role of development aid in supporting micro-credit is tricky. Successful micro-credit institutions such as African Bank in South Africa, Bank Rakyat in Indonesia, and Yunus's own Grameen Bank are all for-profit enterprises, albeit with an underlying social purpose. Not-for-profit NGOs and aid organizations, lacking expertise, risk-management tools, and the local knowledge required to execute micro-credit properly, risk entering markets with mispriced products that drive down returns and diminish the very effectiveness they are trying to take advantage of.

At the Global Micro-credit Summit in Halifax in November, 2006, the Canadian government announced $40 million in funds to be spent on micro-credit programs administered though Oxfam Québec, Développement International Desjardins, and the Canadian Co-operative Association. While the intent is laudable, these are inappropriate channels; the first two organizations in particular do not understand the profit motive that is at the core of successful micro-lending. As a better approach, we recommend that aid agencies fund existing for-profit institutions and focus their efforts on creating environments that encourage their establishment and success.

There a few Canadian organizations that are already pursing some aspects of this approach. One is Calmeadow, a charity that provides affordable, responsive, and sustainable financial services in underdeveloped regions of the world. Calmeadow has two regional micro-finance funds, ProFund Internacional (Latin America) and AfriCap Microfinance Fund (Africa), both of which have been very successful. Another example that deserve to be mentioned is CARE Enterprise Partners (CEP), a part of CARE Canada that operates as a social venture capital firm, incubating model businesses that generate both economic and social value in low-income communities.[3] Like a private-sector venture-capital firm, CEP has an Investment Committee and issues quarterly reports.

Opportunity International (OI) is also a good example of successful microfinance. OI was founded in the early 1970s in the United States with Canadian Ross Clemenger giving out the first official Opportunity International loan to a client in Colombia in 1976. Since then, the organization has grown remarkably with five Support Partners, of which OI Canada is one, serving 40 Implementing Partners in 25 countries. OI Canada was founded in 1997 by David Stiller, who was frustrated with the "inability of relief work to make poor people any less poor." As of 2005, 700,000 families have OI loans and over 850,000 jobs have been created or sustained by OI financing.[4]

Besides providing access to micro-credit, development aid can provide capital to larger entrepreneurs as well. To its credit, Canada is already on the right track in this respect, having recently launched the Canadian Investment Fund

---

3   See CARE Canada website at <www.care.ca/CEP/> for more information.
4   Source for figures is Opportunity International, Canada, 2005; note that these figures are not for OI Canada specifically but for all OI members.

for Africa, a $250 million fund dedicated to making private equity investments in businesses throughout Africa. The fund, managed jointly by well-respected financial firms Cordiant and Actis, comprises a $100 million anchor investment from the Government of Canada with the balance being raised through third parties. Its objective is to spur economic growth by providing risk capital for commercially successful private sector businesses.[5]

Development of human capital

Human capital is as essential as financial capital to creating wealth. We define human capital as the combination of educational attainment, health status, and work experience. Table 15.4 compares the levels of human capital in the top six countries and bottom six countries ranked in the Human Development Index (HDI), using life expectancy as a proxy for both health and work experience, and school enrolment as a measure of educational attainment. It is estimated that human capital constitutes about 80% of the wealth of developed countries (Becker, 1998). In that case it is not hard to imagine the challenge facing the bottom six countries, where school enrolment is one third of what it is in the top six countries and life expectancy roughly half.

What can development aid do to encourage the accumulation of human capital? Currently, most development aid to education is focused on increasing school enrolment. The Millennium Development Goal for education is to ensure that all children can complete primary school by 2015. UNESCO's Education For All (EFA) campaign has similar quantitative goals, as does CIDA's Action Plan on Basic Education. In pursuit of the last, CIDA quadrupled its investments in basic education between 2000 and 2005. Missing from many of these campaigns is a recognition that in many developing countries the quality of education is so low that simply increasing enrolment does not actually have much impact on the real level of human capital (see Pritchett, 2001 for examples and analysis). Since so many other donors are focusing on quantitative enrolment, Canada's development aid could distinguish itself by working aggressively to improve the quality of education at all levels.

There are two effective ways in which Canadian aid could improve real educational outcomes in developing countries. The first is to fund teacher training for primary and secondary schools aggressively. This is a particularly pressing problem in some countries in Africa where the number of qualified teachers is actually falling due to high HIV/AIDS-related mortality. Another is to focus on post-secondary education geared specifically towards entrepreneurship and skills. This area of opportunity is often overlooked by development

---

5 For more information, see <www.cifafund.ca/en/index.html>.

Table 15.4: Indicators of human capital

HDI Rank	Country	Life Expectancy	School Enrolment Ratio
1	Norway	80	100
2	Iceland	81	96
3	Australia	81	n/a
4	Ireland	78	99
5	Sweden	80	97
6	Canada	80	93
	Average of top 6	80	97
1	Central African Republic	39	30
2	Guinea-Bissau	45	37
3	Burkina Faso	48	26
4	Mali	48	35
5	Sierra Leone	41	65
6	Niger	45	22
	Average of bottom 6	44	36

Source: United Nations Development Programme, 2006. School enrolment is all levels.

agencies like CIDA that tend to be preoccupied with basic education. Making Cents International, <www.makingcents.com/>, a for-profit social enterprise started by Canadian Fiona Macaulay, provides training and technology curriculum for micro-entrepreneurs in approximately 40 developing countries. USAID and other development agencies have made good use of these products; CIDA funds would be well spent doing the same. Such initiatives also reinforce micro-credit lending, since equipping micro-entrepreneurs with funds but no skills is a job half done.

Effectively raising the quality—not just the quantity—of education also raises human capital in another way, through its spill-over effect on health. Studies have shown that educated mothers on average raise healthier children; educated youths in countries with a high prevalence of HIV/AIDS are more likely to use condoms; and educated people generally invest more in their own health rather than relying on (often inadequate) government health agencies (Mellington and Cameron, 1999; Gokhale et al., 2004).

Access to technology and information

Technology and access to information are also fundamental tools of wealth creation. The good news is that in this area many developing countries are in a position to "leap-frog" older technologies still used in the developed world and go straight to newer technologies, providing a massive boost to their prospects for productivity and growth. A good example is mobile phones. Grameen Phone, in collaboration with the Grameen Bank, has launched a Village Phone program that aims to place one mobile phone in every village in Bangladesh, providing a public call centre in each. Started less than a decade ago, it is a profitable company with 8.5 million subscribers. Other examples include the "$100 Lap-Top" project started by the technology lab at Massachusetts Institute of Technology (MIT) and Manobi, a mobile and internet value-added service provider operating in the agri-business sector in Senegal.[6]

These examples show that providing access to technology and information can indeed help to reduce poverty if they are low-cost and scalable. Development aid should therefore encourage private-sector initiatives aimed at increasing access to technology and information in developing countries.

Access to markets

Approximately 70% of poor people in developing countries live in rural areas. These people are overwhelmingly farmers and herders. Access to trade markets where they can sell the products of their agriculture is therefore critical to improving their economic prospects. Today, developed countries spend

6   For more examples of technology empowering poverty reduction, see the CGAP: IT Innovation Series at <http://www.cgap.org>.

THE $100 LAP TOP

The development of the $100 Lap Top is a cost effective way of promoting development and bridging the digital divide in poor countries, but it also provides an interesting case study of how effective collaboration between non-profits, governments, business, and academia can act to alleviate poverty in a way that is consistent with the TWC approach.

The $100 Lap Top is the brain child of Nicholas Negroponte, who launched the project at the Massachusetts Institute of Technology (MIT) Media Lab in 2004. Five well-known corporations, Google, Advanced Micro Devices, Red Hat, News Corp., and Brightstar, have each provided expertise and $2 million to fund an NGO, One Laptop Per Child, set up to oversee the project.

Local governments in Brazil, Argentina, Uruguay, Nigeria, Libya, Pakistan, and Thailand have already signed up to buy the lap tops. Even developed country governments in countries such as the US and Australia have expressed interest is using the $100 Lap Top for remote education purposes

approximately $280 billion a year to support their agricultural industries—almost triple what they spend in development aid. As a result, over 3 billion people in developing countries live on less than the $2 a day that the average European cow receives in government subsidies (Hassett and Shapiro, 2003).

Clearly this is immoral, uneconomic, and unsustainable, yet developed countries have stubbornly resisted change. Indeed, as already mentioned, the EU's Common Agricultural Policy and the US government's agro-subsidies proved a major barrier to reaching agreement in the now defunct Doha Round of trade talks. Canada's agricultural subsidies are on about the same level as those of the United States, though considerably lower than those of the European Union. The changes we have recommended to Canada's agricultural program will effectively end large subsidies—mostly borne by Canadian consumers—and help open Canadian markets to poor nations.

As we highlighted in Volume I of this series, *A Canada Strong and Free*, the former Canadian government (compromised by its desire to appease anti-American and anti-globalization interest groups) withheld support for global free trade as an effective way to help poorer nations. Canada's new government has an opportunity to take the initiative and work with other nations in both the G8 and the G20 to resuscitate the Doha talks. If this proves impossible, Canada should judiciously pursue bilateral trade agreements with major trading blocks in developing regions. However, in doing this, we should bear in mind that such agreements are not as desirable as reaching a global agreement under the WTO umbrella or as crucial as Canada's interest in trade with the United States. Moreover, as we have noted, most of these regional agreements face serious hurdles and should not be allowed to interfere with closer regulatory and trade integration with the United States. Thus, while we believe Canada should explore regional agreements, we also believe this should be balanced against the larger interests of a deepening global free trade and our US trade relationship.

Summary of the Tools of Wealth Creation

Table 15.5 provides a summary of the Tools of Wealth Creation. As novel as these may appear in comparison with traditional aid, we believe they are demonstrably more likely to be effective at reducing poverty and delivering help to the less fortunate (as distinct from directing "aid" to Canadian providers of goods and services), and are fully ready to be deployed in the field. Indeed, many experts in development aid philosophically support this approach. John Watson, the President and Chief Executive Officer of CARE Canada, in a recent speech, has suggested many of the same notions (Watson, 2005). The Tools of Wealth Creation are, moreover, versatile. Their usefulness is not limited to other countries where poverty rules. They can be just as effective where poverty persists within Canada—in aboriginal communities, for example.

Table 15.5: A "Tools of Wealth Creation" approach to development

Underlying cause of poverty	Tool of Wealth Creation	Successful example
Lack of legal inclusion in the market system	Property rights	Urban Real Estate Rights Project (Peru)

Resource
The Mystery of Capital, Hernando de Soto, 2000.

Underlying cause of poverty	Tool of Wealth Creation	Successful example
Lack of access to capital	Micro-credit	Calmeadow African Bank Bank Rakyat Grameen Bank

Resources
Banker to the Poor: Micro-Lending and the Battle Against World Poverty, Yunus and Jolis, 1999
The Micro-Finance Revolution: Sustainable Finance for the Poor, Marguerite Robinson, 2001.

Underlying cause of poverty	Tool of Wealth Creation	Successful example
Undeveloped human capital	Education Health Work experience Entrepreneurship	Making Cents BOP entrepreneurs

Resource
The Fortune at the Bottom of the Pyramid: Eradicating Poverty through Profits, C.K. Prahalad, 2006.

Underlying cause of poverty	Tool of Wealth Creation	Successful example
Lack of access to information and technology	Scalable, low cost technological distribution	$100 Lap Top Grameen Phone

Resource
The World is Flat, Thomas Friedman, 2005.

Underlying cause of poverty	Tool of Wealth Creation	Successful example
Lack of access to trade and markets	Free trade	US *African Growth and Opportunity Act* (2000)

Resources
Economic Justice in an Unfair World: Toward a Level Playing Field, Ethan Kapstien, 2006.
Trade Policy and Global Poverty, William Cline, 2004.
In Defense of Globalization, Jagdish Bhagwati, 2004.

PUBLIC-PRIVATE PARTNERSHIPS

Public-private partnerships or "P3s,"have found a growing role in both developed and developing countries. They aim to attract private funding and private-sector skills to what were previously considered public-sector functions. In Canada, well-known P3s include the Bay of Fundy Ferry Services, Nova Scotia's Highway 104 (Cobequid Pass), New Brunswick's Fredericton-Moncton Highway, and water treatment projects in Dartmouth, Moncton, and Edmonton. Other Canadian P3s have initiated projects as diverse as student housing and medical centers. A survey by the Canadian Council for Public-Private Partnerships revealed that Canadians are increasingly comfortable employing P3s to construct, operate, and finance such traditionally public assets as hospitals, hospital services, roads, water treatment facilities, sewage treatment facilities, recreation complexes, public transit, and electricity grids (CCPPP, 2004).

As Canada and other developed countries embrace P3s worth billions of dollars, more are being launched every year in developing countries as well.[7] While not by any means a panacea for every development problem, in certain areas P3s can accomplish ends that otherwise would not be met due to the nature and distribution of the risks they entail. Below we consider two such areas where P3s are appropriate and Canadian aid and expertise should get involved: infrastructure and the development of vaccines.

Infrastructure

Infrastructure investments have unique risks: high fixed and up-front costs and usually strict regulatory environments. In developing countries, these are often further complicated by political, financial, and operational uncertainties. P3s distribute these risks among a number of parties. In addition to spreading risk, they can create a win-win-win-win situation for private companies (foreign and domestic), local governments, aid donors, and the people of the recipient country. As Table 15.6 shows, the dollar value of infrastructure projects in developing countries involving P3s almost doubled between 1995 and 2005—reaching nearly US$96 billion. However, as Figure 15.4 reveals, these were geographically concentrated in Eastern Europe, Asia, and Latin America and sectorally concentrated in telecommunications.

CIDA pays lip service to the potential of infrastructure P3s but it is difficult to find evidence of its involvement with any actual P3 projects. Canada, for example, is one of 14 donors to the Public-Private Infrastructure Advisory Facility (PPIAF), an agency providing technical assistance started in 1999. But this merely supplies technical experts who write reports on what

---

7 See Wettenhall, 2003 for a good overview of P3s in the United Kingdom, Australia, Canada, and other OECD countries.

Table 15.6: Amounts ($US billions) spent on infrastructure projects with private participation (developing countries)

	1995	1996	1997	1998	1999	2000	2001	2002	2003	2004	2005
East Asia and Pacific											
	17.8	27.3	36.2	10.1	12.2	18.2	12.5	9.6	13.3	13.1	13.6
Europe and Central Asia											
	9.5	10.7	14.6	12.2	11.3	25.3	14.1	17.2	11.8	15.1	34.4
Latin America											
	17.1	25.8	49.0	69.3	37.9	39.0	34.6	20.3	16.2	19.8	22.1
Middle East and North Africa											
	0.1	0.1	5.1	3.4	2.9	4.1	4.3	1.6	2.0	7.6	6.7
South Asia											
	3.8	5.7	6.2	2.3	4.6	3.5	4.7	6.0	3.9	11.2	13.6
Sub-Saharan Africa											
	1.7	1.7	3.0	2.2	2.8	2.1	4.0	3.3	5.9	4.0	5.4
TOTAL											
	49.1	71.3	114.1	99.5	71.7	92.2	74.2	58.0	53.1	70.8	95.8

Source: World Bank and PPIAF, PPI Project database. <ppi.worldbank.org/> and <www.ppiaf.org/>.

should be done with P3s, instead of actually doing it. Similarly, CIDA funds courses in some countries on how to make P3s work but does not embark on any itself (IP3, 2007; PPIAF, 2007). According to the OECD aid database, in 2004 Canada spent $20 million on P3s—less than 0.8% of our total aid budget that year.

CIDA's reticence is not for lack of successful P3 models in developing countries. One such example is the construction of the N4 Toll Road from South Africa to Mozambique. This was initiated in 1996 when both post-civil war Mozambique and post-apartheid South Africa wanted to expand their regional trade. More trade demanded better transportation and neither government had the finances to build the required road. The financial and operational risks of such a project were, meanwhile, too high for a private company, multilateral agency, or single aid donor to undertake alone. As a solution, the two countries

Figure 15.4: Geographic and sectoral distribution of public-private partnerships in developing countries, 2005

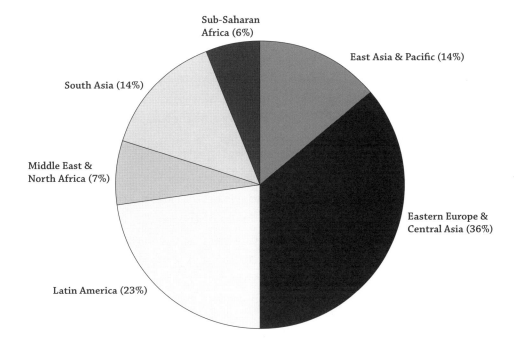

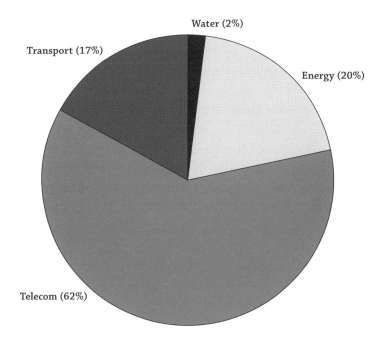

Source: World Bank and PPIAF, PPI Project database, <http://ppi.worldbank.org/>; <http://www.ppiaf.org/>.

formed a P3, financed by equity and debt from construction companies, the South Africa Infrastructure Fund, and private banks.[8] Now complete, the road has improved truck travel between the two countries, expanded trade, encouraged a local tourist industry, and brought follow-on investments (both public and private) in Mozambique.[9]

The main ingredients for a successful P3 include political support, an enabling (corruption-free) regulatory environment, technical expertise, and financing. Rather than host conferences and write reports about P3s, CIDA should focus on financing actual projects and encourage Canadian companies to lend their expertise and equity to them.

Health care and the development of vaccines

Another area where P3s hold potential is health care, particularly in the development of vaccines, which entails many of the same risks as building infrastructure: the high up-front costs of R&D, and the market risk of producing drugs for diseases of poverty. Given the high level of uncertainty attached to both the investment in, and return from, these drugs, diseases such as malaria and TB continue to kill millions of people in developing countries every year.

One solution is for donor governments to use P3s to balance out the risk and reward profile of developing vaccines for these so-called "neglected diseases." One highly effective contribution may take the form of a commitment to purchase a certain dollar value of a vaccine, if a pharmaceutical company can develop it.[10] CIDA need not even establish projects along these lines from scratch; it could easily become an active partner in one or more of a number of P3s already under way. These include the Global Alliance for Vaccines Immunization, the International AIDS Vaccine Initiative, the Medicines for Malaria Venture, and the Global Alliance for Tuberculosis Drug Development. In sum, P3s are not perfect as a development tool; they require structural, political, and financial co-ordination, as well as considerable private-sector expertise, to be worthwhile-. They also require a corruption-free administrative environment. However, successful P3s have produced winning situations for local governments, donors, private companies, and local citizens. Their model should be more widely adopted and supported by Canadian development aid.

---

8   In other P3s, such as the rehabilitation of the Mozambique Port, aid agencies played a key role in providing financing.

9   See Farlam, 2006 for a review of six other successful P3 case studies in Africa. The International Project Finance Association (IPFA) has other examples of successful P3s in Asia, Latin America, and Europe.

10 This idea and others are developed in detail in Kremer and Glennerster, 2004.

TRANSFORMING THE CANADIAN INTERNATIONAL DEVELOPMENT AGENCY

Transforming the Canadian International Development Agency (CIDA) into an agency operated on lines closer to the private sector, that is to say efficiently and with a focus on product, entails a number of steps. We will focus on seven.

1 achieving accountability to stakeholders;
2 improving operational efficiency;
3 replacing a "made-in-Ottawa" approach to aid with an "on-the-ground" approach;
4 adopting a "90-10" rule for choosing recipient countries;
5 buying-in research rather than duplicating existing expertise;
6 creating a marketplace for aid providers; and
7 demanding execution, leadership, and sound management.

Achieving accountability to stakeholders

CIDA's operations are based on what the agency calls a "Business Function Model." Any similarity to actual business largely ends with the name. One "business function" is to "report agency results to stakeholders, including program and project recipients, CIDA management, central agencies, Parliament, and the Canadian public" (CIDA, 2006). While it is perhaps commendable that the taxpayer is at least acknowledged on the list of stakeholders, the average member of the public would most likely be surprised to discover that CIDA spends almost $25 million a year "engaging Canadians" to gain their support for agency programs. CIDA also spends more than ten times as much on the Canadian Partnership Branch, responsible for managing its overall relationship with Canadian private and volunteer-sector partners (CIDA, 2005). While these functions may indeed play a role in stakeholder communications, their combined cost ($317 million) is difficult to explain.

Accountability to Parliament is not much better. CIDA delivers a Departmental Performance Report once a year. In it, the agency fills out its own "report card"— rather like asking a student to grade her own exam. Not surprisingly, of the 31 categories in the most recent report card, on only two items did CIDA give itself a grade of "not yet fully met expectations." On the other 29, it gave itself grades of "exceeded" or "successfully met" expectations. To address these shortcomings, we suggest that an independent third party be given responsibility for completing an annual CIDA "report card" to Parliament and the Canadian public.

Improving operational efficiency

Figure 15.5 shows that since 1990, administrative costs as a percentage of total Canadian official development aid have consistently been higher than in other OECD countries. In 2005, administrative costs, at 6% of ODA, were almost double

Figure 15.5: Administrative costs as a percent of Official Development Assistance (ODA), 1980–2005

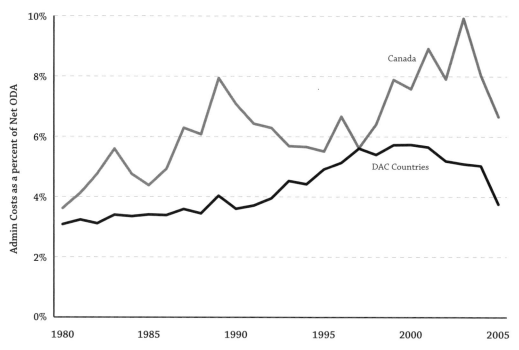

Source: OECD Online ODA database, <http://www.oecd.org/dataoecd/50/17/5037721.htm>.

that of our peers. On an aid budget of $3.7 billion, this means we spent over $100 million on superfluous administrative costs in that year alone. This level of administrative waste is unacceptable. CIDA should make it a priority to bring its administrative cost ratio into line with the OECD-DAC average within two years.

One reason that CIDA's administrative costs are so high may be the geographical sprawl of its programs. This something-for-everybody approach carries a further penalty: it means that Canada's aid achieves a critical mass almost nowhere (OECD, 2002). While the agency appears to be trying to pull its efforts together to some small extent, it continues to boast that "Canadian aid through all channels (including multilateral and partnership) reaches virtually every one of the approximately 120 developing countries in the world." Even excluding multilateral assistance channels, CIDA engages in at least some bilateral programming in approximately 100 countries and maintains field offices in 60 (CIDA, 2005). Some of these are middle-income countries. Why is a relatively small country like Canada, with a limited tax base and resources, trying to help people in every developing country on the planet?

Canada's aid also often goes to the same countries that other large donors help, with the result that our contribution as a proportion of the total aid those countries receive is in some cases almost negligible. For example, as Table 15.7

Table 15.7: Canada's aid contribution in focus countries

	Focus Country Allocation		Country's total ODA ($millions)	Canadian aid as a percent of total aid
	As a percent of total Canadian bilateral aid	$millions		
Bangladesh	4.45	51	1,765	3%
Bolivia	0.7%	8	963	1%
Honduras	0.6%	7	807	1%
Mali	3.5%	40	713	6%
Ghana	3.6%	42	1,706	2%
Ethiopia	3.3%	38	2,291	2%
Mozambique	3.7%	43	1,544	3%
Senegal	1.5%	17	1,322	1%
Tanzania	2.9%	33	2,194	2%
Total/Average	24.2%	279	13,305	2%

Sources: Focus Country aid allocation from CIDA, 2005. Total ODA is from the World Development Indicators (World Bank, 2005) and uses Total ODA in 2004 only, as 2005 is not yet available. Total ODA is reported in $US so the average 2004/2005 $US exchange rate of 0.80 was used for conversion purposes.

shows, CIDA's nine "focus" countries in 2004/05—Bangladesh, Bolivia, Honduras, Mali, Ghana, Ethiopia, Mozambique, Senegal, and Tanzania—received 24% of Canada's total bilateral aid; but in only one of these, Mali, was Canada's share of the total aid the country received over 5%. On average, in the nine "focus" countries, Canada's contribution is approximately 2% of all the aid the country receives. Can we claim to be "focused" on Bolivia, Senegal, and Honduras when we provide only 2% of the total aid these countries receive?

CIDA's aid "focus" must more seriously reflect the meaning of the word. As a guide, we suggest a threshold requiring that Canadian aid be at least 10% of the total in a "focus" country and at least 5% in non-focus Development Partner countries.[11] This degree of concentration compares to the levels other OECD countries achieve. This threshold requirement would leave CIDA with three choices: (1) reduce the total number of countries it is active in; or (2) shift some countries from "focus" to "development partner" status to direct Canadian aid to where it can actually have an impact rather than to countries already overrun with donors trying to make a difference; or (3) a combination of (1) and (2). These changes would go a long way toward making CIDA a more effective, respected, and cost-efficient aid agency.

---

11 We also suggest that a new category of partner be added, conflict-prone countries, whose inclusion and disbursement guidelines are based on different criteria. This recommendation is discussed in more detail below.

The final opportunity for streamlining costs that deserves mention lies within Canada. In addition to its head office in Ottawa, CIDA has three main regional offices in Moncton, Edmonton, and Vancouver and supports six more satellite offices in Calgary, Charlottetown, Halifax, Saskatoon, St. John's, and Winnipeg. CIDA claims these offices provide "convenient direct access" (although for whom is a tantalizing question, considering that its nominal clients are all outside of Canada); but this access comes at an administrative cost that could be put to better use.

Replacing a "made-in-Ottawa" with an "on-the-ground" approach

Currently about 80% of CIDA's 1,500 staff members are located in Ottawa (Goldfarb and Tapp, 2006). CIDA has approximately 60 field offices, which means that on average there are only five people on the ground in each of the countries where the agency operates. This violates a main tenet of good development practice, namely that effectiveness is a function of country-specific knowledge and on-the-ground feedback.

In its Policy Statement on Strengthening Aid Effectiveness, CIDA itself recognized this shortcoming but addressed it with a vague promise to "enhance its field presence in countries selected for enhanced partnerships so that it can effectively deliver new program approaches" (CIDA, 2002). We urge a more assertive commitment to deploy 30% of its staff into the field by 2010 and 40% by 2015. This need not compromise the goal of streamlining CIDA's operational costs. Both the United Kingdom and Denmark have approximately half their staff in the field, and both have administrative cost ratios lower than Canada's (Goldfarb and Tapp, 2006).

Adopting a "90-10" rule

Currently, CIDA gives aid to both low- and middle-income countries, albeit with a bias toward the former. We suggest it adopt instead a "90-10" rule similar to that of the United Kingdom (Barder, 2005), which directs 90% of development aid to low-income countries. We suggest an additional rule: that if a country is an aid donor itself, it not receive ongoing development aid from Canada. This applies today to China and will soon apply to countries like India and Brazil. In November 2006, China agreed to double its aid to Africa by 2009. Why is money from Canadian tax-payers being used to give development aid to China,[12] when China turns around and gives money to Africa? If a country is prosperous enough to be a donor, it should not expect support itself.

---

12   While CIDA does not give official bilateral aid to China, the agency still supports a number of governance, legal, and technical co-operation projects in China. CIDA's China Country Development Programming Framework (CDPF) and a list of projects can be

Using Canadian academic expertise and research capabilities

As with any endeavour, ongoing research into the process of development and effective means to assist it is desirable to guide program managers and direct innovation. Some have recommended that CIDA invest more in this kind of research (Goldfarb and Tapp, 2006). But creating a large in-house research capability is expensive. In CIDA's case, it is also likely to be duplicative. A great deal of pertinent research is already available to CIDA. For example, in 1996 James Wolfensohn, then President of the World Bank, launched a "knowledge bank" that has spent and continues to spend millions of dollars on research and knowledge dissemination in various fields of development.[13]

Among bilateral agencies, the UK development agency has a separate branch called the Central Research Department and USAID has a massive library of research and a specific Knowledge for Development website (USAID, 2006). UN agencies such as UNAIDS, the WHO, the Food and Agricultural Organization, the World Food program, and the UN Development Program, to name but a few, all have research functions. Large multi-national NGOs such as Oxfam, CARE, and World Vision also have their own research capabilities and there are a number of well-regarded development think-tanks such as the Centre for Global Development that provide excellent research on aid topics. In Canada, the publicly funded International Development Research Centre already provides research on four major development themes and has six research offices in developing regions.[14] Given the massive stream of research already available, for CIDA to invest heavily in in-house capabilities seems inefficient at best and wasteful at worst. Instead, in the spirit of enhancing its private-sector orientation, we suggest that CIDA form research "joint ventures" with Canadian institutions and companies noted for their existing expertise in development.

Making a market for aid projects

Nothing inspires efficiency and innovation better than lively competition. CIDA has an opportunity to exploit the power of competition by developing a marketplace for aid delivery. Under this arrangement, both CIDA and private NGOs could tender for project funding; the organization in the best

---

found at <www.acdicida.gc.ca/CIDAWEB/acdicida.nsf/En/JUD-31112026-M6U>. See York, 2006 for a critique of CIDA's continued aid to China.

13 A separate arm of the World Bank is responsible for the execution and coordination of this strategy. See Laporte, 2004 for more information.

14 These themes include; Environment and Natural Resource Management, Information and Communication Technologies for Development, Innovation Policy and Science, and Social and Economic Policy. Regional offices are in Kenya, Senegal, Egypt, India, Singapore, and Uruguay. See International Development Research Centre, 2007 for more detail.

position to fulfill the mandate would receive the assignment and the funds. This market for aid providers would have a number of benefits.

❀ It would remove CIDA's monopoly in Canadian aid and introduce invigorating competition to the domestic development community.

❀ It would encourage specialization. Currently, CIDA has hundreds of projects in over 100 countries, in four main areas with two "cross cutting themes." This scope does not allow for specialization, either by geography or by program. A market approach encourages NGOs to develop a particular level of expertise in certain countries or programs in order to better compete for project funding.

❀ An aid-project marketplace adheres to the principle of "subsidiarity," which leaves to senior levels of government only those functions that cannot be done more effectively and efficiently by smaller and lower levels of organization.

New information technologies would make such a marketplace surprisingly simple to create. CIDA already has a Project Browser Database with over 600 projects listed. The only innovations needed would be to make this proactive (so requests for project proposals are on the site, rather than projects to which funds have already been committed) and to add an element of interactivity, including a bidding process.[15] Contracts would have to set clear performance criteria, with penalties for failure to meet benchmarks, and would require outside auditing, to achieve the efficiency of the private sector.

Demanding execution, leadership, and sound management at CIDA

To conclude, it is important to emphasize that the foregoing reforms will require political will and organizational leadership to achieve. Three parties must take responsibility for their execution: the federal government, the President of CIDA, and the organization's own staff. For the government's part, it must provide a political environment in which reform is a priority. Foreign aid is one of the fastest growing line items in the Canadian budget. In its April 2006 Throne Speech, Prime Minister Harper's government promised "a more effective use of Canadian aid dollars." This commitment must be translated into action and not be allowed to slip down the priority list.

---

15 The World Bank recently started something similar with its Development Marketplace (DM) initiative. DM is not competitive; rather it requires collaboration between individuals with project ideas and organizations, but it could be used as a template for developing an aid marketplace in the Canadian context.

A recent change at the top provides grounds for optimism that CIDA's senior leadership will support reform. In May 2005, Robert Greenhill was appointed President of CIDA. Greenhill, unlike many in the development community who have no private-sector experience, was formerly the President and COO of Bombardier and began his career with McKinsey and Company. Before joining CIDA, he wrote a report entitled *Making a Difference? External Views on Canada's International Impact* (Greenhill, 2005), that outlined Canada's current lack of influence in the world and made dramatic suggestions for improvement. Given this background, outlook, and ability to provide constructive criticism, Mr. Greenhill is well positioned to lead a reformed CIDA. However, he must be able to use his leadership skills to transform CIDA and not be hamstrung by barriers to execution erected by either politicians or bureaucrats.

The third group critical to executing reform is CIDA's own managers and staff. The changes we recommend are largely structural but even the best structure will be ineffective without qualified, committed people working within the organization. Unfortunately, human resources at Canada's development agency currently suffer from a negative chicken-and-egg problem: CIDA is a substandard institution, so it has difficulty attracting and retaining top talent, and because the best Canadian development talents work elsewhere, CIDA continues to under-perform. To break this vicious cycle will take a concerted effort. Canada's development community suffers brain-drain of its brightest talents to more attractive opportunities on the international stage. For example, the Chair of Transparency International is Canadian, the chief of staff at the Clinton Foundation is Canadian, one of the founders of Opportunity International is Canadian, and numerous top professionals at the World Bank, IMF, African,

BUSINESS COUNCIL FOR PEACE: EMPLOYING THE "TOOLS OF WEALTH CREATION" APPROACH IN POST-CONFLICT SITUATIONS

The Business Council for Peace (Bpeace) is a non-profit coalition of volunteer business people in the United States, Canada, Europe, and Australia who apply their business expertise, time, and money to help women build sustainable businesses in war-torn regions. Bpeace believes that entrepreneurship is a foundation for creating hope, stability, and prosperity in post-conflict and conflict-prone regions. The equation, Women + Business = Peace, best sums up the organization's beliefs and goals.

Bpeace is currently active in Rwanda, Afghanistan, and Iraq. They support Rwandan businesswomen engaged in service businesses including a café, conference facilities, a garden center, and beauty salons. The organization also supports Afghani women and Iraqi women engaged in businesses such as textiles, private education, construction-related services including engineering, supply procurement, and water testing.

Bpeace presents an excellent example of a TWC approach that can be applied in post-conflict situations to facilitate the often difficult transition to lasting peace and prosperity.

Inter-American, and Asian Development Banks are also Canadians. Why do people who want to make a global difference in development fields as diverse as HIV/AIDS, environmental protection, justice, corruption, gender equity, finance, and democratic governance, have to go abroad to do so?

To achieve transformation in its operations, CIDA must also sell to top professionals in the Canadian development community a new vision of itself as a transformed organization in which excellence, effectiveness, and innovation are core values. With its operational and management cultures thus transformed, CIDA will become a desirable place to pursue a career, replacing the chicken-and-egg problem with a virtuous cycle of achievement and recruiting success.

REFORMING EMERGENCY AID

Emergency aid takes two common forms: disaster aid and food aid. While Canada's record in disaster aid is admirable, our record on food aid is dismal. Until 2005, 90% of the food aid this country offered was required to be sourced from Canada. This has since been reduced to 50%, but is still among the highest of proportions of tied food aid among OECD countries. Our suggestions for reforming food aid are threefold. First, untie all food aid and allow it to be sourced from the provider best able to deliver the quantity and quality of food required in the timeliest manner. Rather than concentrate administrative efforts on procuring subsidies for Canadian farmers, CIDA should focus on the logistics of getting the food to where it is needed. Second, Canada should refocus its effort on rural development to attack the root causes of the need for food aid. According to Oxfam, Canada's current aid spending on rural development programs is less than half what it was 15 years ago (Oxfam, 2006). A renewed focus on rural development, employing the Tools of Wealth Creation, would empower people increasingly to feed themselves rather than rely on continuous aid from countries like Canada.[16] Finally, Canada should support existing mechanisms (and explore creating its own) that use insurance markets to offset the environmental risks that often lead to food crises. This approach was pioneered by the World Food Program (WFP) in Ethiopia. The WFP took out an insurance policy with French insurer, Axa, at the cost of approximately $1 million. If rainfall in Ethiopia dips below a certain level during a given growing season, Axa will immediately pay out $7.1 million on

---

16 Under the TWC approach this could include providing enhanced access to capital, technology, and markets for farmers, and increasing educational initiatives in rural areas.

the policy (Lacey, 2006)—money that the WFP can use to purchase emergency food supplies. This market-based approach to managing food security risks is far superior to the traditional one, in which people die needlessly of hunger while the WFP and other agencies scramble to drum up relief from donor countries.

REFORMING POST-CONFLICT AID

Afghanistan is currently the main recipient of Canada's post-conflict aid (albeit with plenty of conflict mixed in). Here, therefore, we make some general recommendations with respect to post-conflict aid but pay particular attention to the Afghan mission. Steps Canada could take to improve post-conflict aid include:

- using aid to prevent conflict;
- recognizing a new paradigm of conflict and post-conflict aid;
- demanding accountability for post-conflict aid disbursements and giving the military responsibility for aid delivery if necessary;
- repositioning the deployment of aid and peacekeeping assets;
- using Canadian expertise in building and sustaining democratic institutions in strong, sustainable federal systems; and
- improving the timing of post-conflict aid.

WHAT DO OUTSIDERS THINK OF CANADA'S ROLE IN THE WORLD?
Prior to becoming President of CIDA, Robert Greenhill researched and published a comprehensive report titled *Making a Difference? External Views on Canada's International Impact* (Greenhill, 2005). Respondents collaborated under the condition of anonymity. Some of comments, quoted below, provide a sobering reflection on Canada's impact on the world, as seen by non-Canadians.

"Where has Canada made a significant difference over the past 15 years? Nothing comes to mind."

"Canada will continue to be irrelevant unless there is a political will to change. Today it adopts high moral standards from a safe distance."

"In the '70s and '80s, Canada belonged to like-minded countries making a difference in development. Canada was truly one of the leaders. Canada has totally lost that in the past 15 years."

"The current trends are against Canada's influence."

A reformed CIDA could be an effective tool in both alleviating poverty and improving the sub-standard perception of Canadian contributions on the world stage.

Using aid to prevent conflict

Wars are not only tragic in terms of causing the loss and degradation of human life; they are also terribly expensive in economic terms. Paul Collier, a conflict expert at Oxford University, calculates that the average civil war in a low-income country costs $54 billion (UK-IDC, 2006). The magnitude of this number suggests that, if aid money can provide an ounce of conflict prevention in a fragile state so that war does not erupt, it would be worth much more than a pound of post-conflict cure. To that end, we suggest that CIDA, in addition to realigning its general activity onto a shorter list of "focus" countries as prescribed above, include three conflict-prone countries on its focus list. Understandably it is more difficult to execute aid projects in conflict-prone countries. With that in mind, inclusion of these countries on CIDA's priority list and third-party evaluation of its programs there should employ criteria specific to conflict-prone environments, rather than those used for general development aid. This will ensure that CIDA is not penalized for supporting conflict-prone states.

Recognizing the new paradigm of post-conflict aid

The terms "pre-conflict aid" and "post-conflict aid" imply a chronology that does not necessarily exist in current situations. For example, Canadian troops are on the ground in Afghanistan trying to achieve peace while at the same time engaging in post-conflict-like reconstruction and development programs. The same is true of US military involvement and development aid in Iraq. This may also become a reality in the Darfur region of Sudan, where massive amount of humanitarian and post-conflict types of aid are needed even though peace has not been achieved.

Thus, in discussing aid to conflict-prone and failed or failing states, it is important to appreciate that many of today's conflicts are complex, long, drawn-out affairs in which the distinction between "pre-" and "post-" hostilities is moot. Achieving peace and providing aid may be simultaneous rather than sequential endeavours. Governments engaged in both the funding and operational aspects of aid must recognize this.

Demanding accountability for post-conflict aid disbursements

Afghanistan is currently Canada's top post-conflict aid priority. Ongoing violence in the Afghan theatre, however, makes it an excellent case study in the lack of accountability and barriers to effective aid delivery in such situations. In October 2006, Brigadier-General A.J. Howard testified before the Senate Committee on National Security and Defence. He praised the work of Canadian troops in Afghanistan but commented that a number of aid projects were being held up because they were still waiting for funding from CIDA. Upon further inquiry, the committee found that of $44 million in Canadian development aid that has gone into Afghanistan so far, only $3 million has gone to Kandahar, where the vast majority of Canadian troops are located and Canada's military operations are focused (Senate of Canada, 2006).

Efforts to discover why CIDA's disbursements in Kandahar have been delayed have produced no reasonable explanation. In a letter to the Senate Committee on this topic, Minister of International Co-operation Josée Verner wrote: "The bulk of CIDA's development assistance to Afghanistan goes to National programs delivered through the central government. Some of these programs are active in Kandahar province; however, at this stage we cannot give specific figures as to how much of Canadian money in support of these programs goes to Kandahar province" (Senate of Canada, Standing Committee on National Security and Defence, 2006: Appendix XI). This lack of accountability is unacceptable. If CIDA cannot adequately administer post-conflict aid, its responsibility should be transferred to the military. The Senate report, *Managing Turmoil: The Need to Upgrade Canadian Foreign Aid and Military Strength to Deal with Massive Change*, also recommended transferring aid responsibility to the military if CIDA and other aid organizations are unable to fulfill their role (Senate of Canada, 2006). Unsurprisingly, NGOs such as OXFAM Canada and CARE Canada are strongly against this. They claim that mixing military and aid operations in Afghanistan will confuse the Afghan population. This objection appears to be no more than institutional territoriality. There is little evidence to show that villagers care where support comes from, as long as it addresses their humanitarian needs and arrives in a timely manner.

Geographical alignment of aid and peacekeeping: Focus on Africa

Peacekeeping forces are critical to provide the secure environment within which any type of post-conflict aid can hope to succeed. According to Collier and Hoeffler (2002), there is a 39% chance that peace will collapse within the first five years after a conflict, and a 32% chance that it will collapse in the following five years. Canada has a proud history of peacekeeping. Our former Prime Minister, Lester B. Pearson, is generally regarded as having invented modern peacekeeping when he proposed the first United Nations Emergency Force to end the Suez Crisis in 1956. Canadians today uphold this legacy with pride but must balance it with a realistic appraisal of modern geopolitical, humanitarian, and economic realities.

According to the *Human Security Report*, as of 2003, Africa accounted for over one third of all state-based conflicts, 90% of non-state conflicts, and over

50% of all conflicts worldwide (Human Security Centre, 2005). As we noted above, the continent is also the major focus of Canadian aid initiatives. Over half of CIDA's focus countries are in Africa. Canada has pledged to double aid to the region by 2008/09 and has established a $500 million "Canada Fund for Africa."

Remarkably, despite the fact that Africa receives the majority of Canadian aid and sustains over half of the world's conflicts, only 64 Canadian staff officers, ceasefire observers, and military trainers serve there, supporting a mere three peacekeeping operations, one of which (Sierra Leone) is winding down (CBC, 2006). This is a striking incongruence between the countries where Canadians are engaged, or may engage, in warfare, and those to which we have allocated our aid. It could be reduced by increasing Canada's overall budget for post-conflict aid and including conflict-prone countries in CIDA's focus.

Institution building: Exporting "POGG"

The best-known phrase in Canada's constitutional lexicon is "Peace, Order, and Good Government"—somewhat unfortunately abbreviated by some constitutional scholars into its acronym, "POGG." It should perhaps not entirely surprise the citizens of a country that has managed to avoid serious internal conflict for 140 years over the most violent century in human history, that this same formula is the cornerstone of re-establishing post-conflict societies.

Many of the reforms we suggested earlier to revitalize Canadian democracy, such as civic education, reform of the election process, and a more fully developed political infrastructure, apply even more strongly to new democracies struggling for footing on soil churned by conflict. If we can put our own house in better order, demonstrating to the world the best model of democracy in a strong federal system, we will have a great deal to contribute to post-conflict societies eager for a taste of POGG. Some organizations already exist to transfer expertise in this area. CANADEM, with assistance and funding from Foreign Affairs Canada's Human Security Program, has a roster of over 7,500 rapid-reaction experts prepared to deliver technical assistance in governance. Similarly, CIDA's Canada Corps facilitates the efforts of Canadians to promote democratic institutions in developing and fragile states.[17]

These organizations suffer a major shortcoming however. They generally take a top-down view of institution building and governance. For example, CANADEM recently sent an election monitoring team to Haiti through the International Mission for Monitoring Haitian Elections. But what good is election monitoring if the underlying framework of democracy is missing?

---

17 The Canadian Peacebuilding Coordinating Committee also acts as an umbrella organization for those involved in peace-building initiatives.

Similarly, Canada Corps projects include strengthening the capacity of the Ministry of Women's and Children's Affairs in Bangladesh and improving the responsiveness of African parliaments through the Africa-Canada Parliamentary Strengthening Program. But these are elevated endeavours aimed at elites. They do not address the underpinnings of a strong democratic system such as basic civic education, building political parties, running campaigns, or fostering free and fair forms of political communication (television, radio, newspapers, internet, and so on).

This again resonates with the "Tools of Wealth Creation" approach to reducing poverty. Considerable evidence shows that open markets go hand in hand with stable, peaceful democracy. Causality research shows that free markets "cause" democratic and other civic freedoms that in turn "cause" economic freedom. In other words, a virtuous circle is created (see Griswold, 2004). The mechanics are easy to see. When a regime has the power to determine its citizens' ability to feed, clothe, house, and educate themselves and their families, when it controls whether they can hold a job, get a promotion, or move to another town for advancement, when it can restrict their economic freedom in these or any other ways, then that regime has all the tools it needs to suppress their political and civic freedoms as well—at least until life becomes unbearable and violence a persuasive alternative.

Free markets give people economic independence and lessen their dependence on government, empowering them to claim other freedoms. No nation that lacks free markets has ever supported stable political and civil freedoms. On the other hand, no nation that enjoys economic freedom has ever failed to evolve towards civil and political freedoms, with only two exceptions— Singapore and Hong Kong, on which the jury of history may still be out.

Free markets, as empirical research shows, also spur peaceful solutions by creating a positive rather than a zero-sum economy. Growth in non-market economies is typically weak, non-existent, or even negative (Zimbabwe offers a contemporary case in point). This creates a zero-sum economy in which one person's gain is another's loss and conflict almost inevitable. The only ways to secure a larger slice of the static pie are rent-seeking, political power, or, not uncommonly, some variety of brute force. In a market economy by contrast, individuals typically gain when others do better, because those others either become better customers or more efficient producers of goods and services the first individual wants. In the process, the market economy grows, increasing the pie and everyone's prospects of getting a slice. Its citizens enjoy a stake in that growth, hope for the future, and thus have all the reasons in the world to seek peaceful solutions (see, for example, Gartzke, 2005).

That virtuous cycle is the reason why the Tools of Wealth Creation are equally tools of peace creation. As such, we recommend that post-conflict aid aimed at building democratic infrastructure work from the bottom up with a focus on the Tools of Wealth Creation, rather than from the top down with a focus on elites. We believe this will have a more lasting effect and generate more substantial peace (as well as financial) dividends for post-conflict societies.

Improving the timing of post-conflict aid

Finally, it is important to consider the timing of post-conflict aid. There is no such thing as a quick war and a quick peace. To its credit, the Harper government seems to realize this in Afghanistan. In the Prime Minister's speech to the UN in September 2006, he stated "The challenges facing Afghanistan are enormous. There will be no quick fixes." This mindset is absolutely necessary when embarking on post-conflict and reconstruction aid. Collier and Dollar (2002) highlight one of the most common mistakes: providing too much aid immediately after peace is achieved, when institutional and human capacity is low, and then removing the aid just as the country has gained the capacity to use it effectively. He suggests that reconstruction aid instead "taper in" rather than "taper off." Canada's commitments to post-conflict aid should be made for the long haul; our aid should rise as recipients' capacity improves (up to the point of "saturation" we noted earlier), rather than withdraw as soon as the first signs of success appear.

FISCAL AND POLITICAL IMPLICATIONS

The Canadian government has committed to raising its aid budget to 0.7% of GDP by 2015. Why adopt a random, analytically arbitrary monetary target rather than a reasoned, evidence-based target keyed to results? In addition to the oft-noted absence of any fiscal, macroeconomic, or empirical basis for this 0.7% target (Moss, Pettersson and van de Walle, 2006), it is flawed from a deeper perspective. The commitment targets money to be spent; it says nothing of how, or how well, it is used. Where is the incentive to improve, or even achieve, poverty reduction or development when more aid money flows each year regardless of its effectiveness? This is the epitome of the preference for activity over results. Instead of adopting an arbitrary spending goal, Canada should develop an evidence-based goal for our foreign aid.

William Easterly, in his paper "The Cartel of Good Intentions: The Problem of Bureaucracy in Foreign Aid" (2002), draws attention to the risks to both donor and recipient countries of qualifying aid by funds dispersed rather than services provided. He goes on to show how this encourages aid agencies including CIDA to focus on activities with low return but high visibility such as producing glossy reports and hosting conferences, rather than those with high return and low visibility that actually reduce poverty.

CONCLUSIONS: GIVING SO OTHERS MAY NO LONGER NEED

Point-seven percent of our GDP may or may not be the right amount of money for Canadians to spend trying to alleviate poverty and reduce suffering in the world beyond our borders. What is inarguable is that it is the wrong way to look at the value or sufficiency of our effort. This chapter has identified the crippling flaws to this input-oriented way of thinking about development aid. It has also identified numerous opportunities to transform Canada's practice of foreign aid into something much closer to what we believe Canadians have in mind when, in large numbers, they express their support for it: effective, focused, appropriate aid that empowers the world's disadvantaged to rebuild shattered societies and escape poverty once and for all. In short, foreign aid that really helps.

RECOMMENDATIONS

15.1   Adopt the "Tools of Wealth Creation" as the centerpiece of development aid, to equip poor people with the resources to pull themselves out of poverty. These include:
   * property rights;
   * access to capital;
   * human capital development;
   * access to technology; and
   * access to trade markets.

15.2   Use Public-Private Partnerships, where appropriate, to undertake projects that would otherwise be infeasible in developing countries and create multiple winners among local governments, donors, the private sector, and local citizens. P3s are particularly suited to infrastructure and vaccine development.

15.3   Strengthen internationally active NGOs in Canada by encouraging consolidation and economies of scale and specialization in the sector.

15.4   Transform CIDA by:
   * requiring increased accountability to both the government and the Canadian public;
   * improving operational efficiency;
   * replacing a "made-in-Ottawa" (manager-led) approach to aid with an "on-the-ground" (client-focused) approach;
   * adopting a "90-10" rule;
   * buying-in research rather than duplicating existing expertise;

* creating a market place for aid projects; and
* demanding execution, leadership, and sound management at CIDA.

15.5   Reform food aid by:
* completely untying food aid;
* refocusing efforts on rural development; and
* supporting market-based approaches to managing environmental risks, such as drought insurance.

15.6   Improve post-conflict aid by:
* recognizing the new paradigm of conflict- and post-conflict aid;
* increasing the amount of aid allocated to both conflict-prone nations and post-conflict situations;
* demanding accountability for post-conflict aid disbursements and giving the military responsibility for aid delivery if necessary;
* realigning Canada's aid and peacekeeping priorities to focus on Africa;
* using aid money and Canadian expertise to facilitate bottom-up institution building and governance initiatives in post-conflict nations; and
* improving the timing of post-conflict aid.

15.7   Adopt a reasoned, evidence-based foreign aid budget target rather than the current random, analytically arbitrary monetary target of 0.7% of GDP by 2015.

CONCLUSION
LOOKING AHEAD

Climb with us in your imagination to some high viewpoint and open your eyes to what the future could hold for Canada and for you. What do you see? We see a country offering its citizens the highest quality of life in the world, sustained by the best-performing economy in the world. We see a nation that has become the best-governed democratic federation in the world and highly respected as an international leader.

And what is required from our citizens and governments to make this vision a reality? From citizens, acceptance of greater responsibility for our own well-being and that of others, productive participation in Canada's economy, active involvement in the democratic governance of our local community and country, and a willingness to accept and support the discharging of Canada's international responsibilities. And from governments? Decisions, laws, and public policies based on sound principles, in particular the principles of freedom, responsibility, compassion, democracy, and well-balanced federalism.

The vision and policy recommendations put forward in this summary volume of *A Canada Strong and Free* represent the best efforts of Canada's largest market-oriented think tank, the Fraser Institute, and two experienced political practitioners with a passion for the development of forward-looking public policy based on conservative principles. Can the vision and the policy recommendations of this volume be strengthened and improved upon? Of course they can! We invite your participation in doing so by supporting the ongoing work of The Fraser Institute.

And can the application and adoption of the principles and policies recommended in this volume be strengthened and expanded? They can and they must be, if our vision of what Canada can and should be is ever to become a practical reality. For example, in Canada the application of the principles of economic freedom and free markets are furthest advanced with respect to the operations of our economy and the conduct of our international trade.

But full realization of the benefits of the application of these principles is still seriously hampered by the excessive financial demands and regulatory constraints of oversized and protectionist federal and provincial governments. And the proper and rigorous application of market principles to the protection and conservation of Canada's magnificent physical environment has scarcely even begun.

With respect to achieving the appropriate balances between the roles of the public and private sectors and the various levels of government, especially with respect to the provision of social services, Canadians should be largely satisfied with what has been achieved in the area of K-12 education and with the current direction of welfare reform. But the principles of subsidiarity and "rebalancing" have still not been rigorously applied to the provision of either health care or child care—both of which must be dramatically improved if Canadians are ever to enjoy the highest quality of life in the world—nor to the revitalization of "have not" provinces nor to remedying the tragic conditions faced by on-reserve aboriginals.

With respect to the revitalization of democracy in Canada, democratic reform in general is proceeding at a snail's pace. In most jurisdictions, only a fraction of the measures listed on our "democratic reform menu" are under active consideration and even fewer have actually been implemented.

And with respect to refocusing and reorienting Canada's foreign policy, we are still a long way from becoming the champions of international trade liberalization or of the Tools of Wealth Creation approach to foreign aid called for by our vision of Canada as an international leader.

In other words, much remains to be done to strengthen the application and adoption of the principles and policies put forward in this volume. We conclude by inviting your continued interest and support of the work of The Fraser Institute, and the efforts of all those committed to the principles and policies required to achieve *A Canada Strong and Free*.

REFERENCES

ACE Project (2004). *Citizens' Initiatives*. <focus.aceproject.org/direct-democracy/citizen-initiatives>, as of October 26, 2004.

Adelman, C. (2003). "The Privatization of Foreign Aid: Reassessing National Largesse." *Foreign Affairs*, 82, 6 (November/December): 9–14.

Afonso, Antonio, Ledger Schuknecht, and Vito Tanzi (2005). "Public Sector Efficiency: An International Comparison." *Public Choice* 123: 321–47.

Alberta, International and Intergovernmental Relations (2003). *Memorandum of Understanding: Alberta/British Columbia Partnership on Child Welfare*. <www.iir.gov.ab.ca/canadian_intergovernmental_relations/pdfs/(4.2.1.5)%20AB-BC%20Child_Welfare_MOU.pdf>.

Alberta, International and Intergovernmental Relations (2004). *Alberta-British Columbia Memorandum of Understanding: Environmental Cooperation and Harmonization*. <www.iir.gov.ab.ca/canadian_intergovernmental_relations/documents/Environmental_Cooperation_MOU.pdf>.

Alberta, International and Intergovernmental Relations (2005). *British Columbia-Alberta Memorandum of Understanding: Bilateral Water Management Agreement Negotiations*. <www.iir.gov.ab.ca/canadian_intergovernmental_relations/documents/WaterManagementNegotiatingMOU_March22005_FINAL.pdf>.

Alesina, A., and B. Weder (2002). "Do Corrupt Governments Receive less Foreign Aid?" *American Economic Review* 92, 4: 1126–37.

Alesina, A., and D. Dollar (2000). "Who Gives Foreign Aid to Whom and Why?" *Journal of Economic Growth* 5, 1 (March): 33–63.

Alesina, Alberto, Giuseppe Nicoletti, Silvia Ardagna, and Fabio Schiantarelli (2005). "Regulation and Investment." *Journal of the European Economic Association* 3, 4 (June): 791–825.

Alesina, Alberto, Silvia Ardagna, Roberto Perotti, and Fabio Schiantarelli (2002). "Fiscal Policy, Profits, and Investment." *American Economic Review* 92, 3 (June): 571–89.

Allan, T.R.S. (1993). *Law, Liberty and Justice: The Legal Foundations of British Constitutionalism*. Clarendon Press.

Allard, Jean R. (2002). *The Rebirth of Big Bear's People: The Road to Freedom*. Frontier Centre for Public Policy.

Altenstetter, Christa, and James Warner Björkman, eds. (1997). *Health Policy Reform, National Variations, and Globalization*. MacMillan Press.

Anderson, Terry (1998). "The Rising Tide of Water Markets." Presented at *Property Rights, Economics and Environment*, seminar at Aix-en-Provence, France. <www.environnement-propriete.org/ english/1998/pdf_dowload/anderson.pdf>.

Anderson, Terry (2004). "Markets and the Environment: Friends or Foes?" *Case Western Reserve Law Review* 55, 1.

Anderson, Terry L., Bruce L. Benson, and Thomas E. Flanagan (2006). *Self-Determination: The Other Path for Native Americans*. Stanford University Press.

Anderson, Terry, and Pamela Snyder (1997). *Priming the Invisible Pump*. Policy Series PS-9. Property and Environment Research Center.

Archer, Keith, Roger Gibbins, Rainer Knopff, and Leslie Pal (1999). *Parameters of Power: Canada's Political Institutions*. 2nd ed. Thompson Nelson.

Asher, Mukul G (1995). *Compulsory Savings in Singapore: An Alternative to the Welfare State*. NCPA Policy Report No. 198. National Center for Policy Analysis.

Asher, Mukul G (1999). *Pension Scheme in Singapore: Case Study and Implications*. EPW Special Articles.

Asia Pacific Foundation of Canada (2002). Generous at Heart, Prudent at Pocket. *Foreign Aid and Trade: What Do Canadians Think?* APF Canada.

Auerbach, Alan J. (1983). "Taxation, Corporate Financial Policy and the Cost of Capital." *Journal of Economic Literature* 21: 905–40.

Auerbach, Alan J. (1996). "Tax Reform, Capital Allocation, Efficiency, and Growth." In Henry Aaron and William Gale, edd., *Economic Effects of Fundamental Tax Reform* (Brookings Institution Press).

Bach, Stanley (2003). *Platypus and Parliament: The Australian Senate in Theory and Practice*. Department of the Senate, Parliament House.

Baghwati, J. (2004). *In Defence of Globalization*. Oxford University Press.

Barder, O. (2005). *Reforming Development Assitance: Lessons from the UK*. Working Paper No. 70. Centre for Global Development.

Barro, Robert (1990). "Government Spending in a Simple Model of Endogenous Growth." *Journal of Political Economy* 98, 5: S103–S125.

Barro, Robert (1991). "Economic Growth in a Cross Section of Countries." *Quarterly Journal of Economics* 106, 2 (May): 407–43.

Bassanini, Andrea, and Ekkehard Ernst (2002). *Labour Market Institutions, Product Market Regulations and Innovation: Cross-Country Evidence*. Economics Department Working Paper 316. Organisation for Economic Co-operation and Development.

Battle, Ken (1998). *Transformation: Canadian Social Policy, 1985–2001*. The North American Institute.

Baylor, Maximilian, and Louis Beausejour (2004). *Taxation and Economic Efficiency: Results from a Canadian CGE Model*. Department of Finance Working Paper. [Canada] Department of Finance.

BC Citizens' Assembly on Electoral Reform (2004). *Droop Quota (Formula)*. <www.citizensassembly.bc.ca/public/learning_resources/glossary/2004/csharman-10_0412141107-017>.

Beaulieu, Eugene, Jim Gaisford, and Jim Higginson (2003). *Interprovincial Trade Barriers in Canada: How Far Have We Come? Where Should We Go?* The Van Horne Institute.

Beaulieu, Eugene, Kenneth J. McKenzie, Jimmy Stephane Vu, and Jean-Francois Wen (2004). *Effective Tax Rates and the Formation of Manufacturing Enterprises in Canada*. Fraser Institute Digital Publication (January). <www.fraserinstitute.org/shared/readmore.asp?sNav=pb&id=638>.

Becker, G. (1998). "Human Capital and Poverty." *Religion and Liberty* 8, 1. <www.acton.org/publicat/randl/print_article.php?id=258>.

Becsi, Zsolt (1996). "Do State and Local Taxes Affect Relative State Growth?" *Economic Review* 81, 2 (March/April): 18–36.

Belsky, J., and J. Casidy (1994). "Attachment: Theory and Evidence." In M. Rutter and D. Hay, eds., *Development through Life: A Handbook for Clinicians* (Blackwell Scientific Publications): 549–71.

Benson, Bruce, and Ronald Johnson (1986). "The Lagged Impact of State and Local Taxes on Economic Activity and Political Behaviour." *Economic Inquiry* 24 (July): 389–401.

Berggren, Niclas (1999). "Economic Freedom and Equality: Friends or Foes?" *Public Choice* 100, 3/4 (September): 203–23.

Bibby, Reginald W. (2004). *The Future Families Project: A Survey of Canadian Hopes and Dreams*. Section 5, "Parenting and Parents." The Vanier Institute of the Family.

Bishop, John (1999). "How Provincial Diploma Exams Improve Student Learning." *Fraser Forum* (September).

Blank, Rebecca M., and P. Ruggles (1994). "Short-Term Recidivism among Public-Assistance Recipients." *American Economic Review* 84, 2: 49–53.

Blouin, Patric, M-J Couchesne, and Isabelle Thony (2006). "Summary Public School Indicators for the Provinces and Territories, 1997-2003." Statistics Canada.

Blumenthal, Sidney (1988). *Rise of the Counter-Establishment: From Conservative Ideology to Political Power*. HarperCollins Canada.

Boessenkool, Kenneth J. (1997). *Back to Work: Learning from the Alberta Welfare Experiment*. C.D. Howe Institute Commentary (April). C.D. Howe Institute.

Bosetti, L., R. O'Reilly, and D. Gereluk (1998). "Public Choices and Public Education: The Impact of Alberta Charter Schools." Paper presented at the Annual Meeting of the American Educational Research Association, San Diego, CA.

Bowles, Linda (1994). "The Weaning Process." *Washington Times* (December 20): A16.

Boyer, J. Patrick (1992). *Direct Democracy in Canada: The History and Future of Referendums*. Dundurn.

British Columbia Ministry of Human Resources, Economic Analysis Branch (2003). *MHR Exit Survey—Winter 2003*. <www.mhr.gov.bc.ca/research/reports/MHR_Q4.pdf>, as of October 2003.

British Columbia, Department of Finance (2005a). *Budget and Fiscal Plan 2005/06*. Government of British Columbia.

British Columbia, Department of Finance (2005b). *September Update: Budget and Fiscal Plan 2005/06*. Government of British Columbia.

British Columbia, Ministry of Economic Development (2006). *Trade, Investment and Labour Mobility Agreement between British Columbia and Alberta*. <www.gov.bc.ca/ecdev/down/BC-AB_TILMA_Agreement-signed.pdf>.

British Columbia, Ministry of State for Intergovernmental Relations (2005). *Quebec and British Columbia Sign Agreement on Francophone Affairs*. News release (November 23). <www2.news.gov.bc.ca/news_releases_2005-2009/2005OTP0135-001080.htm>.

Broder, P. (2001). *The Legal Definition of Charity and Canada Customs Revenue Agency's Charitable Registration Process*. The Canadian Centre for Philanthropy, Public Affairs. <www.imaginecanada.ca/Files/publicaffairs/Definition.pdf>.

Brodie, Ian (2001). "Interest Group Litigation and the Embedded State: Canada's Court Challenges Program." *Canadian Journal of Political Science* 34, 2 (June): 357–76.

Brodie, Ian (2002). *Friends of the Court: The Privileging of Interest Group Litigants in Canada*. State University of New York Press.

Brookshire, David, Bonnie Colby, Mary Ewers, and Philip Ganderton (2004). "Market Prices for Water in the Semi-Arid West." *Water Resources Research* 40.

Brown, R., and Y. Guillemette (2003). "Tax Treatment of Charitable Donations: How Much is Enough?" C.D Howe Institute Backgrounder 70 (February). <www.cdhowe.org/pdf/backgrounder_70.pdf>.

Burchinal, Margaret R. (1999). "Child Care Experiences and Developmental Outcomes." *Annals of American Academy of Political Science* 563 (May): 73–97.

Burney, Derek (2005). "Canada-US Relations: Are We Getting it Right?" The Ranchmen's Club, Calgary (November 17).

Burnside, Craig and David Dollar (2000). *Aid, Policies, and Growth*. World Bank.

Burnside, Craig and David Dollar (2004). *Aid, Policies and Growth: Revisiting the Evidence*. World Bank.

Bushnik, Tracey (2006). *Child Care in Canada*. Children and Youth Research Paper Series. Catalogue no. 89-599-MIE (no. 003). Statistics Canada.

Bussière, Patrick, Fernando Cartwright, and Tamara Knighto (2004). *Measuring Up: Canadian Results of the OECD PISA Study—The Performance of Canada's Youth in Mathematics, Reading, Science and Problem Solving: 2003 First Findings for Canadians Aged 15*. Canada, Minister of Industry.

Cai, Jinyong, and Jagadeesh Gokhale (1997). "The Welfare Loss from a Capital Income Tax." *Federal Reserve Bank of Cleveland Economic Review* 33, 1: 2–10.

Canada Council on Social Development [CCSD] (2004). *Child Care for a Change!* Conference Proceedings. Winnipeg, MB (November 12-14, 2004). <www.ccsd. ca/subsites/child care/cc-proceedings.pdf>.

Canada Revenue Agency (2003). *Policy Statement: Political Activities*. Reference # CPS-022. <www.cra-arc.gc.ca/tax/charities/policy/cps/cps-022-e.html>.

Canada Revenue Agency (2006). *Your Canada Child Tax Benefit*. T4114. <www.cra-arc. gc.ca/E/pub/tg/t4114/README.html>.

Canada, Access to Information Review Task Force (2002). *Access to Information: Making it Work for Canadians*. Report of the Access to Information Review Task Force (June). Treasury Board Secretariat. <www.atirtf-geai.gc.ca/accessReport-e.pdf>.

Canada, Department of Finance (2004a). *Budget 2004*. Government of Canada.

Canada, Department of Finance (2004b). *Tax Expenditures and Evaluations 2004*. <www.fin.gc.ca/toce/2004/taxexp04_e.html>.

Canada, Department of Finance (2005). *The Budget Plan 2005*. <www.fin.gc.ca/ budget05/pdf/bp2005e.pdf>.

Canada, Department of Finance (2005). *The Federal Budget 2005*. Department of Finance.

Canada, Department of Finance (2005a). *Budget 2005*. Government of Canada.

Canada, Department of Finance (2005b). *The Economic and Fiscal Update*. Government of Canada.

Canada, Department of Finance (2006). *The Budget Plan 2006*. Government of Canada.

Canada, Department of Finance (2007). *The Budget Plan 2005*. Ottawa: Department of Finance.

Canada, Department of Justice [DoJ] (2005/April). *A Comprehensive Framework for Access to Information Reform: A Discussion Paper*.

Canada, Foreign Affairs and International Trade (2005). *Canada's International Policy Statement: A Role of Pride and Influence in the World*. <geo.international.gc.ca/ cip-pic/ips/overview-en.asp>.

Canada, House of Commons (2005). *Standing Orders of the House of Commons*. (June 30). <www.parl.gc.ca/information/about/process/house/standingorders/toc-e.htm>

Canada, Intergovernmental Affairs, Privy Council Office (2001). *The Charlottetown Accord (1992) (Unofficial Text), Summary*. <www.pco-bcp.gc.ca/aia/default.asp?Language= E&page=consfile&sub=TheHistoryofConstitution&Doc=charlottetown_e.htm>.

Canada, Office of the Auditor General [OAG] (1998/April). *Report of the Auditor General of Canada*.

Canada, Office of the Auditor General [OAG] (2003/November). *Report of the Auditor General of Canada*.

Canada, Office of the Auditor General [OAG] (2005/November). *Report of the Auditor General of Canada*.

Canada, Privy Council Office (2006). *Government Directive on Regulating*. <www.regulation.gc.ca/default.asp?Page=report&Language=E&doc=report_e.htm>

Canada, Royal Commission on Dominion-Provincial Relations (1940). *Report of the Royal Commission on Dominion-Provincial Relations*. "Rowell-Sirois Report." King's Printer.

Canada, Royal Commission on the Economic Union and Development Prospects for Canada [Macdonald Commission] (1985). *Report on the Economic Union and Development Prospects for Canada*. Supply and Services.

Canadian Border Services Agency (2006). *Customs Tariff, Department Consolidation*. <cbsa-asfc.gc.ca/general/publications/customs_tariff-e.html>.

Canadian Broadcasting Corp. [CBC] (2006). "Senator Slams Sparse Canadian Military Presence in Africa." *CBC News* (September 26). <www.cbc.ca/canada/story/2006/09/26/militaryafrica.html>.

Canadian Chamber of Commerce (2004). *Obstacles to Free Trade in Canada: A Study on Internal Trade Barriers* (November).

Canadian Council for Public-Private Partnerships [CCPPP] (2004). *National Public Opinion Survey on Public-Private Partnerships*. <www.pppcouncil.ca/publications.asp#Surveys>.

Canadian International Development Agency [CIDA] (2002). *Policy Statement on Strengthening Aid Effectiveness*. <www.acdi-cida.gc.ca/CIDAWEB/acdicida.nsf/En/STE-32015515-SG4>.

Canadian International Development Agency [CIDA] (2003). *CIDA's Policy on Private Sector Development*. <www.acdi-cida.gc.ca/CIDAWEB/acdicida.nsf/En/REN-218124828-P9B>.

Canadian International Development Agency [CIDA] (2005). *Canadian International Development Agency: Estimates 2005–2006. Part III: Report on Plans and Priorities*. <www.tbs-sct.gc.ca/est-pre/20052006/CIDA-ACDI/CIDA-ACDIr56_e.asp>.

Canadian International Development Agency [CIDA] (2006). *CIDA's Business Process Road Map*. Version 2.5. <www.acdi-cida.gc.ca/CIDAWEB/acdicida.nsf/En/JUD-131105815-LQY>.

Canadian Parliamentary Review (1996). "Committee Systems in Quebec and Ontario: Part 1: Structure and Organization." *Canadian Parliamentary Review* 19, 1 (Spring): 25–30.

Canadian Press/Leger Marketing (2003). *Canadians and Back to School*. August 25. Montreal.

Cao, Jian (1996). *Welfare Recipiency and Welfare Recidivism: An Analysis of the NLSY Data*. Institute for Research on Poverty.

Carpay, John (2005/2006). "A Voice for Freedom in Canada's Courts." *Fraser Forum* (December/January): 15–16. <www.fraserinstitute.org/admin/books/chapterfiles/Dec05ffCarpay.pdf#>.

CBC News Online (2004). *Indepth: Canadian Government—Canada and Public Inquiries.* <www.cbc.ca/news/background/cdngovernment/inquiries.html>.

Centre for Global Development [CGD] (2006). *Commitment to Development Index.* <www.cgdev.org/section/initiatives/_active/cdi>.

CEPA (2005). "The Importance of Timely Construction." Presentation by David MacInnes, President, Canadian Pipeline Association (October 2005).

Certified General Accountants Association of Canada (2006). *Making Trade Dispute Resolution in Canada Work: Certified General Accountants' Experience with Canada's Agreement on Internal Trade* (April). <www.cga-online.org/servlet/portal/serve/Library/News+and+Media/_Product/ca_rep_2006-05_ait.pdf>.

Chambers of Commerce of Ireland (2003). "Chambers Warn of Strain Labour Shortages Are Placing on Business." Chambers of Commerce.

Chao, Johnny C.P., and Herbert G. Grubel (1998). "Optimal Levels of Spending and Taxation in Canada." In Herbert G. Grubel, ed., *How To Use the Fiscal Surplus: What Is the Optimal Size of Government?* (The Fraser Institute): 53–68.

Chief Electoral Officer of Canada (1997). *Report of the Chief Electoral Officer of Canada on the 36th General Election.* <www.elections.ca/gen/rep/ceo/ceoreport_e.pdf>.

Chief Electoral Officer of Canada (2000). *Thirty-Seventh General Election 2000: Official Voting Results.* <www.elections.ca/gen/rep/re2/SynopsisPart1_e.pdf>.

Chirinko, Robert, and Andrew Meyer (1997). "The User Cost of Capital and Investment Spending: Implications for Canadian Firms." In Paul J. N. Halpern, ed., *Financing Growth in Canada* (University of Calgary Press): 17–69.

Chirinko, Robert, Steven M. Fazzari, and Andrew P. Meyer (1999). "How Responsive Is Business Capital Formation to Its User Cost? An Exploration with Micro Data." *Journal of Public Economics* 74: 53–80.

Clarke, Rory, and Eileen Capponi (2004). OECD in *Figures: 2004 Edition.* OECD.

Clemens, Jason, and Niels Veldhuis (2005). *Growing Small Businesses in Canada: Removing the Tax Barrier.* Studies in Entrepreneurship & Markets 1 (December). The Fraser Institute.

Clemens, Jason, and Niels Veldhuis (2007). *Beyond Equalization: Examining Fiscal Transfers in a Broader Context.* The Fraser Institute

Clemens, Jason, Joel Emes, and Rodger Scott (2002). *The Corporate Capital Tax: Canada's Most Damaging Tax.* Public Policy Sources 56 (April). The Fraser Institute.

Clemens, Jason, Jonathan Hayes, Mark Mullins, Niels Veldhuis, and Christopher Glover (2005). *Government Failure in Canada, 2005 Report: A Review of the Auditor General's Reports, 1992-2005.* Public Policy Sources 86. The Fraser Institute. <www.fraserinstitute.org/shared/readmore.asp?sNav=pb&id=800>.

Clemens, Jason, Niels Veldhuis and Milagros Palacios (2007). *Tax Efficiency: Not All Taxes Are Created Equal.* Studies in Economic Prosperity 4. The Fraser Institute

Clemens, M., and T. Moss (2005). *Ghost of 0.7%: Origins and Relevance of the International Aid Target*. Working paper 68. Centre for Global Development.

Clemens, M., S. Radelet, and R. Bhavnani (2004). *Counting Chickens When They Hatch: The Short-Term Effect of Aid on Growth*. Working paper 44. Centre for Global Development.

Cleverley, William O., and Roger K. Harvey (1992). "Is There a Link between Hospital Profit and Quality?" *Health Care Financial Management* (September) 46, 9: 40, 42, 44–45.

Cline, W. (2004). *Trade Policy and Global Poverty*. Peter G. Peterson Institute for International Economics.

Cnaan, Ram A. (2002). *The Invisible Caring Hand: American Congregations and the Provision of Welfare*. New York University Press.

Cohen, Stewart, and T. Neale, eds. (2006). *Participatory Integrated Assessment of Water Management and Climate Change in the Okanagan Basin, British Columbia*. Environment Canada and University of British Columbia.

Collier, P., and A. Hoeffler (2002). "Aid, Policy and Peace: Reducing the Risks of Civil Conflict." *Defence and Peace Economics* 13, 6: 435–50.

Collier, P., and A. Hoeffler (2006a). "Military Expenditure in Post-Conflict Societies." *Economics of Governance* 7, 1: 89–107.

Collier, P., and A. Hoeffler (2006b). *Post-Conflict Risks*. Working Paper 2006-12. Centre for the Study of African Economics.

Collier, P., and D. Dollar (2002). "Aid Allocation and Poverty Reduction." *European Economic Review* 45, 1: 1–26.

Commission d'étude sur les services de santé et les services sociaux (2001). *Les Solutions Émergentes*. Gouvernement du Québec. <www.cessss.gouv.qc.ca/pdf/ fr/00-109.pdf >, as of July 7, 2003.

Commission on Environmental Cooperation, The (2003). *The North American Mosaic: A State of the Environment Report*.

[Committee on Internal Trade] (1995). *Agreement on Internal Trade*. <www.ait-aci.ca/ index_en/ait.htm>.

COMPAS (1998). "Canadian Public Opinion on Families and Public Policy." Report to Southam News and the National Foundation for Family Research and Education (NFFRE). November 23. COMPAS, Inc. <www.fact.on.ca/compas/ compas.htm>.

COMPAS (2003). "Ontario Provincial Election Report for Global TV, National Post, Ottawa Citizen and Windsor Star." May 29. COMPAS, Inc. <www.compas.ca/ data/030521-GlobalOnProvElection-E.pdf>.

COMPAS (2004). *Inter-Provincial Trade Barriers: Seriously Damaging to the Economy and Standard of Living and Almost as Harmful as Canada-U.S. Trade Barriers*. BDO Dunwoody/Chamber Weekly CEO/Business Leader Poll in the *Financial Post*, for publication September 13, 2004. COMPAS, Inc.

Conference Board of Canada (2005). *An Impact Assessment of the BC/Alberta Trade, Investment and Labour Mobility Agreement*. The Conference Board of Canada. <www.gov.bc.ca/ecdev/popt/media_room/bc_ab_trade_investment_mobility_agreement.htm>, as of March 20, 2007.

Conservative Party of Canada (2006). *Stand Up for Canada: Conservative Party of Canada Federal Election Platform 2006*. Conservative Party of Canada. <www.conservative.ca/media/20060113-Platform.pdf>.

Copelan, Brian R. (1998). "Economics and the Environment: The Recent Canadian Experience and Prospects for the Future." In *Canada in the 21st Century*. (Industry Canada).

Cordon, Sandra (2006). "McLachlin Backs Appointment Process." *The Globe and Mail* (February 4): A12.

Council of Atlantic Premiers (1996). *The Atlantic Procurement Agreement: A Memorandum of Agreement on the Reduction of Interprovincial Trade Barriers Relating to Public Procurement*. <www.cap-cpma.ca/images/pdf/eng/APAEnglish.pdf>.

Council of Atlantic Premiers (2000). *Memorandum of Understanding on Atlantic Canada Cooperation*. <www.cap-cpma.ca/images/pdf/eng/capmou.pdf>.

Council of Ministers of Education, Canada [CMEC] (2005). [Website] <www.cmec.ca/index.en.html>.

Council on Foreign Relations (2005). *Building a North American Community: Report of an Independent Task Force*. Independent Task Force Report 53. Council on Foreign Relations. <www.cfr.org/pub8102/independent_task_force_report/building_a_north_american_community.php>.

Court Challenges Program of Canada (2005). *Annual Report 2004–2005*. <www.ccppcj.ca/documents/Annual-Report-2004-2005.pdf>.

Cowley, Peter, and Stephen Easton (2004). *Report Card on Aboriginal Education in British Columbia: 2004 Edition*. Studies in Education Policy. The Fraser Institute.

Cowley, Peter, and Stephen Easton (2006). *Report Card on Aboriginal Education in British Columbia: 2006 Edition*. Studies in Education Policy. The Fraser Institute.

Cummins, Jason, Kevin Hassett, and Glen Hubbard (1996). "Tax Reforms and Investment: A Cross-country Comparison." *Journal of Public Economics* 62, 1-2: 237–73.

Currie, Janet, and Duncan Thomas (1997). "Do the Benefits of Early Childhood Education Last?" *Policy Options* (July-Aug).

Dade, C. (2006). *The Privatization of Foreign Development Assistance*. FOCAL policy paper (July). Canadian Foundation for the Americas (FOCAL). <www.focal.ca/pdf/focal_privatization_jul06.pdf>.

Daigle, Réal, et al. (2006) "Impacts of Sea Level Rise and Climate Change on the Coastal Zone of Southeastern New Brunswick." Environment Canada.

Dales, John H. (1966a). "Protection, Immigration and Canadian Nationalism." In Peter Russell, ed., *Nationalism in Canada* (McGraw-Hill): 164–77.

Dales, John H. (1966b). *The Protective Tariff in Canada's Development*. University of Toronto Press.

Darby, Paul, Kip Beckman, Yves St-Maurice, and Dan Lemaire (2006). *Death by a Thousand Paper Cuts: The Effect of Barriers to Competition on Canadian Productivity*. The Conference Board of Canada.

Dawson, John W. (1998). "Institutions, Investment, and Growth: New Cross-Country and Panel Data Evidence." *Economic Inquiry* 36 (October): 603–19.

Dawson, MacGregor R., W.F. Dawson, and Norman Ward (1989). *Democratic Government in Canada*. University of Toronto Press.

de Moor, André, and Peter Calamai (1997). *Subsidizing Our Demise: Undermining the Earth with Public Funds*. Earth Council.

de Soto, Hernando (2000). *The Mystery of Capital: Why Capitalism Triumphs in the West and Fails Everywhere Else*. Penguin.

Department of Finance (2006). *Advantage Canada: Building a Strong Economy for Canadians*. Government of Canada

Department of Finance Canada (2006). *Advantage Canada: Building a Strong Economy For Canadians*.

Department of Finance Canada (2007). *Major Transfers to Provinces and Territories*. <www.fin.gc.ca/FEDPROV/mtpe.html>.

Devarajan, Shantayanan, David Dollar, and Torgny Holmgren, eds. (2001). *Aid and Reform in Africa: Lessons from Ten Case Studies*. World Bank.

Dickerson, Mark O., and Thomas Flanagan (2006). *An Introduction to Government and Politics: A Conceptual Approach*. 7th ed. Thompson Nelson.

DiLorenzo, Thomas J. (1984). *The Myth of Government Job Creation*. Policy Analysis. The Cato Institute. <www.cato.org/pubs/pas/pa048es.html>, as of October 2003.

Djankov, Simeon, Rafael La Porta, Florencio Lepez-de-Silanes, and Andrei Shleifer (2002). "The Regulation of Entry." *Quarterly Journal of Economics* 117, 1 (February): 1–37.

Dobell, Peter (2003). "The Obstacles to Empowering MPs and MLAs and What It Would Take to Empower Them." In Gordon Gibson, ed., *Fixing Canadian Democracy* (The Fraser Institute): 83–95.

Docherty, David C. (2004). "Could the Rebels Find A Cause? House of Commons Reform in the Chrétien Era." *Review of Constitutional Studies* 9, 1–2: 283–302.

Docherty, David C., and Stephen White (2004). "Parliamentary Democracy in Canada." *Parliamentary Affairs* 57, 3: 613–29.

Dodenhoff, David (1998). *Privatizing Welfare in Wisconsin: Ending Administrative Entitlements—W-2s Untold Story*. Wisconsin Policy Research Institute.

Dodge, David (2006). "Global Economic Forces and the Need for Adjustment." Remarks by David Dodge, Governor of the Bank of Canada, to the Chambre de commerce du Montréal métropolitain and the Fédération des chambres de commerce du Québec, Montréal, QC (June 21).

Doucouliagos, Chris, and Mehmet Ali Ulubasoglu (2006). "Economic Freedom and Economic Growth: Does Specification Make a Difference?" *European Journal of Political Economy* 22, 1: 60–81.

Dymond, Bill, and Michael Hart (2004). "Canada and the New American Empire: Asking the Right Questions." *Policy Options* (June/July): 65–72.

Eagles, Munroe, Harold Jansen, Anthony Sayers, and Lisa Young (2005). "Financing Federal Nomination Contests in Canada—An Overview of the 2004 Experience." Paper presented to the Annual Meeting of the Canadian Political Science Association, London, Ontario. <www.partyfinance.ca/publications/Nominations.pdf>.

Easterly, W. (2002). "The Cartel of Good Intentions: The Problem of Bureaucracy in Foreign Aid." *Policy Reform* 5, 4: 223–50.

Easterly, W. (2003). "Can Foreign Aid Buy Growth?" *Journal of Economic Perspectives* 17, 3: 23–48.

Easterly, W. (2006). *The White Man's Burden.* Penguin.

Easterly, William (2003). "Can Foreign Aid Buy Growth?" *Journal of Economic Perspectives* 17, 3: 23–48.

Easton, Steven T., and Michael A. Walker (1997). "Income, Growth, and Economic Freedom." *American Economic Review* 87, 2 (May): 328–32.

Economist (2005) "Rescuing Environmentalism. Are You Being Served?" *The Economist* (April 23, 2005).

Edwards, Sebastian and Alejandra Cox Edwards (2000). *Economic Reforms and Labor Markets: Policy Issues and Lessons from Chile.* NBER Working Paper 7646. National Bureau of Economic Research.

Elections BC (2002). *Guide to the Initiative Process.* <www.elections.bc.ca/guidebooks/869.pdf>; <www.elections.bc.ca/init/i_guide.html>.

Elections BC (2003). *Report of the Chief Electoral Officer on the Recall Process in British Columbia.* <www.elections.bc.ca/rpt/rclrpt03.pdf>.

Elections BC (2005). *Statement of Votes: Referendum on Electoral Reform* (May 17). <www.elections.bc.ca/elections/sov05/refSOV05/SOV-Refcomplete.pdf>.

Elections Canada (2003). *Electoral Reform—Political Financing.* <www.elections.ca/content.asp?section=loi&document=major&dir=re3&lang=e&textonly=false>.

Elections Canada (2004). *Chief Electoral Officer Announces Application of Supreme Court Decision on Third Parties.* Press Release. <www.elections.ca/content.asp?section=med&document=may1804&dir=pre&lang=e&textonly=false>.

Elections Canada (2004). *Elections Canada: Past Elections* (September 16). Elections Canada Online. <www.elections.ca/>.

Elections PEI (2005). *Plebiscite on Mixed Member Proportional Representation System—Official Results.* Elections Prince Edward Island. <www.electionspei.ca/plebiscites/pr/results/detailed/index.php>.

Emes, Joel, and Dexter Samida (1997). "Canada's Tax on Economic Growth." Unpublished manuscript, The Fraser Institute.

Emes, Joel, and Jason Clemens (2001). *Flat Tax: Principles and Issues*. Critical Issues Bulletins (April). The Fraser Institute.

Epp, Charles R. (1998). *The Rights Revolution*. University of Chicago Press.

Esmail, Nadeem, and Michael Walker (2004). *How Good Is Canadian Health Care?* Critical Issues Bulletin. The Fraser Institute.

Esmail, Nadeem, and Michael Walker (2005a). *Waiting Your Turn: Hospital Waiting Lists in Canada, 15th edition*. The Fraser Institute.

Esmail, Nadeem, and Michael Walker (2005b). *How Good is Canadian Health Care? 2005 Report*. The Fraser Institute.

Esmail, Nadeem, and Michael Walker (2006). *How Good is Canadian Health Care? 2006 Report: An International Comparison of Health Care Systems*. Fraser Institute Digital Publication. <http://www.fraserinstitute.org/shared/readmore.asp?sNav=pb&id=877>

Esmail, Nadeem, Niels Veldhuis, Amela Karabegovic, and Jason Clemens (2005). *Migration of Seniors, Health Care Spending, and Fiscal Pressure*. The Fraser Institute (February).

Expert Panel on Equalization and Territorial Financing Formula (EPETFF) (2006). *Achieving a National Purpose: Putting Equalization Back on Track*. May 2006. Government of Canada, Federal Department of Finance. <www.eqtff-pfft.ca/>.

Farlam, P. (2006). *Working Together Assessing Public–Private Partnerships in Africa*. NEPAD Policy Focus report 2. South African Institute of International Affairs:

Farr, W. Ken, Richard A. Lord, and J. Larry Wolfenbarger (1998). "Economic Freedom, Political Freedom and Economic Well-Being: A Causality Analysis." *Cato Journal* 18, 2 (Fall): 247–62.

Farrell, David M. (2001). *Electoral Systems: A Comparative Introduction*. Palgrave.

Fazzari, Steven, R. Glenn Hubbard, and Bruce Petersen (1988). "Investment, Financing Decisions, and Tax Policy." *American Economic Review* 78, 2: 200–05.

Feachem, Richard G.A., Neelam K. Sekhri, and Karen L. White (2002). "Getting More for Their Dollar: A Comparison of the NHS with California's Kaiser Permanente." *British Medical Journal* 324: 135–41.

Feldstein, Martin (1999). "Tax Avoidance and the Deadweight Loss of the Income Tax." *Review of Economics and Statistics* 81, 4: 674–80.

Ferguson, Brian S. (2002). *Profits and the Hospital Sector: What Does the Literature Really Say?* Atlantic Institute for Market Studies. <www.aims.ca/commentary/profits.pdf>.

Ferrara, Peter J., et al. (1995). *Private Alternatives to Social Security in Other Countries*. NCPA Policy Report 200 (October). National Center for Policy Analysis.

Ferson, M.J. (1994). "Control of Infections in Child Care." *Medical Journal of Australia* 161: 615–18.

Flanagan, Tom (1998). "Alternative Vote: An Electoral System for Canada." *Inroads: The Canadian Journal of Opinion* 7: 73–78.

Flanagan, Tom (2000). *First Nations? Second Thoughts.* McGill-Queen's University Press.

Flanagan, Tom, and Christopher Alcantara (2002). *Individual Property Rights on Canadian Indian Reserves.* Public Policy Source 60. The Fraser Institute. <www.fraserinstitute.org/admin/books/files/property-rights.pdf>.

Folster, Stefan, and Magnus Henrekson (2001). "Growth Effects of Government Expenditure and Taxation in Rich Countries." *European Economic Review* 45: 1501–20.

Fossedal, Gregory A. (2002). *Direct Democracy in Switzerland.* Transaction.

Frenette, M., and G. Picot (2003). *Life after Welfare: The Economic Well-Being of Welfare Leavers in Canada during the 1990s.* Analytical Studies Research Paper Series 192. Statistics Canada.

Friedman, T. (2005). *The World Is Flat: A Brief History of the 21st Century.* Farrar, Straus and Giroux.

Friendly, Martha, and Jane Beach (2005). *Early Childhood Education and Care in Canada 2004.* Child Care Resource and Research Unit (CCRU). <www.childcarecanada.org>.

Gabel, Todd, Jason Clemens, and Sylvia LeRoy (2004). *Welfare Reform in Ontario: A Report Card.* Fraser Institute Digital Publication. The Fraser Institute. <www.fraserinstitute.org>.

Gagné, Lynda G. (2003). *Parental Work, Child-Care Use and Young Children's Cognitive Outcomes.* Statistics Canada Catalogue No. 89-594-XIE. Ministry of Industry.

Gartzke, Eric (2005). Economic Freedom and Peace." In James Gwartney and Robert Lawson, *Economic Freedom of the World: 2005 Annual Report.* Vancouver: The Fraser Institute: 29–44. <www.fraserinstitute.org/shared/readmore.asp?sNav=pb&id=789>.

General Accounting Office [GAO] (1997). "Head Start: Research Provides Little Information on Impact of Current Program." Report to the Chairman, Committee on the Budget, House of Representatives (April). <www.gao.gov/archive/1997/he97059.pdf>.

Gibson, Gordon (2002). *Report on the Constitution of the Citizens' Assembly on Electoral Reform.* Citizens' Assembly on Electoral Reform. <www.citizensassembly.bc.ca/resources/gibson_report.pdf>.

Ginsburg, Tom (2003). *Judicial Review in New Democracies: Constitutional Courts in Asian Cases.* Cambridge University Press.

Glennon, Robert (2006). "The Quest for More Water: Why Markets Are Inevitable." Property and Environment Research Center.

Godin, Keith, Milagros Palacios, Jason Clemens, Niels Veldhuis, and Amela Karabegović (2006). *An Empirical Comparison of Labour Relations Laws in Canada and the United States.* Studies in Labour Markets 2. The Fraser Institute.

Gokhale, M., et al. (2004). "Female Literacy: The Multifactorial Influence on Child Health in India." *Ecology of Food and Nutrition* 43, 4: 257–78.

Goldfarb, Danielle, and Stephen Tapp (2006). *How Can Canada Improve Its Development Aid? Lessons from Other Agencies.* C.D. Howe Institute.

Goldfarb, Danielle, and William Robson (2003). *Risky Business: US Border Security and the Threat to Canadian Exports.* CD Howe Institute.

"Gomery Commission" (Commission of Inquiry into the Sponsorship Program and Advertising Activities) (2005). *Who is Responsible? Fact Finding Report* (November 1). Canada, Minister of Public Works and Government Services.

"Gomery Commission" (Commission of Inquiry into the Sponsorship Program and Advertising Activities) (2006). *Restoring Accountability: Recommendations* (February 1). Canada, Minister of Public Works and Government Services.

Goolsbee, Austan (1998). "Investment Tax Incentives, Prices, and the Supply of Capital Goods." *Quarterly Journal of Economics* 93, 1: 121–48.

Goolsbee, Austan (2004a). "Taxes and the Quality of Capital." *Journal of Public Economics* 88: 519–43.

Goolsbee, Austan (2004b). "The Impact of the Corporate Income Tax: Evidence from State Organizational Form Data." *Journal of Public Economics* 88: 2283–99.

Gotlieb, Allan (1991). *"I'll Be with You in a Minute, Mr. Ambassador": The Education of a Canadian Diplomat in Washington.* University of Toronto Press.

Gotlieb, Allan (2003). "A Grand Bargain with the US." *National Post* (March 5): A16.

Government of Alberta (2007). *Throne Speech 2007* (March 7).

Government of British Columbia (2006a). *BC - AB Agreement Fact Sheet - Procurement.* Ministry of Economic Development. <www.gov.bc.ca/ecdev/popt/media_room/bc_ab_trade_investment_mobility_agreement.htm>, as of March 20, 2007.

Government of British Columbia (2006b). *Trade, Investment and Labour Mobility Agreement between British Columbia and Alberta.* Ministry of Economic Development. <www.gov.bc.ca/ecdev/popt/media_room/bc_ab_trade_investment_mobility_agreement.htm>, as of March 20, 2007.

Government of British Columbia (2007). *TILMA Occupation Listing - April 2007. Victoria:* Ministry of Economic Development. <www.gov.bc.ca/ecdev/popt/media_room/bc_ab_trade_investment_mobility_agreement.htm>, as of May 4, 2007.

Government of Canada (2004). *Tax Expenditures and Evaluations—2004.* <www.fin.gc.ca/toce/2004/taxexp04_e.html>.

Government of Canada (2005a). *Early Childhood Development Activities and Expenditures/ Early Learning and Child Care Activities and Expenditures.* Government of Canada. <socialunion.gc.ca/ecd/2004/english/page00.html>.

Government of Canada (2005b). *The Budget Plan 2005.* Department of Finance Canada. <www.fin.gc.ca/budget05/pdf/bp2005e.pdf>.

Government of Canada (2006a). *Tax and Expenditure Evaluations 2006.* <www.fin.gc.ca/toce/2006/taxexp_e.html>.

Government of Canada (2006b). *The Budget Plan 2006: Focusing on Priorities.* Department of Finance Canada. <www.fin.gc.ca/budget06/pdf/bp2006e.pdf>.

Government of Canada (2007). *The Budget Plan 2007: Aspire to a Stronger, Safer, Better Canada*. Department of Finance Canada. <www.budget.gc.ca/2007/pdf/bp2007e.pdf>.

Government of Manitoba (2005a). *Moving Forward: Governments of Canada and Manitoba Sign an Agreement on Early Learning and Child Care*. News Release (April 29). <www.gov.mb.ca/chc/press/top/2005/04/2005-04-29-07.html>.

Government of Manitoba (2005b). *Moving Forward on Early Learning and Child Care: Manitoba's Action Plan—Next Steps*. Government of Manitoba. <www.gov.mb.ca/fs/child care/moving_forward.html>.

Government of Ontario, Office of the Provincial Auditor (2001). *2001 Annual Report*. VFM Section 3.06. Queen's Printer for Ontario

Government of Quebec (1999). *La Ministère de la Famille et de l'Enfance. Rapport Annuel 1998–1999*. Les Publications du Quebec. <www.mfacf.gouv.qc.ca/ministere/rapports_annuels_en.asp>.

Government of Quebec (2004). *Public Accounts, 2003–2004. Volume 2*. Finances Quebec. <www.finances.gouv.qc.ca/en/documents/publications/pdf/vol2-2003-2004.pdf>.

Grady, Patrick, and Kathleen Macmillan (1998). "Why Is Interprovincial Trade Down and International Trade Up?" *Canadian Business Economics* (November): 26–35.

Graham, John R. (2002). "Dead Capital on Ontario's Hospitals." *Fraser Forum* (April): 23–24.

Granatstein, J.L. (2003). "The Importance of Being Less Earnest: Promoting Canada's National Interests through Tighter Ties with the U.S." C.D. Howe Institute Benefactors Lecture, Toronto (October 21).

Gravelle, Jane (1989). "Differential Taxation of Capital Income: Another Look at the 1986 Tax Reform Act." *National Tax Journal* 42, 4: 441–63.

Gravelle, Jane (2004). "The Corporate Tax: Where Has It Been and Where Is It Going?" *National Tax Journal* 57, 4: 903–23.

Gravelle, Jane, and Laurence Kotlikoff (1993). "Corporate Tax Incidence and Inefficiency when Corporate and Noncorporate Goods Are Close Substitutes." *Economic Inquiry* 31, 4: 501–16.

Greene, Ian, Carl Baar, Peter McCormick, George Szablowski, and Martin Thomas (1998). *Final Appeal: Decision-Making in Canadian Courts of Appeal*. Lorimar.

Greenhill, R. (2005). *Making a Difference? External Views on Canada's International Impact*. The interim report of the Global Voices Project. <www.ciia.org/XVoices_Int_Report.pdf>.

Grier, Kevin, and Gordon Tullock (1989). "An Empirical Analysis of Cross-national Economic Growth, 1951–80." *Journal of Monetary Economics* 24: 259–76.

Griffiths, Rudyard, and Greg Lyle (2005). "Why Young People Don't Vote." Editorial. *National Post* (December 13). <www.thedemocracyproject.ca/holding/why-young-people-don2019t-vote>.

Griswold, Daniel T. (2004). *Trading Tyranny for Freedom: How Open Markets Till the Soil for Democracy*. Trade Policy Analysis 26 (January). Cato Institute. <www.freetrade.org/pubs/pas/tpa-026es.html>

Griswold, Daniel (2005). "Wreaking Environmental Harm – Another Case Against Farm Subsidies." Property and Environment Research Center.

Grogger, J., and C. Michalopoulos (2003). "Welfare Dynamics under Time Limits." *Journal of Political Economy* 3, 3: 530–53.

Grossman, Philip (1988). "Government and Economic Growth: A Non-Linear Relationship." *Public Choice* 56: 193–200.

Grubel, Herbert G. (1998a). "Economic Freedom and Human Welfare: Some Empirical Findings." *Cato Journal* 18, 2 (Fall): 287–304.

Grubel, Herbert G., ed. (1998b). *How to Use the Fiscal Surplus: What Is the Optimal Size of Government?* The Fraser Institute.

Grubel, Herbert G. (2000). *Unlocking Canadian Capital: The Case for Capital Gains Tax Reform*. The Fraser Institute.

Grubel, Herbert G., ed. (2001). *International Evidence on the Effects of Having No Capital Gains Taxes*. The Fraser Institute.

Grubel, Herbert G., ed. (2003). *Tax Reform in Canada: Our Path to Greater Prosperity*. The Fraser Institute.

Grubel, Herbert G. (2005). *Immigration and the Welfare State in Canada: Growing Conflicts, Constructive Solutions*. Public Policy Sources 84. The Fraser Institute.

Gwartney, James, and Robert Lawson (2006). *Economic Freedom of the World: 2006 Annual Report*. The Fraser Institute. <www.freetheworld.com>.

Gwartney, James, and Robert Lawson (2007). *Economic Freedom of the World: 2007 Annual Report*. The Fraser Institute. <www.freetheworld.com>.

Gwartney, James, Chuck Skipton, and Robert Lawson (2001). "Trade Openness, Income Levels, and Economic Growth." In James Gwartney and Robert Lawson, *Economic Freedom of the World: 2001 Annual Report* (The Fraser Institute): 71–87.

Gwartney, James, Randall Holcombe, and Robert Lawson (1998). "The Scope of Government and the Wealth of Nations." *Cato Journal* 18, 2 (Fall): 163–90.

Gwartney, James, Robert Lawson, and Walter Block (1996). *Economic Freedom of the World: 1975–1995*. The Fraser Institute. <www.freetheworld.com>.

Hall, Robert E., and Alvin Rabushka (1995). *The Flat Tax*. Hoover Institution Press.

Hamilton, Alexander, James Madison, and John Jay [1787] (2003). *The Federalist Papers*. Bantam Dell.

Hamilton, Gayle, S. Freedman, L. Gennetian, C. Michalopoulos, J. Walter, D. Adams-Ciardullo, and A. Gassman-Pines (2001). *National Evaluation of Welfare-to-Work Strategies: How Effective Are Different Welfare-to-Work Approaches? Five-Year Adult and Child Impacts for Eleven Programs*. US Department of Health and Human Services, Administration for Children and Families, Office of the Assistant Secretary for Planning and Evaluation; US Department of Education, Office of the Under Secretary, Office of Vocational and Adult Education.

Hansen, H., and F. Tarp (2000). "Aid Effectiveness Disputed." *Journal of International Development* 12: 375–98.

Harding, Lesley (1998). *Case Studies: America Works, USA* (May). <www.sustainability.org.uk/info/casestudies/america.htm>, as of October, 2003.

Harris, K. (2005). "New Law 'Flawed'—Whistleblower Claims: Measures Won't Protect Civil Servants." *Edmonton Sun* (November 2): 31.

Harris, Mike, and Preston Manning (2005a). *A Canada Strong and Free*. The Fraser Institute.

Harris, Mike, and Preston Manning (2005b). A Canada Strong and Free, Volume II. *Caring for Canadians in a Canada Strong and Free*. The Fraser Institute.

Harris, Mike, and Preston Manning (2006a). *Rebalanced and Revitalized: A Canada Strong and Free*. A Canada Strong and Free, Volume III. The Fraser Institute.

Harris, Mike, and Preston Manning (2006b). *Building Prosperity in a Canada Strong & Free*. A Canada Strong and Free, Volume IV. The Fraser Institute.

Harris, Mike, and Preston Manning (2007). *International Leadership by a Canada Strong and Free*. A Canada Strong and Free, Volume V. The Fraser Institute.

Hart, Michael (1998). *Globalization and Standardization: Does a Global Economy Need Global Rules?* Regulatory Affairs and Standards Policy Directorate, Industry Canada

Hart, Michael (2004). "Lessons from Canada's History as a Trading Nation." *Fraser Forum* (June): 6–8.

Hart, Michael (2005). *Escaping the Trap of Agricultural Supply Management*. C.D. Howe Institute Backgrounder 90 (April). C.D. Howe Institute.

Hart, Michael (2006). *Steer or Drift? Taking Charge of Canada-US Regulatory Convergence*. C.D. Howe Institute Commentary 229. C.D. Howe Institute.

Hart, Michael, and Bill Dymond (2006). "Waiting for Conservative Trade Policy." *Policy Options* 27, 8 (October): 63–69.

Hassett, K., and R. Shapiro (2003). "How Europe Sows Misery in Africa." *Washington Post* (June 22). <www.globalpolicy.org/socecon/ffd/2003/0623cap.htm>.

Hawken, Paul, Amory Lovins and L. Hunter Lovins (2000). *Natural Capitalism: Creating the Next Industrial Revolution*. Back Bay Press.

Helliwell, John F. (2002). *Globalization and Well-Being*. UBC Press.

Helliwell, John F., and John McCallum (1995). "National Borders Still Matter for Trade." *Policy Options* 16: 44–48.

Helms, L. Jay (1985). "The Effect of State and Local Taxes on Economic Growth: A Time Series-Cross Section Approach." *Review of Economics and Statistics* 67, 4: 574–82.

Henderson, David (1994). "Putting 'Trade Blocs' into Perspective." In Vincent Cable and David Henderson, eds., *Trade Blocs? The Future of Regional Integration.* (Royal Institute of International Affairs): 179–98.

Hendricks, Kenneth, Raphael Amit, and Diana Whistler (1997). *Business Taxation of Small and Medium-sized Enterprises in Canada.* Working Paper 97-11. Prepared for the Technical Committee on Business Taxation. [Canada] Department of Finance.

Hepburn, Claudia R., and Robert Van Belle (2003). *The Canadian Education Freedom Index.* Studies in Education Policy (September). The Fraser Institute.

Hepburn, Claudia, and Robert Van Belle (unpublished). "Ten Case Studies of School Choice in Canada." Available from the author.

Hiebert, Janet L. (2004). *Charter Conflicts: What Is Parliament's Role?* McGill-Queens University Press.

Hirschl, Ran (2004). *Towards Juristocracy: The Origins and Consequences of New Institutionalism.* Harvard University Press.

Holmes, John W. (1989). "The Disillusioning of the Relationship: Epitaph of a Decade." In Lansing Lamont and J. Duncan Edmunds, eds., *Friends So Different: Essays on Canada and the United States in the 1980s* (University of Ottawa Press for the Americas Society): 308–18.

Holtz-Eakin, Douglas, and Donald Marples (2001a). *Distortion Costs of Taxing Wealth Accumulation: Income versus Estate Taxes.* NBER working paper 8261. National Bureau of Economic Research.

Holtz-Eakin, Douglas, and Donald Marples (2001b). *Estate Taxes, Labour Supply, and Economic Efficiency.* Center for Policy Research Special Report. American Council for Capital Formation.

Howett, Richard, and Kristiana Hansen (2005). "The Evolving Western Water Markets." *Choices.* American Agricultural Economics Association.

Hoxby, Caroline M. (2001). "How School Choice Affects the Achievement of Public School Students." Paper prepared for the Koret Task Force meeting at the Hoover Institution, Stanford, CA (September 20–21, 2001). <post.economics.harvard.edu/faculty/hoxby/papers/choice_sep01.pdf>.

Hsia, David C., and Cathaleen A. Ahern (1992). "Good Quality Care Increases Hospital Profits under Prospective Payment." *Health Care Financing Review* 13, 3 (Spring): 17–24. <www.epw.org.in/34-52/sa4.htm>, as of August 3, 2001.

Hufbauer, Gary (2005). "Inconsistency between Diagnosis and Treatment." *Journal of International Economic Law* 8, 2 (June): 291–97.

Huffman, James L. (1993). "NAFTA and Water: Dare We Talk about Water Markets?" In A.R. Riggs and Tom Velk, eds., *Beyond NAFTA: An Economic, Political and Sociological Perspective* (Studies on the Economic Future of North America, The Fraser Institute).

Human Resources and Skills Development Canada [HRSDC] (1999). *1998 Employment Insurance Monitoring and Assessment Report*. <www.hrsdc.gc.ca/asp/gateway. asp?hr=en/ei/reports/eimar.shtml&hs=ada>.

Human Resources and Skills Development Canada [HRSDC] (2000). *1999 Employment Insurance Monitoring and Assessment Report*. <www.hrsdc.gc.ca/asp/gateway. asp?hr=en/ei/reports/eimar.shtml&hs=ada>.

Human Resources and Skills Development Canada [HRSDC] (2001). *2000 Employment Insurance Monitoring and Assessment Report*. <www.hrsdc.gc.ca/asp/gateway. asp?hr=en/ei/reports/eimar.shtml&hs=ada>.

Human Resources and Skills Development Canada [HRSDC] (2002). *2001 Employment Insurance Monitoring and Assessment Report*. <www.hrsdc.gc.ca/asp/gateway. asp?hr=en/ei/reports/eimar.shtml&hs=ada>.

Human Resources and Skills Development Canada [HRSDC] (2003). *2002 Employment Insurance Monitoring and Assessment Report*. <www.hrsdc.gc.ca/asp/gateway. asp?hr=en/ei/reports/eimar.shtml&hs=ada>.

Human Resources and Skills Development Canada [HRSDC] (2004a). *2003 Employment Insurance Monitoring and Assessment Report*. <www.hrsdc.gc.ca/asp/gateway. asp?hr=en/ei/reports/eimar.shtml&hs=ada>.

Human Resources and Skills Development Canada [HRSDC] (2004b). *Chief Actuary's Outlook on the Employment Insurance Account for 2005*. Actuarial Services HRSDC, October. <www.hrsdc.gc.ca/en/ei/reports/pr2005.pdf>.

Human Resources and Skills Development Canada [HRSDC] (2005). *2004 Employment Insurance Monitoring and Assessment Report*. <www.hrsdc.gc.ca/asp/gateway. asp?hr=en/ei/reports/eimar.shtml&hs=ada>.

Human Resources and Skills Development Canada [HRSDC] (2007). *Employment Insurance Monitoring and Assessment Report 2006*. <www.hrsdc.gc.ca/en/ei/ reports/eimar_2006.pdf>.

Human Security Centre (2005). *Human Security Report 2005: War and Peace in the 21st Century*. Liu Institute for Global Issues, University of British Columbia. <www. humansecurityreport.info/>.

Hyndman, N., and R. Anderson (1995). "The Use of Performance Information in External Reporting: An Empirical Study of UK Executive Agencies." *Financial Accountability and Management* 11 (February 1): 1–17.

Imagine Canada (2006a). *A Portrait of Religious Organizations in Canada*. Imagine Canada.

Imagine Canada (2006b). *A Portrait of Social Service Organizations in Canada*. Imagine Canada.

Indian and Northern Affairs Canada (2004). *Restructuring the Relationship*. <www. ainc-inac.gc.ca/ch/rcap/rpt/rel_e.html>.

Industry Canada (2005). *Trade Data Online*. <strategis.ic.gc.ca>, as of March 11, 2005.

Institute for Public-Private Partnerships, Inc. [IP3] (2007). PPP *Skills and Competency Development: Online Training Programme*. <www.ip3.org/projects/2520_01.htm>.

Instituto Peruano de Economía [IPE] (2001). *Proyecto de Derechos de Propiedad Urbana Promoción del Crédito y las Inversiones*. <www.cofopri.gob.pe/pdpu/versioningles/pdf/1.pdf>.

International Development Research Centre [IDRC] (2007). *About IDRC*. <www.idrc.ca/en/ev-8513-201-1-DO_TOPIC.html#2>.

International Institute for Strategic Studies (2002). *The Military Balance 2002–2003*. Oxford University Press.

International Monetary Fund (2005). *World Economic Outlook: Building Institutions* (September). <www.imf.org/external/pubs/ft/weo/2005/02/index.htm>

Irwin, Douglas A. (1996). *Against the Tide: An Intellectual History of Free Trade*. Princeton University Press.

Jones, Laura (2002). "Measuring the Regulatory Burden: The First Step towards Accountability." *Fraser Forum* (January): 9, 15.

Jones, Laura, and Stephen Graf (2001). *Canada's Regulatory Burden. How Many Regulations? At What Cost?* Fraser Forum Special Issue (August).

Jorgensen, Dale W., and Kun-Young Yun (1991). "The Excess Burden of Taxation in the United States." *Journal of Accounting and Finance* 6: 487–508.

Kapstein, E. (2006). *Economic Justice in an Unfair World: Toward a Level Playing Field*. Princeton University Press.

Karabegović, Amela, and Fred McMahon (2005). *Economic Freedom of North America: 2005 Annual Report*. The Fraser Institute.

Karabegović, Amela, and Jason Clemens (2005). "Ending Child Labour—Bans Aren't the Solution." *Fraser Forum* (March): 25–26.

Kaufmann, D., and P. Siegelbaum (1997). "Privatization and Corruption in the Transition." *Journal of International Affairs* 50: 419–49.

Kesselman, Jonathan R (2004). *Mandatory Retirement and Older Workers: Encouraging Longer Working Lives*. C.D. Howe Institute.

Kesselman, Jonathan R., and Finn Poschmann (2001a). *A New Option for Retirement Savings: Tax Prepaid Savings Plans*. Commentary. The Pension Papers 149 (February). C.D. Howe Institute.

Kesselman, Jonathan R., and Finn Poschmann (2001b). Expanding the Recognition of Personal Savings in the Canadian Tax System. *Canadian Tax Journal* 49, 1: 40–101.

Kheiriddin, Tasha, and Adam Daifallah (2005). *Rescuing Canada's Right: Blueprint for a Conservative Revolution*. John Wiley & Sons Canada.

King, R.G., and S. Rebelo (1990). "Public Policy and Economic Growth: Developing Neoclassical Implications." *Journal of Political Economy* 98, 5: 126–50.

Knopff, Rainer, and F.L. Morton (1992). *Charter Politics*. Nelson Canada.

Knox, Robert (1998). "Economic Integration in Canada through the Agreement on Internal Trade" In Harvey Lazar, ed., *Canada: The State of the Federation 1997: Non-constitutional Renewal* (Institute of Intergovernmental Relations, Queen's University, Kingston; McGill-Queen's University Press): 137–67.

Knox, Robert, and Amela Karabegović (forthcoming). *Myths and Realities of TILMA.* The Fraser Institute.

Kremer, M., and R. Glennerster (2004). *Strong Medicine: Creating Incentives for Pharmaceutical Research on Neglected Diseases.* Princeton University Press.

Labour Mobility Coordination Group (2001). *Report on Implementation of the Labour Mobility Chapter of the Agreement on Internal Trade.* Forum of Labour Market Ministers. <www11.hrsdc.gc.ca/en/cs/sp/hrsdc/lmp/mobility/2001-000049/page00.shtml>, as of May 4, 2007.

Lacey, Marc (2006). "Food Aid Program Takes Out Insurance on Ethiopia Weather." *New York Times* (March 8). <http://select.nytimes.com/gst/abstract.html?res=F70F12FF39550C7B8CDDAA0894DE404482&n=Top%2fNews%2fBusiness%2fCompanies%2fAXA>.

Laghi, Brian (2004). "Harper Plan for Elected Senate gets Major Boost: New Brunswick's Lord Says He'll Hold Vote if Tory Leader Defeats Martin on June 28." *Globe and Mail* (June 17): A1.

Laporte, Bruno (2004). *The Knowledge Bank in Action.* World Bank. <siteresources.worldbank.org/WBI/Resources/KnowledgeBankOct2004.pdf>.

Lefebvre, Pierre (2004). "Quebec's Innovative Early Childhood Education and Care Policy and Its Weaknesses." *Policy Options* (March). IRPP.

Lefebvre, Pierre, and Philip Merrigan (2002). "The Effect of Child Care and Early Education Arrangement on Developmental Outcomes of Young Children." *Canadian Public Policy* 28, 2 (June): 159–86.

Lefebvre, Pierre, and Philip Merrigan (2003). *Assessing Family Policy in Canada.* IRPP Choices 9, 5 (June).

Lensink, R., and H. White (2001). "Are There Negative Returns to Aid?" *Journal of Development Studies* 37 (August): 42–65.

LeRoy, Sylvia (2005). "Don't Abandon Successful Welfare Reforms." *Fraser Forum* (February): 3–4.

LeRoy, Sylvia, and Greg Gudelot (2004/2005). "Gratitude in Motion: Best Practices Help Tackle Homelessness." *Fraser Forum* (December/January): 15–18.

LeRoy, Sylvia, and Milagros Palacios (2006). *Generosity in Canada and the United States: The 2006 Generosity Index.* Fraser Institute Digital Publication (December). The Fraser Institute. <http://www.fraserinstitute.org/shared/readmore.asp?sNav=pb&id=878>.

Lewis III, Howard, and J. David Richardson (2001). *Why Global Commitment Really Matters.* Institute for International Economics.

Liu, Liqun, and Andrew Rettenmaier (2004). "The Excess Burden of the Social Security Tax." *Public Finance Review* 32, 6: 631–50.

Locke, John [1690] (1980). *The Second Treatise of Government*. C.B. Macpherson, ed. Hackett.

Lortie, Pierre (1991). *Royal Commission on Electoral Reform and Party Financing*. Minister of Supply and Services Canada.

Mackie, Richard (2004). "Runciman Urges Election of Senators." *The Globe and Mail* (April 30): A7.

Mackness, William (1999). *Canadian Public Spending: The Case for Smaller More Efficient Government*. Public Policy Source 13. The Fraser Institute.

Macrory, Patrick (2002). "Another Chapter in the Lumber Saga." *National Post* (October 10): A19

Magnuson, Katherine A., Christopher J. Ruhm, and Jane Waldfogel (2004). *Does Prekindergarten Improve School Preparation and Performance?* NBER Working Paper 10452 (April). National Bureau of Economic Research. <www.nber.org/papers/w10452>.

Mandela, Nelson (1998). Speaking to the Canadian Parliament. Hansard number 125, 36th Parliament, 1st Session, September 24, 1998. <www2.parl.gc.ca/HousePublications/Publication.aspx?Language=E&Mode=1&Parl=36&Ses=1&DocId=2332831>.

Manfredi, Christopher P. (2001). *Judicial Power and the Charter: Canada and the Paradox of Liberal Constitutionalism*. 2nd ed. Oxford University Press.

Manfredi, Christopher (2005/2006). "Strategic Litigation and Policy Reform: Costs and Benefits." *Fraser Forum* (December/January): 9–10. <www.fraserinstitute.org/admin/books/chapterfiles/Dec05ffManfredi.pdf#>.

Manitoba, Information Services (2002). *Manitoba and New Brunswick Sign Co-operation Agreement*. News Release (January 23). <www.gov.mb.ca/chc/press/top/2002/01/2002-01-23-02.html>.

Manley, John (2005). Speech to Conference on Canada-United States Relations, Centre for Trade Policy and Law (November 4). <www.ctpl.ca>.

Manning, Preston (2002). *Think Big: My Adventures in Life and Democracy*. McClelland & Stewart.

Manning, Preston (2005). "Give Canada a Chance." Speech at the Toronto Roundtable on Democratic Infrastructure (Sept. 17). <www.manningcentre.ca>.

Mansur, Eric, and Sheila Olmstead (2006). "The Value of Scarce Water: Measuring the Inefficiency of Municipal Regulations." AEI-Brookings Joint Center for Regulatory Studies.

Marquis, Pierre (1993). *Referendums in Canada: The Effect of Populist Decision-Making on Representative Democracy*. <www.parl.gc.ca/information/library/PRBpubs/bp328-e.htm>.

Mason, Dwight (2005). *The Canada-United States Relationship: Is There a View from Washington?* Commentary (December). Royal Canadian Military Institute.

Mbaku, John Mukum, ed. (1999). *Preparing Africa for the Twenty-First Century: Strategies for Peaceful Co-existence and Sustainable Development*. Ashgage.

McArthur, William (1996). "Private Hospitals Improve Public Sector Health Care." *Fraser Forum* (December): 24–26.

McCallum, John (1995). "National Borders Matter: Canada-US Regional Trade Patterns." *American Economic Review* 3: 615–23.

McKey, Ruth, et al. (1985). "The Impact of Head Start on Children, Families, and Communities." HHS 85-31193 (June). US Department of Health and Human Services.

McMahon, Fred (2000a). *Road to Growth*. Atlantic Institute for Market Studies.

McMahon, Fred (2000b). *Retreat from Growth: Atlantic Canada and the Negative Sum Economy*. Atlantic Institute for Market Studies.

McMahon, Fred, and Martin Zelder (2002). *Making Health Spending Work*. Public Policy Source 54. The Fraser Institute.

Megginson, William L., and Jeffery M. Netter (2001). "From State to Market: A Survey of Empirical Studies on Privatization." *Journal of Economic Literature* 39, 2: 321–89.

Mellington, N., and L. Cameron (1999). "Female Education and Child Mortality in Indonesia." *Bulletin of Indonesian Economic Studies, Taylor and Francis Journals* 35, 3: 115–44.

Mendelsohn, Matthew, and Andrew Parkin (2001). "Introducing Direct Democracy in Canada." *Choices: Strengthening Canadian Democracy* 7, 5 (June): 3–38. <www.irpp.org/choices/archive/vol7no5.pdf>.

Meyer, Daniel R., and M. Cancian (1996). "Life after Welfare." *Public Welfare* 54: 25–29.

Michalski, Joseph H. (1999). *Values and Preferences for the "Best Policy Mix" for Canadian Children*. CPRN Discussion Paper No. F/05 (May).

Mihlar, F., and D. Smith (1997). *Government-Sponsored Training Programs: Failure in the United States, Lessons for Canada*. Critical Issues Bulletin (December). The Fraser Institute.

Milner, Henry (2001). *Civic Literacy in Comparative Context: Why Canadians Should be Concerned*. IRPP Policy Matters 2, 2. Institute for Research on Public Policy.

Milner, Henry (2004). *First Past the Post? Progress Report on Electoral Reform Initiatives in Canadian Provinces*. IRPP Policy Matters 5, 9. Institute for Research on Public Policy.

Milner, Henry (2005). *Fixing Canada's Unfixed Election Dates: A "Political Season" to Reduce the Democratic Deficit*. IRPP Policy Matters 6, 6. Institute for Research on Public Policy.

Ministry of Community and Social Services [MCSS], Government of Ontario (1999). *Government's Private Sector Initiative Creates New Jobs for Ontario Works Participants in Sudbury*. News Release (March 15). Communications and Marketing Branch.

Ministry of Community, Family, and Children's Services [MCFCS], Government of Ontario (2000). *Zero Tolerance for Welfare Fraud.* Backgrounder (January 18).

Ministry of Community, Family, and Children's Services [MCFCS], Government of Ontario (2001). *Ontario Works Policy Directives, September 2001.* <www.cfcs.gov.on.ca/CFCS/en/programs/IES/OntarioWorks/Publications/ow-policydirectives.htm>, as of October 2003.

Mintz, Jack M. (2006) *The 2006 Tax Competitiveness Report: Proposals for Pro-Growth Tax Reform.* C.D. Howe Institute Commentary 239 (September 2006).

Mintz, Jack M., Duanjie Chen, Yvan Guillemette, and Finn Poschmann (2005). *The 2005 Tax Competitiveness Report: Unleashing the Canadian Tiger.* CD Howe Institute.

Mohanty, Nirmal, and Shreekant Gupta (2002). *Breaking the Gridlock in Water Reforms through Water Markets: International Experience and Implementation Issues for India.* Liberty Institute (New Delhi). <http://www.libertyindia.org/policy_reports/water_markets_2002.pdf>.

Moon, Rachel T. (2000). "Sudden Infant Death Syndrome in Child Care Settings." *Pediatrics* 106: 295–300.

Morton, F.L. (2003). "Can Judicial Supremacy Be Stopped?" *Policy Options* (October): 25–29.

Morton, F.L. (2004). "Reforming the Judicial Appointment Process for the Supreme Court of Canada." Presentation to the Standing Committee on Justice and Human Rights, House of Commons, Ottawa (April 1).

Morton F.L. (2006). "Judicial Appointments in Post-Charter Canada: A System in Transition." In Kate Malleson and Peter H. Russell, eds., *Appointing Judges in an Age of Judicial Power: Critical Perspectives from Around the World* (University of Toronto Press).

Morton, F.L., and Rainer Knopff (2000). *The Charter Revolution and the Court Party.* Broadview Press.

Moss, T., G. Pettersson, and N. van de Walle (2006). *An Aid-Institutions Paradox? A Review Essay on Aid Dependency and State Building in Sub-Saharan Africa.* Working Paper 74. Center for Global Development.

Mullins, Mark (2005). *Accounting for Gomery: The Money Links between the Federal Government, Political Parties, and Private Interests.* Fraser Institute Digital Publication (July). <www.fraserinstitute.org/shared/readmore.asp?sNav=pb&id=777>.

National Center for Policy Analysis (2000). *Idea House.* <www.ncpa.org/hotlines/juvcrm/d2.html>, as of October 2003.

National Council of Welfare [NCW] (2004). *Fact Sheet: Welfare Recipients.* <www.ncwcnbes.net/htmdocument/principales/numberwelfare_e.htm>.

National Council on Welfare [NCW] (2006). *Welfare Incomes 2005.* <www.ncwcnbes.net/documents/researchpublications/ResearchProjects/WelfareIncomes/2005Report_Summer2006/ReportENG.pdf>.

New York State Department of Labor (1997). "Memorandum from Pete Landsberg to John Haley" (June 11).

New, Michael J. (2002). *Welfare Reform That Works: Explaining the Welfare Caseload Decline, 1996–2000*. The Cato Institute.

NICHD Early Child Care Research Network (1996). "Characteristics of Infant Child Care: Factors Contributing to Positive Caregiving." *Early Childhood Research Quarterly* 11: 269–306.

NICHD Early Child Care Research Network (2003). "Does Amount of Time Spent in Child Care Predict Socioemotional Adjustment During the Transition to Kindergarten?" *Child Development* 74, 4: 976–1005.

Nicol, Lorraine (2005). "Irrigation Water Markets in Southern Alberta." MA Thesis prepared for Department of Economics, University of Lethbridge (unpublished).

Nicoletti, Giuseppe, and Stefano Scarpetta (2003). "Regulation, Productivity and Growth: OECD Evidence." *Economic Policy* 18, 36 (April): 9–72.

Northwest Territories, Dep't of Executive (2003). *Northwest Territories-Alberta Memorandum of Understanding for Cooperation and Development*. <www.executive.gov.nt.ca/documents/AlbertaMOU-2003.pdf>.

Nye, Joe (2002). Evidence (May 2). *Partners in North America: Advancing Canada's Relations with the United States*, Report of the House of Commons Standing Committee on Foreign Affairs and International Trade (December).

O'Farrell, P.N (1990). *Small Manufacturing Competitiveness and Performance: An Analysis of Matched Pairs in Nova Scotia and New England*. In association with Gardner Pinfold Consultants. Commissioned by the Nova Scotia Department of Industry, Trade and Technology, and Atlantic Canada Opportunities Agency.

O'Grady, Dennis (2002). Phosphorus Trading in the South Nation River Watershed, Ontario, Canada. CH2M Hill Canada, Ltd.

O'Neal, Brian (1993). *Electoral Systems*. Parliamentary Information and Research Service. <www.parl.gc.ca/information/library/PRBpubs/bp334-e.htm>.

Office of the Superintendent of Financial Institutions Canada (2004). *Actuarial Report (21st) on the Canada Pension Plan*. Office of the Chief Actuary.

Olsen, Darcy Ann (2005). "Is Preschool Good for Children?" *Fraser Forum* (May): 5–6.

Ontario Institute for Studies in Education at the University of Toronto (OISE/UT) (2004). *Public Attitudes towards Education in Ontario, 2004*. <www.oise.utoronto.ca/OISE-Survey/specialTopics.html>.

Ontario, Ministry of Community and Social Services (2006). *Ontario Regulation 134/98. Ontario Works Act, 1997*. <www.cfcs.gov.on.ca/CFCS/en/programs/IES/OntarioWorks/Legislation/default.htm>.

Opportunity International, Canada (2005). *History: The Opportunity International Timeline*. <www.opportunitycanada.ca/learn/history.html>.

Organisation for Economic Co-operation and Development [OECD] (1996). *Shaping the 21st Century: The Contribution of Development Cooperation*. <www.oecd.org/dataoecd/23/35/2508761.pdf>.

Organisation for Economic Co-operation and Development [OECD] (1997). *OECD Economic Survey: Canada*. OECD.

Organisation for Economic Co-operation and Development [OECD] (1998). *Open Markets Matter: The Benefits of Investment Liberalisation*. OECD.

Organisation for Economic Co-operation and Development [OECD] (2001). *Education at a Glance*. OECD

Organisation for Economic Co-operation and Development [OECD] (2002). Canada (2002), *D[evelopment] A[ssistance]C[ommittee] Peer Review*, 2002. <www.oecd.org/document/61/0,2340,en_2649_37413_2409533_1_1_1_37413,00.html>.

Organisation for Economic Co-operation and Development [OECD] (2003). *Public Sector Transparency and the International Investor*. OECD.

Organisation for Economic Co-operation and Development [OECD] (2005a). *Aid Flows Top USD 100 Billion in 2005*. <www.oecd.org/document/40/0,2340,en_2649_34447_36418344_1_1_1_1,00.html>.

Organisation for Economic Co-operation and Development [OECD] (2005b). *Education at a Glance*. OECD. <www.oecd.org/document/34/0,3343,en_2649_201185_35289570_1_1_1_1,00.html>.

Organisation for Economic Co-operation and Development [OECD] (2005c). *Revenue Statistics 1965–2004*. OECD.

Organisation for Economic Co-operation and Development [OECD] (2006a). *OECD Economic Outlook 80* (December). OECD.

Organisation for Economic Co-operation and Development [OECD] (2006b). *Revenue Statistics, 1965–2005*. OECD.

Organisation for Economic Co-operation and Development [OECD] (2007). *Going for Growth, 2007*. OECD.

Ouchi, William (2004). "Academic Freedom." *Education Next* (Winter). <www.educationnext.org/2004/21.html>.

Owens, Dennis (2000). *The Search for Aboriginal Property Rights*. Frontier Centre for Public Policy. <www.fcpp.org/policy_series/aboriginal_policy_rights.html>.

Owens, Dennis (2002). *Deconstructing the Aboriginal Problem*. Frontier Centre for Public Policy. <www.fcpp.org/main/publication_detail.php?PubID=170>.

Oxfam Canada (2005). *Flexibility for Local Purchase - Oxfam Applauds Changes in Food Aid Rules*. Press release (September 22). <www.oxfam.ca/news-and-publications/pressroom/press-releases/flexibilityfor-local-purchase-oxfam-applauds-changes-in-food-aid-rules>.

Oxfam Canada (2006). *You Can't Eat Promises*. Press Release (October 30). <www.oxfam.ca/news-and-publications/pressroom/press-releases/oxfam-you-can2019t-eat-promises>.

Palacios, Milagros, and Jeremy Brown (2005). "Saving Rivers Through Water Transfers." *Fraser Forum* (July/August): 25–26.

Palacios, Milagros, and Niels Veldhuis (2006). *Canadian Government Debt 2006: A Guide to the Indebtedness of Canada and the Provinces.* The Fraser Institute.

Pammett, Jon H., and Lawrence LeDuc (2003). "Explaining the Turnout Decline in Canadian Federal Elections: A New Survey of Non-voters." Elections Canada.

Parsons, Graham (1994). *Internal Trade and Economic Cooperation: Down to the Wire on an Internal Trade Agreement.* Canada West Foundation.

Pauly, Mark V. (1968). "The Economics of Moral Hazard: Comment." *The American Economic Review* 58: 531–37.

Peden, Edgar (1991). "Productivity in the United States and Its Relationship to Government Activity: An Analysis of 57 Years, 1929–1986." *Public Choice* 69: 153–73.

Peden, Edgar, and Michael Bradley (1989). "Government Size, Productivity, and Economic Growth: The Post-War Experience." *Public Choice* 61: 229–45.

Pinera, Jose (1998). "The Chilean Model." *Journal of the Institute of Economic Affairs* 18, 1 (March): 24–28.

Piott, Steven L. (2003). *Giving Voters a Voice: The Origins of the Initiative and Referendum in America.* University of Missouri Press.

Porter, E. Michael, Klaus Schwab, Xavier Sala-i-Martin, and Augusto Lopez-Claros (2004). *Global Competitiveness Report 2004–2005.* World Economic Forum. <www.palgrave.com/products/Catalogue.aspx?is=1403949131>.

Prahalad, C. (2006). *The Fortune at the Bottom of the Pyramid: Eradicating Poverty through Profits.* Wharton School Publishing.

Pritchett, L. (2001). "Where Has All the Education Gone?" *World Bank Economic Review* 15, 3: 367–91.

Public-Private Infrastructure Advisory Facility [PPIAF] (2007). *The Public-Private Infrastructure Advisory Facility.* [Description of organization.] <www.ppiaf.org/>.

Radelet, S. (2006). *A Primer on Foreign Aid.* Working paper 92. Centre for Global Development.

Rajan, R., and A. Subramanian (2005). *Aid and Growth, What Does the Cross-Country Evidence Really Show?* IMF working paper 127. International Monetary Fund.

Ramsay, Cynthia (1998). *Medical Savings Accounts: Universal, Accessible, Portable and Comprehensive Health Care for Canadians.* Critical Issues Bulletins. The Fraser Institute.

Razin, Assaf, and Chin-Wa Yuen (1996). "Capital Income Taxation and Long-Run Growth: New Perspectives." *Journal of Public Economics* 59: 239–63.

Rector, Robert (1997). *Wisconsin's Welfare Miracle.* <www.heritage.org/Research/Welfare/index.cfm>, as of October 2003.

Rector, R., and S. Youssef (1999). *The Determinants of Welfare Caseload Decline.* The Heritage Foundation.

Reid, John (2001). *Annual Report Information Commissioner 2000–2001*. Minister of Public Works and Government Services Canada. <www.infocom.gc.ca/reports/2000-2001-e.asp>.

Reid, John (2002). *Response to the Report of the Access to Information Review Task Force: A Special Report to Parliament*. Minister of Public Works and Government Services Canada. <www.infocom.gc.ca/reports/2002special-e.asp>

Reid, John (2005). *Annual Report Information Commissioner 2004-2005*. Minister of Public Works and Government Services Canada. <www.infocom.gc.ca/reports/2004-2005-e.asp>.

Reid, Scott (1996). "Penumbras for the People: Placing Judicial Supremacy under Popular Control." In Anthony A. Peacock, ed., *Rethinking the Constitution: Perspectives on Canadian Constitutional Reform, Interpretation and Theory* (Oxford University Press): 186–213.

Reid, Scott (2005). "The Road to Electoral Reform." *Canadian Parliamentary Review* 28, 3 (Autumn): 4–8.

Reidl, B., and R. Rector (2002). *Myths and Facts: Why Successful Welfare Reform Must Strengthen Work Requirements*. The Heritage Foundation.

Reynolds, Andrew (1998). *First Past the Post—Advantages*. ACE Project.

Reynolds, Andrew, and Ben Reilly (1997). *MPP—Disadvantages*. ACE Project.

Rhoads, Steven E. (2004). *Taking Sex Differences Seriously*. Encounter Books.

Richards, John (2006). *Creating Choices*. C.D. Howe Institute.

Riddell, Chris, Peter Kuhn, Jason Clemens, and Milagros Palacios (2006). *Long-Term Effects of Generous Unemployment Insurance: Historical Study of New Brunswick and Maine, 1940–1990*. The Fraser Institute.

Ritter, J. (2000). "Know Thine Enemy: Information and Democratic Foreign Policy." In B. Finel and K. Lord, eds., *Power and Conflict in the Age of Transparency* (St. Martin's Press): 339–61.

Roach, Kent (2001). *The Supreme Court on Trial: Judicial Activism or Democratic Dialogue?* Irwin Law.

Robinson, M. (2001). *The Microfinance Revolution: Sustainable Finance for the Poor*. World Bank.

Roodman, David, and Scott Standley (2006). *Tax Policies to Promote Private Giving in DAC Countries*. Working paper no. 82. Centre for Global Development.

Rooney, Jennifer, Donna Lero, Karen Korabik, and Denise L. Whitehead (2003). *Self-Employment for Women: Policy Options that Promote Equality and Economic Opportunities*. Status of Women Canada.

Roy, Francine (2006). "From She to She [sic]: Changing Patterns of Women in the Canadian Labour Force." *Canadian Economic Observer* 19, 6 (june; catalogue no. 11-010-XPB): 3.1–3.9. <http://www.statcan.ca/english/freepub/11-010-XIB/11-010-XIB2006006.pdf>.

Royal Canadian Mounted Police [RCMP] (2005). *Peacekeeping Missions and the Police in Canada: An Impact Study of Civilian Police Officers and Police Services.* Executive summary. <www.rcmp-grc.gc.ca/peacekeeping/missions_study_e.htm>.

Ruggiero, Renato (1996). "The Road Ahead: International Trade Policy in the Era of the WTO." Sylvia Ostry Foundation Lecture, Ottawa (May 28). Reproduced in Sylvia Ostry, ed. (2003), *At the Global Crossroads: The Sylvia Ostry Foundation Lectures* (McGill-Queen's University Press).

Rugman, Alan M., and John Kirton (2000). "NAFTA, Environmental Regulations and Firm Strategies: An Update with Chapter 11 Cases." Paper presented at the conference, *Strengthening Canada's Environmental Community through International Regime Reform: Twenty-First Century Challenges,* Munk Centre for International Studies, University of Toronto (November 16–18). <www.envireform.utoronto.ca/old-site/pdf/Rugman/nafta.pdf>.

Russell, Peter H. (1983). "The Political Purposes of the Canadian Charter of Rights and Freedoms." *Canadian Bar Review* 61: 30–54.

Rutter, Michael (1995). "Clinical Implications of Attachment Concepts: Retrospect and Prospect." *Journal of Child Psychological Psychiatry* 36: 549–71.

Sachs, J. (2005). *The End of Poverty: Economic Possibilities for Our Time.* Penguin Press.

Sala-i-Martin, Xavier (2002). *The Disturbing "Rise" of Global Income Inequality.* NBER Working Paper 8904 (April). <papers.nber.org/papers/w8904>.

Saskatchewan Justice (2005). *The Referendum and Plebiscite Act.* Saskatchewan Justice. <www.saskjustice.gov.sk.ca/legislation/summaries/referendumact.shtml>.

Saunders, Cheryl (2003). "The Australian Republic: Act I." In F. Leslie Seidle and David C. Docherty, eds., *Reforming Parliamentary Democracy* (McGill-Queens University Press): 56–82.

Savoie, Donald J. (1999). *Governing from the Centre: The Concentration of Power in Canadian Politics.* University of Toronto Press.

Sayers, Anthony M., and Lisa Young (2004). *Election Campaign and Party Financing in Canada.* Democratic Audit of Australia, Australian National University. <arts.anu.edu.au/democraticaudit/papers/20040908_sayers_young_elect_finance.pdf>.

Schafer, Chris, Joel Emes, and Jason Clemens (2001). *Surveying US and Canadian Welfare Reform.* Critical Issues Bulletin. The Fraser Institute.

Schindler, David, and William F. Donahue (2006). "An Impending Water Crisis in Canada's Western Prairie Provinces." *Proceedings of the National Academy of Sciences.* National Academy of Sciences.

Schleyer, Renato Gazmuri (1994). Chile's Market-Oriented Water Policy: Institutional Aspects and Achievements. In Guy Le Moigne, D. William Easter, Walter Ochs, and Sandra Giltner, eds., *Water Policy and Water Markets: Selected papers and Proceedings from the World Bank's Ninth Annual Irrigation and Drainage Seminar, Annapolis, Maryland, December 8-10, 1992* [Technical Paper 249] (World Bank).

Schuknecht, Ludger, and Vito Tanzi (2005). *Reforming Public Expenditure in Industrialised Countries: Are There Trade-Offs?* Working paper 435 (February). European Central Bank.

Scully, Gerald W. (1989). "The Size of the State, Economic Growth and the Efficient Utilization of National Resources." *Public Choice* 63: 149–64.

Scully, Gerald W. (1991). *Tax Rates, Tax Revenues and Economic Growth.* Policy Report 98. National Center for Policy Analysis.

Scully, Gerald W. (1994). *What Is the Optimal Size of Government in the United States?* Policy Report 188. National Center for Policy Analysis.

Scully, Gerald W. (1995). "The 'Growth Tax' in the United States." *Public Choice* 85: 71–80.

Scully, Gerald W. (1998). *Measuring the Burden of High Taxes.* Policy Report 215. National Center for Policy Analysis.

Scully, Gerald W. (2000). *Public Spending and Social Progress.* Policy Report 232. National Center for Policy Analysis.

Segal, Hugh (2003). "Canada in Transition: Facing the Shift from Global Middle Power to Senior Regional Power." Key-note Address to Russian Association of Canadian Studies, Moscow (June 26). <www.irpp.org>.

Senate of Canada, Standing Committee on National Security and Defence (2006). *Managing Turmoil: The Need to Upgrade Canadian Foreign Aid and Military Strength to Deal with Massive Change.* An Interim Report of the Standing Senate Committee on National Security and Defence (July). <www.parl.gc.ca/39/1/parlbus/commbus/senate/com-e/defe-e/rep-e/rep04nov06-e.pdf>, as of October 2006.

Shugart, Matthew Soberg, and Martin P. Wattenberg, eds. (2001). *Mixed-Member Electoral Systems: The Best of Both Worlds?* Oxford University Press.

Siegle, J.T. (2001). "Democratization and Economic Growth: The Contribution of Accountability Institutions." Ph.D. dissertation. School of Public Affairs, University of Maryland.

Simpson, Jeffery (2001). *Friendly Dictatorship: Reflections on Canadian Democracy.* McClelland & Stewart.

Smith, Adam [1759] (2002). *The Theory of Moral Sentiments.* Cambridge Texts in the History of Philosophy. Cambridge University Press.

Smith, David E. (2003). *The Canadian Senate in Bicameral Perspective.* University of Toronto Press.

Smith, Graeme (2006). "An Oasis of Relative Calm in a Sea of Violence." *Globe and Mail* (June 23): A11.

Smith, Jennifer. (2003). "Debating Reform of Canada's Parliament." In F. Leslie Seidle and David C. Docherty, eds., *Reforming Parliamentary Democracy* (McGill-Queens University Press): 150–68.

Social Development Canada (2006). *Social Security Statistics Canada and the Provinces, 1978-79 to 2002-03.* <www.sdc.gc.ca/en/cs/sp/sdc/socpol/tables/page00.shtml>. Updated by special request.

Stafford, Janine (2002). *A Profile of the Child Care Services Industry.* Catalogue No. 63-016-XPB (September). Ministry of Industry, Statistics Canada, Service Industries Division.

Stairs, Denis, David J. Bercuson, Mark Entwistle, and J.L. Granatstein (2005). *In the National Interest: Canadian Foreign Policy in an Insecure World.* Canadian Defence and Foreign Affairs Institute.

Statistics Canada (1998). *Interprovincial Trade in Canada, 1984–1996.* Statistics Canada.

Statistics Canada (2000). *Interprovincial and International Trade in Canada, 1992–1998* (June). Statistics Canada.

Statistics Canada (2001a). *Population Projections for Canada, Provinces, and Territories 2000–2026.* Statistics Canada.

Statistics Canada (2001b). "Trends in the Use of Private Education." *The Daily* (July 4). <www.statcan.ca/Daily/English/010704/d010704.pdf>.

Statistics Canada (2002). *Provincial Trade Patterns.* Statistics Canada.

Statistics Canada (2004a). *Cornerstones of Community: Highlights of the National Survey of Nonprofit and Voluntary Organizations.* Catalogue no. 61-533-XPE. Ministry of Industry.

Statistics Canada (2004b). "Employment Insurance Coverage Survey." *The Daily* (June 22). <www.statcan.ca/Daily/English/040622/d040622c.htm>.

Statistics Canada (2004c). *The Performance of Interprovincial and International Exports by Province and Territory since 1992* (March). Statistics Canada.

Statistics Canada (2005a). *Annual Demographic Statistics.* Catalogue No. 91-213-XIB (March 31).

Statistics Canada (2005b). "Child Care." *The Daily* (February 7). <www.statcan.ca/Daily/English/050207/d050207b.htm>.

Statistics Canada (2005c). "Employment Insurance Coverage Survey." *The Daily* (June 22). <www.statcan.ca/Daily/English/050622/d050622d.htm>.

Statistics Canada (2005d). *Provincial Economic Accounts 1981–2004.*

Statistics Canada (2006a). *Caring Canadians, Involved Canadians: Highlights from the 2004 Canada Survey of Giving, Volunteering and Participating.* Catalogue 71-542-XPE/71-542-XIE (June). <www.statcan.ca/bsolc/english/bsolc?catno=71-542-X#olcinfopanel>.

Statistics Canada (2006b). Provincial Economic Accounts. Statistics Canada.

Statistics Canada (2006c). *The Daily: Canada's Population by Age and Sex* (October 26).

Statistics Canada, Public Institutions Division (2003). Financial Management System. Statistics Canada.

Statistics Canada, Public Institutions Division (2004). *Financial Management System*. Statistics Canada.

Statistics Canada, Public Institutions Division (2005). *Financial Management System*. Statistics Canada.

Statistics Canada, Public Institutions Division (2006). *Financial Management System*. Statistics Canada.

Statistics Canada, Public Institutions Division (2007). *Financial Management System*. Statistics Canada.

Sterling, Norman (2000). "Recent Committee Reforms in Ontario." *Canadian Parliamentary Review* 23, 2 (Summer): 6–10.

Stone-Sweet, Alec (2000). *Governing with Judges: Constitutional Politics in Europe.* Oxford University Press.

Stone-Sweet, Alec (2004). *The Judicial Construction of Europe.* Oxford University Press.

Strategic Council (2002). *A Family Snapshot: Canadian Attitudes on the Family.* Focus on the Family Canada.

Student Vote (2004). *Student Vote 2004: Post-Election Analysis.* <www.studentvote.ca/pages.php?pageid=3>.

Sturgess, Gary L., and Michael Wright (1993). *Water Rights in Rural New South Wales: The Evolution of a Property Rights System.* Centre for Independent Studies.

Svensson, J. (2005). "8 Questions about Corruption." *Journal of Economic Perspectives* 19, 5: 19–42.

Tanzi, Vito (1995). *Government Role and the Efficiency of Policy Instruments.* IMF Working Paper. International Monetary Fund.

Tanzi, Vito (2005). "The Economic Role of the State in the 21st Century." *Cato Journal* 25, 3 (Fall): 617–38.

Tanzi, Vito, and Ludger Schuknecht (1997a). "Reconsidering the Fiscal Role of Government: The International Perspective." *American Economic Review* 87: 164–68.

Tanzi, Vito, and Ludger Schuknecht (1997b). "Reforming Government: An Overview of the Recent Experience." *European Journal of Political Economy* 13: 395–417.

Tanzi, Vito, and Ludger Schuknecht (1998a). "Can Small Governments Secure Economic and Social Well-Being?" In Herbert Grubel, ed., *How to Use the Fiscal Surplus: What is the Optimal Size of Government?* (The Fraser Institute): 69–92.

Tanzi, Vito, and Ludger Schuknecht (1998b). "The Growth of Government and the Reform of the State in Industrial Countries." In Andres Solimano, ed., *Social Inequality* (Michigan University Press).

The 105th American Assembly (2005). *Renewing the US-Canada Relationship. American Assembly.* New York: Arden House (February 3-6).

The Economist (2006). "The New Titans: A Survey of the World Economy." (September 16).

Thompson, D. (1999). "Democratic Secrecy." *Political Science Quarterly* 114, 2: 181–93.

Tomal, Annette (1998). "The Relationship between Hospital Mortality Rates, and Hospital, Market and Patient Characteristics." *Applied Economics* 30: 717–25.

Toronto Star (2004). "Gun Registry Costs $2B, CBC Reports." *Toronto Star* (Feb. 14): A6.

Transparency International (2005). *Corruption Perceptions Index 2005.* Transparency International Surveys. <ww1.transparency.org/surveys/index.html#cpi>, as of March 2, 2006.

Treff, Karin, and David B. Perry (2001). *Finances of the Nation, 2000.* Canadian Tax Foundation.

Treff, Karin, and David B. Perry (2002). *Finances of the Nation, 2001.* Canadian Tax Foundation.

Treff, Karin, and David B. Perry (2006). *Finances of the Nation, 2005.* Canadian Tax Foundation.

Tumlir, Jan (1985). *Protectionism: Trade Policy in Democratic Societies.* American Enterprise Institute.

Turner, William (2004). "The Commoditization and Marketing of Water." WaterBank.com

Uhr, J. (1998). *Deliberative Democracy in Australia.* Cambridge University Press.

United Kingdom, House of Commons, International Development Committee [UK-IDC] (2006). *Conflict and Development: Peacebuilding and Post-conflict Reconstruction.* Sixth Report of Session 2005–06, Volume I. HC 923-I. <www.publications.parliament.uk/pa/cm200506/cmselect/cmintdev/923/923i.pdf>.

United Nations. *United Nations Declaration of Human Rights*, Article 26.

United Nations (2005). *Investing in Development: A Practical Guide to Achieve the Millennium Development Goals.* United Nations.

United Nations Development Programme [UNDP] (2006). *Human Development Report 2006. Beyond scarcity: Power, Poverty and the Global Water Crisis.* <hdr.undp.org/hdr2006/pdfs/report/HDR06-complete.pdf>.

United States, Bureau of Labour Statistics (2005). *Foreign Labour Statistics.* <data.bls.gov/>, as of March 7, 2005.

United States, Bureau of Labor Statistics (2007). *International Programs.* <http://www.bls.gov/bls/proghome.htm#INT>.

United States Department of Health and Human Services, The Administration for Children and Families [USHHS] (2003). *Temporary Assistance for Needy Families Program (TANF): Fifth Annual Report to Congress.* United States Department of Health and Human Services, February. <www.acf.dhhs.gov/programs/ofa/annualreport5/>, as of October 2003.

United States General Accounting Office [USGAO] (1978). *Job Training Programs Need More Effective Management.* United States General Accounting Office.

United States General Accounting Office [USGAO] (1979). *Moving Participants from Public Service Programs into Unsubsidized Jobs Needs More Attention.* United States General Accounting Office.

United States General Accounting Office [USGAO] (1980). *Labor Should Make Sure CETA Programs Have Effective Employability Development Systems.* United States General Accounting Office.

US Department of Commerce, Bureau of Economic Analysis (2006). Various data series. <www.bea.gov/>.

US Department of Commerce, Bureau of Economic Analysis (2007). Various data series. <www.bea.gov/>.

US Government Accountability Office [US GAO] (2005). *Tax Policy: Summary of Estimates of the Costs of the Federal Tax System*. GAO.

USAID (2006). *Knowledge for Development* .<knowledge.usaid.gov/>.

Vaillancourt, Francois (1989). *The Administrative and Compliance Costs of the Personal Income Tax and Payroll Tax System in Canada, 1986*. Canadian Tax Paper No. 86. Canadian Tax Foundation.

Vander Ploeg, Casey (1996). *Assembly '96: Summary Report*. Canada West Foundation. <www.cwf.ca/abcalcwf/doc.nsf/(Publications)/7190EA588919D3EA87256BD1 00783092/$file/199701.pdf>.

Vander Ploeg, Casey (2003). "Constituent Assemblies as Vehicles for Change." In Gordon Gibson, ed., *Fixing Canadian Democracy* (The Fraser Institute): 219–28.

Vander Ploeg, Casey, and Peter McCormick (1997). *Meaningful Consultation: A Contradiction in Terms?* Canada West Foundation. <www.cwf.ca/abcalcwf/doc. nsf/(Publications)/4EEF79027424864887256BD30002D75E/$file/199712.pdf>.

Vedder, Richard K. (1993). *Economic Impact of Government Spending: A 50-State Analysis*. Policy Report 178. National Center for Policy Analysis.

Vedder, Richard K., and Lowell E. Gallaway (1998). "Government Size and Economic Growth." Paper prepared for the Joint Economic Committee of the US Congress.

Veldhuis, Niels (2006). "Presentation to The British Columbia Provincial Sales Tax Review Panel, January 19, 2006." The Fraser Institute. Available upon request.

Veldhuis, Neils, and Jason Clemens (2004). "Does Canada Have a Marriage Tax Penalty?" *Fraser Forum* (March): 9–12.

Veldhuis, Niels, and Jason Clemens (2006). *Productivity, Prosperity, and Business Taxes*. Studies in Economic Prosperity 3. The Fraser Institute.

Veldhuis, Neils, Joel Emes, and Michael Walker (2003). *Tax Facts 13*. Vancouver, BC: The Fraser Institute.

Veldhuis, Niels, Keith Godin, and Jason Clemens (2007). *The Economic Costs of Capital Gains Taxes*. Studies in Entrepreneurship and Markets. The Fraser Institute. Vancouver: BC.

Walker, Michael A. (1997). "Is There an Ideal Size of Government and What Is It?" Presentation at Annual Congress of the Friedrich Naumann Stiftung.

Washington Alliance for a Competitive Economy (2003) "The Northern Colorado Water Conservancy District" in *Water Case Study: Water for a Growing Economy*. Olympia: Association of Washington Business.

Watson, J. (2005). "Markets, Democracy and the Alleviation of Poverty." Notes for an address at the World Presidents' Organization.

Weidenbaum, Murray L., and Robert DeFina (1976). *The Cost of Federal Regulation of Economic Activity*. Competitive Enterprise Institute.

Wettenhall, R. (2003). "The Rhetoric and Reality of Public-Private Partnerships." *Public Organization Review: A Global Journal* 3: 77–107.

Wheelan, Charles (2002). *Naked Economics: Undressing the Dismal Science*. Norton.

Wilson, Thomas A. (2003). "An Evaluation of Business Taxes in Canada." In Herbert Grubel, ed., *Tax Reform in Canada: Our Path to Greater Prosperity* (The Fraser Institute): 111–38.

Windsor Star (2005). "Split Decision on Child Care." *Windsor Star* (February 12): A9.

Wooldridge, Adrian, and John Micklethwait (2004). *Right Nation*. Penguin.

World Bank (2004). *World Development Indicators Online*. <www.worldbank.org/>.

World Bank (2005). *Doing Business: Benchmarking Business Regulations* [database]. <www.doingbusiness.org/>.

World Bank (2005). *World Development Indicators, 2005*. <devdata.worldbank.org/wdi2005/Cover.htm>.

World Economic Forum (various issues). *Global Competitiveness Report*. <http://www.weforum.org/en/initiatives/gcp/index.htm>.

Wößmann, Ludgar (2000). *Schooling Resources, Educational Institutions, and Student Performance: The International Evidence*. Kiel Working Paper No. 983. The Kiel Institute of World Economics.

York, G. (2006). "CIDA Quietly Keeps Up Cash Flow to China." *Globe and Mail* (November 24). <www.theglobeandmail.com/servlet/story/LAC.20061124.CIDA24/TPStory/International>.

Yunus, M., and A. Jolis (1999). *Banker to the Poor: Micro-Lending and the Battle against World Poverty*. Public Affairs.

Zelder, Martin (2000). *How Private Hospital Competition Can Improve Canadian Healthcare*. Public Policy Source 35. The Fraser Institute.